W9-DIN-244

PERSISTENCE AND CHANGE

*Proceedings of the First International Conference
On Event Perception*

To James J. Gibson and Gunnar Johansson, two friends in science, whose exemplary work inspired the conference on which this book is based, and whose exemplary lives as scientists continue to inspire us all, we respectfully and affectionately dedicate this second volume in the series, Resources for Ecological Psychology.

PERSISTENCE AND CHANGE

*Proceedings of the First International Conference
On Event Perception*

Edited by

William H. Warren, Jr.
Brown University

Robert E. Shaw
University of Connecticut

LEA LAWRENCE ERLBAUM ASSOCIATES, PUBLISHERS
1985   Hillsdale, New Jersey   London

Copyright © 1985 by Lawrence Erlbaum Associates, Inc.
All rights reserved. No part of this book may be reproduced in
any form, by photostat, microform, retrieval system, or any other
means, without the prior written permission of the publisher.

Lawrence Erlbaum Associates, Inc., Publishers
365 Broadway
Hillsdale, New Jersey 07642

Library of Congress Cataloging in Publication Data

International Conference on Event Perception (1st :
  1981 : University of Connecticut)
  Persistence and change.

  Bibliography: p.
  Includes index.
  1. Perception—Congresses. 2. Change (Psychology)—
Congresses. I. Warren, William H., Jr. II. Shaw,
Robert E. III. Title.
BF311.I566 1981   153.7'5   84-13704
ISBN 0-89859-391-3

Printed in the United States of America

RESOURCES FOR ECOLOGICAL PSYCHOLOGY

A series of volumes edited by:
Robert E. Shaw, William M. Mace, and Michael T. Turvey

Resources for Ecological Psychology

Edited by Robert E. Shaw, William M. Mace
and Michael T. Turvey

This series of volumes is dedicated to furthering the development of psychology as a branch of ecological science. In its broadest sense, ecology is a multidisciplinary approach to the study of living systems, their environments, and the recipiocity that has evolved between the two. Traditionally, ecological science emphasizes the study of the biological bases of *energy* transactions between animals and their physical environments across cellular, organismic, and population scales. Ecological psychology complements this traditional focus by emphasizing the study of *information* transactions between living systems and their environments, especially as they pertain to perceiving situations of significance to planning and execution of purposes activated in an environment.

The late James J. Gibson used the term *ecological psychology* to emphasize this animal-environment mutuality for the study of problems of perception. He believed that analyzing the environment to be perceived was just as much a part of the psychologist's task as analyzing animals themselves, and hence that the "physical" concepts applied to the environment and the "biological" and "psychological" concepts applied to organisms would have to be tailored to one another in a larger system of mutual constraint. His early interest in the applied problems of landing airplanes and driving automobiles led him to pioneer the study of the perceptual guidance of action.

The work of Nicolai Bernstein in biomechanics and physiology presents a complementary approach to problems of the coordination and control of movement. His work suggests that action, too, cannot be studied without reference to the environment, and that physical and biological concepts must be developed together. The coupling of Gibson's ideas with those of Bernstein forms a natural basis for looking at the traditional psychological topics of perceiving, acting, and knowing as activities of ecosystems rather than isolated animals.

The purpose of this series is to form a useful collection, a resource, for people who wish to learn about ecological psychology and for those who wish to contribute to its development. The series will include original research, collected papers, reports of conferences and symposia, theoretical monographs, technical handbooks, and works from the many diciplines relevant to ecological psychology.

Dedication

To James J. Gibson, whose pioneering work in ecological
psychology has opened new vistas in psychology and
related sciences, we respectfully dedicate this series.

Contents

Preface

The First International Conference on Event Perception was held at the University of Connecticut, June 7–12, 1981, to recognize a newly burgeoning field of research and theory that is beginning to make its impact felt in the perceptual sciences at large. We remember, early on in the planning, brainstorming for the names of relevant scientists—and overflowing the blackboard. We plotted the frequency of publications on the subject from the 1930's to the present, and came up with an exponential curve. Those we surveyed about the idea of a conference unanimously agreed that the time was ripe. On this basis we decided to organize a modest working conference in order to help consolidate current thinking on the topic, crystallize outstanding questions and enduring issues, and suggest an agenda for future research.

The common insight behind an "event" approach is that, unlike most perceptual psychologists' stimulus displays, the natural world doesn't usually sit still for a perceiver, nor does a perceiver typically sit still when exploring his or her surroundings. Our perceptual encounters with the world are dominated by events, or changes in structure over time. But far from complicating the act of perceiving, such transformations appear to yield more efficient, stable, and veridical perception, by providing more information about the object or event observed.

This insight was championed in 1950 independently by Gunnar Johansson, whom we were pleased to have with us at the meeting, and by the late James J. Gibson. These two figures towered over the conference, and it is to them that we respectfully and affectionately dedicate its proceedings. The idea suggested to both men new approaches to classic problems of perception—the perceptual constancies, perceiving the three-dimensional structure of objects, the muddle of perceptual ambiguity and illusion—and it introduced new and fascinating problems as well, such as the perception of change. Since that time the event concept has come to influence work not only in psychology, but also artificial intelligence, biology, philosophy, and applied research. Although the availability of spatio–temporal information apparently makes life easier for the perceiver, it poses new and difficult challenges, both formal and methodological, for the scientist—and therein lies the subject matter of this volume.

The idea of a "working conference" was to combine major statements by researchers in the field with topic oriented work groups, in order to structure discussion of issues. By holding the 75 participants captive in rural Connecticut for five days, considerable heat and not infrequent light was generated. The Storrs weather was unusually kind, the company very congenial, and a high level of enthusiasm was maintained through the sessions, meals, parties, and dormitory debates. A number of themes emerged in the course of the meeting and they run as a subtext through these proceedings. They include the so-called "Johansson conjecture" that mathematically complex displays tend to yield simple and stable perception (and vice versa for simple displays), suggesting that what is "complex" for our mathematics may not be so for our visual systems; the distinction (if any) between the perception of "slow" and "fast" events; the distinction (if any) between the perceptual and cognitive apprehension of events; and the role of physical systems models in psychological theory.

The resulting collection of papers includes major addresses, commentary, and work group reports. The introduction by Warren and Shaw provides an overview of event research from an ecological point of view. Historically, the focus of event perception research has been in vision, and the papers by Johansson, Mace, Lappin, and Todd carry on this line of development, including comparisons of Johansson's and Gibson's approaches, the formal description of optical information, and the constraints that spatio–temporal symmetries might place on theories of mechanism. Benedikt and Burnham then illustrate how a formal optical analysis can be applied to the practical problems of designing architectural environments.

A more recent development has been the extension of event concepts into the acoustic domain. Jenkins' paper illustrates the promise of research in the neglected area of auditory event perception, while Studdert-Kennedy evaluates the relevance of the event approach for speech perception research, and Verbrugge considers its application to higher level language processes. Another exciting development is the link being forged between visual event perception and problems in the control and coordination of movement. The paper by Kugler, Turvey, Carello, and Shaw considers the theoretical problem of regulating dynamic action systems by means of spatio–temporal information, and the novel dialogue between von Hofsten and Lee discusses some recent research on the visual control of movement. Finally, in the last section we present reports from the conference work groups. These are not transcripts, but discursive summaries of each group's discussion. They attempt to distill the prevailing issues in each topic area, and often serve as "state of the art" summaries of research in these fields.

Support for the conference was provided by the University of Connecticut Research Foundation, and we thank Hugh Clark for his efforts. Organization of the conference would not have been possible without the help of Linda Ferrell, and that of John Farling and the staff of the University of Connecticut Conference Center. We would also like to thank the advisory panel for their consultation: Michael Arbib, Eleanor Gibson, James Jenkins, Joseph Lappin, David Lee, Sverker Runeson, and Michael Studdert-Kennedy. An important talk on event epistemology was also delivered at the conference by Professor Alvin Goldman, University of Illinois, to whom we express our appreciation.

We hope that this volume will not only provide an introduction to the enduring problems and current approaches in the field of event perception, but will also convey a sense of the excitement that permeated the conference and that drives us to pursue this newly opening area of research.

William H. Warren, Jr.
Robert E. Shaw

Foreword

On a June day eleven years ago, a one week conference began in Ithaca, New York, called "The Workshop on Ecological Optics." About forty people attended, many of them students or ex-students of James Gibson, who organized the co-ference. But others came, too. Among them were Robert Shaw, David Lee, Gunnar Janssen, and Sverker Runeson. Much of the discussion centered on events and the necessity of treating them if we are to understand how a nonstatic world is perceived, and in this sense it was a kind of forerunner of the Conference on Event Perception that this book commemorates.

But in another sense this Conference is very different, and I believe it is worth pointing out some of the ways, since many potential readers will tend to identify it with Gibson's ecological approach to perception. His approach is indeed represented here but so are other points of view. That comes out in the report of work groups and some of the papers; for example, in Mace's paper "Johansson's Approach to Visual Event Perception—Gibson's Perspective." Mace emphasizes that an event, for Gibson, was an environmental change that is specified in many kinds of ambient arrays, providing structural properties detectable by smelling, touching, listening, tasting, hearing, and so on. A proximal stimulus array of the kind one might try to portray via computerized display is not an event in Gibson's sense of a change in the surface layout of an animal's environment. Mace makes this point and others that contrast differences of definition and theory that sparked many of the Conference's most interesting discussions.

Let it be said, however, that these contrasting opinions and the arguments to which they gave rise would not have occurred at any other conference or meeting that I have attended in recent years, or that I am likely to attend. I cannot imagine a discussion of how slow vs. fast events would be treated in perceptual theory at, say, the Psychonomic Society. Therein lies, for me, the value of this conference. Over 80 people, mostly psychologists, were gathered, all of whom were concerned with the way human perception provides us with knowledge of events.

Events as sources of information about the world are the most neglected topic in traditional theories of perception, which in fact seldom mention them. But Gibson's ecological approach emphasizes that they are not the only sources of information—so are places, objects and people, and at a more basic level of description, the substances and surfaces of things in the world and their relations to one another. Indeed, it is a disturbance in the structural relations of surfaces and substances that constitutes an event for Gibson, not "motion" as people sometimes assume. How we perceive motions of things, of people, and of missiles and targets of various kinds and act appropriately in relation to them at the right time, even as we are moving ourselves, is nevertheless a fascinating problem in event perception, and a number of presentations at the Conference dealt with it. These presentations mostly differ radically from older papers on motion perception in the psychological literature, papers on apparent motion for example, because the observer is no longer assumed to be sitting passively in a laboratory chair, but to be acting (interacting) continuously in a kind of reciprocal give and take correspondence with the changing scene, the action itself changing the scene. The papers by Lee and von Hofsten, and Kugler, Turvey, Carello, and Shaw highlight this important shift in approach to the perception of motion.

Indeed, the phrase "perception of motion" has become a sort of anachronism. We do not perceive motion as such, according to the ecological approach to event perception, but rather change occurring within an event, as Warren and Shaw stressed. Forrest Lee Dimmick, in the Titchenerian tradition, may have had confidence in his introspective description of motion as a "gray flash," but the ecological approach to event perception finds this an inadequate description of a perceived event. Even more inadequate is the traditional treatment of stimulus information, which the ecological approach presumes to be in correspondence with the event itself. It has become abundantly clear, as James Gibson pointed out at the Workshop on Ecological Optics, that the stimulus information for motion is not motion on the retina but a structural change in the ambient optic array that specifies a change in the surface layout of a place or a person or object in the layout.

That perception of motion is not the only focus of an ecological approach to event perception was made particularly clear by the inclusion in the conference program of a paper by Jenkins on acoustic events and one by Studdert-Kennedy on speech perception. Both papers are fascinating and bring acoustic and speech events uncompromisingly within the fold of an ecological approach to event perception. This is a very new angle, one that was not treated at all, of course, in the Workshop on Ecological Optics, but the new areas for theorizing and research thus opened up are in complete harmony with the ecological approach.

This harmony is notable in the stress in these papers on the false scents laid in the past by elementaristic and static approaches to acoustic and especially to speech events.

Both speakers pointed out the necessity for a more dynamic treatment, taking account of the functional significance of these events and the way the sources (the real events) are specified in the acoustic array. How is it, Jenkins asked, that an M.D. listening to someone's heart via a stethoscope hears a heart beating, not just sounds? Or as Studdert-Kennedy pointed out, we have failed to recognize that what is represented in the speech signal is information about its source, invariants that specify it. The invariants are not "in the head," as theorists have sometimes thought, but in dynamic structural relations in the signal, analogous perhaps to the relations in the point light displays that Johansson used in his research on perception of biological motion.

Theoretical emphases in the papers on acoustic and linguistic events, including Verbrugge's paper on meaningful aspects of language, were similar to those in the papers on visually perceived events or events in general. Most events, after all, offer rich information for the perceiver which he does not normally break down according to pickup systems, so we can expect some similarity of invariant properties between systems. The importance of a functional treatment of event perception and what an event affords for the guidance of action; the dynamic and relativistic nature of the information as it specifies an event; and the fact that the source (the real event) is specified in stimulus information, and is not arbitrary or random in its correspondence with the perceived event, were recurrent emphases. In connection with the last point, it was often suggested that there is no need for mediation by "intelligence," a view which was sometimes referred to as "taking out a loan on intelligence." On the contrary, as several speakers suggested, if we are to look somewhere for knowledge to fill in gaps that now pose questions, the ecological approach should seek answers in the evolution of the organism as it has adapted to its environment and its ecological niche.

The poverty of research on event perception was occasionally referred to, but considering the brief time that it has been a working area for research, I do not agree with the accusation. Outstanding research is described in the papers: Johannson on perception of biological motion, Lee on "time to contact," and Runeson on mechanical events and perceived "causality" and "intention," to mention only a few examples. Furthermore, the research resources already available in the literature are actually much richer than the primarily theoretical papers might seem to imply, and so are the potential questions for research to address.

The Conference's work groups in some cases, at least, did consider research resources and questions for research: Where there is existing research, and what questions, in the light of the Conference, may be usefully pursued. The group to which I belonged, on Development, did just this after a little rather futile argument on questions such as how an event should be defined. The group came up with good questions and with a sense that there is already a fairly rich body of evidence from the ecological approach that is relevant to event perception in the developmental literature. From our view (my bias is very transparent), work in the developmental area is sufficient to justify having given Development a spot on the main program. Another time, maybe.

Another time is, indeed, indicated. As I review in my mind the five days of this Conference, it seems well worth a second round in a couple of years. Points of view differed, but that makes for good discussion. There was time to talk individually and to get acquainted with many people, all of whom were keenly interested in the topic of the Conference. The Conference will help to consolidate as well as expand a new way of thinking about perception which is already revolutionizing the field.

Eleanor J. Gibson
Cornell University
Ithaca, New York
August, 1981

PERSISTENCE AND CHANGE

Proceedings of the First International Conference
On Event Perception

1 Events and Encounters as Units of Analysis for Ecological Psychology

William H. Warren, Jr.
Brown University

Robert E. Shaw
University of Connecticut

A crucial decision faced by any scientific program is, quite simply, deciding what scale of things to look at. Tacitly or explicitly, a unit of analysis is selected—preferably one appropriate to the phenomena of interest. Choosing a unit that is too large makes the phenomena unanalyzable. Indeed, such over-zealous holism leaves the scientist little to say beyond pointing to the thing itself and expressing naked appreciation. Consider an attempt to explain the tides at the scale of planetary units of gravitational attraction. Because this unit of analysis is too coarse to differentiate the components of the Earth-moon system, and because the tidal effects of other planets are miniscule, the regular swelling of the waters cannot be explained.

The more common problem, however, has been fostered by atomism—choosing a unit of analysis that is too small, and thereby eliminating crucial higher-order relations. This often leads to immense computational complexity that requires the introduction of arbitrary constraints to artificially simplify the phenomenon in question. Unfortunately, this strategy creates unnecessary, but unassailable, paradoxes regarding the system's behavior, and inevitably leads to either of two undesirable outcomes: Forces of unknown origin are postulated to be acting on the system from without, or equally mysterious capabilities are attributed to the system itself. We have seen the former problem arise in Newtonian physics in the guise of the "action-at-a-distance" concept, and analogously in psychology in the uncritical acceptance of ESP. The latter problem survives in the notions of decision-making homunculi or executive motor programs. These theoretical ploys, like an attempt to explain the tides in earth-bound units of force that ignore the moon, must ultimately be considered magical, for in describing only a partial system they miss fundamental systemic relations and consequently

1

yield circular explanations appealing to a hidden redescription of the phenomenon itself.

We convened this Conference out of a belief in the significance of a theory of events for psychology. The participants each arrived at this belief in their own way, and found the concept of an event useful, even indispensable, in their work. That this concept has proven recalcitrant under diverse scrutiny provides, perhaps, the best evidence of its worth.

We presume to suggest, however, that in spite of the obvious intuitive appeal the concept holds, it remains a somewhat dark idea in need of much clarification. Quite independent of any doctrinaire use to which we as individuals might choose to put the concept, we should come to some agreement on what an event is, how information about events might be described, and ultimately methods by which such information could be measured.

UNITS OF ANALYSIS IN PSYCHOLOGY

Many thinkers have searched for the proper unit of analysis for psychology. From Descartes' sensations, to Locke's ideas, to punctate stimuli, cues, features, templates, and structural descriptions, these units have all had three aspects in common: They have been conceived as *static* in form, *fixed* at a given scale size, and *elemental,* to be related by compounding or concatenation to assemble larger wholes.

Apparently, the major reason for this conception of the psychological unit is a traditionally accepted view of nature as frozen in a timeless Euclidean space, or as staticized by the infinitesmal snapshots of Newton's calculus of physics. This static "snapshot" view of perception has been abetted by the more contemporary metaphor of the eye as a camera (which in turn must make the cortex into a screening room—instead of James' theatrical stage—for the perceiver's homunculus). Historically, the assumption that static cues or images provide the raw materials for perception mandated the pictorial stimulus, the reduction screen, the bite bar, and the tachistoscope for experimental methodology, accumulating data which, of necessity, reinforced the original assumption.

As a consequence of static images being held primary, the perception of motion or change was considered derivative or secondary, one in a list of auxiliary phenomena. Under this view, successive snapshots of events are thought to be processed sequentially and the motion inferred or cognitively interpolated between frames, a filmstrip in the cortical theater from which the homunculus somehow derives the phenomenological experience of motion. Hence, cinematic or stroboscopic motion became the model for the perception of real motion—a curious reversal of affairs—while other types of change were seldom studied at all. The claim that change grows out of nonchange presents a philosophical conundrum of the first order, and as Shaw & Pittenger (1978) have argued elsewhere, the attempted solution of comparing successive images and inferring their difference relations runs into logical paradoxes, such as the Höffding problem (e.g., Neisser, 1967). To compute a change between images, homologous elements in related images must be compared. But to identify which images are related and which elements homologous, the processing system must either have prior knowledge about the change—the very thing that is to be computed—or must embody other knowledge and heuristics and perform extensive computations in order to identify homologous elements (see Marr, 1980). Little wonder that the field of event perception, plagued by contradictions, failed to flourish.

THE DISCOVERY OF OPTICAL FLOW

However, a few early students of vision such as Mach, Exner, and Wertheimer had the insight to insist that motion be treated as a primary perceptual form, and not as something derived from more "basic" static forms. For the current metaphor that optical stimulation is better conceived as a *flow* than as a sequence of pictures, we shall forever be indebted to the work of J. J. Gibson and Gunnar Johansson, who in 1950 independently began turning the tide of scientific opinion on the matter. The theme of this Conference is evidence of our respect for their contribution and support of their vision.

For Gibson, it began with the realization that permitting the observer or the observed scene to *move* made certain supposed problems of spatial perception appear to vanish. The recognition of this fact first came during his famous studies of aircraft landing, in which he discovered that a flier's orientation and heading with respect to the earth's surface were given in patterns of optical change (Gibson, 1947, 1950; Gibson, Olum, & Rosenblatt, 1955). In collaboration with Eleanor Gibson and others over the next decade, this discoverey of optical transformations was extended to the classical problem of depth perception, recast as the separation of surfaces in a layout (Gibson, Gibson, Smith, & Flock, 1959); the problem of rigid shape perception, studied via *change* in a shadow caster (Gibson, 1957; Gibson & Gibson, 1957); the novel problem of perceiving a style of change itself (von Fieandt & Gibson, 1959); the perception of surface slant (Flock, 1964); and the visual guidance of locomotion (Gibson, 1958). Although the research was charting new territory and the theoretical base was under constant revision, the consistent finding was that perceptual ambiguity was resolved under transformation. In fact, it might be said that choosing improper (static) units of analysis actually served to create paradoxes of depth perception, size and shape constancy, Necker cube ambiguity, Ames illusions, and so on. The introduction of spatio–temporal change revealed a richness of perceptual information available under natural circumstances that made the recourse to inference or other mediation unnecessary, and this result provided the experimental foundation for the later development of Gibson's theory of direct perception (Gibson, 1961, 1966; Michaels & Carello, 1981).

For Johansson, a related discovery was in the making: That patterns of optical change not only disambiguate, but could by themselves induce, structural relations among components of a display. As Johansson stated his working hypothesis in 1950, "The organization of the event wholes, as regards formation of groups, etc., is primarily determined by the temporal relations between the elements" (p. 15). The 1950 book was a careful study of the effects of systematically varying the oscillatory paths of motion and phase relations of two to six dots on a projection screen, and produced a number of startling discoveries. Rather than perceiving independent motions, dots that moved in phase in a common direction were not only grouped together, as according to the Gestalt law of "common fate," but appeared to be linked by a rigid rod. In some cases, rotations of complex objects in three dimensions were seen, such as a revolving crank axle or orbital motions about a rotating axis. Such observations led Johansson to his renowned vector analysis of motion perception, namely, that common motions composed of simultaneous equal vector components provide a frame of reference for the remaining components of motion. Using this principle, Johansson was able to predict the perceptual effects of novel moving dot displays (see also Johansson, 1958, 1974a, this volume).

In subsequent papers, Johansson focussed on applications of vector analysis to the problem of perceiving three–dimensional rotations from changes in the frontal plane, whether simple harmonic motion (Johansson, 1958), elliptical paths analyzed as conic sections (Johansson, 1974b), or changes in the length and orientation of a line (Johansson & Jansson, 1968). To explain his observations, he was led to the position that the visual system seeks rigidity; otherwise relative motions in the frontal plane would be seen as elastic two–dimensional motions instead of rigid three–dimensional rotations. This in turn led him and Gunnar Jansson to study the conditions under which nonrigid transformations such as bending, stretching, and deformation are perceived (Jansson, 1977; Jansson & Johansson, 1973; Jansson & Runeson, 1977; Johansson, 1964), which we will return to shortly. Most recently, the compelling effects of point-light walkers (Johansson, 1973) have galvanized a wide interest in event perception as a subject matter in its own right (see Cutting & Kozlowski, 1977; Cutting, Proffitt, & Kozlowski, 1978; Runeson & Frykholm, 1981).

As the work of Gibson and Johansson progressed, characteristic aspects emerged to distinguish their approaches, although the seeds of the later departures were germinating in 1950 (see Mace, this volume). Gibson had begun by studying optic patterns producible by the motions of real objects and observers; Johansson had begun by manipulating detached "proximal" variables per se. Consequently, Gibson came to emphasize the information available about a cluttered layout of surfaces in the accretion and deletion of dense optical textures, whereas Johansson developed his vector analysis using displays with a few points or object outlines. The fruit of these differences was the contrast between Gibson's optic invariants and Johansson's vectors; and the bases these concepts provided for, repsectively, the theory of direct perception of the natural world (Gibson, 1966) and the hypothesis of hard-wired "decoding principles" automatically applied to visual input by the organism (Johansson, 1964; Johansson & Jansson, 1968). This, their most serious divergence, was discussed openly in an exchange of letters after Gibson's visit to Uppsala in 1968 (Johansson, 1970; Gibson, 1970)—a rare model of gentlemanly debate.

In 1958, Johansson believed that the two methods of optic analysis were identical: "What are my motion vectors other than higher-order variables in Gibson's meaning of the term?" (p. 368). In cases where different vector descriptions of the same display were possible, one was perceptually selected on the basis of a minimum principle or past experience. In 1964, however, Johansson concluded that there was "*no specific information*" in the two–dimensional projection plane that would distinguish elastic two–dimensional shape and size changes from rigid three–dimensional motions, and consequently the visual system must possess certain interpretive principles to guarantee veridical perception, such as a preference for rigidity. By the 1970 exchange, it was clear that Johansson could not accept a theory of direct perception based on what he felt was equivocal information.

We would suggest that this disagreement was really a consequence of the earlier choices: Each man was true to his observations, but different things were being observed. Minimal displays that lend themselves to two competing vector descriptions may indeed be equivocal, but sufficiently rich displays are not. We would prefer to model perceptual processes on the basis of rich rather than minimal information because the natural environment is rich, and it, not the laboratory, provides the context for evolution and attunement. The issue is whether either type of display contains information of some kind to distinguish rigid from nonrigid motions without requiring auxiliary principles, and the results of Todd (1982) and others suggest that this may indeed be the case. Common vector components may be construed as a species of higher order invariant that is implicated in rigid displacements, but it is one among several, such as changes in the nested structure of an optic array that are not necessarily reducible to the continuous motions of points (see Mace, this volume).

Yet despite such differences, it is the overriding commonality in Gibson's and Johansson's approaches that yields their legacy: An insistence that spatio–temporal change—events—be taken as the only viable starting point for perceptual theory. As Johansson observed in 1958, "Change of excitation has been shown to be a *necessary* condition for visual perception," (p. 359). It is the distinguishing character of events as units of analysis that we would now like to pursue.

EVENTS AS UNITS OF ANALYSIS

Change

At the risk of repeating ourselves, the first thing that distinguishes events from other units of analysis is that they are intrinsically spatio–temporal rather than merely spatial in nature. In keeping with Einstein's vision, Shaw & Pittenger (1978) defined an event as, "a minimal change of some specified type wrought over an object or object-complex within a determinate region of space–time." By recognizing that events partake of change over time, psychology belatedly accepts the truth of Minkowski's (1908) post-relativity dictum that, "henceforth, space by itself, and time by itself, are doomed to fade away into mere shadows, and only a kind of union of the two will preserve an independent reality."

In other words, events are primary, and empty time and static space are derivative. The universe is in process, and objects may be considered only as more or less persistent regions in an onslaught of spatio–temporal change. The transformations wrought have different time courses, and the slower ones leave what appear from our perspective as stable or permanent properties. Hence the words "structure" and "change" are perspectival terms, for persistence in an event must be defined relative to the time course of the perceiver. The bright orange leaf that is transient for us is a permanent fixture for the 24–hour life span of the insect that lands upon it, and the mountainside that appears to us eternal will, in time, be levelled by erosion. Most basically, then, events exhibit some form of *persistence* that we call an object or layout, and some *style of change* defined over it. As noted earlier, what is interesting perceptually is that events are sources of information for proper perceivers, both about the objects and the changes they undergo.

Change-Specified Structure. Not only may information about structural properties be isolated by subjecting an object to changes like rotation, but structure itself is definable in terms of what is preserved and what is destroyed under different transformations. An automobile remains an automobile as it moves, turns, or is pushed off a cliff by its frustrated owner; its rigid shape is destroyed when it crashes at the bottom; and it finally relinquishes its automobile-structure when it is melted down for scrap. In a frozen image, everything is "structural"; it requires change to define the uniquely persistent properties. Our favorite illustration of this profound fact is a film by Gibson in which a randomly textured square is translated across a randomly textured background—and when the action is stopped, the square vanishes into the optical camouflage of the background (Gibson, 1968; Gibson, Kaplan, Reynolds & Wheeler, 1969). The structure in this case only exists in the textural difference relations defined over time; the square as such is not defined in any individually frozen frame. Furthermore, no amount of looking at successive frames on the film strip can divine those difference relations or homologous elements perceptually; the perception of the event is dependent on certain spatio–temporal conditions. The same is true of Johansson's point-light walkers: Only a jumble of lights is seen in a single image or over a series of static images, but a coherent figure pops to life under a brief transformation. An hour's meditation on this effect is worth a week of event theory!

Besides Johansson's work, other examples of change-specified structure include Metzger's (1953) original rotating-pegs display, the Wallach and O'Connell (1953) kinetic depth effect, and Lappin, Doner, and Kottas' (1980) experiment in which the three–dimensional shape of an object is not detected until the object is rotated (see also Braunstein, 1976; Andersen & Braunstein, 1983). Similarly, Kaplan (1969) and Mace and Shaw (1974) have shown that optical change will disambiguate the relative layout of surfaces in depth. Recent work in computer vision has produced new computational approaches to the problem of obtaining "structure from motion" (Ullman, 1979; Marr, 1980; 1982). The goal of such studies is not just the demonstration of change-specified structure, but the identification of the optical information that specifies structure, and this is a problem that is by no means solved (see Lappin, this volume; Todd, this volume).

Change-Specified Change.   Work on the perception of the style of change specified by a transforming display, other than simple motion or rigid rotation, is a relatively recent offspring of the event approach. For example, the ground-breaking experiment of von Fieandt & Gibson (1959) showed that observers reliably distinguish rigid rotation in depth from elastic stretching and compression. Recent work by Eleanor Gibson and her coworkers has demonstrated that infants make a similar distinction (Gibson, Owsley, & Johnson, 1978; Gibson, Owsley, Walker, & Megaw-Nyce, 1979), and, as mentioned earlier, Jansson and his colleagues have pursued the proximal patterns that distinguish stretching, bending, and folding. Research on biological motion since Michotte's (1946/ 1963) original "caterpillar locomotion" display has found that many styles of change can be perceptually identified, from walking, running, dancing, and gymnastics of point-light people (Johansson, 1973) to distinguishing cranio-facial growth patterns from other types of nonrigid transformations (Mark, 1979; Mark, Todd, & Shaw, 1981; Pittenger & Shaw, 1975; Pittenger, Shaw, & Mark, 1980). Successful characterizations of the optical information for these events should help evaluate the claim that styles of change characteristic of both slow and fast events are directly specified rather than inferred.

Because stable shapes typically result from event processes, static images or pictures of many natural phenomena logically point beyond themselves to the larger events in which they are embedded. Natural objects are formed and re-formed by ongoing dynamic processes such as growth, decay, geologic upheaval, weathering and erosion, manipulation and tool use, and so on. Any object is an artifact of its formation and evolution, and in fact owes its very structure to such processes. A photograph of a human face is a fragmentary record of its history, bearing the marks and scars of the slow and fast events in which faces participate—hominid evolution, individual growth, the emotion being expressed, the word just uttered. Hence, to understand a natural object such as a face, and even to understand a snapshot of a face, the object must be considered as an ongoing, if slow, event. The popular alternative, trying to understand an object that is fundamentally in process through snapshots, is, we believe, fruitless. Bringing the concept of change into our characterization of perceptual phenomena, therefore, is akin to bringing the moon into an explanation of the tides—in no other way can adequate explanations of perception be found.

Event Periods

A second fact that must be incorporated into our event theories is that the periods of different events may be quite variable, ranging from the assiduously slow growth, blossoming, and wilting of a flower to the rapid flight of a baseball from pitcher to batter. In other words, the style of change associated with one event may act over intervals longer or shorter than those of other events, and may occupy a narrower or broader region of space–time. This is the second thing that distinguishes events from other units of analysis, for there can be no *fixed* unit of change, or fixed spatio–temporal scale, over which all events are defined.

It is over these intrinsically determined periods that events must be characterized and perceptual information described and measured. A test of this proposition is straightforward: If the perceptual sampling of an event is restricted to something less than the required period, then the event will not be seen for what it is; either the style of change will not remain specified, or the identity of the structure undergoing the change will be lost. For instance, Shaw has shown that a stroboscopically illuminated event consisting of a rotating cube will appear to be neither a rotation nor a cube when the frequency of the strobing yields a sequence of perceptual samples whose successive order is arhythmic with respect to the periodic character of the event (Shaw, McIntyre, & Mace, 1974). Thus, by stroboscopically illuminating a rhythmic event, not only may you alter the quantitative aspects of the style of change (such as speed, direction, and even "freezing" of rotation), but you can so alter the nature of the event that *what* is happening to *what* is no longer specified.

As suggested earlier, the apparent duration of structure and the apparent rate of change are perspectival concepts, dependent upon the relationship between the event-periodic structures of the world and the perceiver. If we glance at the second hand of a clock, we see it sweep over the clockface texture while we see the minute hand and hour hand in a frozen configuration. But what if we looked at the minute hand longer or more carefully? Or what if we built an oversized Big

Ben with a 120-mile circumference? Then the tip of the hour hand would move at a rate of 10 mph, clearly a detectable pace. The obvious principle involved is that the rate of angular velocity of the end of a lever is a function of its distance from the fulcrum. Alternatively, we might achieve the same effect by looking at the tip of the hour hand of a watch through a powerful microscope. Astronomers, likewise, who see no effect of the rotation of the Earth on the relative motion of stars by naked eye, readily perceive such motion under the magnification and reduced field of a telescope.

Thus, we see that the perceptual information for the rate of an event is perspectival and not absolute. Excruciatingly "slow" events have their displacements specified by the same variables of information as the motions of apparently "fast" ones. *Only a single continuous parameter, a scale change, distinguishes the information for slow events from that for fast events.* The effects on the observer may be nonlinear—from a perceived "motion" to a perceived "displacement"—but the description of the event itself should not be (Shaw & Pittenger, 1978). Furthermore, if we accept Gibson's description of perceiving as the pickup of information over time, both fast and slow events may be *perceived* as long as information specifying them is available to the observer, whatever its time scale (but see Johansson, this volume; Mace, this volume). Hence the distinction between perceptual information for slow and fast events, under this thesis, is but a nonlinear effect of continuous scale change (see Perspective III, Chapter 18, this volume).

3 Nesting

Third, events of different periods may overlap within the same region of space–time, that is, natural events come *nested,* like the scenes and acts of a play. Following the Gibsons, we must recognize that events of importance for perceivers are defined at ecologically appropriate scales, or levels of nesting. The relevant level of nesting is determined by the significance of events at that level for the needs and activities of the perceiving animal. For the hungry animal, the event of interest is the apple dropping from the tree; for the apple picker, it is the ripening of the fruit; and for the orchard manager, it is the life cycle of the tree. Similarly, we may attend to the momentary smile or frown of a friend, his daily growth of beard, the change in his height or weight over the years, or the still more gradual erosion of facial contours as aging takes its toll over a lifetime. Perceptual information for events at different levels of nesting must be available simultaneously, but can be attended to separately.

The nesting of simpler events may give rise to complex events not necessarily reducible to their simpler elements—although in some trivial cases they may be. Surely an American football game includes a number of plays, but the game as such is a higher order event that involves more than the concatenation of plays; it involves winning or losing, timing of quarters, referee rulings, and other superordinate properties not manifested in the subevents of individual plays. Thus we must recognize this complication in our event theory: Nested events are logically, if not materially, independent; therefore, they cannot be scaled to any single level of elemental units for analysis, static or otherwise. Rather we must strive to understand the spatio–temporal interval of an event at many different scales of analysis: slower and faster, larger and smaller, so long as we stay within the bounds of ecological relevance.

ENCOUNTERS AS UNITS OF ANALYSIS

Gibson (1979) makes it clear that, for taxonomic purposes, his use of the term "event" is restricted to external environmental occurrences that do not involve activities of the observer. Thus, the term covers mechanical changes in the layout of surfaces and objects, chemical changes in surface color and texture, and changes in surface existence (e.g. evaporation or decomposition), but not changes in the point of observation or other actions on the part of the perceiver. However, an observer's own movements do constitute changes in structure over time, and as Gibson himself demonstrated, the events of self-locomotion and limb movement are visually perceived. Thus, we agree with Johansson (this volume) that the general concept of an *event* should be liberalized to include the physical *acts* of the perceiver.

Gibson (1979) used the term *ecological event* for those external events that occur at an ecological scale, intermediate between the microscopic and cosmic extremes. Such events are those of significance for an organism's behavior, involving the surfaces and objects of the terrestrial environment, and hence are potentially perceptible by organisms. Following this notion, let us introduce the concept of an *encounter*[1], that is, an ecological event in which an animal participates either as an actor or as a perceiver preparatory to action. We define an action as an intentional behavior. Hence, encounters are events pregnant with information relevant to the control of action. For example, when a tree falls alone in the forest, this ecological event produces certain mechanical, optical, and acoustical disturbances. On the other hand, when an observer is present in the forest, detects the disturbances, and prepares to escape the toppling tree, that participation in the ecological event creates an encounter. The information specifying the properties of such events is crucial for the perceptual guidance and attunement of actions. Thus, encounters wed the acting-and-perceiving organism to the environment in the service of the organisms's needs and intentions (Shaw & Turvey, 1981; Shaw, Turvey, & Mace, 1981; Turvey, Shaw, Reed, & Mace, 1981).

---

[1]Gibson (1979, p. 231–2) used the word "encounter" somewhat informally to refer to an organism's behavioral interactions with an object, based on what the object afforded for activity.

We argue that organism-environment encounters are the proper units of analysis for psychology, and it is descriptions of information for ecological events and the control of activity at this scale of space–time that are required for our science. We should select events for study pragmatically, not arbitrarily or for methodological convenience, selecting those that have consequences for the observer's activity and well-being in the natural environment. Hence, the encounter as a unit of analysis is not something that can be coded into units of sensory activity, like features or spatial frequencies; the unit is not in the nervous system, rather, the participant's nervous system is in the unit (or in Mace's [1977] words, "Ask not what's inside your head, but what your head's inside of"). This was the primary insight of American functionalism taken into the pragmatist movement by Dewey and Bentley in their concept of transaction, a concept whose roots go back to Peirce's notion of "thirdness" (Shaw & Turvey, 1981). Gibson was a student of E. B. Holt, who himself was a student of James, who in turn borrowed so much from Peirce. Thus, from Peirce to Gibson we have the scholarly conduit through which this great insight flows down to us, and whose ramifications are yet to be fathomed.

In other words, what an animal is and how it can participate in encounters indicates those events worthy of our attention and likely to lead to meaningful psychological theory. This is a pragmatic criterion for our science, for we believe that perception/action systems are pragmatically designed and built for ecological tasks. Ecological events must ultimately be described in relation to encounters, with reference to both the animal and the environment. This principle of animal-environment mutuality lies at the heart of Gibson's ecological approach to psychology.

Gibson coined the term *affordance* to characterize the animal-referent description of objects and events, and much consternation has ensued (e.g., Fodor & Pylyshyn, 1981; Turvey, Shaw, Reed, & Mace, 1981). So far, however, very little research has been directed toward the study of affordances, presumably because the concept has proven somewhat elusive. What makes the concept of an affordance somewhat difficult to grasp is the failure to shift our thinking about perceptual information from arbitrarily selected or neutral units of analysis to ecologically appropriate ones. In fact, affordances are no more mysterious than physical properties, such as weight and size, or rate and rhythm. Affordances are measurable material properties of the environment construed *functionally*, as they serve an animal's actions, facilitate its adaptations, and support its intentions.

What makes affordances different from physical properties in isolation is that they are defined and measured relationally, with respect to an intentional act. For example, rather than simply measuring the dimensions of a chair, one refers those dimensions in part to the body size and weight of the sitter. This determines whether the chair affords the specific encounter of comfortable sitting, or perhaps sitting at all, by the person in question. What makes a rock "throwable" or a stairway "climbable" or a food "edible" is likewise the existence of a perceiving agent with certain action capabilities, or *effectivities* (Turvey & Shaw, 1979). In essence, affordances simply describe the use-value of things for an animal with particular action capabilities, and are best characterized by making "intrinsic" measurements of one in terms of the other (Shaw & Cutting, 1980; Warren & Shaw, 1981; Warren, 1982, in press).

In sum, every disposition of an animal for some action coimplicates a disposition of some environmental structure to support that action. These dual dispositions are the essence of animal-environment mutuality. Hence, every affordance names a category of potential encounters, and affordances provide a useful way of packaging event information into ecologically appropriate units for theoretical analysis and empirical study, in keeping with the functionalist approach of pragmatic realism. (For a detailed discussion of controlled collisions as a species of encounters, see Kugler et. al., this volume.)

INFORMATION

Although it remains a serious challenge to explain how the environment imparts structure to energy by the laws of physics, it is even more difficult to explain how such structured energy distributions constitute useful information for an active perceiver. In the case of vision, the optical pattern at a point of observation is due to the lawful scatter-reflection of incident light from the surroundings, and transformations of that optic array are induced by motions of the surfaces themselves or movements of the perceiver. The fundamental hypothesis put forth by Gibson is that *information exists as invariant aspects of these patterns and changes in the energy distribution.*

As a development of this view, following a suggestion by the noted philosopher Ernst Cassirer (1944) in his seminal paper, *The Concept of Group and the Theory of Perception,* Shaw and others examined the role of symmetry groups in event perception (Shaw, McIntyre, & Mace, 1974; Shaw & Wilson, 1976). They concluded that such groups may indeed be useful in describing the invariant aspects of energy distributions underlying the information for perception.

The mathematical intuition that group theory may ultimately prove helpful in guiding our thinking about event perception has its roots at the heart of the 20th Century revolution in physics. The group-theoretic techniques developed by Felix Klein, David Hilbert, Emmy Noether, Hermann Weyl, and Eugene Wigner, and incorporated into special relativity and quantum physics to characterize energy invariants, might prove invaluable to psychologists who are seeking to characterize informational invariants. The problem is that the applications of group theory to the macro scale of events in relativity physics, and to the micro scale of events in quantum physics, do not appear appropriate for the terrestrial scale at which humans perceive and act. What is needed is a group theory adapted to the invariant structure of events at that in-between scale that Gibson called "ecological physics."

But given that an ecological approach selects the appropriate scale of analysis, why is the concept of an event still so difficult to make formally explicit and scientifically useful? The history of science suggests to us that what appears intuitively simple in nature may prove virtually impossible to characterize until certain prerequisite concepts are introduced. Apparently, the greater the ramifications of a concept, the greater the entropy produced in a science by the frequent but casual use of the term. Perhaps the terms "information" and "event" in psychology may require the same lengthy and careful debate as did such terms as "matter," "energy," and "elasticity" in physics before the alchemy of scientific criticism transmuted them from base ideas to valuable explanatory concepts. The concept of elasticity is a case in point. Few scientists could make sense of Thomas Young's formulation of the idea until Augustin Cauchy introduced the concepts of stress and strain, which proved prerequisite to its understanding.

The pair of prerequisite concepts that we wish to offer as aids to understanding the notion of an event are what we have referred to elsewhere (e.g., Pittenger & Shaw, 1975) as *transformational* and *structural invariants*—terms coined to describe, respectively, the precise information for the style of change characteristic of an event, and the information for those structural properties that remain constant under that change. In what follows our goal will be to persuade you that these two concepts are sufficiently rich to encompass any kind of event, and sufficiently precise to guide both theory and research. The extent to which our proposal proves fruitful, of course, is a matter that only time and diligence will decide.

see p. 246

THE APPLICATION OF GROUP THEORY TO EVENT PERCEPTION

Specifically, our proposal is that a particular pair of transformational and structural invariants constitutes a formal description of the information that specifies a certain type of event. It is by virtue of these invariants that information for an event might be characterized and ultimately measured.

Before giving details, let us consider the abstract form of the argument. We propose that the specification of a particular event requires two things: First, a *symmetry-preserving* operation that defines the structural invariant of the event, that is, that designates the properties that remain invariant under the style of change. Second, a *symmetry-breaking* operation that designates certain other properties that are systematically destroyed under all instances of the style of change, defining the transformational invariant of the event. Furthermore, the nature of the structural properties of objects is revealed to us by observing events in which they remain constant contrasted with events in which they change; hence, a generic group, in which two contrasting events with reciprocal symmetry-preserving and symmetry-breaking operations stand as *dual anti-symmetric subgroups*, must be defined for perceptual theory. Although this type of analysis identifies the structural and transformational invariants specific to an event, it remains for the study of ecological optics, acoustics, or haptics to determine exactly how they are manifested in the optic, acoustic, or haptic array.

For example, consider an object such as a book on a flat surface such as a table top. The book may be slid over the table by rotating and translating it. Since such displacements do not change the shape of the book we call them *rigid* transformations. The set of rigid transformations forms a mathematical group, in the usual sense that more complex displacements can be composed of sequences of rotations and translations. Sets of such basic transformations that can be so combined without creating new styles of change are said to have the first important property of groups, that of *closure*. If space permitted, we could show how the set of rigid transformations, or displacements, also satisfies the other properties of mathematical group: Second, that, each displacement has an *inverse*, or opposite, displacement that nullifies its effect; third, that for all displacements there exists an *identity* or "do nothing" operation that leaves everything unchanged; and fourth, that the way complex sequences of displacements are applied satisfies the *associative* property of combination.

Now consider the subgroup of rotations. What are the structural properties of the book that remain invariant, or "symmetrical," under this operation? First, what is typically called the "rigid shape" of the object is constant (this term can be generalized to include other object properties such as size, color, and texture as well). Second, the book's location remains constant, as a fixed point is maintained under the transformation. Hence, rotation can be considered a symmetry-preserving operation with respect to rigidity and location. A mathematical description of the information that specifies these properties is the structural invariant of the event.

It is not enough, however, to know that such properties remain constant; to specify the style of change, the properties that vary must be known. Rotation is clearly a symmetry-breaking operation with respect to the object's orientation. Hence, the destruction of only the property of orientation is unique to the rotational style of change, and when formally characterized it comprises the transformational invariant of the rotation event. Taken together, the structural and transformational invariants provide complete formal description of the perceptual information that is unique and specific to the event of a rotating book; and it is only through the counterpoint of symmetry-preserving and symmetry-breaking operations that the event is thereby specified. For brevity we often say that structural and transformational invariants specify an event or are the information for an event, but we must be cautious, lest these formal descriptions of information become confused with the invariant properties of the energy distributions themselves—a mistaking of the description for the thing described.

In a deeper sense, however, the nature of structural properties is not revealed to us by their constancy. We perceive by contrasts. In order for a property dimension to be made visible, we must observe some systematic variation along that dimension; in order to know an object, we must subject it to all sorts of transformations and see how it behaves. A particular event is but one such interrogation. This is why we might expect fish to be the last creatures on earth to discover the properties of water, and why a world full of objects of the same shape would teach us nothing about shape as a property dimension. Thus, information completely specifying a structural property requires contrasting variation in that property, and we propose that it is provided by two *dual anti-symmetric subgroups* of events—"antisymmetric" in that what one preserves the other destroys, "dual" in the strict mathematical sense that they have contrasting, reciprocal effects along a single dimension of change.

Returning to our example, let us ask: What are the reciprocal effects of rotating and translating the book on the table? That is, what structural properties does each change and leave invariant? Put simply, where we have seen that rotation changes the orientation of the object but not its location, translation does the reverse—changes its location but not its orientation. Hence, rotation and translation are antisymmetric in their effects on location and orientation, for the symmetry that rotation *preserves* is exactly that which translation *breaks*, and vice versa. Hence, these two dual events make visible the structural properties of location and orientation via their contrasting effects.

As for the structural property of rigidity under displacement, the essence of the concept is that the distances between arbitrary points on the displaced object remain constant: Under translation, every point is moved by equal parallel vectors, and under rotation, every point is moved by equal angular vectors. Thus, both operations are symmetry-preserving with respect to rigid shape. To reveal the structural aspects of rigidity or shape to an observer, therefore, by our hypothesis nonrigid transformations or disparate shapes must also be observed.

We may further show that rotation and translation are nested under a higher-order class of events, that of rigid displacements, by virtue of sharing a higher-order transformational invariant. As we have seen, both styles of change leave the rigid shape of the object invariant, and hence are symmetry-preserving with respect to shape. However, although rotation maintains a fixed point, neither preserves a fixed *line* of points, and hence both are symmetry-breaking with respect to a fixed line. This defines a new transformational invariant specific to the generic group of rigid displacements, uniting the events of rotation and translation (see Fig 1.1).

If we are correct in our proposals, it follows that every type of event should have a dual with which it can be contrasted. Let us consider an additional

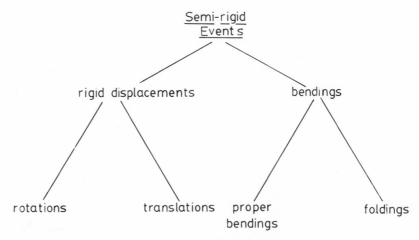

FIG. 1.1 Structure of dual antisymmetric subgroups nested within generic groups. The properties preserved and destroyed under each type of event determine its structural and transformational invariants.

example in order to demonstrate the generality of the analysis. We draw on Jansson & Runeson's (1977) experimental study of bending events that alter the curvature of a surface without stretch or strain. They and their subjects divided bending events into two sub-classes called *proper-bending* and *folding*. Following the current line of argument, we suggest that bending events comprise a group with proper-bending and folding represented as dual antisymmetric subgroups, each preserving what the other destroys.

By way of illustration let us return to our book, still sitting on the table. The opening and closing of the book can be considered a folding style of change in which two rigid half-surfaces rotate independently about a fixed axis or "crease," like a hinge. As the book's hard cover does not bend, the structural property preserved under folding is the *degree of curvature* of each half-surface. A proper-bending style of change, on the other hand, is defined as the smooth flexion of the surface, resulting in a change of curvature over the whole surface, rather than a simple creasing along one axis. Thus folding is symmetry-preserving with respect to the degree of curvature of the half-surfaces, while proper-bending is symmetry-breaking with respect to the same property. It is this contrast which distinguishes the two transformational invariants characteristic of these two styles of change.

On the other hand, since folding involves rotation around a fixed axis, it divides the surface into two independent parts, or half-surfaces. This is not true of proper-bending, since the flexing of one portion of the surface continuously redefines the curvature of the whole. Thus we might say that where proper-bending is symmetry-preserving with respect to flexion or the *continuity of curvature*, folding breaks that symmetry, disrupting curvature in a discontinuous manner at the crease. In sum, folding preserves degree of curvature and destroys continuity of curvature, while proper-bending does the opposite, and again we find dual, antisymmetric transformations whose styles of change differ in both what properties are left invariant and what properties are systematically changed. This subtlety in description is easily misunderstood (e.g., Cutting, 1983) and therefore deserves careful attention.

It now remains to show how proper-bending and folding may be united under a more generic group operation called *bending,* by identifying a higher order style of change. In the case of folding, as we have noted, the line of points on the crease remains fixed. Similarly (by extension of Brouwer's fixed point theorem), when a surface undergoes proper-bending, it flexes relative to a line of fixed points. Hence both proper-bending and folding events are symmetry-preserving with respect to a line of fixed points, and both are obviously symmetry-breaking with respect to surface rigidity. This defines a common transformational invariant, uniting the two events under a generic bending group (see Fig. 1.1).

Now let us quickly show that, relatively speaking, bending events and rigid displacements are themselves nested within a higher event structure that we might call "semirigid" events. Whereas displacements preserve rigidity, bendings do not. On the other hand, although bendings preserve a line of fixed points, we have noted that displacements do not. Hence, with respect to the structural properties of rigidity and line of fixed points, displacements and bendings are antisymmetric duals: What one preserves the other destroys. But what is the higher order transformational invariant shared by these two styles of change? They are united in the generic group of "semirigid" events whose transformational invariant is characterized by the breaking of all symmetries listed earlier while preserving a new higher order property called Gaussian curvature. This is simply the preservation of arc lengths and angles between points on a surface, such that no figure drawn on the surface itself is stretched or compressed under the transformation. In this way, bending events and rigid displacements are united under a common style of change, and together comprise the generic group of semirigid events (Fig. 1.1). It can further be shown that semirigid events are duals with the group of events known as "strains," which involve the stretching and compressing of surfaces—but that is another story. It is reasonable to conclude that the concepts of event groups, symmetry-breaking and preserving operations, and transformational and structural invariants provide a general but precise means for systematically characterizing events and their perceptual specification.

EVENT DYNAMICS

Most of our discussion up to this point has described events in terms of pure motion and change. We have spoken of styles of change defined over structure, such as displacements, bending, stretching, three–dimensional rotation, and the motions of the joints during locomotion. The formal structure of such events can be given a rate-independent, *geometric* description, as we have attempted with the application of group theory. By scaling them with respect to time, however, these motions may also be given a satisfactory rate-dependent, or *kinematic* description in terms of velocity, acceleration, jerk, and so on, as Johansson's vector analysis or Gibson's rates of texture deletion have implied. But, being concerned with ecological events, we are forced to leave this disembodied world of spatio–temporal abstraction and confront the material one. Most of the events that occur around us are *not* free to vary along arbitrary kinematic dimensions. Rather they are governed by specific terrestrial constraints such as gravitational force, the friction between surfaces, the elasticity of common objects, and the rate at which living organisms can dissipate energy, variables that restrict the possible kinematic patterns of change. Runeson (1977) rightly drew our attention to the *dynamics*[2] of natural events in his dissertation on collision events, and much recent work has pursued this new direction.

This does not mean, however, that we are forced to give up event-groups as a classification scheme for perceived events. On the contrary, we should seek ways in which to incorporate dynamic variables (e.g., forces, masses, frictions) into our kinematic event descriptions, just as our field has struggled to incorporate change into static geometric, or snapshot descriptions. Although this is a most difficult task, a significant intuitive beginning has been made (see Johansson, this volume). Let us end by considering how events might be redefined to accommodate the more realistic restrictions imposed by dynamics.

To set any object in motion, or to bring about any mechanical, chemical, or biological change, work must be done and hence, energy expended. Specifically, potential or free energy (energy available to perform work) is transformed into kinetic energy (that bound up in doing work on a body or dissipated as heat). More concretely, transformations between forms of energy may occur, as when chemical energy is converted to mechanical energy and heat in a muscle or an automobile engine, or electrical energy is converted to light and heat when a lamp is turned on. As the textbooks note, the presence of energy is only revealed to an observer when some kind of *change* takes place. Hence, the energy concept plays the role of a structural invariant whose constancy (i.e., conservation) is revealed by some transformation. Where there's smoke there's fire: An ecological event implicates the transformation of energy.

---

[2]Modern physics texts typically divide mechanics into two branches, the study of the equilibrium mechanics of stationary bodies (*statics*) and the study of motion. This latter field is in turn broken down into the study of motion exclusive of mass and force (*kinematics*) and the study of the relationship between motion and the forces affecting motion (*dynamics* or *kinetics*). The terms ''dynamics'' and ''kinetics'' are used interchangeably both for this latter area, and for the general study of moving bodies. In this paper we opt to follow Runeson (1977) in using ''dynamics'' in the more limited sense to refer to the study of the relation between motion and force.

Consequently, we propose to redefine events dynamically, as follows: *An event is a minimal change in an energy potential (or between energy potentials) within some intrinsically determined region of space–time.* This definition improves on our earlier kinematic one by grounding its formal relations in the dynamical processes of physical systems. As animals we are bathed in a sea of energy, with an ebb and flow not merely of change but of change determined by potential flux. Hence, we may say that the ultimate limit on any terrestrial event is the rate of dissipation of free energy in the event system. This suggests an approach to the concept of event periods, for the so-called "relaxation times" of different events are determined by the masses and energies involved.

The central question for an ecological theory of event perception thus becomes, *how do dynamics condition perception*? This question immediately takes on two forms. When applied to *ecological events,* the issue is one of how the dynamic properties of a distal event are specified to an observer. When applied to *encounters,* the issue is one of how an animal comes to participate successfully in a dynamic encounter, that is, how the energy expenditure required for a goal-directed action is perceptually specified to the actor. This contrast is illustrated by the example of seeing someone else lift a heavy object (e.g., Runeson & Frykholm, 1981) as opposed to seeing how we must lift it ourselves.

In both cases, the logic of the argument can be stated rather simply: Ecological events are governed by dynamic law; organisms participate in events (whether as observers or perceptually-guided actors) and survive; hence, perception must be constrained by dynamic law. The crucial and difficult link in the argument is, of course, the relationship between energy and information. It is here that the problem of the semantics of perception—that is, how optical and acoustical patterns can be said to have meaning, or *be information,* for a particular animal—must be attacked. Thus our question about how dynamics condition perception may be reformulated as follows: How is the infomation specific to an event related to the energy bound up in that event, and to the work that must be done by the animal in an encounter? (see Kugler, Turvey, Carello, & Shaw, this volume). Initially, we must consider how the unfolding of a dynamic event *structures* or patterns light and sound in particular ways for particular perceiver/actors.

The Dynamics of Ecological Events

Gibson argued that information should be described as invariant structure in an energy distribution. A particular surface layout or event yields a unique transformation of pattern in light and sound, available for detection by a perceiver. But as Runeson (1977) pointed out, optically specified events pose a conundrum: Even though events must involve the dynamics of energy transformation, changes in an optical pattern can only be described kinematically, either in terms of motions on an optic projection surface or in terms of temporal changes in optical structure. The mapping from dynamic event to kinematic pattern thus appears to collapse a dimension, much as the dimension of "depth" was believed to be lost in a flat retinal image, for dynamic variables such as mass, friction, elasticity, and energy are not present in the kinematic description. Higher-order aspects of other events, such as their animacy and intentionality, are similarly "lost" in a kinematic array. Can observers actually perceive the dynamic, animate, and intentional properties of a distal event, or only its motion?

A number of well-known experiments suggest that such higher-order properties are commonly perceived. For example, Michotte's (1946/1963) classic work on the perception of causality can perhaps best be understood as a study of apparently open systems in which the dynamic law of conservation of momentum in collisions is violated (see also Natsoulas, 1960, 1961). Crudely, assuming approximately equal masses for objects of equal size in a display, an object that is struck by another and that moves off at a nonconserving velocity is seen as being the source of the additional energy in the system, and the result is a "triggering" effect of self-propulsion. Michotte's related studies of locomotion and Johansson's experiments with point-light walkers demonstrate that animacy can also be perceived in appropriately constrained kinematic displays. Finally, Heider and Simmel's (1944) film of interacting geometric shapes illustrates that intentional behavior is perceived as well, and some of the relevant variables of motion have been identified by Bassili (1976).

Most instructive are several studies that indicate that perceivers *cannot help but* be constrained by event dynamics, even when specifically instructed to attend to the kinematic properties of a display. When viewers are asked to report on the motion of a body moving from rest, Runeson (1974, 1975) found that an object gradually accelerated to a constant velocity is perceived as moving at a constant speed throughout, while an object starting with an instantaneous constant velocity is perceived as making an initial jump followed by deceleration to a constant velocity. Such findings are peculiar in terms of the perception of velocity per se, but are consistent with the dynamics of natural "start events," in which massive bodies like animals or falling trees achieve motion only through gradual acceleration, never with an instantaneous velocity. Hence, what looks "natural" is a gradually accelerating body. In this case, apparently, perception is constrained by the dynamics of terrestrial events. Analogously, in Gibson's film of nonreversible events such as crashing surf and cookie-eating, we suggest that many of the reversed cases look funny or unnatural or even animate precisely because they violate specific dynamic constraints, running up energy gradients rather than down them (Gibson & Kaushall, 1973).

To prevent "dynamic event perception" from being reduced to "motion perception plus inference," however, it must be shown that even though dynamic properties are not themselves present in the optic array they are *specified* by the array kinematics. Runeson (1977) first made this point clear, and by way of example he showed that completely general kinematic information for the dynamic properties of elasticity and relative mass in collisions could be derived from the law of conservation of momentum. In subsequent experiments at the University of Connecticut, we found highly accurate judgments of elasticity in a bouncing ball display (Warren, Kim, & Husney, in preparation), and drew some preliminary conclusions about the optical information supporting—within certain ranges—accurate judgments of relative mass in collision events (Todd & Warren, 1983). Similarly, Shaw, Mark, Jenkins, and Mingolla (1982) have argued that the perception of cranio-facial growth and judgments of facial attractiveness are contingent upon the confluence of potentials (gravitational, muscular, masticatory, cellular growth, etc.) acting within certain ranges over time to shape the profile. Hence, perception is not merely conditioned by event dynamics, but by dynamics construed *at an ecological scale,* within terrestrial ranges of values. In sum, there is evidence to indicate that the perception of ecological events is indeed constrained by the dynamic laws under which such events unfold, via regularities in the kinematics of change in the optic array.

The Dynamics of Encounters

Considering that organisms must function in a dynamically governed world, their actions should be guided by information about the energetics of the encounters in which they participate. This applies both to the control of activity in which the animal is actively engaged, and to the specification of possibilities for action, or affordances, prior to their realization.

The problem of motor control and coordination can be seen as a version of the general problem of the arising of order and regularity in complex systems, and recent approaches to this problem in physics can be mined for their applications in psychology (see Kugler et. al., this volume; Warren & Kelso, this volume). Borrowing on these developments, Kugler, Kelso, and Turvey (1980, 1981) and Kugler and Turvey (in press) have argued that the regulation of activity may be an a posteriori consequence of the dynamics of the animal-environment system, rather than dictated a priori by commands or programs in the motor system. Following Iberall (1977), they have characterized the actor as a collection of thermodynamic engines that, when taken together with environmental constraints, give rise to stabilities, or preferred regions of minimal energy dissipation, which can act to establish parameter values for the motor system. Thus, they have been able to predict the preferred frequencies of a cyclical motor activity, the uni- and bi-manual swinging of hammers with varying masses and lengths, and to specify the timing and quantity of energy required to maintain the activity, on the basis of an analysis of the stabilities of the person-pendulum system. Adjusting the frequency of hammering, walking, running, bicycling, etc. under different conditions acts to maintain the system in a stable state, although the constraints can be temporarily violated at some cost to the actor. In these cases, activity is regulated by the dynamics of the encounter, enabling the animal to participate successfully and economically by sensing and taking advantage of seams in the energy distribution. We believe this to be currently the most promising conception of *propriospecific* information in the guidance of movement.

We have been drawing upon a dynamic approach to understand how the perception of the opportunities for action (affordances) is configured by the energy demands of those actions. First, given that any activity requires energy expenditure and that a course of action is selected on the basis of visual information, *exterospecific* information about the work involved should be available not only during, but prior to activity. In other words, Kugler and Turvey (in press) address the problem of how to best swing a given hammer; the affordance problem is how to choose the best hammer to swing. Secondly, to realize a particular affordance by performing precise movements (like reaching for and grasping a hammer), a specific quantity of energy must be degraded over the musculature, and this, too, must be specified in advance. The work involved and the motor parameterization required will of necessity vary with the size and structure of the actor, that is, with the *dynamic fit* between animal and environment, and hence such information must be "body scaled," or intrinsically scaled to the individual (Lee, 1980; Warren, 1982; Warren & Shaw, 1981).

Consider a cat that leaps from the floor onto a platform of some kind, an action performed with precision and grace whether the target is a low, wide chair or a high, narrow windowsill. First of all, the cat must perceive that the platform is "leapable," within the reach of its action system. Second, it must be the case that there is visual information available to tune the cat's action system to the requirements of the particular act. In other words, the motor parameters governing the dissipation of energy over the cat's particular limb structure must be tuned to move its particular body mass over a particular distance in a gravitational field. In experiments on humans undergoing self-initiated falls from standing position onto a tilted platform, Dietz & Noth (1978) found that the onset of EMG activity in the arm muscles preparatory to landing was under visual control *and* that the rate of increase and peak level of activity was proportional to the distance of the fall. Hence, muscle activity prior to landing is proportional to the uncoming force at impact, and is visually controlled. In sum, the dynamic consequences of an act, the required work, must somehow be visually specified.

Recently, we have been studying the ordinary activity of climbing stairs to explore the relationship between perception and action, affordances and effectivities, and information and energy (Warren, 1982, in press). We found that an affordance such as an optimally "climbable" stairway is determined by the dynamic fit between climber and stair. On the one hand, as the riser height of a stair increases relative to the leg length of a particular climber, more energy must be expended to move the body mass through a given vertical distance, or to perform a given amount of "ecological" work. On the other hand, as riser height decreases, more energy is expended in a greater number of step cycles to do the same amount of work. These two competing factors act to establish an optimal point of minimum energy cost for the animal-environment system, an optimum riser height that is a constant proportion of leg length. If perceivers are sensitive to the energy demands of possible activities, their visually guided choices of stairways with different dimensions should reflect these optimal points of energy efficiency. Indeed, we found that observers of varying limb dimensions visually prefer those stairways that optimally match their body size. Hence, they are perceiving an affordance of "climbability" as specified by the optimal point in the animal-environment system, which is inherently meaningful for action in terms of energy expenditure.

We have shown formally that stairway dimensions are optically specified to an observer in body-scaled terms, and hence the observer has information about the fit between his or her leg and the stair. However, we do not wish to rule out the role of experience, or the participation in previous encounters, in the attunement of the visual system to the available information about subsequent activity. Under this view, perceptual learning might involve active exploration of the energy manifold over a spatio–temporal interval sufficient to determine its topology or shape and identify its optimal points. These points pick out the values of optical variables that specify unclimbable and optimal stairways to a perceiver.

CONCLUSION

In this chapter we have identified some of the major problems and sampled a few important directions of current research in the fledgling field of event perception. This overview has led us to conclude that the study of events is not just another problem area but one in which questions arise of fundamental importance to all areas of perceptual research. We have seen how the incorporation of temporal variables into formerly spatial theories of perception has transformed not just the theories, but the formulation of the problems, giving birth to our field of event perception. We have here suggested that a successful approach to the problem of how a meaningful environment is perceived and acted within must further incorporate dynamic variables—that both ecological events and encounters should be reconstrued not just spatio–temporally, but dynamically. Energy potentials configure events, the consequent optical and acoustic information available about them, our possibilities for action, and ultimately the phenomena of perception that are the driving concern of this conference. In closing, we would like to echo Gunnar Johansson's remark that some day there will be no diciplinary distinction between "event perception" and "perception" in general, for spatio–temporal—and dynamic—variables will be understood as crucial to any explanation of the phenomena at hand.

REFERENCES

Andersen, G. J. & Braunstein, M. L. Dynamic occlusion in the perception of rotation in depth. *Perception & Psychophysics*, 1983, *34*, 356–362.

Bassili, J. N. Temporal and spatial contingencies in the perception of social events. *Journal of Personality and Social Psychology*, 1976, *33*, 680–685.

Braunstein, M. L. *Depth perception through motion.* New York: Academic Press, 1976.

Cassirer, E. The concept of group and the theory of perception. *Philosophy and Phenomenological Research*, 1944, *5*, 1–35.

Cutting, J. E. Four assumptions about invariance in perception. *Journal of Experimental Psychology: Human Perception and Performance*, 1983, *9*, 310–317.

Cutting, J. E., & Kozlowski, L. T. Recognizing friends by their walk: Gait perception without familiarity cues. *Bulletin of the Psychonomic Society*, 1977, *9*, 333–356.

Cutting, J. E., Proffit, D. R., & Kozlowski, L. T. A biomechanical invariant for gait perception. *Journal of Experimental Psychology: Human Perception and Performance*, 1978, *4*, 357–372.

Dietz, V., & Noth, J. Pre-innervation and stretch responses of triceps bracchii in man falling with and without visual control. *Brain Research*, 1978, *142*, 576–579.

Fieandt, K. von, & Gibson, J. J. The sensitivity of the eye to two kinds of continuous transformation of a shadow pattern. *Journal of Experimental Psychology*, 1959, *57*, 344–347.

Flock, H. R. Some conditions sufficient for accurate monocular perception of moving surface slant. *Journal of Experimental Psychology*, 1964, *67*, 560–572.

Foder, J. A. & Pylyshyn, Z. W. How direct is visual perception? Some reflections on Gibson's "Ecological Approach." *Cognition*, 1981, *9*, 139–196.

Gibson, E. J., Gibson, J. J., Smith, O. W., & Flock, H. R. Motion parallax as a determinant of perceived depth. *Journal of Experimental Psychology*, 1959, *58*, 40–51.

Gibson, E. J., Owsley, C. J., & Johnston, J. Perception of invariants by five-month-old infants: Differentiation of two types of motion. *Developmental Psychology*, 1978, *14*, 407–415.

Gibson, E. J., Owsley, C. J., Walker, A., & Megaw-Nyce, J. Development of the perception of invariants: substance and shape. *Perception*, 1979, *8*, 609–619.

Gibson, J. J. *Motion picture testing and research.* AAF Aviation Psychology Research Report No. 7. Washington, D.C.: Government Printing Office, 1947.

Gibson, J. J. *The perception of the visual world.* Boston: Houghton Mifflin, 1950.

Gibson, J. J. Optical motions and transformations as stimuli for visual perception. *Psychological Review*, 1957, *54*, 288–295.

Gibson, J. J. Visually controlled locomotion and visual orientation in animals. *British Journal of Psychology*, 1958, *49*, 182–194.

Gibson, J. J. Ecological optics. *Vision Research*, 1961, *1*, 253–262.

Gibson, J. J. *The senses considered as perceptual systems.* Boston: Houghton Mifflin, 1966.

Gibson, J. J. *The change from visible to invisible: A study of optical transitions* (motion picture). State College, PA: Psychological Cinema Register, 1968.

Gibson, J. J., Kaplan, G., Reynolds, H., & Wheeler, K. The change from visible to invisible: A study of optical transitions. *Perception & Psychophysics*, 1969, *5*, 113–116.

Gibson, J. J. On theories for visual space perception. A reply to Johansson. *Scandinavian Journal of Psychology*, 1970, *11*, 75–79.

Gibson, J. J. *The ecological approach to visual perception.* Boston: Houghton Mifflin, 1979.

Gibson, J. J., & Gibson, E. J. Continuous perspective transformations and the perception of rigid motion. *Journal of Experimental Psychology*, 1957, *54*, 129–138.

Gibson, J. J. & Kaushall, P. *Reversible and irreversible events* (motion picture). State College, PA: Psychological Cinema Register, 1973.

Gibson, J. J., Olum, P., & Rosenblatt, F. Parallax and perspective during aircraft landing. *American Journal of Psychology*, 1955, *68*, 372–385.

Heider, F., & Simmel, M. An experimental study of apparent behavior. *American Journal of Psychology*, 1944, *57*, 243–259.

Iberall, A. S. A field and circuit thermodynamics for integrative physiology. I. Introduction to general notions. *American Journal of Physiology*, 1977, *233*, R171–R180.

Jansson, G. Perceived bending and stretching motions from a line of points. *Scandinavian Journal of Psychology*, 1977, *18*, 209–215.

Jansson, G., & Johansson, G. Visual perception of bending motion. *Perception*, 1973, *2*, 321–326.

Jansson, G., & Runeson, S. Perceived bending motions from a quadrangle changing form. *Perception*, 1977, *6*, 595–600.

Johansson, G. *Configurations in event perception.* Uppsala: Aimqvist & Wiksell, 1950.

Johansson, G. Rigidity, stability and motion in perceptual space. *Acta Psychology*, 1958, *14*, 359–370.

Johansson, G. Perception of motion and changing form. *Journal of Scandinavian Psychology*, 1964, *5*, 181–208.

Johansson, G. On theories for visual space perception. A letter to Gibson. *Scandinavian Journal of Psychology*, 1970, *11*, 67–74.

Johansson, G. Visual perception of biological motion and a model for its analysis. *Perception and Psychophysics*, 1973, *14*, 201–211.

Johansson, G. Vector analysis in visual perception of rolling motion: A quantitative approach. *Psychologie Forschung*, 1974, *36*, 311–319. (a)

Johansson, G. Visual perception of rotary motion as transformation of conic sections. *Psychologia*, 1974, *17*, 226–237. (b)

Johansson, G., & Jansson, G. Perceived rotary motion from changes in a straight line. *Perception and Psychophysics*, 1968, *4*, 165–170.

Kaplan, G. A. Kinetic disruption of optical texture: The perception of depth at an edge. *Perception & Psychophysics*, 1969, *6*, 193–198.

Kugler, P. N., Kelso, J. A. S., & Turvey, M. T. On the concept of coordinative structures as dissipative structures. I. Theoretical lines of convergence. In G. E. Stelmach & J. Requin (Eds.), *Tutorials in motor behavior*. Amsterdam: North Holland, 1980.

Kugler, P. N., Kelso, J. A. S., & Turvey, M. T. On the control and coordinating of naturally developing systems. In J. A. S. Kelso & J. E. Clark (Eds.), *The development of movement control and coordination*. New York: John Wiley, 1981.

Kugler, P. N. & Turvey, M. T. *Information, natural law, and the self-assembly of rhythmic movement.* Hillsdale, NJ: Erlbaum, in press.

Lappin, J. S., Doner, J. F., & Kottas, B. L. Minimal conditions for the visual detection of structure and motion in three dimensions. *Science*, 1980, *209*, 717–719.

Lee, D. N. Visuo-motor coordination in space–time. In G. E. Stelmach & J. Requin (Eds.), *Tutorials in motor behavior*. North-Holland Publishing Co., 1980.

Mace, W. M. James Gibson strategy for perceiving: Ask not what's inside your head but what your head is inside of. In R. E. Shaw & J. Bransford (Eds.), *Perceiving, Acting and Knowing: Toward an Ecological Psychology*. Hillsdale NJ: Lawrence Erlbaum Associates, 1977.

Mace, W. M., & Shaw, R. E. Simple kinetic information for transparent depth. *Perception and Psychophysics*, 1974, *15*, 201–209.

Mark, L. S. *A transformational approach toward understanding the perception of growing faces.* Doctoral dissertation, University of Connecticut, 1979.

Mark, L. S., Todd, J. T., & Shaw, R. E. The perception of growth: How different styles of change are distinguished. *Journal of Experimental Psychology: Human Perception and Performance*, 1981, *7*, 355–368.

Marr, D. Visual information processing: The structure and creation of visual representations. *Philosophical Transactions of the Royal Society of London*, 1980, *B290*, 199–218.

Marr, D. *Vision.* San Francisco: W. H. Freeman, 1982.

Metzger, W. *Gesetze des Sehens.* Frankfort am Main: Waldemar Knamer, 1953.

Michaels, C. F., & Carello, C. *Direct perception.* Englewood Cliffs, NJ: Prentice-Hall, 1981.

Michotte, A. *The perception of causality.* London: Methuen, 1963. (Originally published in French, 1946).

Minkowski, H. *Space and time.* Address delivered at the 80th Assembly of German Natural Scientists and Physicians, Cologne, Sept. 21, 1908.

Natsoulas, T. Judgments of velocity and weight in a causal situation. *American Journal of Psychology,* 1960, *73,* 404–410.

Natsoulas, T. Principles of momentum and kinetic energy in the perception of causality. *American Journal of Psychology,* 1961, *74,* 394–402.

Neisser, U. *Cognitive Psychology.* New York: Appleton-Century-Crofts, 1967.

Pittenger, J. B., & Shaw, R. E. Aging faces as viscal-elastic events: Implications for a theory of non-rigid shape perception. *Journal of Experimental Psychology: Human Perception and Performance,* 1975, *1,* 374–382.

Pittenger, J. B., Shaw, R. E., & Mark, L. S. Perceptual information for the age level of faces as a higher order invariant of growth. *Journal of Experimental Psychology: Human Perception and Performance,* 1979, *5,* 478–493.

Runeson, S. Constant velocity—not perceived as such. *Psychological Research,* 1974, *37,* 3–23.

Runeson, S. Visual prediction of collision with natural and nonnatural motion functions. *Perception and Psychophysics,* 1975, *18,* 261–266.

Runeson, S. *On visual perception of dynamic events.* Doctoral dissertation, University of Uppsala, Sweden, 1977.

Runeson, S., & Frykholm, G. Visual perception of lifted weight. *Journal of Experimental Psychology: Human Perception and Performance,* 1981, *4,* 733–740.

Shaw, R. E., & Cutting, J. E. Constraints on language events: Clues from an ecological theory of event perception. In U. Bellugi & M. Studdert-Kennedy (Eds.), *Signed language and spoken language: Biological constraints on linguistic form.* Dahlem Konferenzen, Weinheim/Deerfield Beach, Fla./Basel: Verlag Chemie, 1980.

Shaw, R. E., McIntyre, M., & Mace, W. M. The role of symmetry in event perception. In MacLeod, R. B. & Pick, H. L. (Eds.), *Perception: Essays in honor of James J. Gibson.* Ithaca: Cornell University Press, 1974.

Shaw, R. E., Mark, L. S., Jenkins, D. H., & Mingolla, E. A dynamic geometry for predicting growth of gross craniofacial morphology. In A. Dixon & B. Sarnat (Eds.), *Proceedings of an international conference on mechanisms and influences on bone growth,* 1982.

Shaw, R. E., & Pittenger, J. B. Perceiving change. In H. Pick & E. Saltzman (Eds.), *Modes of perceiving and processing information.* Hillsdale, NJ: Lawrence Erlbaum Associates, 1978.

Shaw, R. E., & Turvey, M. T. Coalitions as models for ecosystems: A realist perspective on perceptual organization. In Kubovy, M. & Pomerantz, J. (Eds.), *Perceptual Organization.* Hillsdale, NJ: Lawrence Erlbaum Associates, 1981.

Shaw, R. E., Turvey, M. T., & Mace, W. M. Ecological psychology: The consequence of a committment to realism. In W. Weimer & D. Palermo (Eds.), *Cognition and the symbolic processes, II.* Hillsdale, NJ: Erlbaum, 1981.

Shaw, R. E., & Wilson, B. E. Generative conceptual knowledge: How we know what we know. In D. Klahr (Ed.), *Carnegie-Mellon symposium on information processing: Cognition and instruction.* Hillsdale, NJ: Lawrence Erlbaum Associates, 1976.

Todd, J. T. Visual information about rigid and nonrigid motion: A geometric analysis. *Journal of Experimental Psychology: Human Perception and Performance,* 1982, *8,* 238–252.

Todd, J. T., & Warren, W. H. Visual perception of relative mass in dynamic events. *Perception,* 1983.

Turvey, M. T. & Shaw, R. E. The primacy of perceiving: An ecological reformulation of perception for understanding memory. In L. G. Nilsson (Ed.), *Perspectives on memory research.* Hillsdale, NJ: Erlbaum, 1979.

Turvey, M. T., Shaw, R. E., Reed, E. S., & Mace, W. M. Ecological laws of perceiving and
acting: In reply to Fodor and Pylyshyn. *Cognition,* 1981, *9,* 237–304.

Ullman, S. *The interpretation of visual motion.* Cambridge, MA: MIT Press, 1979.

Wallach, H., & O'Connell, D. N. The kinetic depth effect. *Journal of Experimental Psychology,*
1953, *45,* 205–217.

Warren, W. H. *A biodynamic basis for perception and action in bipedal climbing.* Doctoral dissertation, University of Connecticut, 1982. (University Microfilms No. 8309263)

Warren, W. H. Perceiving affordances: The visual guidance of stair climbing. *Journal of Experimental Psychology: Human Perception and Performance,* in press.

Warren, W. H., Kim, E. E., & Husney, R. The way the ball bounces: Visual perception of elasticity
and control of the bounce pass. In preparation.

Warren, W. H., & Shaw, R. E. Psychophysics and ecometrics. *Behavioral and Brain Sciences,*
1981, *4,* 209–210.

2 About Visual Event Perception

Gunnar Johansson
University of Uppsala
Sweden

ABOUT VISUAL EVENT PERCEPTION

A basic problem in the study of visual perception is how reflected light, focused onto a vertebrate's retina, can evoke perception of a three–dimensional distal world, the animal's own displacements in this world, and the motion of other organisms and objects. This problem, and my attempts to solve it, are the concerns of this chapter.

In the past, psychologists generally have treated this as if it were a problem only for human vision. In contrast to this approach, I take a biological perspective, and therefore discuss visual space perception in terms that are valid for the lens-and-retina eyes of all vertebrate species.

The theme is "event perception" and I would like to begin by making clear what this concept is intended to cover and what is it not. In my monograph *Configurations in Event Perception* (1950) the concept was introduced in a programmatic way. In the present treatment of vision, "event perception" will refer to the *immediate and spontaneous outcome from suprathreshold changes in the optic array* stemming from: (1) distal motion; or (2) changes in brightness and color.

I am aware that this definition of the term "event perception" as referring only to something ongoing implies a restriction of the ordinary content of the word "event." In my terminology, it covers the meaning of the German word *geschehen*, but not *begebnis*; in Swedish, *skeende* (an ongoing process), but not *handelse* (a bounded occurrence). (See the analysis in Mace, this volume, regarding the difference between J. J. Gibson's terminology and my own).

The earlier investigation studied the perceptual effects of temporal relations between two or more spatially isolated physical events: groups of dots in motion, surfaces changing their brightness and/or color, etc. My ambition was to find mathematical relations between the displayed events and the concomitant perception. Besides visual effects, analogous auditory and tactual stimulation was investigated. The main outcome of these experiments was that perception of motion is rather exclusively the preferred type of response, irrespective of sensory channel. This perceptual preference for the decoding of simultaneous physical events in terms of a unitary motion explains why the study of visual event perception most often means a study of motion perception.

The framework for my analyses is the well-established paradigm: Distal stimulus → proximal stimulus → percept. Light reflected from the distal environment forms a proximal distribution of energy specified at the optic nodal point of the eye and focused over the scanning retina. This ever-changing distribution of radiant energy is, by means of a so far unexplained type of *neural processing in the visual system,* transformed into a percept. My experimental program has been centered on the proximal stimulus-to-percept component of the above scheme and this preference will continue in the present paper. However, as a necessary background to my analyses I will also discuss the distal component. No one has treated the distal aspects and the distal to proximal relations more consistently than my late friend and deeply admired colleague J. J. Gibson. Therefore, I will find it useful to refer to his work in several connections.

EVENT PERCEPTION AND ECOLOGICAL EVENTS

In Gibson's last book (1979) we encounter as a central concept the term ''ecological event.'' In his terminology this term stands for physical events in the animal's environment which play an important role in its interaction with the environment. As instances of such distal events Gibson mentions movements of other animals, mechanical motions and other changes over time intervals extending from fractions of a second up to long term events like ripening of fruits and aging of human beings (Gibson, 1979, Ch. 6; see also Pittenger & Shaw, 1975; Warren, 1978; Warren & Shaw, this volume). I have defined ''visual event perception'' as *the immediate sensory recording of changes in proximal stimulation.* Evidently, the concept ''ecological event,'' as describing distal changes, is far wider in range than is my corresponding concept ''perceptible event'' on the organism side, a concept denoting events that might potentially be *perceived.* Some ecological events like the running of a dog are perceptible, other like the ripening of a fruit are not. Perceptible events can be described as spatial changes resulting in proximal changes where the rate of change falls between the lower and upper discrimination limens for the sense organ.

How are the nonperceptible "ecological" events recorded by an observer? This interesting problem falls outside my present theme, but I cannot avoid the comment that it must be appropriate to introduce the term *"event cognition"* for this category of mental achievement. The components of this act are described in conventional terms: initial perceptual recording of essential invariances, storing in memory, comparison between memory and perception and finally recognition of basic structural relationships. [For a critique of such "image comparison" models see Shaw & Pittenger, 1978; Warren & Shaw, this volume - The editors.]

Thus, Gibson's term, "ecological events," is far wider in scope than my "event perception" concept. In other respects, however, some types of perceptual events fall outside the domain of ecological events as defined by Gibson; I return to this later.

ABOUT STIMULI FOR VISUAL EVENT PERCEPTION

The perception of motion can be studied under two headings: *self-motion* perception and *object-motion* perception. In our analyses it will be important to distinguish clearly between these two categories because the determining proximal stimulus characteristics differ in a crucial way.

Self-Motion Perception. In an active animal or man the nodal points of the eyes are most often moving relative to the environment. In man this depends on a number of contributing factors, three of which are of immediate interest in the present context. These are: (1) the head is in a more or less pronounced way moving relative to the body; (2) the body is often moving relative to the environment; (3) there is always a body sway when a person lacks a firm back support. The resulting displacements of the nodal points of the eyes relative to the environment will be termed *self-motion* or, alternatively, locomotion or egomotion. Because it takes place in the environment, self-motion will be treated as a distal event. It is easily seen that an active person (or animal) most often produces some degree of self-motion and also—for physical reasons—that self-motion typically represents a continuous motion.

The optic projection through the lens of an eye in self-motion, relative to the environment, generates the proximal stimulus focused onto the retina. The retina itself usually scans this projection with saccadic or pursuit movements. (The slight difference between the optic nodal point of the human eye and its center of rotation is not taken into account here.) Because of the relative motion of eye to environment, this projection generally is ever-changing under self-motion. Thus the proximal stimulus during self-motion generally is a continuous optic flow over the whole retina (cf. Gibson, 1966). The perceptual response to this proximal stimulus normally is *self-motion perception*.

Let us explicitly sum up in terms of our triadic paradigm. Light reflected by a distal, static, three–dimensional environment is focussed onto the retina of an eye as a proximal stimulus. Due to self-motion of the eye, the proximal stimulus takes the form of a continuous optic flow. This optic flow evokes a perception of self-motion relative to the environment.

For our forthcoming analyses it will be of great importance to observe that when the environment is totally rigid and static the optic flow geometrically represents a perspective transformation. This means that in this flow the so-called projective properties stay invariant, irrespective of how the eye moves relative to the environment.

Object-Motion Perception.   So far we have assumed a totally static environment. However, there often exist moving objects, animals, and people in the environment. The projections of these ''objects'' taken individually also generate local flow patterns which overlay the optic flow generated by the self-motion, and are ''mixed'' with this latter flow. (This means that the respective local flows no longer represent perspective projections.) One may also observe one's own body, especially the extremities. These then qualify as objects of perception. For instance, when I see my own hand writing this sentence I perceive the hand as an object in the present technical sense.

This description is easy to grasp when we consider our artificial indoor environment with its absolutely static structure, planar surfaces, horizontal floor and ceiling, vertical walls, rectangularity, and so on. Most object-motions in this type of environment stem from other persons and the transport of objects.

Far more complex is the mathematical structure of projections from the natural open-air environment. In this environment rigidity and static structures are exceptions. Typically, such environments contain trees, bushes and grass moving in the wind; sometimes also streaming water, moving clouds, etc. Thus, static backgrounds (naked rocks, sand deserts, etc.) and rigid motions are exceptions in this type of environment; elastic motion, bending, and form change usually determine the projections into the eye. When we move through this environment we combine the self-motion component in the proximal flow with this tremendously complex nonrigid motion component. From a mathematical point of view the result is like a chaos or is at least mathematically complex to the point of absurdity. Still we know that visual systems from the very early stages of evolutionary development were efficient analyzers of this type of flow. This environment was the ordinary environment for our ancestors as well as for their ancestors, and so on down the evolutionary series. The visual systems of our forerunners (even the most primitive) are, like our own, capable of instantly bringing order in terms of mathematical invariants to this apparent chaos. For the running rabbit this sensory achievement is of absolutely vital importance, as it is for the chasing hungry fox. How can this achievement be theoretically understood? I will return to this discussion.

What Is Static Perception?

The above analysis of the proximal stimulus in terms of different components in an optic flow has a theoretically important consequence. It necessarily implies that in most cases the perception of *stationary objects and a static environment is in fact the result of a sensory processing of an optic flow extended over the whole retina*. The perceptual outcome of this processing is perception of (1) a stationary environment and (2) self-motion relative to this environment. Thus, perception of static objects or pictures means lack of object motion components in the optic flow, and *not* lack of optic flow in the proximal stimulus, as often has been presumed. Perception from static proximal "retinal images" is a very unusual thing. It is mainly found under laboratory conditions and then only momentarily, or perhaps when we are lying in our beds fixating a point in the ceiling. Even then the projection is not an image but a blur (due to the physiological nystagmus, which is an interesting component in the optic flow, not treated here). Ordinarily, perception of static pictures, objects, etc. indicates that the optic flow from the object attended to is perspectively coherent with the rest of the self-motion-generated flow. Therefore, when we perceive something as static, we have a most essential type of event perception—perception of self-motion in a stationary environment. This has often been ignored in the treatment of visual perception.

Readers familiar with Gibson's concept of "ecological events" discussed previously have probably noted another discrepancy between the content of his concept and the definition of "self-motion perception" as a case of event perception. This is a consequence of my proximal approach. Generally, when we perceive our environment we have the perception of our self-motion relative to this environment as an unnoticed background. This common case is discussed later. Contrary to this proximal classification, Gibson's classification of distal ecological events explicitly excludes self-motion (in his terminology, locomotion) from this category. He says: "The events we are concerned with are "external" so a displacement of the point of observation will be excluded because it refers to the locomotion of the potential observer, not to the motion of a surface" (1979, p. 94).

FROM OPTIC FLOW TO EVENT PERCEPTION

Spatial Information in the Optic Flow Field
As Generated by Self-Motion

Traditionally the proximal stimulus, described as a retinal image, has been analyzed in terms of pictorial characteristics, or cues. The implicit assumption behind cue theory is the existence of a stationary projection, the image, in a stationary eye in a static 3–D environment. All of my readers are presumably familiar with the theoretical problems connected with explaining the perception of three–dimensional space in terms of such cues.

The insight outlined in the previous section, that the relevant stimulus for this perception by physical necessity must be described as a continuous flow pattern, has changed this situation in a most important way. Time enters into the paradigm as a new dimension to be added to the two spatial ones, and the analyses must now be carried out in terms of space–time relations. As one of the proponents of a space–time model I am glad to find that this type of analysis of the retinal stimulus has become more common during recent years. An important factor behind this development is the growing interest in event perception not only among students of perception but also in some related branches: the neurophysiology of vision, sensory-motor control, and computer vision.

The change from analyses of pictorial cues to the study of spatio–temporal relations has the great advantage that mathematical models for the optic flow can be applied, which, accepting certain constraints, demonstate that there exists in this flow information about the distal 3–D environment. Consequently a number of such models have been worked out; models which so far, however, are mainly concerned with information about invariant spatial relations in the proximal flow of self-motion in a rigid environment. These models are similar in a fundamental way, namely with respect to the search for relational invariance during projection from one plane to another through a moving polar point. Their mathematical structures, however, differ due to the respective problem settings. I here classify these approaches in three groups: the perceptual theory group, the neuro-physiological approach, and the computer vision approach. Most of the endeavor so far has been concerned with the mathematically simplest case: self-motion through a completely rigid environment.

Gibson, Olum, and Rosenblatt (1955) initiated this work with their analysis of the optical information for a pilot's eye during flying. Basically, his study was an analysis of the perspective transformation at the station point in a central projection when this point is moving relative to a rigid surface (see also Gibson, 1957). Hay (1966), also a psychologist, extended and formalized the analysis of Gibson et al., and Gordon's (1965) papers applied the same type of analysis to visual information during car driving. Lee (1974, 1976) contributed to this development (see also Lee, 1980). Finally, Warren (1976) is another perceptionist who made a significant contribution to the analyses of the optic flow. [A still higher-order space–time geometry for event perception is presented by Kugler et al, this volume. The editors].

The receptive field studies in neurophysiology have opened the doors for physiological studies of the neural aspects of event perception. Nakayama and Loomis (1974) demonstrated in a most interesting way the possibility of understanding self-motion perception in receptive-field terms starting with an optic flow field analysis along the lines of Gibson et al. and Gordon.

With the recent development in computer science we have a new branch, "computer vision." It concerns automata that can move and see. Of course the basic problem in this branch is directly related to our own problem: the problem of "biological vision," concerning information about a 3–D environment at a moving point. This branch has in a few years developed in a highly impressive and interesting way. I refer especially to Marr (1976), Koenderink & van Doorn (1976), Ullman (1979), and Prazdny (1980).

These latter studies are mathematically very specific because of the need to express them in terms of algorithms adapted to processing in a digital computer. Solutions worked out with the computer's "neural system" in mind indicate an important difference between "artificial intelligence" problems and psychological–physiological theorizing. For example, while Nakayama and Loomis (1974) ask for mathematical models that are appropriate for processing in the neural system of vision (their convexity function), the artificial intelligence solutions are aiming at models for optic flow field analysis adapted to the functioning of the digital computer. There certainly exist great differences between these two types of systems.

These differences are so evident that a warning about unwarranted inferences may seem superfluous. However, I am not quite sure. I have found some tendencies among colleagues to offer computer oriented solutions as possible principles for explaining the functioning of the visual system. In my opinion the analyses of optic flow advanced in computer-vision research are of great interest for us as psychologists, but our biological problem about how the visual system abstracts information from this flow is far more intricate than the technical one and must be solved by systematic experimental research on human subjects.

The insight that the digital computer of today can hardly handle even artificial-vision problems is rapidly growing among the specialists in this field. A number of alternatives to the serially working digital computer are also under discussion and development. In this work analogues to what is known about visual processing are sought for. (For a recent review see Lerner 1980.)

As touched on previously, these analyses of self-motion optic flow have another characteristic in common. They represent algebraic analyses of relations in rigid spatial structures, relations that stay invariant in a central projection under any motion of the station point. Thus, these analyses are in various ways dealing with invariances under perspective transformations (to a minor extent the Marr–Ullman model deviates from this scheme by applying local parallel projection). I warned earlier against accepting any one of these models in a literal way as a model for the visual processing of optic information. In my own work I have instead preferred a more general, but also admittedly far more unstructured, model for this processing. This model is geometric rather than algebraic and simply consists of accepting the projective invariances under perspective transformation as a framework for the analysis of the proximal stimulus-to-percept relations. I hope the reason for this attitude will be obvious from my analyses of object-motion perception in a later section. First, however, some comments on a puzzling problem.

Why Is the Environment Perceived
As Stationary in Self-Motion?

In self-motion generated optic flow there exists no information of absolute character. The information available is in terms of relations, for instance spatial relations between eye and environment. Therefore, it is no more correct from a mathematical or logical point of view to specify self-motion generated flow in terms of the perceiver's motion than it would be to choose the perceiver as the reference and describe the world as moving. In the latter case, walking would mean a deliberate moving of the environment under our feet by means of commands to our legs! This kind of speculation may seem ridiculous, but from point of view of perceptual theory it is a serious problem. We must look for an answer to the question stated in the heading. And we cannot refer to perception of our own activity, for the previous example illustrates that this does not solve our problem.

In my opinion, the solution to the problem will be found in a differential functioning of the visual system itself. During the last ten years there has been a new interest in the study of peripheral motion perception. The results of this research are of great importance from a general theoretical point of view. This research, which for the most part has been carried out in physiological laboratories, has most significantly shown that the human retina is not homogeneous over its surface with respect to the perceptual response to a continuous optic flow. Such a stimulus over the peripheral parts of the retina of a stationary eye (the whole retina exclusive of a central area with a radius of about $20°$) regularly evokes the perception of a stationary environment and self-motion. The same type of stimulation over only the central part instead results in the perception of object motion and a stationary perceiver. For a recent review of this research see Dichgans & Brandt (1978).

There has even been proposed a rather well-founded physiological theory saying that the visual system is in fact composed of two subsystems, a very ancient "ambient" one and a younger "focal" one. The ambient subsystem is then described as closely related to the motor system while the focal system is thought of as related to attentional control. These thoughts first were presented in a systematic way by Held (1968), Ingle, (1967), Schneider, (1967), and Trevarthen, (1968).

An earlier theory that self-motion perception was an effect of coherent stimulation over major parts of the retina has been invalidated. It has been established that isolated motion stimulation over very limited parts of the peripheral retina is enough for evoking a perception of passive self-motion. In the extreme case even a single dot in continuous motion over a few degrees of visual angle 70° from the fovea has been found to induce a corresponding perception of self-motion (Johansson, 1977a, 1977b).

Thus, we have material enough to give an answer to our question. Evidently, there exists in the visual system a selective function which induces the perception of self-motion in a stationary environment. The perceptual distinction between object-motion and self-motion is not due to specific differences in the type of stimulus flow but rather stems from a specific visual processing.

INFORMATION IN OPTIC FLOW FIELDS ABOUT OBJECT-MOTION

Object-Motion Mixed With Self-Motion

According to the mathematical analyses mentioned, there exists in self-motion generated flow fields—within certain restrictions—specific information about the 3–D space. A typical restriction (and highly limiting one) in these analyses is that self-motion through a fully static environment is supposed. This limitation, evidently, is conditioned by the mathematical complexity that arises from attempts to include the effects of object-motion in the flow.

After accepting the perspective transformation model initially developed by Gibson (1957), I have in my own theorizing regarded the understanding of self-motion perception as the less intriguing part of our general problem of space and motion perception. Far more problematic is finding an efficient theoretical paradigm where perception of object-motion of different kinds can also be included. However, only an approach to visual space perception along such lines can satisfy the demand for a biologically relevant theory of visual perception.

I will now sketch some basic contours of a theory of how proximal stimulus flow and visual motion perception are related. This theory comprises the perception of object-motion in the form of rigid motion, elastic motion, and form change simultaneously with the self-motion component.

A key to a theory for the visual decoding of this general type of optic flow pattern is given in the principle of flow analysis which I have called *perceptual vector analysis*. This principle has been abstracted from a great number of experimental investigations, both my own and others. Basic data are found in Johansson, (1950, 1958, 1964, 1976), Börjesson and von Hofsten (1972, 1973, 1975, 1977). See also Gogel (1974, 1978), Hochberg and Fallon (1976), Hochberg, Fallon, and Brooks (1977). I have also reviewed and discussed this principle in several other publications (e.g., Johansson, 1975, 1977c, 1978a, 1978b. See also Johansson, von Hofsten, and Jansson 1980). Basically the principle says that optic flow is treated in perceptual processing, not as a flow relative to a fixed reference frame, but rather as a system of relative and common motions within and between hierarchically ordered, moving reference systems.

I will start by analyzing the optic flow in a real situation where a single, rigid, moving object is seen by a moving observer in an otherwise static environment. Let us imagine a situation where a person (for instance, you) in a slowly moving open car is passing a factory wall at the moment that a piece of wallboard is being hoisted in front of the wall. The gaze is directed toward the wall and we assume monocular vision. Under these conditions let the self-motion at a given short interval of time, Δt, produce a horizontal flow over the retina of the passenger. Fig. 2.1 shows, in simplified form, the photographic record of the flow that we would obtain, by substituting for the person's eye a camera with the shutter open during the interval Δt. The continuous line arrows in the figure represent traces produced by rays of light reflected from the structures of the wall and wallboard. They illustrate in vector form the spatio - temporal information projected by the lens of the eye onto the retina.

As the figure shows, the horizontal traces from the wall indicate a horizontal relative motion between the eye and the wall. Interpreted in the same straightfor-

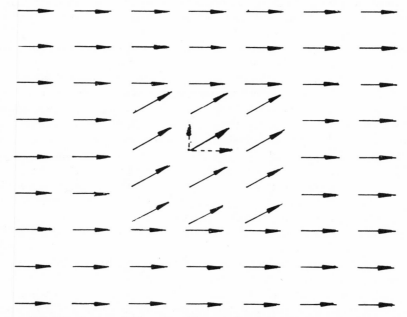

FIG. 2.1   A schematic illustration of the optic flow field at the retinas of a person passing a stationary vertical surface in front of which an object is moving vertically. Continuous lines = vectors representing the optic flow pattern (= the proximal stimulus); dashed lines = example of the perceptual separation of vertical relative component and common horizontal components in the object-generated part of the flow (see text).

...the diagonal arrows from the rectangle representing the wallboard ...ward ...diagonal relative motion between the eye and the board. However, we ...ind...at our visual system in the situation described would not report the board ...erforming a diagonal motion. The board will be seen as moving vertically, ...nd it is simply impossible to see its diagonal motion relative to the eye. Thus, we do not "perceive" the optic flow as such.

The record of the board motion at the eye can be described mathematically as the vector sum of the projection of a horizontal motion relative to the eye (as obtained from the stationary wall) and a vertical motion relative to this horizontally moving reference frame. These two components are indicated in the figure by the dotted vector arrows at one of the wallboard elements. Evidently, this type of mathematical analysis of the flow from the board into two components corresponds to the perception of the scene. It describes the perception of self-motion relative to the wall plus board and of another simultaneous motion, a vertical motion of the board, relative to the wall.

In the optic flow, as projected at the retina, there exist only the horizontal wall-generated vectors and the diagonal wallboard vectors. The perception of two simultaneous motions under the conditions described must be the result of some kind of sensory processing of the proximal flow. It is the mathematical analogue to this processing which I have termed *perceptual vector analysis*.

In accordance with this construction, one of the two vectors into which the proximal flow from the object is analyzed coincides with the self-motion flow from the static parts of the environment. Let us term this motion the *common motion* component. The second vector specifies a motion relative to this common motion or, better, a motion relative to a reference system that is moving in pace with the common motion. This will be called the *relative motion* component.

Our analysis of course has a general applicability in the sense that it is vali... for all types of rigid environments with one or more rigid objects in motion (... well as in the special case where the self-motion component is zero).

Vector Analysis in Object-Motion Perception

Up to this point, my main purpose in presenting the perceptual vector an... has been to demonstrate the existence of such a principle in the per... decoding of optical flow under the conditions of everyday perception. ... concern is to present some direct experimental evidence. The principle o... tual vector analysis was first established in studies on the perceptual ... directly manipulating the proximal flow pattern. In this type of ex... study there exists no distal stimulus. The problem concerns the percep... of manipulating the proximal flow pattern and determining some ge... matical relations between the proximal stimulus and percept. It was... tions of this kind that the principle of perceptual vector analysis w... and found to be a general principle in visual event perception.

Some Experiments

Let me exemplify with some experiments using very simple forms of such
patterns. These are patterns consisting of only two, three, or four spatially
isolated elements, such as dark dots or bright spots in motion against a homogeneous background. Bright spots seen moving in total darkness afford the most
advantageous situation, but the effects are also easily studied with dark spots
against a framed homogeneous bright screen in a visible, structured environment.

Figure 2.2 shows some such motion patterns stemming from Johansson
(1950), a mongraph with a large number of similar experiments. Fig. 2.2(I) is an
often used example and Fig. 2.2(II) and (III) are also rather well known among
students of visual perception, because these patterns have been used in the
educational film on motion perception from my laboratory (Maas, 1970). As
described in the figure captions, the relative motion between the elements and
their common motion component are seen in these examples as two separate
motions. In such simple combinations the common motion usually plays the role
of the perceptual background to the relative motion, the latter being automatically attended to. This relation is similar to the static figure-ground relation, when it
is a question of attensity, with the self-motion as background to the object-
motion.

My initial studies of vector analysis were limited to cases with frontoparallel
motion. This is the special case where central projection and orthogonal analysis
coincide. Later I investigated the perception of object-motion in depth in terms of
vector analysis of the proximal pattern (Johansson, 1964). In a comprehensive
series of investigations Börjesson and von Hofsten have continued along this line
and studied the perceptual effects of a manifold of combinations of direction
motion in two, three, and four element motions. These studies have contributed to our understanding of factors determining perceived type of motion, direction and perception of rigid objects moving in depth versus
non-rigid motion. Also contributions from Hochberg and his associates (Hochberg & Fallon, 1976; Hochberg et al., 1977) are
important together with a number of other related studies.

Perception of Continuously Changing
Geometrical Figures

The behavior of a line segment on a display is an example of a
fundamental type of all geometrical forms. Regarded as the
proximal stimulus the transformation is unspecific; it is not
obvious whether it is the projection of a moving line of
constant length or of a line, the length of which is
changing. The proximal position of the line makes the event

ward way, the diagonal arrows from the rectangle representing the wallboard indicate a diagonal relative motion between the eye and the board. However, we know that our visual system in the situation described would not report the board as performing a diagonal motion. The board will be seen as moving vertically, and it is simply impossible to see its diagonal motion relative to the eye. Thus, we do not "perceive" the optic flow as such.

The record of the board motion at the eye can be described mathematically as the vector sum of the projection of a horizontal motion relative to the eye (as obtained from the stationary wall) and a vertical motion relative to this horizontally moving reference frame. These two components are indicated in the figure by the dotted vector arrows at one of the wallboard elements. Evidently, this type of mathematical analysis of the flow from the board into two components corresponds to the perception of the scene. It describes the perception of self-motion relative to the wall plus board and of another simultaneous motion, a vertical motion of the board, relative to the wall.

In the optic flow, as projected at the retina, there exist only the horizontal wall-generated vectors and the diagonal wallboard vectors. The perception of two simultaneous motions under the conditions described must be the result of some kind of sensory processing of the proximal flow. It is the mathematical analogue to this processing which I have termed *perceptual vector analysis*.

In accordance with this construction, one of the two vectors into which the proximal flow from the object is analyzed coincides with the self-motion flow from the static parts of the environment. Let us term this motion the *common motion* component. The second vector specifies a motion relative to this common motion or, better, a motion relative to a reference system that is moving in pace with the common motion. This will be called the *relative motion* component.

Our analysis of course has a general applicability in the sense that it is valid for all types of rigid environments with one or more rigid objects in motion (as well as in the special case where the self-motion component is zero).

Vector Analysis in Object-Motion Perception

Up to this point, my main purpose in presenting the perceptual vector analysis has been to demonstrate the existence of such a principle in the perceptual decoding of optical flow under the conditions of everyday perception. My next concern is to present some direct experimental evidence. The principle of perceptual vector analysis was first established in studies on the perceptual effects of directly manipulating the proximal flow pattern. In this type of experimental study there exists no distal stimulus. The problem concerns the perceptual effects of manipulating the proximal flow pattern and determining some general mathematical relations between the proximal stimulus and percept. It was in investigations of this kind that the principle of perceptual vector analysis was abstracted and found to be a general principle in visual event perception.

Some Experiments

Let me exemplify with some experiments using very simple forms of such flow patterns. These are patterns consisting of only two, three, or four spatially isolated elements, such as dark dots or bright spots in motion against a homogeneous background. Bright spots seen moving in total darkness afford the most advantageous situation, but the effects are also easily studied with dark spots against a framed homogeneous bright screen in a visible, structured environment.

Figure 2.2 shows some such motion patterns stemming from Johansson (1950), a mongraph with a large number of similar experiments. Fig. 2.2(I) is an often used example and Fig. 2.2(II) and (III) are also rather well known among students of visual perception, because these patterns have been used in the educational film on motion perception from my laboratory (Maas, 1970). As described in the figure captions, the relative motion between the elements and their common motion component are seen in these examples as two separate motions. In such simple combinations the common motion usually plays the role of the perceptual background to the relative motion, the latter being automatically attended to. This relation is similar to the static figure-ground relation, when it is a question of attensity, with the self-motion as background to the object-motion.

The initial studies of vector analysis were limited to cases with frontoparallel motion. This is the special case where central projection and orthogonal analysis coincide. Later I investigated the perception of object-motion in depth in terms of a vector analysis of the proximal pattern (Johansson, 1964). In a comprehensive series of investigations Börjesson and von Hofsten have continued along this line in their study of the perceptual effects of a manifold of combinations of direction and speed in two, three, and four element motions. These studies have contributed to an understanding of factors determining perceived type of motion, direction of perceived motion and perception of rigid objects moving in depth versus perception of nonrigid motion. Also contributions from Hochberg and his associates (Gogel, 1974, 1978; Hochberg & Fallon, 1976; Hochberg et al., 1977) are of immediate interest together with a number of other related studies.

Perceptual Responses to a Continuously Changing Form In Some Simple Geometrical Figures

A continuously growing–shrinking line segment on a display is an example of a simple form of change in the simplest of all geometrical forms. Regarded as the outcome of a central projection, such a transformation is unspecific; it is not possible to say whether the changing pattern is the projection of a moving line of constant length or represents the projection of a line, the length of which is continuously changing. Adding changes of position of the line makes the event

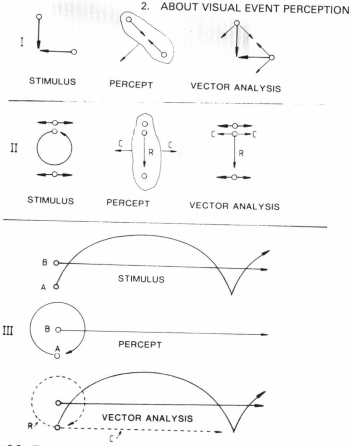

FIG. 2.2   Three example of perceptual vector analysis in simple combinations of motions in dot patterns.

I. Two dots moving toward and away from each other with the same frequency and speed, one along a vertical and the other along a horizontal track. The primary percept is a diagonal motion representing the relative motions between the dots. This system, however, is seen as describing a common motion along the opposite diagonal. Perceptually the common motion mainly acts as a background or frame of reference for the relative motion.

II. A motion pattern consisting of two dots in simple harmonic motion along horizontal tracks and a third dot tracing a circle. The three motion paths are arranged as shown in the figure. The horizontal component in the circular motion has the same frequency, amplitude and phase as the motion of the two other dots. Perceptually this common component (C) is abstracted from the circular motion leaving the second component, the relative motion (R) as a perceived motion up and down along a moving line formed by the three dots. Thus, in this case the percept represents a mathematically correct vector analysis.

III. Also the well known rolling wheel "illusion" exemplifies a correct perceptual vector analysis. The horizontal component in the cycloid (A) which is common with the motion of the hub (B) is seen as a translatory motion (C) and the residual circular component (R) represents the rolling along the track.

more complex, but still such a moving line, when treated as a transformation under central projection, is undetermined.

Combining three lines to form a triangle, with each line cyclically changing in length, direction, and position, introduces a complex change in the simplest of geometrical surfaces. Such patterns can represent the projection of a rigid, moving triangle as well as a triangle changing its form and, thus, like changing lines, it is undetermined in the present meaning.

When we take the next step toward figural complexity, however, by introducing a fourth line, thus producing a changing quadrangle we will find that in general the geometric ambiguity between rigid motion and form changes no longer exists. Only in some special cases can such a transformation be described as the projection of a moving, rigid figure.

Geometrical considerations of this type are of considerable interest in experimental research on the basic principles of the visual decoding of the proximal optic flow pattern. The underlying question of course is: How will the visual system deal with such projectively unspecific proximal events?

The proximal-cue-theoretical answer is that perception of form changes in frontoparallel figures will be perceived. Alternatively, applying the projectively invariant properties of a model brings about the prediction that changing straight lines and triangles always will result in perceptual ambiguity between rigid motion and form change. The changing quadrangle, however, must in all but a few special cases bring about perception of form change.

My colleagues and I at the Uppsala laboratory have carried out a great number of experiments, using as stimuli changing patterns of the type described. We even reduced the figural information still more by using patterns with only two, three, or four dots, leaving to the visual system the task of organizing possible projectively invariant figural relations (Börjesson & von Hofsten, 1972, 1973, 1975, 1977; Johansson, 1964, 1974a,b; Johansson & Jansson, 1968). A radical and most significant theoretical implication of a great number of such experiments is that the visual system nearly always exhibits a strong perceptual tendency to abstract the maximum amount of common motion from the optic flow even when this flow can not represent a rigid object moving in space. In these cases, a specific object motion is perceived while the object simultaneously changes its shape in a specific way. An experiment from my 1964 investigation demonstrates in a straightforward way this perceptual effect.

Fig. 2.3a shows the stimulus pattern used in a reference experiment. It consists of a bright square which continuously changes its size in a cyclical way. The cycle time was about 2 seconds and the figure was growing–shrinking in accordance with the triangular function (max.: min. = 2:1). When interpreted as a perspective transformation, this pattern represents the projection of a square of constant size, moving parallel to the line of vision. (It was also perceived in this way.) In this figure the vector arrows from the corners of the square (as well as all vectors from contour elements) are concurrent toward the point I, the point at infinity of a central projection. Thus, they all represent projections of parallel

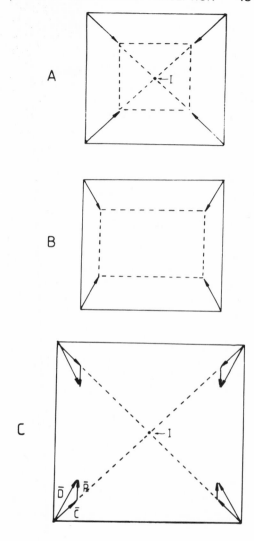

FIG. 2.3   Example of perceptual abstraction of rigid motion and residual form change from a non-perspective proximal form change (see text).

motion tracks. In terms of the perceptual vector analysis this means that they diagram a motion in depth common for all displayed contour elements.

Figure 2.3b illustrates an experimental pattern representing a specific perceptual combination of form change and motion in an object. The amount of horizontal shrinking of the figure is only one half of that in the vertical dimension, and of that in the original figure. Thus, the vectors in this figure are not concurrent; they will not meet at a common point at infinity. This means that the pattern cannot represent a rigid motion. In accordance with our vector model, let us now abstract the component which represents a common motion. This is done in Fig. 2.3c. In this figure, as in Fig. 2.3a, the diagonals represent projections of parallel tracks and therefore the direction of a common motion component. Thus, the point of intersection (I) is the point at infinity for the common motion. Now let us abstract from the displayed vectors ($\bar{D}$) the components $\bar{C}$, directed toward the point I. The residual vectors $\bar{R}$ specify the relative motion component.

In accordance with our theory, the common component in the flow, thus abstracted, should represent perception of a "rigid" motion, a motion acting as a frame of reference for the relative motions. Our diagram specifies it as a sagittal motion with an amplitude that is one half of the original one in Fig. 2.3a. In the experiment this interpretation was found to be valid. The subjects perceived a bright frontal surface moving to and fro in a sagittal direction, with a track length of roughly one half of that seen in the reference experiment.

I may add that about half the subjects perceived the object as changing its shape from a square to a rectangle during the backward phase, and the other half reported seeing a square which rotated about a central horizontal axis.

The result tells us that the visual system of the subjects had automatically extracted a specific common component from the proximal flow. This result strongly supports the theory of perceptual vector analysis. The result from the group of subjects perceiving motion plus form change is especially convincing. Why is just this amount of common motion abstracted from a changing proximal figure when the end result is still a changing figure? Does this not indicate a built-in principle of analysis analogous to the principle of perceptual vector analysis? To me it does.

Perception of Biological Motion

Up to the present, the most convincing demonstrations of perceptual vector analysis as a fundamental principle are found in studies of the perception of those patterns of moving elements that I have called biological motions. These patterns were constructed in an attempt to investigate the generality and efficiency of the common-and-relative motions paradigm. This was done by making the patterns of interaction of elements far more complicated both with respect to their motions and to their hierarchical relations than was the case in the initial experiments. In attempting to construct such patterns, it was convenient to think about motion patterns typical of the animal skeletons of, say, birds, horses or men. Such a skeleton can be described as a set of pendulums connected into four groups, the limbs, which are held together by the flexible spine. As an example, the human arm–hand system represents a six step hierarchy of rigid rods connected by more or less complicated joints. These components interact as a functional unit under many mechanical constraints in a way which, from a kinetic point of view, is extremely complicated.

In my studies of the principle of perceptual vector analysis, I had worked with mechanical motion combinations of a rather simple type. Therefore, I considered the motion patterns of the vertebrate skeleton as a very interesting and tough case and decided to investigate it. I also found it to be of special interest because of its evident biological significance.

Problem.   With the theoretical background sketched, the experimental problem was a straightforward one. Given a number of dots moving in accordance with the motions of the main joints of a human body, as when the person is walking, what type of perception will such a pattern of moving elements evoke? Possible percepts are: (1) a random, unorganized swarm of moving dots; (2) the opposite extreme, namely a perception of a walking human being; or (3) some degree of organization in accordance with the principle under investigation but also a number of temporary spurious interactions between the elements.

Type of Displays.   Human walking, running, etc. were chosen as subjects for the first set of studies. In accordance with the problem setting, only the motions of the main joints (shoulders, elbows, wrists, hips, knees, and ankles), representing end points of the pendulums in the hierarchical arrangement, were displayed. Such displays can be constructed from a set of moving bright spots and recorded in a straightforward manner by video or film in accordance with methods described elsewhere (see Johansson, 1973). The result was a video or film record of 10–12 bright spots moving against a dark background.

Results.   Every observer of a display of the type described immediately perceives a person performing just the motions recorded (walking, dancing, running, etc.). Thousands of viewers of the Motion Perception films from the Uppsala Laboratory (Maas, 1970, 1971) have been amazed at this striking effect. A formal analysis of the perceptual outcome in terms of perceptual vector analysis was carried out by Johansson (1976). It was shown that the percept could be described as a mathematically correct vector analysis in a system of hierarchically related moving reference frames. In this investigation it was also found that the perceptual vector analysis represents a primitive and unconditional way of functioning by the visual system.

Perceptual organization was determined in accordance with this principle at near–threshold levels of spatial resolution (with spots moving a few minutes of arc of visual angle) and of temporal resolution (with displays of .1–.2 seconds). In other words, there never exists a first moment of perception when the display appears unorganized, as an ambiguous configuration undergoing an indeterminate motion.

Thus, the boldest possible prediction in accordance with the theory was verified. The astonishing thing at that time was that the complexity of these patterns did not in any way obstruct the perceptual analysis but rather had a remarkable facilitating effect. Evidently, the great amount of vectorially related information per second was perceptually processed in a parallel way and immediately determined the percept.

A number of later experiments on biological motion perception has further demonstrated a most remarkable capacity of the visual system for abstracting seemingly esoteric information from such patterns. Cutting and his coworkers, in particular, have made this clear. This group has shown for instance that it is possible to recognize friends from their gait when recorded with biological motion techniques (Cutting & Kozlowski, 1977) and even to determine the gender of an actor (Cutting, Profit, & Kozlowski, 1978; Barclay, Cutting & Kozlowski, 1978). They hypothesized that the relevant information for gender is found in the invisible point representing the center for common motion in the dot motion patterns. The location of this point was shown to vary systematically with gender. Cutting (1978) also found that computerized manipulation of this point verified these results, thus demonstrating the incredible capacity of the visual system for abstracting such centers of common motion (see also Börjesson & von Hofsten, 1972, 1973.)

At the Uppsala laboratory, Runeson and Frykholm (1981) have studied the astonighing human ability to abstract a most complex type of information from biological motion patterns. This study was concerned with perception of effort and will be discussed further. Frykholm (personal communication) has continued the studies on both gender detection and identification of persons from such patterns in interesting ways.

SOME THOUGHTS ABOUT BIOLOGICAL MOTION AND PERCEPTUAL THEORY

Let us speculate a little about some theoretically interesting consequences that can be discerned from the results of these biological motion studies.

"Praeterea censeo."   The studies of biological motion have revealed a perceptual ability to abstract highly exact and detailed spatial information from such motion patterns, which have been characterized as exceedingly complicated from a mechanical–mathematical point of view. On the other hand, we also know that experiments with fewer elements and mathematically simple functions not infrequently result in indefinite or ambiguous percepts. In my experimental work on event perception I have frequently observed this effect: There exists a direct relation between mathematical complexity in the stimulus flow on the one hand and perceptual efficiency, specificity, and sensitivity on the other. In my discussions with colleagues about experimental problems it has been something of a *praeterea censeo* for me to mention this effect, which has usually not been recognized. My *censeo* thus is that we in our experimental planning must take

this relation between mathematical (and especially algebraic) complexity and perceptual efficiency into account. We often expect in an unwarranted way mathematical precision and reliability in response to mathematically simple events, and ambiguous, variable responses to mathematically complex ones. We often have been astonished when instead we get the reverse. This has led us to believe that we are dealing with a very sloppy system, or that our theory is inadequate. In my opinion, this vagueness in results is the price we have to pay for our ambition to isolate basic principles underlying the sensory processing of optic flow. What I wish to underline is that mathematical simplicity in this connection implies scanty perceptual material for the analysis (few simultaneous perceptual "bits" of information). In contrast, the tremendous mathematical complexity in biological motion patterns represents a very dense flow of information, a high degree of redundancy, and therefore a greater possibility for exact analysis. Evidently the visual system is constructed especially to deal with optic flows of this type. Or expressed in another way: What is easy for the visual system is complex for our mathematics, and what is mathematically simple is hard for the visual system to deal with.

Biological Motion and Gibson's Ecological Approach.   Biological motion must be regarded as a most essential type of ecological event in Gibson's sense. Recognizing an animal as belonging to a certain species, as being a friend, a mate, a potential prey, a potential enemy, or predator, represents a perceptual ability of vital importance. If we extend the content of the term "biological motion" to include also motion of the vegetation, its ecological importance will stand out still more clearly.

With these reflections as a background, it follows as a matter of course that the instantaneous and perfect reading of all kinds of biological motion patterns is of vital importance for survival. Therefore, it can hardly be astonishing to find that the visual system is so extremely efficient in handling this type of flow pattern, even in our highly impoverished experimental representation of biological motion. We must imagine that visual systems from the earliest stages of their evolution have been neurally organized for efficient decoding of this type of optic flow pattern. Mechanical motions met with in nature, for instance effects of the gravitational force, are mathematically far simpler than are most biological motions and therefore, as stated above, poorer in visual information. Hence, the visual systems may be less efficient in veridical interpretation of such patterns (cf. Runeson, 1977).

VISUAL PERCEPTION OF DYNAMICS

In physics we are used to studying mechanics under three subdisciplines, statics, kinematics and dynamics. Kinematics is the discipline where spatio–temporal changes are specified in terms of velocities and accelerations; force and mass are fundamental concepts in dynamics. With this paradigm as a background, it is easy to find that the study of visual motion perception, with few exceptions, has been concerned with aspects of physical events which, from a systematic point of view, belong to kinematics.

Why have we so neglected the dynamic aspect? From the biological viewpoint which I have pleaded for above and, of course, still more from the closely related "ecological" approach, it is apparent that perceptual information about forces underlying a visual event should be of at least the same importance as the kinematic aspects. A good reason for this apparent bias in favor of kinematics can be found in a counter-question: Can stimuli for perception of dynamics even be specified? Simply asking whether forces really are perceptible may be regarded as far from a rhetorical question. Even if we are willing to answer this question in the affirmative, we must admit that it is justified. As sketched above, it has been possible for the students of motion perception to identify some essential characteristics in the optic flow corresponding to the perception of the distal motions. We must admit, however, that we still have not gone very far along this road, because of the difficulty of identifying the relevant stimulus variables. Identifying stimuli for force perception (if they exist) must by necessity be a still harder task. As far as I know at present, stimuli for perception of force must be sought in certain rather abstract "higher-order" relations in the stimulus flow.

I previously raised the somewhat provocative question of whether stimuli for perception of dynamic aspects of events existed, and thus whether knowledge about forces acting in an event is really immediate perceptual knowledge. Most of my readers know that this was, in fact, Hume's famous problem regarding the perception of causality. We know that Hume's answer was in the negative. However, we also know that Michotte, in his pioneering investigation on causality perception (1946/1963), experimentally attacked this problem—and refuted Hume's deduction.

Michotte's investigation is one of the very few existing experimental studies on the perception of dynamics. It was a first approach and in several instances has been criticized for methodological reasons. Of special importance in our present context is Runeson's (1977) analysis, which demonstrated that in fact Michotte's stimuli were quite inadequate from the point of view of physics. However, in my opinion, Michotte has clearly demonstrated the possibility of strict experimentation with dynamic aspects of event perception. When we also take Runeson's criticism and contributions into consideration, we can state that, at least in some cases, dynamic aspects are perceptible, and that it is possible to identify relevant stimulus variables for the perception of dynamics.

As previously stated, besides the study of perception of causality there exist very few experimental studies on the perception of dynamics. At the Uppsala Laboratory, however, we have from time to time attacked such problems. As early as the sixties, Jansson took up Michotte's problem. Jansson and I conducted studies on the problem of visual perception of the g-force, mostly in the form of pilot studies (Johansson & Jansson, 1967). To my knowledge this was the first attempt to broaden our knowledge of the problem area of dynamics perception. Recently Runeson and Frykholm (1981), in an innovative way, have investigated the perception of weight lifting, which I already have referred to and on which I comment in the next section.

The studies of causality and of g-force perception are concerned with rather simple mechanical events as compared to intricate biological motion patterns. Remembering the principle of the inverse relations between mathematical and perceptual complexity stated previously, it is immediately apparent that biological motion patterns may offer an advantageous method for studying the perception of dynamics, just because of the amount of perceptually available information in the optic flow from such patterns. This is discussed in the next section.

About Perception of Force and Strain From Biological Motion Patterns

As an introduction to this area I will direct your attention to a scene in the Uppsala film on visual motion perception (Maas, 1970, 1971). Those of you who have watched this film probably will remember the scene in which a point-light man is doing pushups. We can see how the elegant and forceful lifting of the body in the beginning of the scene gradually changes and how the pushups become more and more shaky, slow and irregular. We perceive how the actor is growing exhausted and clearly see how hard it is for him during the last pushups to lift his body and straighten his arms. To the extent an observer can perceive muscular effort in this interplay between the ten dots, we must regard it as an indication of the possibility of using biological motion patterns for studies of the perception of dynamics.

As other similar examples I will refer to the studies of perception of gait described earlier (Cutting and Kozlowski, 1977; Frykholm, personal communication). These studies demonstrate a great sensitivity for discriminating very faint differences in complicated biological motion patterns. Furthermore, with a coworker, Lars Bäckström, I have been able to isolate and manipulate certain stimulus variables determining the impression of force in biological motion perception. Such possibilities are of decisive importance for real progress in this field. The great value of Michotte's approach was that he was able, with rather simple methods, to manipulate relevant stimulus variables.

Bäckström and I analysed the pendulum motion at the joints using Fourier spectra. This material made it possible to synthesize walking patterns from an optional number of harmonics in these spectra. As you may imagine, a walking pattern with only the fundamental component seems very different from a human walking style. It looks very mechanical and floating and totally devoid of force. Adding, say, three of the subsequent higher harmonics makes the style of walking humanlike but relaxed and easygoing. Adding still higher frequencies gradually yields the characteristic impression of force in the steps. This indicates that this, and related variations of the pattern of acceleration in the proximal flow pattern, may be a way for finding direct stimulus correlates to force perception. These observations also support the hypothesis that mathematically complex flow patterns are efficient in evoking perception of dynamic properties.

Runeson and Frykholm's Investigation.   So far, I have commented on observations and pilot studies supporting the expectation that biological motion types of stimuli may be advantageous to the study of perception of physical forces. Recently, however, Runeson and Frykholm (1981), in accordance with such observations, have begun research on perception of dynamics in biological motion. They chose to study the possibility of perceiving biological strain or exertion in lifting and carrying boxes weighing 5–28 kg. using the biological motion technique. Subjects observing such displays were able to estimate the relative weights of the boxes from the motion patterns of the twelve joints of the actor with remarkable accuracy. Fig. 2.4 shows their main result with estimated weight plotted against physical weight.

Thus, this experiment demonstrates convincingly that the visual system is highly efficient in abstracting information about dynamic characteristics from biological motions.

With these and some related studies of the dynamic aspects of event perception as a background, we can conclude that these dynamic aspects not only afford a very important area for future research in visual perception but also that it is possible to investigate them in an experimentally fruitful way. This fresh field certainly must be looked upon as a challenge for the new generation of researchers, not yet irreversibly imprinted with the old, sterile theoretical and methodological concepts which in my opinion have had a blocking effect in the past.

SUMMING UP

In this paper I have given a survey of what I regard as some of the most essential problems in the study of visual space perception and have sketched some basic routes towards their solution.

These problems stem from the fact that a moving organism, human or animal, gets specific and useful information about its environment from the optic flow at the eye. My study has not been limited to totally rigid and static man-made environments. Instead the analyses have treated the general type of natural environment, composed of moving, nonrigid structures like trees, bushes, grass,

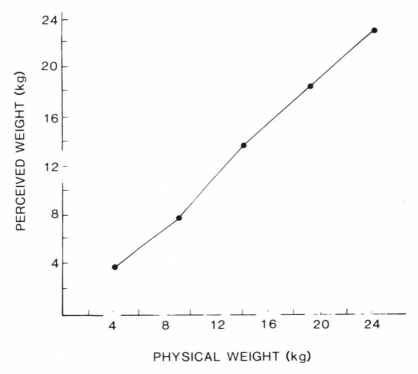

FIG. 2.4   Means of estimates of invisible weights ''lifted'' by biological motion type of dot patterns. From Runeson and Frykholm, 1981 (see text).

water etc., and often humans or other moving animals. For our arboreal ancestors such an everchanging, nonrigid environment must have been the rule.

I have also emphasized that the optic flow is built up from two types of ''distal'' events: (1) motions of the nodal point of the perceiver's eye relative to the environment (self-motion), and (2) motions of objects in the environment. In accordance with such an analysis, we must regard also what usually is termed ''static perception,'' as specified by a background type of event perception, namely self-motion relative to a stationary environment. In this way all visual perception typically contains a component of event perception.

The optic flow at the nodal point of the refracting system of the vertebrate eye carries information about all these spatial changes *in* the environment and *relative to* the environment. The basic term in my proposal is *relative*. What the visual system evidently records are not absolute measures but instead hierarchies of certain spatial relations which stay invariant under change. I have proposed the invariant relations constituting projective geometry as a descriptive framework for our analysis. Automatic perceptual abstraction of invariant relations constituting projective relations, and also invariant relations between invariant relations in sometimes very complex hierarchical systems is supposed. More specifically, I have stressed that this visual decoding of relations can be represented in terms of vector analyses of the proximal optic flow.

I am fully aware that my approach is very unorthodox, to say the least, and also that what I propose in many respects is more similar to a paradigm or a direction for future experimental research than to a fully developed theory. However, even with this limitation—or rather because of it—I think I have a strong point. The system is built on a thorough empirical basis. My statements about the visual "data" treatment are not speculations but are based on systematic research, step by step, over a long period of time. This means that whatever theoretical framework future students of perception should prefer, their description of the visual decoding of optic flow will represent a more or less direct analogy to the system sketched in the present paper.

REFERENCES

Barclay, C. D., Cutting, J. E., & Kozlowski L. T. Temporal and spatial factors in gait perception that influence gender recognition. *Perception & Psychophysics*, 1978, *23*, 145–152.

Börjesson, E., & Hofsten, C. von. Spatial determinants of depth perception in two-dot motion patterns. *Perception & Psychophysics*, 1972, *11*, 263–268.

Böjesson, E., & Hofsten, C. von. Visual perception of motion in depth: Application of a vector model to three-dot motion patterns. *Perception & Psychophysics*, 1973, *13*, 169–179.

Börjesson, E., & Hofsten, C. von. A vector model for perceived object rotation and translation in space. *Psychological Research*, 1975, *38*, 209–230.

Börjesson, E., & Hofsten, C. von. Effects of different motion characteristics on perceived motion in depth. *Scandinavian Journal of Psychology*, 1977, *18*, 203–208.

Cutting, J. E. Generation of synthetic male and female walkers through manipulation of a biomechanical invariant. *Perception*, 1978, *7*, 393–405.

Cutting, J. E., & Kozlowski, L. T. Recognizing friends by their walk: Gait perception without familiarity cues. *Bulletin of the Psychonomic Society*, 1977, *9*, 333–356.

Cutting, J. E., Profitt, D. R., & Kozlowski, L. T. A biomechanical invariant for gait perception. *Journal of Experimental Psychology: Human perception and Performance*, 1978, *4*, 3, 357–372.

Dichgans, J., & Brandt, T. Visual-vestibular interaction: Effects on self-motion perception and postural control. In R. Held, H. Leibowitz, H. L. Teuber (Eds.), *Handbook of sensory physiology*. Vol. VIII Berlin, Heidelberg, New York: Springer-Verlag, 1978.

Frykholm, G. *Perception av kön och identitet* (personal communication) 1981.

Gibson, J. J. Optical motions and transformations as stimuli for visual perception. *Psychological Review*, 1957, *64*, 288–295.

Gibson, J. J. *The senses considered as perceptual systems*. New York, Boston: Houghton Mifflin, 1966.

Gibson, J. J. *An ecological approach to visual perception*. Boston: Houghton Mifflin, 1979.

Gibson, J. J., Olum, P., & Rosenblatt, F. Parallax and perspective during aircraft landings. *American Journal of Psychology*, 1955, *68*, 372–385.

Gogel, W. C. Relative motion and the adjacency principle. *Quarterly Journal of Experimental Psychology*, 1974, *14*, 425–437.

Gogel, W. C. Size, distance and depth perception. In E. C. Carterette, & M. P. Friedman, (Eds.), *Handbook of perception*, Vol. 9. New York: Academic Press, 1978, 299–333.

Gordon, D. A. Static and dynamic visual fields in human space perception. *Journal of Optical Society of America*, 1965, *55*, 1296–1303.

Hay, J. C. Optical motions and space perception: an extension of Gibson's analysis. *Psychological Review*, 1966, *73*, 550–565.

Held, R. Dissociation of visual functions by deprivation and rearrangement. *Psychologische Forschung*, 1968, *31*, 338–348.

Hochberg, J., & Fallon, P. Perceptual analysis of moving pattern. *Science*, 1976, *136*, 1081.

Hochberg, J., Fallon, P., & Brooks, V. Motion organization in "stop action" sequences. *Scandinavian Journal of Psychology*, 1977, *18*, 187–97.

Ingle, D. Two visual mechanisms underlying the behavior of fish. *Psychologische Forschung*, 1967, *31*, 44–51.

Johansson, G. *Configurations in event perception*. Uppsala: Almqvist & Wiksell, 1950.

Johansson, G. Rigidity, stability and motion in perceptual space. *Acta Psychologica*, 1958, *14*, 359–370.

Johansson, G. Perception of motion and changing form. *Scandinavian Journal of Psychology*, 1964, *5*, 181–208.

Johansson, G. Visual perception of biological motion and a model for its analysis. *Perception & Psychophysics*, 1973, *14*, 201–211.

Johansson, G. Projective transformations as determining visual space perception. In R. B. MacLeod & H. L. Pick, Jr. (Eds.) *Perception: Essays in honor of J. J. Gibson*. Ithaca, New York: Cornell University Press, 1974. (a)

Johansson, G. visual perception of rotary motion as transformations of conic sections. *Psychologica*, 1974, *17*, 226–237. (b)

Johansson, G. Visual motion perception. *Scientific American*, June, 1975: 76–88.

Johansson, G. Spatio–temporal differentiation and integration in visual motion perception. *Psychological Research*, 1976, *38*, 379–393.

Johansson, G. Studies on visual perception of locomotion. *Perception* 1977, *6*, 365–376. (a)

Johansson, G *Visual perception of locomotion elicited and controlled by a bright spot moving in the periphery of the visual field*. Department of Psychology, University of Uppsala, Report No. 210, 1977. (b)

Johansson, G. Spatial constancy and motion in visual perception. In Epstein (Ed.) *Stability and constancy in visual perception*. New York: Wiley, 1977. (c)

Johansson, G. About the geometry underlying spontaneous visual decoding of the optical message. In E. L. J. Leeuwenberg & H. F. J. Buffart (Eds.) *Formal theories of visual perception*. New York: Wiley, 1978. (a)

Johansson, G. Visual event perception. In R. Held, H. W. Leibowitz and H. L. Teuber (Eds.) *Perception: Handbook of sensory physiology*, Vol. VIII. Berlin, Heidelberg: Springer-Verlag, 1978. (b)

Johansson, G., & Jansson, G. *The perception of free fall*. Department of Psychology, University of Uppsala. (Mimeograph) 1967.

Johansson, G., & Jansson, G. Perceived rotary motion from changes in a straight line. *Perception & Psychophysics, 4*, 1968.

Johansson, G., Hofsten, C. von, & Jansson, G. Event perception. *Annual Review of Psychology*, 1980, *31*, 21–63.

Koenderink, J. J., & Doorn, A. J. van. Local structure of movement parallax of the plane. *Journal of Optical Society of America*, 1976, *66*, 717–723.

Lee, D. N. Visual information during locomotion. In R. B. MacLeod & H. L. Pick, Jr. (Eds.). *Perception: Essays in honor of James J. Gibson*. Ithaca, New York: Cornell University Press, 1974, 250–267.

Lee, D. N. A theory of visual control of braking based on information about time-to-collision. *Perception*, 1976, *5*, 437–459.

Lee, D. N. Visuo-motor coordination in space–time. In G. E. Stelmach and J. Requin (Eds.) *Tutorials in motor behavior*. North-Holland Publishing Company, 1980.

Lerner, L. J. Computers that see. *IEEE Spectrum*, October, 1980, 28–33.

Maas, J. *Motion perception* I, 1970; II, 1971 (Films). Houghton Mifflin, 1970–71.

Marr, D. Early processing of visual information. *Philosophical Transactions of the Royal Society of London*, 1976, *275*, 483–534.

Michotte, A. *La perception de la causalité*. Louvain: Publ. Univ. English translation, 2nd ed.: *The perception of causality*. London: Methuen, 1963.

Nakayama, K., & Loomis, J. M. Optical velocity patterns, velocity–sensitivity neurons and space perception: a hypothesis. *Perception*, 1974, *3*, 63–80.

Pittenger, J. B., & Shaw, R. E. Aging faces as visual-elastic events. Implication for a theory on non-rigid shape perception. *Journal of Experimental Psychology: Human Perception and Performance*, 1975, *1*, 374–382.

Prazdny, K. Egomotion and relative depth map from optical flow. *Biological Cybernetics*, 1980, *36*, 87–102.

Runeson, S. *On visual perception of dynamic events*. Doctoral dissertation, Department of Psychology, University of Uppsala, 1977.

Runeson, S., & Frykholm, G. Visual perception of lifted weight. *Journal of Experimental Psychology: Human Perception and Performance*, 1981, *7*, 733–740.

Shaw, R. E., & Pittenger, J. B. Perceiving change. In H. Pick & E. Saltzman (Eds.), *Modes of perceiving and processing information*. Hillsdale, NJ: Laurence Erlbaum Associates, 1978.

Schneider, G. E. Contrasting visual-motor functions of tectum and cortex in the golden hamster. *Psychologische Forschung*, 1967, *31*, 52–62.

Trevarthen, C. E. Two mechanisms of vision in primates. *Psychologische Forschung*, 1968, *31*, 299–337.

Ullman, S. The interpretation of structure from motion. *Proceedings of the Royal Society of London:* 1979, B 203, 405–426.

Warren, R. The perception of egomotion. *Journal of Experimental Psychology: Human Perception and Performance*, 1976, *2*, 448–456.

Warren, R. The ecological nature of perceptual systems. In E. C. R. Carterette and M. P. Friedman (Eds.) *Handbook of Perception*, Vol. 10. New York: Academic Press, 1978.

3 Johansson's Approach to Visual Event Perception— Gibson's Perspective

William M. Mace
Trinity College
Hartford, Connecticut

INTRODUCTION

Gunnar Johansson's paper described some of the work which established him as one of our most important perceptual psychologists. Indeed, the idea of a whole conference on event perception might not have arisen without Johansson's contributions. Everyone involved in research on event perception should be grateful for his persistence because it has taken so long for the larger psychological community, particularly in the U.S., to resonate to issues in event perception. A superficial modern history of event perception would note the pioneering work of Mach and Exner, then von Ehrenfels, Wertheimer, Heider, Rubin, Düncker, Michotte, and Johansson's earliest work (Boring, 1942; Johansson, 1978). Out of all this, however, it was not "events" which were given sustained attention, but "motion." Heider (Heider, 1926/1959; Heider & Simmel, 1944), Michotte (Michotte, Thinès, & Crabbé, 1964), and Johansson's contributions, together with, say, those of Benussi, Musatti, Wallach, and Metzger, remained interesting phenomena that were often noted but rarely pursued. The critical conditions for "uptake" have not been satisfied until recently. Thus event perception per se has a history that is arguably as old as most topics in experimental psychology, but its consolidation as a genuine subject matter worth the efforts of research programs, as opposed to a mere collection of entertaining curiosities, owes much to Professor Johansson.

Surely the most important episode in the recent growth of interest in events was Johansson's demonstration that a very few points of light could be transformed from a meaningless jumble into a *walking person* by relative motions of those lights (Johansson, 1973). The richness of what could be seen in these displays attracted widespread interest and continues to astonish people to this day. The availability of film techniques and computer graphics have, of course, contributed enormously to the rise of interest in event perception, but Gunnar Johansson has shown from within psychology that there are actually good problems to which we can apply these technologies.

JOHANSSON IN LIGHT OF GIBSON

Besides Gunnar Johansson, the dominant influence on the thinking of many of the people at this Conference has been James Gibson. I shall examine several of the main ideas in Johansson's paper (this volume) by comparing them with Gibson's. Gibson and Johansson were well acquainted and greatly enjoyed sharpening their ideas on one another. There is even a series of articles, one by Johansson and two by Gibson, which brings their private discussions into public (Johansson, 1970; Gibson, 1970, 1977). The purpose of my paper is to make sure that the comparisons they developed continue to be noted, examined, and elaborated. I shall focus my attention on points raised at this conference in Johansson's paper and will not repeat the emphases of the earlier exchanges. The previous papers are reprinted in the collection of Gibson's papers edited by Reed and Jones (1982).

Similarities

As Gibson and Johansson repeatedly claimed in their long association, their points of agreement outnumbered (or better, outweighed—since neither was given to dwelling on shared opinions) their points of disagreement, particularly when considered relative to the larger community of experimental psychologists. First, they agreed on the superiority of changing displays to static displays for organizing perceptual experience, maintaining that a proper stimulus analysis must be a space–time analysis. They rejected any notion that a theory of static displays should be prior to a theory of dynamic displays. Second, they agreed on the importance of invariants under transformation in perception, as Johansson made clear in his chapter on the constancies in Epstein (1977). Finally they agreed that it is important to perceive one's own locomotion and that perceiving necessarily involves sensitivity to both those aspects of a changing array specific to one's own posture and locomotion, and to those aspects which are independent of the observer. Johansson's vector analyses that separate common from relative motions address this kind of cospecification.

Differences

I shall discuss four salient differences between the two positions in roughly increasing order of importance.

Semantic Differences.   The first difference is terminological and should be dispensed with quickly. As Runeson and Johansson explained at the conference, the English word ''event'' has been used to translate the Swedish word *skeende* which Johansson originally used.

Skeende refers to the ongoing aspect of change, emphasizing flows and repetition as opposed to boundedness, which might be captured by emphasizing a beginning and an end. Calling something a *skeende* emphasizes that it is a temporal occurrence, a process. Another word that could be translated into English as ''event'' is *händelse*. A *händelse* is an occurrence whose existence and dramatic quality is more the issue than its temporal extent. Normal English usage of ''event'' is more like a *händelse* than a *skeende*. Thus we speak of social events, theatrical events, sports events, musical events and so forth. Newspaper articles about highly publicized affairs that prove disappointing may call those affairs nonevents. A train's passage across a highway at a crossing would be a *skeende* if taken as just the motion of the train. But if it were eagerly awaited by a group of train watching enthusiasts, it would be a *händelse* for them, that is, a significant occurrence.

Given these two choices it is clear that a perceptual psychologist who studied the configurations of motions that Johansson did would call them *skeende* in Swedish. After consulting an Oxford professor, he chose the English word ''event'' as the closest translation and has used it in his English writing since 1950. It is his most general term for change. Recently Johansson defined ''event'' as a ''generic concept denoting various kinds of relational change over time in a structure (1978, p. 677).'' He has then found it necessary to distinguish among distal events, proximal events, and perceptual events. The German translations of Johansson have used *Geschehen,* or ''event.'' That is, indeed, the word used by Heider in 1926 subsequently translated into English as 'event' (Heider, 1959).

Both Gibson and Johansson use ''event'' in the sense of *type* of event, as distinct from tokens. They are interested in changes like rolling, walking, approaching, receding, exploding, or melting, in general, not *this* instance or *that* instance. Together I think they deviate somewhat from the more common usage as token. An historical event in a broad sense is a singular happening. History can be thought of as a sequence of noted events, actual occurrences which do not repeat (in traditional western cosmology). *Types* of events (war) recur, but actual events (e.g., the Hundred Years War) make up the minimal nonrepeatable unit. *Händelse* seems to be more of a token word than *skeende*. Even though the token sense of event, as in a historical event, strikes me as more common than the type sense of ''event,'' the context has been clear enough that I have never detected a confusion in the literature.

Gibson defined his terms somewhat differently and did not call all changes in structure events. The word ''event'' for Gibson referred to types of material change in the world, not to all changes of structure and not to changes of structure in the optic array. He noted three major classes of terrestrial events—changes of surface layout or arrangement, changes of surface composition, and changes in surface integrity (1979, chapter 6). A fourth type of material change, changes in the relation between an animal and its environment, from the animal's point of view, was not called an event at all, but an "encounter."[1] Changes in optical structure (or acoustic, haptic, or chemical structure, where relevant) were said to carry information *for* both events and encounters without themselves being events or encounters. Thus Gibson's use of the word "event" became much more restricted than Johansson's, and readers of Gibson's later work (after 1966) should bear this in mind.

Up to this point I see little for Johansson to disagree with, although it is important for the wider audience to appreciate the differences in word use. Johansson's term *skeende* has been his natural term behind the English word "event." It is his most general cover term for change. Gibson's use of "event" has been more specific. Interestingly enough, since Gibson repeatedly stated that an event, as embodied change, must have its own beginning and end, it would appear that what he meant was closer to the Swedish *händelse*. This is not all that the difference in the two positions amounts to. One should not expect perceptual theory to divide neatly along lines established in the Swedish language. But taking this one contrast rather coarsely, it does seem true to say that Gibson was closer to meaning *händelse* than to *skeende* in his meaning for the word "event."

Slow Events.   A more substantial, but still not very deep, distinction between Johansson's and Gibson's positions concerns the status of slow events. Both theorists know full well that all embodied things in this world (mathematical entities aside) change, but at a variety of rates relative to one another. An apple falls to earth much more rapidly than it ripens. Phenomenally we humans find it compelling to say that we perceive falling, but far less compelling to say that we perceive ripening because we do not see the characteristic changes of color and texture of the apple in the span of a typical observational act. At the opposite extreme, we do not say that we perceive the fast motion of the raster that generates a static TV image. Johansson wishes to use this difference to distinguish between perceptible and nonperceptible events. He has confined his interest to the "perceptible" events. From Johansson's point of view, the compelling difference between events whose changes are phenomenally evident and those whose changes are not is sufficient to warrent a division of subject matter into perceived and cognized events. On this view one can perceive the motion of the second hand of an analog watch but not that of the hour hand. That is apprehended by cognition.

---

[1]Lecture at the University of Connecticut, Department of Psychology, October 1, 1976.

Gibson, on the other hand, did not use phenomenal experience as a criterion for delineating subject matter in his latest theorizing. Rather, he used the existence and availability of information. For him cases were divided between those in which information for an event or encounter was available and sufficiently sampled to detect it, and those in which a judgement (or behavioral commitment) was made in the absence of sufficient information or sampling. Thus for Gibson, neither the speed of an event nor the phenomenology is as important as whether or not information is being detected. An extended discussion of the continuity between slow and fast events may be found in Shaw and Pittenger (1978). Gibson was clearly committed to pursuing the pickup of information as a unified topic in a way that differs from Johansson's commitments (see Gibson, 1979, ch. 14). This is a genuine difference between them, but I repeat, not one that by itself divides them very deeply.

Point vs. Texture Displays.   An advantage of Johansson's point-light method lies in the stark contrast between what one can see in the changing displays and what one cannot see in the static displays. The implausibility of discovering the rich structure of the changing pattern from analyses of individual "snapshots" is dramatized every time the film stops and we see just a jumble again. Neither memory, nor knowledge, nor any other "familiarity" account of event perception suggests itself.

Gibson, too, wished to devise displays that dramatized the priority of changing patterns over static ones. However Johansson's point-light method does not lend itself to the study of surfaces, which Gibson also emphasized. To study the specification and transformation of surfaces, Gibson turned to random textures. Gibson's student, George Kaplan (1969), created a series of displays that looked irresistably like opaque surfaces moving over one another as long as the film was running, but like a single undivided surface in any individual frame. This was done by progressively adding or subtracting texture from each successive frame. Gibson (1979) argued that the changes involved in the concealing or revealing of opaque surfaces, occlusion, were fundamental optical properties of real, terrestrial environments. Moreover, he constantly stressed the fact that removing and adding texture were not the sort of changes to be found in projective geometry; hence projective geometry could not be the most general foundation for terrestrial optical theory.

Johansson, less concerned with finding a completely general theory than Gibson, has found projective geometry to be very useful for organizing the phenomena of interest to him and for suggesting new experiments. Gibson often lamented the fact that changes of occlusion were less amenable to analysis and experimentation than Johansson's point-light displays seemed to be, but held that this practical shortcoming did not make the facts of occlusion or their implications any less true.

Although Gibson talked about the information for occlusion in terms of the progressive addition or subtraction of texture, this should be taken only as a preliminary, practical formulation. It is not a final hypothesis, but a step in theory development. The most general principle of changes in the optic array was, for Gibson, what he called simply the disturbance of structure. What was called for then were increasingly precise hypotheses about what constituted relevant disturbances of structure and accompanying invariants for specifying events and encounters. Addition (accretion) or subtraction (deletion) of texture was a step, but such a description taken alone is too presumptive about what counts as texture.

There is a little known phenomenon called omega motion which makes this point nicely (Saucer, 1953, 1954; Tyler, 1973; Zeeman & Roelofs, 1953). Omega motion is simply another phenomenon that can be observed in a standard apparent motion paradigm. The only constraint is that the elements that turn on and off be larger than a point. They may be columns of two or more points, bars, or just discs that are relatively large. How large this "large" should be is a matter for further investigation. Assume we have two bars separated in space. Recall that beta motion is the name for clear apparent motion of a single bar induced by flashing these two bars on and off in sequence. If the alternation is quick enough there is more of a blur and the nature of the moving object is unclear. An observer sees "pure" motion. This is phi. In between, however, at about 2.5–3.5 cycles per second, lies omega motion. There is a figure–ground reversal where the interspace becomes a surface (or a shadow to some) that appears to move back and forth in front of a solid background, the edges of which are *seen* as alternately revealed and concealed. Omega motion, therefore, is an occlusion phenomenon, but the conditions for it are not readily analyzed as the addition and subtraction of texture. Refining a theory of the disturbance of optical structure to include this case along with those that have already been studied is clearly a challenge for the future. Gibson's interests and methods lend themselves to discovering and pursuing such phenomena, whereas Johansson's do not. The two approaches seem complementary in the sense that Gibson's focal interests would not lead one to discover and elaborate Johansson's phenomena either.

Underlying Paradigms of Perception.   I turn now to the most significant of the differences in my discussion. One of the critical aspects of any scientific theory is the canonical situation it is constructed around, such as the motion of a single particle in Newtonian mechanics. What "image" does a theorist have in mind when developing particular scientific concepts? Some properties of these images will be explicit, others strongly hinted at, and still others throughly camouflaged. In perception, most students have adopted the spatial imagery that Johansson mentioned as their canonical model of an instance of perceiving. This is the "Distal-Proximal-Percept" model underlying any linear causal theory of perception and made most explicit by Brunswik, Heider, and Koffka (Gibson, 1970/1982). One takes it that occurrences at a sensory organ (proximal events) are somehow caused by prior spatial–temporal occurrences so that a causal chain going from *distal stimulus* to *proximal stimulus* to *percept* is set up. Professor Johansson has maintained that Gibson emphasized the distal–proximal relation in his ecological approach and that he (Johansson) has stressed the proximal–percept relation.

This does not capture Gibson's approach, however, because Gibson reasoned from a model situation that could not be analyzed as a chain of events from environment to experience. Gibson questioned both the idea of a *stimulus* in perception (1960, 1967) and the proximal–distal metaphor. The clearest idea of what a stimulus might be is that which causes a response, as in the common view of a reflex; a goad or a prod to an animal was Gibson's usual example. A stimulus, properly speaking, is imposed. It *impinges* on one's *receptors*. But of course few people, certainly not Johansson, believe that either a distal or a proximal stimulus really *causes* perception. There are too many slips between the stimulus "givens" and the percepts. Customarily the gap between putative stimulus and percept as response has been filled with internal representations and/or processes, two of whose theoretical functions are to perform the conversion from stimulus to response and to account for failures of the two to correspond. As long as the stimulus–response model acts as a framework for thinking about perception, it will not itself be examined by experiment. Experiments can address the questions: What is the stimulus? What is the response? What lies between the two? They need not be taken to address the question: Is the stimulus–response framework proper? Yet this was one of the primary objects of skepticism for Gibson in his later years. Instead of *stimuli* Gibson offered his idea of *information*, which is pattern (optic, acoustic, etc.) specific to its sources and which is just *there*. Once there, it can be *used* (or obtained) by animals as a functional resource.[2] Gibson's information can be *clarified* by animals at a variety of levels of detail—all of which exist—depending on the interests and capacities of the animal. Gibson was never satisfied that a stimulus–response view could adequately characterize the *exploratory* and *guidance* functions of perceiving. The S–R mold has been far better suited to characterizing the classification and identification functions of perception. To draw the sharpest contrast, the S–R view has the environment doing something (impinging on, stimulating, etc.) to the animal, whereas Gibson thought of the animal as doing something (clarifying, obtaining, investigating, using) to the environment. Even though he distinguished between performatory and exploratory activities, it must be emphasized that his notion of exploration was also quite performance oriented when compared to more typical theories of attention. Gibson often insisted that he alone had a theory of perception which supposed a truly active observer. More

---

[2]The resource image is Ed Reed's.

traditional approaches sometimes say they have active theories but mean it in a Leibniz–Kant sense of mental activity, the sort of thing meant to reconcile stimulus and response relations, not to contravene them (see Gibson, 1976, 1979, ch. 14; Richards, 1976).

Johansson has been able to make progress on problems of interest to him without rejecting the S–R framework, just as Gibson did in earlier times when he was pursuing a psychophysical program. Johansson does not seem to worry about the details of his framework (that would be like philosophy) as long as it helps him devise interesting experiments and demonstrations. Gibson rejected the S–R paradigm because he concluded it was *false,* even though he too found it a more pliable paradigm than his own for experiments.

The spatial aspect of the distal-proximal-percept metaphor may itself be questioned futher. John Dewey had questioned it (1896), Gibson's mentor, E. B. Holt questioned it (Holt, 1915) and Gibson himself was finally questioning it by the 1960s (Gibson 1970–1982). What these critics pointed out, after William James, was that there is a critical distinction between links in a physical causal chain and objects of action and perception. Holt argued that even for physics proximity was not the primary relation. He maintained that the prior question of a science was "what is an object or animal *doing?*" Answering the question, for him, required finding the proper objects of the action or motion. It raised the question, "of what is behavior a constant function?" Thus a Newtonian falling body is lawfully understood relative to the center of the earth rather than various successive places measured by a meter stick that it might be falling past. Holt noted that, in distal-proximal terms, that of which behavior is a constant function seemed to recede further toward the distal end as one considers living matter relative to nonliving, and "higher" organisms relative to "lower." A rock, then, is Newtonian, but a plant may move toward some value along a light gradient, and Little Red Riding Hood goes to grandmother's house. The idea that physically proximal "objects" are not to be confused with objects of action or perception is embodied in the distinction between physical and epistemic (or intentional) objects discussed by Shaw & Bransford (1977). Some of Gibson's more explicit reasons for rejecting the distal-proximal metaphor were stated at the 1970 conference on Ecological Optics (1970/1982). He listed five:

1. Surfaces can be distinguished from light emitters as sources of structured light. Treatments in terms of proximal stimuli concentrate on light at the eye and therefore cannot make this distinction.
2. The distal "object" can never itself *be* a stimulus, but the term "stimulus" is often used ambiguously to refer to both.
3. Gibson's pet idea of the 1950s, that texture gradients were proximal stimuli for slant relative to the line of sight, did not empirically work out.
4. The more general notion of "higher order variables of stimulation" seemed unclear and unlikely to become more clear.

5. Gibson's analyses of motion (1968) led him to the conclusion that the retina should not be taken as a frame of reference for defining what was meant by "motion." Distal-proximal thinking, on the other hand, would seem to have no choice but to consider the motion of points relative to the retina as primary "stimulus" for the perception of motion.

The alternative "picture" of the relevant model of visual perception that Gibson developed (analogues would also hold for other modes of perceiving) was that of an *ambient* optic array, something for animals to be *inside of* or *immersed in*. It is then something that can be sampled from, consistent with the explanatory imagery I tried to convey in the earlier discussion of the S–R portion of the perceptual paradigm. He thought of the structure of the optic array in terms of nested solid angles packed up against one another. Taken in this way, an optic array is a plenum; it is filled. There are no empty spaces. Thus there can be no points, no motions of points, no velocities or accelerations of points. Rather, there are changes in the overall structure of the plenum. Some of these changes, and their underlying invariants, may *specify* the motions of detached objects in the air, but this is not to be confused with the idea that isolated points of light moving relative to the retina are the underlying stimuli for an environmental event of a similar description.

Gibson's latter day ecological theorizing may be termed a *terrestrial materialism* as well as a realism. He stressed not only the primacy of surfaces as the behaviorally relevant interface between substances and media, but the absolute priority of the surface of the earth, bounded by the sky, as the frame of reference for understanding both perception and action. Johansson has often used his studies of embedded frames of reference to argue against Gibson, but it is important to realize that for Gibson the ground is the *ultimate* frame of reference in which events and encounters, in particular, are nested—if not the *only* frame of reference.

I have dwelled on this last difference as the major one because the distal-proximal stimulus analysis is so rarely questioned that it is often taken as a truism, or at worst, an innocent working assumption. Even though Gibson and Johansson stimulated and supported one another for nearly 30 years, Johansson has not acknowledged how radical a change of approach to perception Gibson was advocating.

Having staked out Gibson's ground, I return to Johansson's. At this Conference he has been humble and has heaped praise on Gibson. Even though this paper follows his lead and emphasizes Gibson's ideas, it is not meant to yield fully to Johansson's modesty. The world of experimental psychology is just beginning to catch up with Gunnar (Restle, 1979; Cutting, 1981). His career has been fertile with fascinating phenomena. By giving psychologists robust, tantalizing displays to investigate, he has surely done more to establish the autonomy of event perception than the cleverest of theories could do at this time.

REFERENCES

Boring, E. G. *Sensation and perception in the history of experimental psychology.* NY: Appleton-Century-Crofts, 1942.

Cutting, J. Coding theory adapted to gait perception. *Journal of Experimental Psychology: Human Perception and Performance,* 1981, *7,* 71–87.

Dewey, J. The reflex arc concept in psychology. *Psychological Review,* 1896, *3,* 357–370.

Epstein, W. (Ed.) *Stability and constancy in visual perception.* New York: Wiley, 1977.

Gibson, J. J. The concept of the stimulus in psychology. *American Psychologist,* 1960, *15,* 694–703.

Gibson, J. J. On the proper meaning of the term "stimulus." *Psychological Review,* 1967, *74,* 533–534.

Gibson, J. J. What gives rise to the perception of motion? *Psychological Review,* 1968, *75,* 335–346.

Gibson, J. J. On theories for visual space perception. A letter to Johansson. *Scandinavian Journal of Psychology,* 1970, *11,* 75–79.

Gibson, J. J. A history of the ideas behind ecological optics. Transscribed and edited by A. G. Barrand and M. Riegle, 1970. Reprinted in E. Reed & R. Jones (Eds.) *Reasons for realism. Selected papers of James J. Gibson.* Hillsdale, N. J.: Lawrence Erlbaum Associates 1982.

Gibson J. J. The myth of passive perception. A reply to Richards. *Philosophy and Phenomenological Research,* 1976, *37,* 234–238.

Gibson, J. J. On the analysis of change in the optic array. *Scandinavian Journal of Psychology,* 1977, *18,* 161–163.

Gibson, J. J. *The ecological approach to visual perception.* Boston: Houghton Mifflin, 1979.

Heider, F. Ding und medium. *Symposion,* 1926, *1,* 109–157. Translation reprinted as Thing and medium. *Psychological Issues,* 1959, *1,* (3), 1–34.

Heider, F., & Simmel, M. An experimental study of apparent behavior. *American Journal of Psychology,* 1944, *57,* 243–259.

Holt, E. B. Response and cognition. I. The specific-response relation. *The Journal of Philosophy (Psychology, and Scientific Methods),* 1915, *12,* 365–373.

Johansson, G. On theories for visual space perception. A letter to Gibson. *Scandinavian Journal of Psychology,* 1970, *11,* 67–74.

Johansson, G. Visual perception of biological motion and a model for its analysis. *Perception & Psychophysics,* 1973, *14,* 201–211.

Johansson, G. Visual event perception. In R. Held, H. W. Leibowitz, & H. L. Teuber (Eds.) *Perception: Handbook of sensory physiology,* Vol, VIII. Berlin, Heidelberg: Springer-Verlag, 1978.

Kaplan, G. Kinetic disruption of optical texture: The perception of depth at an edge. *Perception & Psychophysics,* 1969, *6,* 193–198.

Michotte, A., Thinès, G., & Crabbé, G. Les compléments amodaux des structures perceptives. In *Studia psychologica.* Louvain: Publications Université de Louvain, 1964.

Reed, E., & Jones, R. (Eds.) *Reasons for realism: Selected papers of James J. Gibson.* Hillsdale, N. J.: Lawrence Erlbaum Associates, 1982.

Restle, F. Coding theory of the perception of motion configurations. *Psychological Review,* 1979, *80,* 1–24.

Richards, R. J. Gibson's theory of perception: A criticism of Mueller's specific nerve energies hypothesis. *Philosophy and Phenomenological Research,* 1976, *37,* 221–234.

Saucer, R. T. The nature of perceptual processes. *Science,* 1953, *117,* 556–558.

Saucer, R. T. Processes of motion perception. *Science,* 1954, *120,* 806–807.

Schiff, W. Perception of impending collision. *Psychological Monographs,* 1965, *79,* No. 604.

Shaw, R. E., & Bransford, J. Introduction: Psychological approaches to the problem of knowledge. In R. Shaw & J. Bransford (Eds.) *Perceiving acting, and knowing.* Hillsdale, N. J.: Lawrence Erlbaum Associates, 1977.

Shaw, R. E., & Pittenger, J. Perceiving change. In H. Pick & E. Saltzman(Eds.) *Modes of perceiving.* Hillsdale, N. J.: Lawrence Erlbaum Associates, 1978.

Tyler, C. W. Temporal characteristics in apparent movement: Omega movement vs. phi movement. *Quarterly Journal of Experimental Psychology,* 1973, *25,* 182–192.

Zeeman, W. P. C., & Roelofs, C. O. Some aspects of apparent motion. *Acta Psychologica,* 1953, *9,* 158–181.

4 Reflections on Gunnar Johansson's Perspective On the Visual Measurement of Space and Time

Joseph S. Lappin
Vanderbilt University

INTRODUCTION

It is indeed a pleasant responsibility to reflect on Gunnar Johansson's thorough and thoughtful review of the "Perception of Motion, Dynamics and Biological Events." I admire Gunnar's expression of these problems, and I am grateful for his having given us this paper.

As a reflector, my role is best served by operating not as an ideal mirror but as one with some variations in perspective—some twists, turns, holes, and highlights. If the transformations are not too severe, they may aid in the detection of some of the invariant aspects across both perspectives.

I will focus on three problems involved in the phenomena that Gunnar has reviewed:

1. *Measurement:* How does the visual nervous system measure the spatio–temporal structure of the environment?

2. *Statistics and topology:* How do perceived geometrical structures derive from the statistical coherence of complex stimulus patterns composed of multiple discrete surfaces and motions?

3. *Mechanisms:* What possible mechanisms and processes can explain the structural correspondence between perception, experience, and environmental events?

MEASUREMENT

Of all the services that our visual systems provide for us, perhaps the most important is measurement of the geometric structure of the visual world. Such measurement is fundamental to almost every instance of visual-motor coordination and visual pattern recognition. For example, in running through an outfield to meet a swiftly falling baseball, in guiding a car through speeding freeway traffic, in recognizing the faces of friends in a crowded room, or in performing any of a thousand everyday activities so routine we scarcely think of them, human perceivers exhibit astonishingly precise knowledge of the detailed structure and dynamics of environmental objects and events. As the observer moves through the environment, the perceived metric structure of environmental objects and events typically remains invariant under continuing transformations of the proximal stimulation projected on the retina. Despite their familiarity, these phenomena may be regarded among the most magnificent of nature's achievements, and they deserve our admiration and attention as students of perception. Indeed, our appreciation of the visual measurement of space and motion has been very greatly enhanced by the experiments of Gunnar Johansson and his colleagues.

Although visual space perception is not ordinarily considered as a process of measurement, this generalization of the concept of measurement seems valid and useful. Measurement is usually considered as a procedure for assigning numbers to represent empirical relations, but the same general conception can be extended to other systems for representing metric relations. In visual perception, for example, observers usually exhibit accurate knowledge of the 3–D spatial structure and location of environmental objects. The format in which spatial relations are ''represented'' in the visual nervous system is unknown, of course, but mathematical characteristics of the perceived relations among objects are certainly testable by psychophysical techniques. Observers' judgments about spatial relations may sometimes be inconsistent or ''incorrect'' (as defined by reference to a ruler, for example) when stimuli are embedded in illusory or insufficient contextual structure, but the perceived spatial relations can still be determined psychophysically. Indeed, Gunnar Johansson's experiments have provided valuable information about the nature of visual measurement.

Before examining Johansson's findings, it will be useful to briefly review the general logical structure of formal theories of measurement, particularly as described by Krantz, Luce, Suppes, and Tversky (1971) for the assignment of numbers of empirical structures. First, measurement should be understood to involve the mapping of one *relational structure* (defined as a set of elements and some relations among them) into another relational structure. That is, relations are mapped into relations.

Formal theories of measurement are explications of the characteristics of this representation of one relational structure by another. There are three basic aspects: *representation, uniqueness,* and *meaningfulness.* The representation problem is to specify necessary and sufficient conditions for a given empirical relational structure to be represented by another relational structure. The uniqueness problem is to specify the uniqueness of the representation in terms of permissible transformations of the representational elements that will preserve the empirical relations. For example, an ordinal measurement scale is one in which the assignment of numbers is unique only up to a monotonic transformation, and a ratio scale permits a numerical assignment unique up to multiplication by a scalar constant. The meaningfulness problem is to specify the permissible transformations of the empirical objects and events under which their qualitative relational structure remains invariant (see Luce, 1978). That is, if any given empirical relationship constitutes a meaningful basis for some metric representation, then the qualitative empirical relation must remain invariant under ostensibly irrelevant changes in the specific conditions of measurement and must combine in meaningful lawful relationships with measures of other empirical variables.

The *psychophysical* representation problem involves specifying the geometric relations that can be visually perceived in a given set of physical stimulus patterns and the conditions under which these relations can be perceived. Thus, an important part of Johansson's contribution to the understanding of visual measurement is what he has shown us about the perceivable geometric relations in optical patterns and about the limited amount of stimulus structure required to perceive these relations. Specifically, Gunnar has shown us that the space–time patterns of *change* or *transformation* among a small set of moving points of light are sufficient to provide rapid and rich visual information about the 3–D structure and motion of a large variety of both rigid and nonrigid objects. As mentioned above, we cannot say just how the nervous system represents the metric information about such patterns, but we may presume that the representation is in a form that is commensurate with that used for the control of bodily action and with certain aspects of the memory retention of information about similar groups of patterns previously experienced under very different optical conditions. Warren (1982) has recently provided important evidence and rationale in support of the idea that metric information about the environment must involve the same variables and units of measure as the information that controls actions of the skeletal muscles.

Psychophysical analogs of the uniqueness problem involve specifying the consistency and accuracy of behavioral responses to the metric structure of stimulus patterns as well as the convergence of various response measures on the same perceived structure of stimulus relations. Although this uniqueness aspect of visual measurement has not been investigated explicitly in Johansson's research and writing, he has provided important evidence pertaining to the precision of visual measurement and to its stability under changes in viewing positions.

The meaningfulness problem in visual measurement is analogous to a corresponding problem in other scientific applications (see Krantz, Luce, Suppes, & Tversky, 1971, ch. 10; Luce, 1978). The problem is to specify the class of quantitative statements or laws that can legitimately be formulated about a set of objects or events on the basis of particular qualitative empirical observations.

One might in principle measure a large number of different empirical properties of a set of objects, but what are the valid quantitative representations of these properties, and which of them express functionally meaningful relationships suitable for the formulation of laws? In vision the question is which of the innumerable possible measures of optical patterns will constitute perceptually meaningful geometric relations for the guidance of actions and the recognition of objects and events?

Luce (1978) has demonstrated that the answer to the former question, pertaining to the formulation of numerical laws in classical physics, is that meaningful numerical laws (those that are "dimensionally invariant") correspond to qualitative relations that remain invariant under automorphisms of the measurement structure (defined as the empirical relational structure and its numerical representation). As it applies to vision, this seems to correspond to the idea that meaningful measures are those that remain invariant under optical transformations produced by irrelevant changes in the observational conditions. Meaningful measures of shape, for example, should be invariant under perspective changes in viewing position, and measures of surface color should be invariant under changes in ambient lighting. Now one of the principal results so beautifully demonstrated in Johansson's research is that perspective transformations constitute an extraordinarily rich source of visual information about the geometric structure of environmental objects and events. Thus, vision seems to derive some of its measures of spatial structure from those qualitative optical relationships that remain invariant under perspective transformations.

A basic aspect of the meaningfulness problem in formal measurement theory that is especially relevant to visual measurement concerns the reference standard against which the empirical structures are measured. The most familiar class of measurement procedures, illustrated by the use of a ruler, is *extensive* measurement—where the empirical structure is measured by counting the number of concantenated standard units required to match it. The reference system in this case is extrinsic to the structure being measured.

A second class of procedures to represent geometric relations has been called "functional" (Platt, 1958) or "intrinsic" (Shaw & Cutting, 1980; Warren, 1982). Here, geometric relations are represented in terms of *symmetry* (i.e., invariance, self congruence) under transformations that map the empirical structure onto itself. That is, the reference standard is intrinsic to the empirical structure being measured. Platt (1958) pointed out that the construction of many geometric structures both in nature and technology is functionally controlled by primitive but precise processes involving convergence toward symmetry under transformation: A circular arc may be traced out on a beach by the wind twisting tall grass through the sand; precision optical lenses are produced by rubbing two rough pieces of glass against each other in a random sequence of planar translations and rotations. Conjoint measurement (Luce & Tukey, 1964; Krantz, Luce, Suppes, & Tversky, 1971) may also be regarded as an example of functional measurement—where interval-scaled measures of two independently manipulated experimental variables may be constructed from the invariance of certain ordinal relations in the data structure under the group of translations of the values of the two manipulated variables.

Platt (1958, 1960) hypothesized that visual representations of geometric relations such as collinearity, parallelism, etc. might be obtained from a similar type of functional geometry through invariance under eye movements. Although Platt's specific hypothesis about the role of eye movements has been experimentally disconfirmed, a significant body of research by Johansson and others on the visual perception of form and motion points to the basic role of functional geometry in visual measurement.

Let us now examine more closely the characteristics of visual measurement. A first question concerns the reference system by which the structure of stimulation is measured. Traditionally, the perception of environmental structure has been implicitly assumed to be derived from the application of prior knowledge and heuristics to a retinal image with well-defined structure in 2–D space and time. Johansson's experiments on the perceptual organization of point-light displays, however, clearly indicate that something is wrong with this conception: The precision and speed with which metric relations in space–time can be perceived in reduced and unfamiliar stimulus patterns is irreconcilable with the hypothesis that the perception of environmental structure requires additional information extrinsic to the stimulus pattern.

Indeed, elementary properties of visual anatomy and physiology indicate that we should be skeptical of the assumption that the 2–D retinal image has a well-defined structure in which positions and distances of stimulus components are specified by reference to anatomical positions in the visual nervous system. The anatomy and physiology of the visual system seem inappropriate for providing such metric information. First, the anatomical organization of receptors, neurons, receptive fields, etc., varies widely over the visual field, whereas the perceived metric structure of the visual world remains fairly constant as the eyes scan the environment. Second, neural response characteristics vary widely among individual receptors and neurons and are strongly influenced by the intensity and spectral characteristics of the stimulation, but the perceived metric structure remains invariant under changes in ambient illumination. Third, the metric structure of environmental objects and events is measured in the 3–D space of the environment rather than the 2–D space of the retina. Experimental evidence demonstrates that indeed it is only the 3–D and not the 2–D structure that observers see (Johansson, 1964; Lappin & Fuqua, 1983; Lappin & Preble, 1975). Fourth, motion of the proximal retinal stimulus is produced both by motion of the object in its environment and by motions of the observer's eyes and body, but these two sources of motion are usually perceptually distinguished from each other. In general, the anatomy and physiology of the visual system provide few immediately obvious clues about how the visual system measures the patterns of stimulation. Evidently, the assumption that vision employs an extensive measurement system is untenable.

Rather than measuring the world by reference to the anatomical structure of the retina, neural information about the metric structure and dynamics of the world should derive mainly from the organization of the world itself, reflecting as little as possible the prior organization of the observer's sensory apparatus. As Warren (1982) has shown, however, effective visual-motor control demands that measures of environmental structure be commensurate with the information used to control movements of the observer's body. Coordination of bodily movements with environmental events seems to require that the position of the observer's body and the forces required to change that position be specified in the same dimensions and units of measure as those used for representing the environmental structure. Johansson makes a similar point (this volume) in emphasizing that measures are needed for both environmental structure and for the position and motion of the observer. Such measures of the relationship between the observer and the environment, however, do not require that the world be extensively measured by reference to the observer. Instead, as Warren has suggested (personal communication), measures of the environment, the observer, and the observer-environment relationship are probably intrinsic to the observer-environment system. Many of these measures can probably be obtained directly from the dynamics of the projected optical stimulation (Gibson, 1979; Koenderink & van Doorn, 1981), though some may well depend on the activity of the observer.

To illustrate the visual measurement of an object moving in an environmental frame of reference, consider a running tennis player who is preparing to return an approaching tennis ball. The player's perception of the tennis ball moving in relation to the court and net involves measures of object motion relative to the 3–D environment, but these measures must be abstracted from the changing 2–D retinal stimulus patterns that are altered by movements of the observer's eyes and body. That is, *the perceived motion of the environmental event must remain invariant under the bodily motion of the perceiver.* Moreover, such sports as tennis and baseball often provide less than .5 seconds of time for the player to measure the trajectory of the ball and to coordinate his own motion with that of the ball so that the two motions intersect at the proper point in both space and time. Experimental evidence about the speed and precision with which such visual measures can be recovered from even small amounts of stimulus data is offered by Johansson's well-known research with point-light displays. Consider, for example, the movies of biological motion designed by Johansson and Cutting and their colleagues (e.g., Barclay, Cutting, & Kozlowski, 1978; Cutting & Kozlowski, 1977; Johansson, 1973; Maas, 1970, 1971)—where human walkers can be visually identified in brief displays of a few spots of light attached to the trunk and limbs. The 3–D structure and motion of a given part of the body, say the forearm, may be perceived more or less independently of the motion of the rest of the body in 3–D space: Swinging of the forearm at the elbow may be seen while the whole arm is moving at the shoulder and the whole body is bending at the waist, dancing over the ground and so forth. That is, measures of the local structure and motion of individual components of the pattern remain invariant under global motions of the whole structure. The speed and precision of these measures is suggested by the fact that individual walkers and subtle details of their structure and dynamics can be recognized in brief displays (less than 1 second) of the motion of only a few (less than 10) spots of light arranged in an unfamiliar pattern (Johansson, 1973, 1976; Cutting & Kozlowski, 1977). Indeed, the astonishing effectiveness with which the visual system can extract information from nothing more than spatial and temporal geometric relations in brief and unfamiliar patterns has become increasingly evident from a rapidly growing body of experimental research (e.g., Burr & Ross, 1979; Julesz, 1971; Lappin, Doner, & Kottas, 1980; Lappin & Fuqua, 1983; Lehmkuhle & Fox, 1980; Restle, 1979; Runeson & Frykholm, 1981; Todd, 1981; Uttal, Fitzgerald, & Eskin, 1975).

If we consider the implications of such performance capabilities, then we must conclude that visual measures of the 3–D structure and motion of environmental objects can be derived from the projective transformations of retinal stimulus patterns produced by motions of the observer or by objects within the 3–D world. That is, the transformation must specify the metric structure that remains invariant under the transformation. These invariants in the changing stimulus patterns must be what vision measures.

Now the symmetry group in which 3–D structures and motions remain invariant under relative motions of the observer and environment is closely related to the *Lorentz group* that specifies the space–time structure of the propagation of physical forces in the "special theory of relativity"—where the velocity of propagation (e.g., of light) remains invariant under inertial motions (those at a constant velocity in a constant direction) of the observer. All physical laws must obey a symmetry given by invariance under Lorentz transformations of the spatial and temporal coordinates:

$$dx_A^2 + dy_A^2 + dz_A^2 - c^2dt_A^2 = dx_B^2 + dy_B^2 + dz_B^2 - c^2dt_B^2 \qquad (1)$$

where the dx^2, dy^2, dz^2, and dt^2 terms represent the squared differences in orthogonal spatial and temporal coordinates of two points in the path of the propagation, where the A and B subscripts designate two different coordinate systems associated with two observers who may be travelling in different directions with different velocities, and where c^2 is the squared velocity of light that is a constant for both observers. Einstein's (1905/1952) use of this equation in describing the structure of electromagnetic propagation beautifully illustrates the power of functional measurement. Einstein's strategy was to begin with the symmetry of the physical event and then derive the metric structure of space and time required to preserve this symmetry.

Evidently, the invariant structure of the visual world may be derived from a similar functional equivalence under the projective transformations associated with motion parallax and binocular parallax. This visual symmetry can be described as:

$$dx_A^2 + dy_A^2 + (dz_A^2) - v^2 dt_A^2 = dx_B^2 + dy_B^2 + (dz_B^2) - v^2 dt_B^2 \qquad (2)$$

where the components terms have essentially the same meaning as before, but with two exceptions: First, the (dz^2) term is enclosed in parentheses to indicate that distances in depth away from the observer are not directly given in the single stationary retinal projection (ignoring for the present the significant contribution from various pictorial cues). The difference between these two terms, $(dz_A^2) - (dz_B^2)$, can be determined by the value required to preserve the symmetry of the equation. Second, in place of the constant velocity of light, c, we now have a variable velocity, v, associated with the motion of an environmental object. For the coordinate transformations associated with binocular parallax, the A and B subscripts would designate the disparate views of the two eyes. For motion parallax, the two subscripts could designate two successive views by the same eye moving in relation to the viewed objects.

Several types of recent experimental evidence support the hypothesis that in vision, as in physics, spatial and temporal variables are functionally interrelated in shaping the perception of coherent structure and motion. One example of particular relevance to the Lorentzian model described above is an experiment by Burr and Ross (1979) on the role of temporal disparity in stereopsis. Using dynamic random dot stereograms with no spatial disparity ($dx_L^2 = dx_R^2$ and $dy_L^2 = dy_R^2$), temporal interocular disparities of less than .5 msec. were shown to suffice for producing detectable displacements in depth of a moving target, with the magnitude of apparent displacements increasing with the velocity of motion. That is, this experiment seems to have validated the Lorentzian functional relation

$$v^2 (dt_R^2 - dt_L^2) = dz_R^2 - dz_L^2 \qquad (3)$$

for stereoacuity. Recent experiments by Burr (1979) and Morgan (1980) have also documented a similar form of trade-off between spatial and temporal displacements in vernier acuity tasks. The hypothesis that velocity plays a more fundamental role in vision than do either spatial or temporal extents as such has been supported in an experiment by Lappin, Bell, Harm, and Kottas (1975), who found the velocity of a briefly moving target to be more accurately discriminated than either the spatial or temporal displacements that determined its velocity. Analogous results have also been obtained by McKee (1981) in experiments on acuity for temporal intervals in moving patterns. In still another experimental paradigm, Falzett and Lappin (1983) found that spatial and temporal extents had additive and interchangeable effects on the detectability of both stationary and moving targets embedded in dynamic visual noise, with no qualitative difference in the detectability of stationary and moving forms. Altogether, it seems clear that the visual system fuses both space and time in the perception of form and motion.

The picture that emerges from this evidence is compatible with the general hypothesis that the visual system measures the structure of environmental objects and events by the symmetries they produce in the spatio–temporal patterns of retinal stimulation. Of course this is but another coloring of the same picture that James Gibson and Gunnar Johansson have been painting for several years now. As Gibson (1957) put it, "the transformation that a form undergoes may be as important for perception as the form that undergoes the transformation." Evidently, what is perceived is symmetry in space–time.

It bears mention, however, that the preceding discussion of visual measurement is restricted to the *kinematics* of visual patterns. One of the important points of Johansson's review of the perception of biological motion and events is that vision succeeds in measuring not only kinematic structure but also the *dynamics* of environmental events (see especially Runeson & Frykholm, 1981). One simple illustration of this idea may be obtained by rotating a point-light display of a human walker 180 degrees, so that the feet are moving at the top of the display and the head and shoulders are at the bottom. Whereas the human figure is immediately recognizable in the normal orientation, it is essentially unrecognizable in the rotated display, even after being identified as an inverted human walker (Robert Fox, personal communication). The kinematic structure of both displays is the same, but the perceptions are quite different. It is certainly an oversimplification to suggest that the visual system detects the constancy of *velocity* as indicated by analogy with the Lorentz equation. More abstract symmetries must be detectable, involving force, causation, intention, effort, resistance, and so forth. Marvelous indeed!

STATISTICS AND TOPOLOGY

This discussion of the geometry of visual patterns has also been oversimplified in another important respect: The variability and ambiguities of natural stimulus patterns have been overlooked. In point of fact, the retinal patterns of optical data provided by most natural environments are extraordinarily variable in their intensities, contours, motions, surface orientations, numbers and spacing of separate objects, and so on. Representative stationary examples of such patterns are shown in Fig. 4.1 and 4.2. When such patterns are described not in terms of already organized objects and motions but in terms of the distribution of intensities over a dense set of discrete points, then the complexities of such massive arrays of data may well seem overwhelming. The computational ambiguities in deriving a coherent global organization of environmental objects from the local relationships in projected optical patterns have been made especially evident by research on computer vision. The general computational problem lies in attributing the observed variabilities in projected arrays of optical data to specific parameters of environmental structure. Satisfactory general solutions for this problem

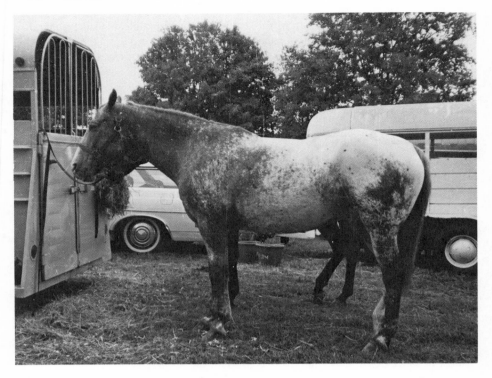

FIG. 4.1.   A stationary optical pattern typifying the geometric complexity of everyday visual patterns captured at a single moment in time. A major computational problem in interpreting such patterns is to determine the connectedness relations among neighboring points. The global structure of 3-D surfaces and objects must derive from these local relations and cannot in general provide an *a priori* framework for interpreting the local relations. (Photo courtesy of T. S. Lappin)

have remained elusive and much more subtle and difficult than initially anticipated.

A fundamental problem in constructing a global geometric representation of a projected optical pattern is *topological*—partitioning the data points into subsets of connected points associated with the same structure characterized by the same or smoothly changing parameter values. The measurement problem cannot be isolated from this connectedness problem. Measures of local geometric relations depend on the global organization of connections in space and time.

On those rare occasions when the stimulus pattern consists only of a single closed surface presented as a sharply contrasting figure against a homogeneous background, the topological problem is simple. But the problem rapidly grows more difficult as uncertainties about the number and identity of objects increase,

FIG. 4.2.   A stationary optical pattern sectioned from a dynamic visual scene.
The exposure time was approximately 17 msec. Determining the global structure
of connectedness and metric relations among neighboring points is complicated by
the fact that these local relations are rapidly changing.

as contours and surfaces are partially hidden by one another, as intensities vary
due to the direction of ambient lighting, and so forth. Neighboring data points are
not necessarily associated with the same structure, and points belonging to the
same structure are often separated in space and time. The massive size and
awesome variability of retinal data arrays are potentially associated with corresponding ambiguities in measuring the structural parameters of environmental
objects and events. The problem is: How is global structure derived from local
geometric relations when the measurement of local relations depends on the
global organization of environmental structure?

Despite these formidable computational difficulties, biological vision systems
seem to revel in the use of more and more data. Gunnar (this volume) offers the
provocative observation that "what is simple for the visual system is complex for
our mathematics, and what is mathematically simple is hard to deal with for the
visual system." Presumably, mathematical complexity refers here to the amount
and variability of the projected optical data. Roughly speaking, as the ratio of the
number of data points to the number of independent parameters grows larger—as
the redundancy increases—the speed and accuracy of recognizing environmental

structure also increase. From a statistical point of view, this appears readily understandable: Larger sets of data lend greater confidence to the testing of hypotheses. The rub, of course, is that visual hypotheses about metric relations are often not well defined before the data have been received, and the data are not well defined in the absence of their structural organization.[1] Measures of geometric relations are dependent on statistical analysis, and conversely; neither problem can be defined or solved independently of the other.

Gunnar's observation about the poor correspondence between mathematical complexity and visual complexity actually serves to point out a significant weakness in the foundations of our current understanding of vision: We do not yet know how to quantify the organizational complexity of arbitrarily selected visual patterns described only in terms of the spatio–temporal distribution of intensity values. That is, we lack a general theory of the geometric information for vision. In many special cases, of course, we can specify organizational complexity— when the optical patterns are selected from a restricted set with known structural parameters. In most research on visual perception, however, the descriptions of stimulus patterns tacitly embody a *prior* knowledge of the relevant structural organization defined in terms of distal environmental structure rather than proximal values of elementary physical variables. But if we lack a truly objective description of the information provided to vision then we shall not get very far in understanding how it is processed.

The importance of statistical variables in controlling the perceptual organization of complex spatio–temporal patterns has been clearly demonstrated in numerous experiments with moving and stereoscopic patterns composed of large numbers of random elements. The detectability of both motion (Julesz & Chang, 1980; Lappin & Bell, 1976; Lappin & Kottas, 1981) and stereoscopic depth (Tyler & Julesz, 1980) increase monotonically with the number of correlated target elements in successive (moving) or simultaneous (stereoscopic) frames. To a first approximation, the increase in detectability is proportional to the square root of the number of elements—as if all of the correlated target elements contribute independently to the global organization (see review by Julesz & Schumer, 1981). Additional suggestions that vision operates somewhat as a linear detector of statistical structure have been provided by Lappin and Kottas (1981), who found the detectability of apparent motion in dynamic random-dot

---

[1]In theological and philosophical contexts, this problem of the circularity of interpretation is known as *hermeneutics*—named for the Greek god Hermes, who among other functions served as the herald and messenger of the gods, rendering their symbols understandable by mortals. The term is applied especially to the interpretation of sacred texts, where God's or a writer's intended meaning must be deciphered from the surface structure of words composed in another cultural context. The hermeneutic process is composed of some mixture of two opposing attitudes or processes: The hermeneutics of belief—of faith, recognition, recollection, restoration of meaning—and the hermeneutics of doubt—of critical analysis, skepticism, and removal of meaning. Ricoeur (1970) provides a detailed discussion of this process and its application in psychoanalysis.

patterns to be directly proportional to the overall coherence (as measured by autocorrelation) of patterns in both space and time, with the spatial and temporal components contributing equivalently and interchangeably. Similarly, the dependence of stereopsis on the binocular cross correlation in random-element stereograms has been documented in Julesz's extensive research (see Julesz, 1971).

Thus, in the situations represented by the preceding experiments, the visual system seems to operate as an approximately linear detector of both spatial and temporal coherence. Coherence is a statistical property. The amount of coherence in a pattern can be measured by an autocorrelation function, which measures the correlation of a pattern with itself. Suppose that $f(x,y,t)$ is a pattern of optical energy defined over two spatial dimensions and time; and suppose that M is a transformation which maps the pattern into a new set of coordinates in the same space—M might be a translation, a rotation, a projective transformation, or in principle any transformation that maps the set of points in the X, Y, T space onto itself. In vision, the relevant transformation group may correspond to motions in 3–D space and their projections onto a 2–D plane. That is, M is a member of a group of transformations. The autocorrelation of the pattern $f(x,y,t)$ under the transformation of M may then be defined as

$$A(M) = \iiint f(x,y,t){\cdot}M[f(x,y,t)] \; dxdydt \qquad (4)$$

It may be noted that the autocorrelation is defined on the transformation M rather than on points in the X, Y, T space in which the original pattern is defined. In most applications, one considers not only a single value of the autocorrelation for a single transformation, but a complete autocorrelation function defined over the whole transformation group of which M is a member.

Thus, autocorrelation is a statistical measure of a geometric property, linking statistics and symmetry groups. It is also important to understand that the autocorrelation function is a linear function of the input pattern; an autocorrelation detector is a linear system, the output of which is proportional to the coherence of the input. No organization or information appears at the output of a linear system that was not contained in its input. If one considers stimulus patterns composed of signal plus noise, then the output signal/noise ratio is directly proportional to the input signal/noise ratio; multiple signals are simply additive in their effects. The autocorrelation function is also a close relative of the Fourier transform; both are linear measures of the periodic structure of the patterns.

Many aspects of perception could be easily understood if vision were representable simply as a linear operation, but this is not a sufficient description. Nonlinear effects occur in the perceptual organization of many stimulus patterns, reflecting *cooperative* interactions among separate components of the pattern of neural activity. The approximately linear behavior occurs when the geometric organization is simple and homogeneous—e.g., when a uniformly textured and densely connected surface is translated in a constant direction and velocity over neighboring regions of space and time. When the geometric organization of the pattern is not uniform, however, nonlinear cooperative effects have been well documented in the perceptual organization of stereoscopic (e.g., Julesz, 1978; Tyler & Julesz, 1976), moving (Doner, Lappin, & Perfetto, 1984; Julesz & Chang, 1980; Lappin, Doner, & Kottas, 1980; Lappin & Staller, 1981), and stationary spatial patterns (Julesz & Burt, 1979). When patterns are composed of two superimposed but inconsistent organizations, mutual interference rather than simple linear additivity of their perceptual effects has been obtained (Julesz & Chang, 1976; Lappin & Kottas, 1981). Julesz (1978) provides a thorough review of cooperative phenomena in stereopsis and their implications about underlying mechanisms. Despite the striking capability of vision to operate as a linear system in detecting coherence of many stimulus patterns, vision is certainly not a linear system. In general, the statistical and geometric variables interact in determining the perceptual organization of many stimulus patterns.

The nonlinear organizational phenomena in vision seem to arise in the process of determining the topological structure of connectedness in complex patterns— i.e., partitioning patterns into separate regions or surfaces of mutually connected components. When the stimulus pattern is segmented into multiple discrete substructures, the speed and accuracy of perceptual organization may be markedly reduced.

From a statistical point of view, it is not difficult to see why this might occur. Suppose, for example, that a set of patterns was characterized by n substructures or dimensions of variation in structural parameters. The total number of alternative patterns would increase exponentially with n: If there were k alternative parameter values on each of the n dimensions, there would be k^n alternative patterns to be discriminated. Additionally, if there were a constant number of data points in each pattern (larger than k^n), then the average number of data points associated with each substructure would be inversely proportional to n, and the statistical uncertainty of the estimate of each parameter value would be directly proportional to $\sqrt{n}$. Therefore, the time required to identify the structural parameters of a particular pattern should increase monotonically with $\sqrt{n}k^n$. The measurement ambiguities associated with uncertainties about structural parameters may be even greater in many situations. Suppose one knew beforehand the identities of each of the component substructures in a pattern, but did not know how they were arranged in a particular pattern—analogous to the situation where one knows all of the students in a class but does not know how they will arrange themselves in the available seats on any particular occasion. If there are m possible locations on each of n component substructures, the number of alternative patterns would increase factorially, $m!/(m - n)!$ if $m > n$, and $n!/(n - m)!$ if $n > m$. Of course these are idealized models, probably not representative of biological vision systems, but they suggest why increasing the structural complexity of the stimulus patterns should be expected to produce large increases in the processing time or amount of data required to identify a given pattern.

One suspects, however, that biological vision systems are not so adversely affected by uncertainties about structural parameters as suggested by the preceding models. The geometric constraints imposed by the connectedness relations among neighboring points in space–time probably provide considerable information about the metric structure of retinal data patterns. Additionally, prior knowledge about the set of potential structural relations, as derived from previous experiences in a particular environment, probably places significant constraints on the set of alternative patterns that must be discriminated. In any case, both theoretical and empirical research on this problem is sparse. We do not yet know how to quantify complexity, nor do we understand its perceptual effects.

Several researchers have begun to make some headway in this fundamental problem area, however. Perhaps the most general and promising line of work is that of Julesz (cf. 1981) on the application of statistical geometry to the perceptual segregation of densely textured 2–D patterns. In a study of this problem spanning nearly twenty years, Julesz has found that the great majority of cases of "spontaneous" (or "preattentive") segregation of textured arrays into areas of discriminably different textures have derived from differences in the *second-order statistics* of the patterns. Second-order statistics are defined by line segments joining pairs of points in a pattern. Two patterns have different second-order statistics if the lengths or orientations or combinations of intensities at the ends of the line segments have different relative frequencies in the two patterns. The second-order statistics give a general description that determines the autocorrelation function and the Fourier spectrum of the pattern, although the converse is not true (Julesz, 1981). The nth-order statistics are defined by the relative frequencies of n-sided polygons. With only a few but significant exceptions, Julesz has found that textures differing in third and higher order statistics are not immediately discriminable without attentional scanning. According to Julesz, those textures with iso–second-order statistics that are immediately discriminable involve the detection of a few conspicuous local features, called "textons," which include elongated blobs (of given width and orientation) and quasi-collinear structures.

What is particularly important about Julesz's research program is the development of a general theory for quantifying the geometric and statistical properties of complex patterns together with experimental methods for generating densely textured patterns with specific geometric properties. Psychophysical measures of the discrimination of these patterns then provide measures of the perceptual segregation produced by that geometric property. Although Beck, Prazdny, and Rosenfeld (1981) have raised questions about the validity of some of Julesz's conclusions and have proposed an alternative model based entirely on the detection of differences in the relative frequency of local feature elements, the conceptual and experimental tools for investigating these problems have been considerably advanced by Julesz's research.

A somewhat different but promising theory for quantifying the organizational complexity of complex patterns has been developed recently by Jonathan Doner (in preparation) at Vanderbilt. Doner's method is also based on statistical properties of textured patterns, but is defined by the relative frequencies of local intensity combinations in 2 × 2 quartets of neighboring positions in a lattice.

These and other efforts to quantify the statistical characteristics of geometric information in complex patterns (e.g., Restle, 1979) are encouraging developments. Additional progress in understanding the geometrical complexity of visual patterns may be anticipated in the foreseeable future. More theoretical research is needed, coupled with more experimental work in testing theoretical schemes against a wider range of geometric structures including 3–D and moving patterns. Perhaps the visual system applies a form of statistical geometry to the analysis of vector manifolds in space–time that is similar to the statistical geometry that it seems to apply to the analysis of 2–D spatial textures. Indeed, this seems to be just the direction that Gunnar has been taking us with his ideas about the role of vector analysis in vision. We have much more to learn, however.

MECHANISMS

If, as the preceding discussions have suggested, visual measures of geometric relations in space–time are based on symmetries in dynamic retinal stimulus patterns, and if these measures of local geometric relations depend on global statistical analyses, then the neural mechanisms by which these processes occur seem to be well-hidden from currently available experimental and theoretical tools. What would a neural mechanism that detected symmetries of metric structure look like? Would we recognize one if we saw it? How do global neural patterns modify the representation of local geometric relations?

Even if the preceding suggestions about visual measurement are valid, they are not necessarily very satisfying as explanations. The hypothesis that visual measurement is based on the symmetry of dynamic stimulus patterns might be regarded as more descriptive than explanatory. Isn't this just the phenomenon that demands an explanation? Can we be said to understand these phenomena if we do not know how they arise from neural mechanisms? Attitudes of individual researchers will differ on this question, but certainly many will not feel satisfied without some more specific knowledge of the underlying neural mechanisms.

Identification of these mechanisms seems quite problematic, however, with the presently available conceptual, experimental, and analytic tools of contemporary electrophysiology and anatomy. Electrophysiological studies of the visual system have usually been concerned with the receptive field properties of single neurons, but it seems inconceivable that the perceptual organization of Johansson's point-light displays could be explained in these terms. Surely, the visual measurement of metric structure in these patterns must involve space–time relations among multiple neurons. Simultaneous recordings from multiple individual neurons, however, are very difficult with modern techniques. Even if such data were available, what relationships in the recordings from multiple neurons would constitute critical evidence with which to identify and describe the neural mechanisms? Clearly, there is a sizeable gap between the empirical data and the conceptual framework with which to interpret the data.

Three roughly formed hypotheses (or attitudes) about the underlying neural mechanisms are the following: First, the neural representation of metric relations via the symmetries of stimulus patterns might be regarded as an axiomatic correspondence between neural and perceptual (phenomenological) events that is simply true by definition. Perhaps there is no more primitive property of the neural representation. So long as the neural events can provide an approximately linear or piece wise linear representation of the geometry of the retinal stimulus patterns, without distorting the information contained in those patterns, then perhaps all the information required for representing metric structure has been provided. Just what experimental data would confirm this hypothesis is certainly not clear, but rejection would seem possible only by demonstrating some more primitive property of neural events correlated with the perceptual structure of stimulation. Present knowledge about visual physiology and perception offers no obvious reason in principle why this hypothesis should be rejected.

Second, the perception of metric structure in stimulus patterns might derive from a more geometric isomorphism between perceptual and neural events involving cooperative relations among neighboring points of neural activity. Of course, this is the hypothesis proposed by Gestalt psychologists (e.g., Koffka, 1935). Although the Gestalt hypothesis of psychoneural isomorphism was premature in being untestable by the neurophysiological methods then available, and although electrophysiological data on receptive field properties of single neurons are thought by many to reject this hypothesis, rejection of the hypothesis may well have been premature. Kaas (1977), for example, has noted that the ubiquitous topographical representations of receptor surfaces in the sensory cortex suggest that there is validity to the Gestalt hypothesis: Maintaining the spatial connectivity of neighboring points of sensory activity apparently is important to sensory function, probably to permit cooperative interactions among neighboring neurons driven by neighboring points of stimulation. Furthermore, researchers in computer science have recently become increasingly attracted to the computational effectiveness of cooperative relaxation algorithms in finding global constraints on local relations (e.g., Zucker, Leclerc, & Mohammed, 1981).

A third alternative is that neural organizations of sensory activity derive in part from feedback from higher sensory and motor centers and ultimately from the functional coordination of an animal with its environment. That is, perceptual organization may be coordinated with action, as Gibson (1979) and Shaw and Turvey (1981) have proposed. Of course this hypothesis is not necessarily incompatible with the second hypothesis. The general question concerns the relative importance of feedback from subsequent neural representations and of cooperative interactions between neural events at the same synaptic and neuronal levels. Perhaps an appropriate mixture of these two types of cooperative processes provides the mechanism by which the brain enables global constraints to influence local geometric relations.

FINAL REFLECTION

As a final reflection, we owe Gunnar Johansson considerable gratitude for the rich view he has helped to develop of the visual measurement of spatial and temporal relations. We are also obliged, however, to continue with much more research to seek answers to the intriguing questions that Gunnar's research has illuminated.

ACKNOWLEDGMENT

Preparation of this paper was supported in part by National Science Foundation Grants BNS-7805857 and BNS-8112473.

REFERENCES

Barclay, C. D., Cutting, J. E., & Kozlowski, L. T. Temporal and spatial factors in gait perception that influence gender recognition. *Perception & Psychophysics,* 1978, *23,* 145–152.

Beck, J., Prazdny, S., & Rosenfeld, A. *A theory of textural segmentation.* Computer Science Technical Report Series, University of Maryland, No. TR-1083. 1981.

Burr, D. C. Acuity for apparent venier offset. *Vision Research,* 1979, *19,* 835–837.

Burr, D. C., & Ross, J. How does binocular delay give information about depth? *Vision Research,* 1979, *19,* 523–532.

Cutting, J. E., & Kozlowski, L. T. Recognizing friends by their walk: Gait perception without familiarity cues. *Bulletin of the Psychonomic Society,* 1977, *9,* 333–356.

Doner, J. F. Toward a theory of processing: I. Quantification of stimulus organization. In preparation.

Doner, J., Lappin, J., & Perfetto, G. The detection of three-dimensional structure in moving optical patterns. *Journal of Experimental Psychology: Human Perception and Performance,* 1984, *10,* 1–11.

Einstein, A. The electrodynamics of moving bodies. *Annalen der Physik,* 1905, *17.* Translated and reprinted in H. A. Lorentz, A. Einstein, H. Minkowski, & H. Weyl. *The principle of relativity.* New York: Dover, 1952.

Falzett, M., & Lappin, J. S. Detection of visual forms in space and time. *Vision Research,* 1983, *23,* 181–189.

Gibson, J. J. Optical motions and transformations as stimuli for visual perception. *Psychological Review,* 1957, *64,* 288–295.

Gibson, J. J. *The ecological approach to visual perception.* Boston: Houghton Mifflin, 1979.

Johansson, G. Perception of motion and changing form. *Scandinavian Journal of Psychology,* 1964, *5,* 181–208.

Johansson, G. Visual perception of biological motion and a model for its analysis. *Perception & Psychophysics*, 1973, *14*, 201–211.

Johansson, G. Spatio–temporal differentiation and integration in visual motion perception. *Psychological Research*, 1976, *38*, 379–393.

Julesz, B. *Foundations of cyclopean perception*. Chicago: University of Chicago Press, 1971.

Julesz, B. Global stereopsis: Cooperative phenomena in stereoscopic depth perception. In R. Held, H. W. Leibowitz, & H. L. Teuber (Eds.), *Handbook of Sensory Physiology, Vol. 8: Perception*. Berlin: Springer, 1978, *8*, 215–256.

Julesz, B. Textons, the elements of texture perception, and their interaction. *Nature*, 1981, *290*, 91–97.

Julesz, B., & Burt, P. Cooperativity of nearby micropatterns in texture discrimination. *Bulletin of the Psychonomic Society* (Suppl.), 1979, *14*, 242.

Julesz, B., & Chang, J. J. Interaction between pools of disparity detectors tuned to different disparities. *Biological Cybernetics*, 1976, *22*, 107–119.

Julesz, B., & Chang, J. J. Disparity limits for random-dot cinematograms for movement and form detection, and a learning effect. *Journal of Optical Society of America*, 1980, *70*, 624.

Julesz, B., & Schumer, R. A. Early visual perception. *Annual Review of Psychology*, 1981, *32*, 575–627.

Kaas, J. Sensory representation in animals. In G. S. Stent (Ed.), *Function and formation of neural systems*. Berlin: Dahlem Konferenzen, 1977.

Koenderink, J. J., & van Doorn, A. J. Exterospecific component of the motion parallax field. *Journal of Optical Society of America*, 1981, *71*, 953–957.

Koffka, K. *Principles of Gestalt Psychology*. New York: Harcourt, Brace, & World: 1935.

Krantz, D. H., Luce, R. D., Suppes, P., & Tversky, A. *Foundations of measurement*. New York: Academic Press, 1971.

Lappin, J. S., & Bell, H. H. The detection of coherence in moving random-dot patterns. *Vision Research*, 1976, *16*, 161–168.

Lappin, J. S., Bell, H. H., Harm, O. J., & Kottas, B. L. On the relation between time and space in the visual discrimination of velocity. *Journal of Experimental Psychology: Human Perception and Performance*, 1975, *1*, 383–394.

Lappin, J. S., Doner, J. F., & Kottas, B. L. Minimal conditions for the visual detection of structure and motion in three dimensions. *Science*, 1980, *209*, 717–719.

Lappin, J. S., & Fuqua, M. A. Accurate visual measurement and three–dimensional moving patterns. *Science*, 1983, *221*, 480–482.

Lappin, J. S., & Kottas, B. L. Perceptual coherence of moving random-dot patterns. *Acta Psychologica*, 1981, *48*, 163–174.

Lappin, J. S., & Preble, L. D. A demonstration of shape constancy. *Perception & Psychophysics*, 1975, *17*, 439–444.

Lappin, J. S., & Staller, J. D. Prior knowledge does not facilitate the perceptual organization of dynamic random-dot patterns. *Perception & Psychophysics*, 1981, *29*, 445–456.

Lehmkuhle, S., & Fox, R. Effect of depth separation on metacontrast masking. *Journal of Experimental Psychology: Human Perception and Performance*, 1980, *6*, 605–621.

Luce, R. D. Dimensionally invariant numerical laws correspond to meaningful qualitative relations. *Philosophy of Science*, 1978, *45*, 1–16.

Luce, R. D., & Tukey, J. W. Simultaneous conjoint measurement: a new type of fundamental measurement. *Journal of Mathematical Psychology*, 1964, *1*, 1–27.

Maas, J. B. *Motion perception I, II* (Films). Boston: Houghton Mifflin, 1970, 1971.

McKee, S. P. A local mechanism for differential velocity detection. *Vision Research*, 1981, *21*, 491–500.

Morgan, M. J. Spatio–temporal filtering and the interpolation effect in apparent motion. *Perception*, 1980, *9*, 161–174.

Platt, J. R. Functional geometry and the determination of pattern in mosaic receptors. In H. P. Yockey, R. L. Platzman, & H. Quastler (Eds.), *Information theory in biology*. New York: Pergamon, 1958.

Platt, J. R. How we see straight lines. *Scientific American*, June, 1960.

Restle, F. Coding theory of motion configurations. *Psychological Review*, 1979, *86*, 1–24.

Ricoeur, P. *Freud and philosophy: An essay on interpretation*. New Haven: Yale University Press, 1970.

Runeson, S., & Frykholm, G. Visual perception of lifted weight. *Journal of Experimental Psychology: Human Perception and Performance*, 1981, *7*, 733–740.

Shaw, R. E., & Cutting, J. E. Constraints on language events: Cues from an ecological theory of event perception. In U. Bellugi & M. Studdert-Kennedy (Eds.), *Signed language and spoken language: Biological constraints on linguistic form*. Dahlem Konferenzen, Weinheim: Verlag Chemie, 1980.

Shaw, R., & Turvey, M. T. Coalitions as models for ecosystems: A realist perspective on perceptual organization. In M. Kubovy & J. Pomerantz (Eds.), *Perceptual organization*. Hillsdale, NJ: Lawrence Erlbaum Associates, 1981.

Todd, J. T. Visual information about moving objects. *Journal of Experimental Psychology: Human Perception and Performance*, 1981, *7*, 795–810.

Tyler, C. W., & Julesz, B. The neural transfer characteristics (Neurontropy) for binocular stochastic stimulation. *Biological Cybernetics*, 1976, *23*, 33–37.

Tyler, C. W., & Julesz, B. On the depth of the cyclopean retina. *Experimental Brain Research*, 1980, *40*, 196–202.

Uttal, W. R., Fitzgerald, J., & Eskin, T. E. Rotation and translation effects on stereoscopic acuity. *Vision Research*, 1975, *15*, 939–944.

Warren, W. H. *A biodynamic basis for perception and action in bipedal climbing*. Ph.D. dissertation, University of Connecticut, Storrs, 1982. (University Microfilms No. 8309263)

Zucker, S. W., Leclerc, Y. G., & Mohammed, J. L. Continuous Relaxation and local maxima selection: Conditions for equivalence. *IEEE Transactions on Pattern Analysis and Machine Intelligence*, 1981, *PAMI–3*, 117–127.

5 Formal Theories of Visual Information

James T. Todd
Brandeis University

During the past several years there has been a growing scientific interest in how biological systems obtain information from visual stimulation. Although this is one of the oldest areas of research in experimental psychology, it has been given a new impetus in recent years by a number of technological developments. One important factor that has facilitated research in perceptual psychology is the increasing availability of laboratory computer graphics systems. It is now possible, for example, to control the structure of complex visual displays using mathematical models to manipulate shading or to generate patterns of movement. Other research in the field of artificial intelligence has been stimulated by the practical applications of building man-made systems that can mimic or enhance the perceptual capabilities of biological organisms. Many people believe that it may soon be possible, for example, to construct visual processing systems that can forecast weather from satellite photographs or control the movements of robots.

An important problem for all of these research activities is to develop a formal, mathematical analysis of how the structure of light at a point of observation relates to objects and events in the surrounding environment. There are many contrasting approaches to this problem. Indeed, there have been fundamental disagreements among different theorists that have resulted in heated controversy (e.g., see Ullman, 1980). The present paper will examine some of these different methods of analyzing visual information in an attempt to understand their individual advantages and limitations. The paper is organized into two parts: Part 1 describes four general assumptions about the nature of light and visual stimulation. Part 2 compares several alternative methods of analyzing the structure of light to obtain useful information about objects and events in the surrounding environment.

PART 1: BASIC ASSUMPTIONS

Assumption 1

Light is reflected from surfaces in all directions. This assumption is seldom stated explicitly in most analyses of visual information (see, however, Gibson, 1966; Torrance & Sparrow, 1967), but it is unavoidable, if we are to conclude that an unobstructed object can be seen from any vantage point. A crude model of how light reaches the eye is shown in Fig. 5.1. Surfaces in the environment are illuminated by light that originates from a luminous body such as an incandescent lamp or the sun. The reflected light from all visible portions of the environment converges at a point of observation forming an intricately structured cone of visual solid angles (see Gibson, 1979). It is the structure of this cone that provides a perceptual system with visual information. The process of reflection in a cluttered environment is extraordinarily complex. The amount of light that

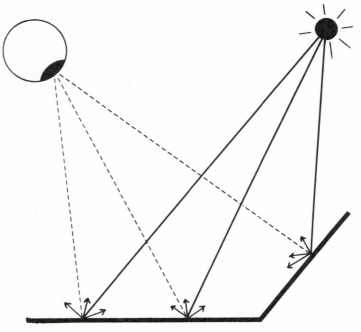

FIG. 5.1   A schematic model of how reflected light converges at a point of observation

reflects from a particular surface region in any given direction depends on the chemical composition of the surface and its orientation with respect to the light source; the positions and spectral compositions of all luminous bodies that are illuminating the surface; and the positions, orientations, and chemical compositions of all nonluminous bodies that can illuminate the surface indirectly through the process of reflection. Our current knowledge of how light interacts with surfaces in a complex environment is quite limited. Most analyses of visual information assume that identifiable features of objects such as edges and vertices are somehow delineated in the cone of visual solid angles, but the precise manner in which this is achieved has yet to be elaborated.

Assumption 2

The structure of light at a point of observation can be described mathematically by analyzing how the visual solid angles intersect with a hypothetical projection surface. Although all existing analyses of visual information are based on some variation of this assumption, there are important distinctions among different theories involving the shape of the projection surface and the relative orientations of the incoming light rays. Consider the issue of shape. For many theorists the most intuitive way of analyzing visual information is to adopt a hemispherical projection surface, because that is the approximate shape of the human retina. It is important to keep in mind, however, that the structure of light does not depend on the specific anatomical structure of the human eye, and could be analyzed just as easily using some other form of projection surface such as a plane (e.g., Longuet-Higgens & Prazdny, 1980) or a cylinder (e.g., Lee, 1974). For the purposes of a formal analysis, the choice of a projection surface is purely a matter of mathematical convenience, since a description of visual information in terms of one projection surface can always be uniquely transformed into a description in terms of any other. A more important distinction among existing theories involves the relative orientations of the incoming light rays as they intersect the projection surface toward the point of observation. Consider the two diagrams depicted in Fig. 5.2. In Fig. 5.2A, the incoming light rays intersect the projection surface at oblique angles to one another as they converge on the point of observation a relatively short distance away. This is called a polar or central projection. In Fig. 5.2B, on the other hand, the light rays converge at a point that is infinitely far from the projection surface so that they all travel along parallel trajectories. This is called a parallel or orthographic projection. Although a perfect parallel projection can never be achieved under natural viewing conditions, it is closely approximated whenever the size of an object is smaller than one tenth its distance from the point of observation. Thus, analyses based on parallel projection are only relevant to human vision when an object is relatively small or is viewed from a relatively long distance. Analyses based on polar projection have no restrictions on viewing distance from a purely mathematical

A   B

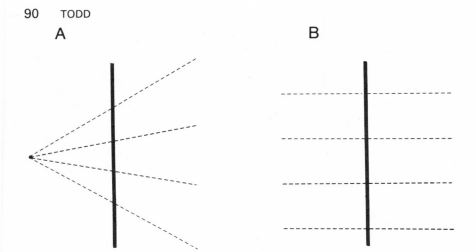

FIG.5.2   Two models of how light rays (dotted lines) can intersect a planar
projection surface (solid lines). Under polar projection (A), the light rays intersect
the surface at oblique angles. Under parallel projection (B), the light rays intersect
the surface at right angles along parallel trajectories.

point of view. However, because the tolerance for measurement error becomes
smaller and smaller as viewing distance increases, they are only useful in practice for objects that are relatively large or a small distance from the point of
observation. There is an overwhelming amount of evidence that human observers
can accurately perceive the layout of the environment under either parallel or
polar projection, but a theoretical explanation for this high degree of flexability
remains a mystery.

Assumption 3

*Within any cross section of a cone of visual solid angles there are distinguishable
units called optic elements.* The most common form of this assumption, on
which most existing analyses of visual information are implicitly based, is that
the structure of light can be modeled as a sparsely packed array of Euclidean
points that are distinguished from one another by their positions in space and
time. The primary attraction of this approach is that it allows one to employ the
standard techniques of projective geometry. Unfortunately, however, a closer
examination reveals that it is fundamentally incompatible with Assumption 1. If
light reflects from surfaces in all directions, and the layout of surfaces in the
environment is continuous, then the structure of light must be infinitely dense
(Gibson, 1966). If optic elements had no other properties except position, then
the visual projection of any complex event would be indistinguishable from a
Ganzfeld. A more reasonable model of the pattern of light on a projection surface
is shown in Fig. 5.3. The surface is divided into several regions, each of which

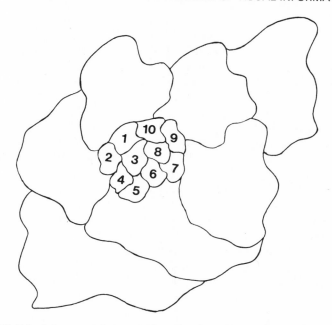

FIG. 5.3   A hypothetical pattern of optic elements on a visual projection surface.
Each bounded region represents an optic element with a uniform spectral composition that is distinct from its neighbors. The elements numbered 1 through 10 form
a higher order unit, since they are all significantly smaller than the elements that
surround them.

has a uniform spectral composition that is distinct from its neighbors. In other
words, any pair of points in neighboring regions (e.g., regions 5 and 6 in Fig.
5.3) have measurably different spectral compositions, and any pair of points in
the same region have identical spectral compositions within appropriate limits of
measurement. Each distinct region constitutes an optic element. It is important to
recognize that an optic element has considerably more structure than a Euclidean
point. Different elements can be distinguished from one another by a variety of
properties including size, shape, position and spectral composition. They can
also be grouped together to form higher order units (see Fig. 5.3). Thus, the
structure of light is really a hierarchy of structures that can be described at many
different scales of analysis (cf. Todd, 1982). Existing theories of visual information have not taken advantage of this richness of structure. Individual theorists
have focussed on specific properties of optic elements, such as position (e.g.,
Ullman, 1979), shape (e.g., Ikeuchi, 1980) or spectral composition (e.g., Horn,
1975), at a particular scale of analysis. As a result, the generality of these
theories has been quite limited.

Assumption 4

The environment which surrounds a point of observation is subject to physical constraints. As was pointed out by Bishop George Berkeley almost 300 years ago, any given structure on a two–dimensional surface is projectively equivalent to an infinite number of possible structures in three–space. Berkeley concluded on the basis of this mathematical fact that visual perception of a three–dimensional environment would be impossible without having additional information provided by other sensory modalities (but see Turvey, 1977). Unlike Berkeley, modern theorists have recognized that there are physical constraints within a natural environment that limit the domain of structures to be considered. There are a wide variety of these constraints that have been postulated for the analysis of visual information. It has been assumed, for example, that the reflectance properties of a given surface must be either homogeneous or stochastically regular over its entire extent (Flock, 1964; Gibson, 1950; Horn, 1975); that an object cannot hang suspended in midair without a visible means of support (Sedgwick, 1973); that objects cannot spontaneously become visible or invisible unless they are occluded by other objects (Braunstein, Anderson & Riefer, 1982; Kaplan, 1969); and that objects cannot be deformed in a manner that is projectively equivalent to a rigid motion (Lee, 1974; Todd, 1981, 1982; Ullman, 1979). Some of the constraints that have been employed in the analysis of visual information are extremely limited in their domain of application. In the analysis of image shading, for example, it is typically assumed that the reflectance of a surface and the position and spectral composition of the light source are known (Horn, 1975; Ikeuchi & Horn, 1981; Woodham, 1978). Although these analyses are obviously inappropriate for the study of human vision (see Todd & Mingolla, 1983), they may prove useful for designing robot visual systems to operate in restricted contexts.

PART 2: METHODS OF ANALYSIS

All existing analyses of visual information are based on some variation of the four assumptions described above. They all deal with reflected light, broken down into elementary units, on some type of projection surface, within a particular context of constraint. These assumptions establish the ground rules for a formal analysis, but they do not by themselves constitute a complete theory of visual information. In order to be informative, the structure of light must covary in some lawful manner with the structure of objects and events in a natural environment. An adequate theory of visual information must provide an explicit account of that covariation. From the standpoint of perceptual theory, it must allow us to predict how a given set of displays will be perceived by human observers. From the standpoint of artificial intelligence, it must allow us to construct a functioning system that can respond appropriately to visual inputs. These criteria for evaluating a theory of visual information are not identical, since a functioning robot need not operate in exactly the same way as a human being. The criteria are quite similar in another sense, however, since they both require an unambiguously defined procedure (i.e., an algorithm) that formally maps the structure of light onto the structure of the environment within some plausible set of constraints.

There have been many techniques proposed in the literature for analyzing visual information, ranging in mathematical sophistication from simple algebra to symmetry-group theory and tensor calculus. In the discussion that follows, these analyses will be described in terms of the particular aspects of optic structure on which they are designed to operate.

Analyses Based on Element Homologies

One way of extracting meaningful information from the structure of light is to find a set of homologous optic elements under different viewing conditions that all correspond to a particular local region of the environment. If changes in the environment are sufficiently constrained, then the three–dimensional structure of any local region can be visually specified by changes in its projected image. Analyses based on homologous elements are especially common in theories of binocular vision (e.g., Marr & Poggio, 1976). Since each eye views the world from a slightly different vantage point, the corresponding optic elements for a given region of the environment will be located at different positions on the two projection surfaces. Similar analyses can also be used in monocular vision to determine the three–dimensional structure of an object in motion (e.g., Ullman, 1979). Although there is only one point of observation, it is possible to compare the projections of a given region at different moments in time. An interesting extension of this approach has recently been suggested by Woodham (1978) for the analysis of image shading. Woodham has shown that the three–dimensional structure of a stationary object can be determined by a monocular-visual system if the light source is moving. As in the analysis of object motion, the homologous elements are defined on a single projection surface at different moments in time. In this case, however, the elements differ from one another in spectral composition rather than position.

A fundamental difficulty for all homology theories is to decide which of the optic elements under different viewing conditions actually correspond to the same region of the environment. There are two basic solutions to this problem that have been proposed in a variety of different contexts, such as apparent motion and binocular vision. One approach is based on the assumption that optic elements can vary along many different dimensions, and that some of their properties will be unaffected by any given change in viewing conditions. Woodham's analysis of image shading provides an especially simple example. Consider an optic element that corresponds to a particular local region of the environment. The spectral composition of this element may be dramatically altered by movement of the light source, but its position on the projection surface will remain invariant. Thus, in this particular context, homologous elements can be easily identified by their positions. An alternative approach to this problem is based on the assumption that neighboring optic elements on the projection surface will generally correspond to neighboring regions of the environment. If changes in the environment are continuous, then the "disparity" among homologous elements should vary smoothly almost everywhere across the projection surface—except, for example, at occluding boundaries. Within this context of constraint, homologous elements can be identified by an optimization procedure that minimizes the disparity differences for neighboring elements over the entire projection surface (cf Marr & Poggi, 1976, 1978, 1979; Ullman, 1979).

Analyses Based on Local Neighborhoods of Elements

Although relationships among homologous elements have a broad range of potential applications for the study of vision, there are many other aspects of visual information that do not require a change in viewing conditions. This is demonstrated quite clearly by our ability to perceive the three-dimensional organization of a natural scene from a single photograph. One common technique for analyzing the structure of light at a single vantage point is to examine the relationships within a local neighborhood of optic elements. This technique was first developed by James Gibson (1950) in an attempt to describe how people perceive surface orientation. Gibson based his analysis on two assumptions: First, that most natural surfaces have a characteristic texture that is "stochastically regular" (see Gibson, 1979); and second, that the elements of surface texture are in one-to-one correspondence with the elements of optical texture within a cone of visual solid angles. On the basis of these assumptions, Gibson argued that there is a fixed relation between the slant of a physical surface and the gradient of texture density among its corresponding optic elements (see Fig. 5.4). A gradient is a mathematical concept that describes the rate of change of one variable with respect to others in the direction of maximum change. In other words, it is a vector quantity that describes how a group of neighboring elements are related along some particular dimension. Although Gibson's original analysis was exclusively concerned with gradients of texture density, subsequent research has demonstrated that observers are also sensitive to gradients of texture size and shape (e.g., Flock & Moscatelli, 1964; Phillips, 1970). In addition, more recent analyses have shown that gradients of image intensity can provide information about the orientation of a surface (Horn, 1975; Ikeuchi & Horn, 1981; Woodham, 1981) and the direction of illumination (Pentland, 1982).

    In the analysis of optical texture and shading, the concept of a gradient is used to describe how the density or intensity of a configuration of optic elements changes with respect to position on the projection surface in the direction of

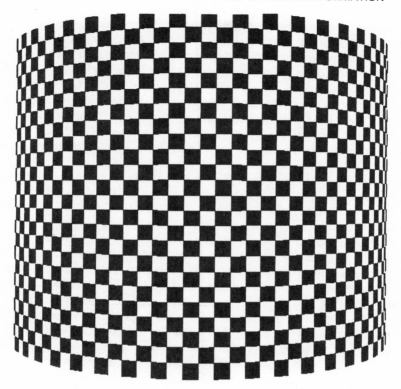

FIG. 5.4   The pattern of optical texture produced under polar projection by a checkerboard cylinder.

maximum change. Other analyses, however, make use of a different type of gradient called a velocity to describe how the position of a single optic element changes with respect to time in the direction of maximum change. It is important to keep in mind that a gradient can only be defined within an arbitrarily small local neighborhood of elements. In the case of a velocity, the neighboring elements exist within a local region of space–time. The related concept of displacement also describes a change in position with respect to time, but is not a gradient, since it does not require the existence of local neighborhoods. In general, analyses of apparent motion (e.g., Ullman, 1979) often employ the concept of displacement, whereas analyses of continuous motion (e.g., Lee, 1974, Longuet-Higgens & Prazdny, 1980; Todd, 1981) are more likely to employ the concept of velocity.

Analyses Based on the Global Organization of Elements

The structure of light can be defined formally at many different scales of analysis. The concept of a gradient allows us to examine the fine details within a local neighborhood of optic elements, but there is other information at a more global level of analysis in the specific patterns by which optic elements are organized over the entire projection surface. A particularly common technique for analyzing the global structure of light involves the concept of an optical flow field, first introduced by James Gibson in 1950. Gibson noted that an observer's movements relative to the environment produce well defined patterns of projected motion, in which the optic elements seem to ''flow'' over the projection surface. For example, consider the pattern of optical flow that is produced when an observer moves over a planar ground surface along a rectilinear trajectory (see Fig. 5.5a). Although each optic element has a different velocity, they all diverge in a graded fashion from a single point at the horizon. There are several aspects of this particular flow field that are potentially informative. The fact that all of the velocity vectors are oriented towards a fixed point indicates that the observer is undergoing rectilinear motion; the smooth linear increase in all directions from the point of divergence indicates that the observer is moving relative to a planar surface; the fact that the point of divergence is on the horizon indicates that the observer is moving parallel to the surface; and the position of the point of divergence along the horizon indicates the specific direction in which the observer is heading. Other types of motion produce quite different patterns of optical flow. Fig. 5.5b, for example, shows the pattern of flow that is produced by circular motion over a planar ground surface. Although these diagrams are intended to depict an observer's movement relative to other objects in the environment, there is no reason why similar diagrams could not be used to represent the global organization of texture fields, intensity fields or binocular-disparity fields.

A   B

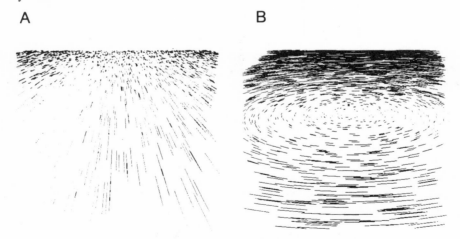

FIG. 5.5   The patterns of optical flow produced under polar projection by rectilinear motion over a planar ground suface (A), and circular motion over a planar ground surface (B).

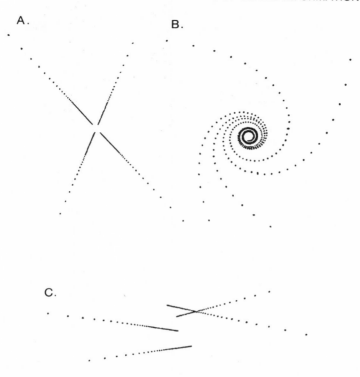

FIG. 5.6   The image trajectories under polar projection of a rigid configuration of four points translating in depth (A), a rigid configuration of four points translating in depth and rotating about an axis that is perpendicular to the projection surface (B), and a nonrigid configuration of four points translating in different directions (C).

Another technique for describing the global structure of light is to specify the trajectories of optic elements over an extended region of space–time. Gunnar Johansson was the first to argue that motion trajectories are appropriate units of analysis for the study of visual information. Within this context, he has analyzed the complex pattern of motion in a point-light walker display as a nested set of pendular trajectories (Johansson, 1973; see also Cutting, 1978, 1981). He has described how rotary motion causes optic elements to move along elliptical trajectories (Johansson, 1974a; see also Eriksson, 1974), and how rolling motions can be defined in terms of trochoidal trajectories (Johansson, 1974b). A similar approach has also been adopted by Restle (1979). His coding theory, which is based on the parameters for generating an elliptical trajectory, can accurately predict how a set of moving elements will be perceived within hierarchically nested frames of reference. Todd (1982) has extended this analysis by demonstrating how the geometric relations among a set of projected trajectories can be used to specify the three–dimensional structure of an object, and perceptually meaningful categories of motion such as rigid and nonrigid (see Fig. 5.6).

Analyses Based on the Organization of Identifiable Features

Some analyses of visual information are designed to operate only after more primitive analyses have identified the optical projections of specific features of environmental structure. For example, Sedgwick (1973) has shown that when an object is in contact with an unbounded, planar ground surface, its height above the ground is visually specified by a relationship between its projected size and position relative to the horizon (see Fig. 5.7a). In order to apply this analysis,

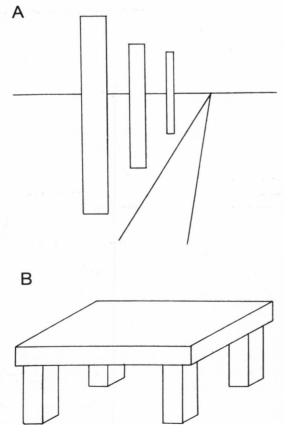

FIG. 5.7 The three-dimensional structure of a complex scene can often be specified by a configuration of line segments on a visual projection surface. In (A), the height of each rectangular object is specified by a relation between its projected size and position relative to the horizon. (The object to the right is the tallest of the three.) In (B), the relations among the line segments specify a large rectangular object that is supported by four smaller rectangular objects.

however, it is necessary to distinguish among the optic elements that correspond to the object, the ground and the sky. This is not a trivial requirement. Although human observers apparently have little difficulty identifying bounded regions within a cone of visual solid angles, there are at present no adequate theories of how this is accomplished.

Other analyses in the field of artificial intelligence are also designed to operate on identifiable features. Indeed, many of the scene-analysis programs used in computer vision research receive coded representations of line drawings as inputs rather than real visual images. This is typically justified by assuming that some earlier process has identified the lines and junctions on a visual projection surface that correspond to the edges and vertices of opaque, plane-faced polyhedra in three–dimensional space (see Fig. 5.7b). One famous program written by Guzman (1968) classifies line junctions on a visual projection surface into a relatively small number of categories. The result of this classification is generally ambiguous, because each type of line junction can have many possible three–dimensional interpretations. However, because there are severe topological constraints on how the line junctions can be connected to one another, the number of possible interpretations for the entire configuration is reduced dramatically. Subsequent research has demonstrated that whatever ambiguities remain can often be eliminated by taking into account additional constraints on the relative orientations of lines on the projection surface (Mackworth, 1973) or the projected boundaries of cast shadows (Waltz, 1975).

CONCLUSIONS

There are many different ways of analyzing visual information. It is possible to deal with either the local or global aspects of optical structure; with monocular or binocular vision; with a moving or stationary point of observation; and under either parallel or polar projection. The important thing to note about the different approaches described above is that they all have a limited domain of application. There is no general theory of visual information that can cope simultaneously with texture, shading, motion and stereopsis, at both near and far viewing distances, and at both local and global scales of analysis. Nor is it likely that such a general theory will be developed in the foreseeable future. The current trend of research in both perceptual psychology and artificial intelligence is toward increasing modularization. That is to say, different types of visual functions seem to require qualitatively different methods of analysis.

How then should we evaluate the theoretical significance of any one approach? Let us first consider this problem from the perspective of artificial intelligence. One obvious criterion for evaluating a theory of visual information is the generality of its assumptions. An analysis that assumes, for example, that all objects are illuminated by a single point-light source will generally be less useful than some other analysis that works for any type of illumination. This does not suggest that restrictive analyses are without value for all possible applications—only that more general analyses are preferred, other things being equal. A second important criterion for evaluating a theory of visual information is its complexity. Any analysis that can be carried out with a few simple operations will generally be more useful than some other technique that requires many hours of computer time. Finally, we must also consider how easily an analysis can be implemented into an actual working system. Any technique that requires the solution to an unsolved problem will generally be less useful than an analysis that can be carried out efficiently using existing technologies.

From the perspective of perceptual theory, however, none of these criteria are directly relevant, since all that really matters is how well a theory conforms to the perceptual capabilities of human observers. Perhaps the most important characteristic of formal analyses of visual information is that they have testable implications—they deal with specific aspects of optical structure within specific contexts of constraint. If the necessary conditions for performing an analysis are not satisfied, it will inevitably produce erroneous results, oftentimes in a predictable manner (e.g., Todd & Warren, 1982). Thus, in order to demonstrate the psychological validity of any theory of visual information, it is necessary to show that the mathematical limitations of the theory are consistent with the perceptual limitations of actual human observers. Unfortunately, although there has been an explosion of mathematical analyses during the past decade, there have been relatively few attempts to examine their empirical implications. One of the exceptions to this general trend is the elegant work of Marr and Poggio (1979) on the computational theory of human stereo vision. After developing a formal mathematical analysis, these authors describe a number of psychophysical and neurophysiological predictions, which, if found to be false, would invalidate the analysis as a possible theory of human stereopsis. Our knowledge of perception in general would be greatly enhanced if other researchers would adopt a similar strategy.

REFERENCES

Braunstein, M. L., Anderson, G. J. & Reifer, D. M. The use of occlusion to resolve ambiguity in parallel projections. *Perception and Psychophysics*, 1982, *31*, 261–267.

Cutting, J. E. Generation of male and female walkers through the manipulation of a biomechanical invariant. *Perception*, 1978, *7*, 393–405.

Cutting, J. E. Coding theory adapted to gait perception. *Journal of Experimental Psychology: Human Perception and Performance*, 1981, *7*, 71–87.

Eriksson, S. E. A theory of veridical space perception. *Scandanavian Journal of Psychology*, 1974, *15*, 225–235.

Flock, H. R. A possible optical basis for monocular slant perception. *Psychological Review*, 1964, *71*, 380–391.

Flock, H. R., & Moscatelli, A. Variables of surface texture and accuracy of space perception. *Perceptual and Motor Skills*, 1964, *19*, 327–334.

Gibson, J. J. *The perception of the visual world.* Boston: Houghton Mifflin, 1950.

Gibson, J. J. *The senses considered as perceptual systems.* Boston: Houghton Mifflin, 1966.

Gibson, J. J. *The ecological approach to visual perception.* Boston: Houghton Mifflin, 1979.

Guzman, A. *Computer recognition of three–dimensional objects in a visual scene.* Ph. D. thesis, MAC–TR–59, Project MAC, Massachusetts Institute of Technology, Cambridge, Mass., 1968.

Horn, B. K. P. Obtaining shape from shading information. In P. H. Winston (Ed.), *The psychology of computer vision.* New York: McGraw-Hill, 1975.

Ikeuchi, K. *Shape from regular patterns.* Technical Report AI–TR–567, Artificial Intelligence Laboratory, Massachusetts Institute of Technology, Cambridge, Mass., 1980.

Ikeuchi, K., & Horn, B. K. P. Numerical shape from shading and occluding boundaries. *Artificial Intelligence,* 1981, *17,* 141–184.

Johansson, G. Visual perception of biological motion and a model for its analysis. *Perception and Psychophysics,* 1973, *14,* 201–211.

Johansson, G. Visual perception of rotary motions as transformations of conic sections—a contribution to the theory of visual space perception. *Psychologia,* 1974, *17,* 226–237. (a)

Johansson, G. Vector analysis in visual perception of rolling motion: A quantitative approach. *Psychologische Forschung,* 1974, *36,* 311–319. (b)

Kaplan, G. A. Kinetic disruption of optical texture: The perception of depth at an edge. *Perception and Psychophysics,* 1969, *6,* 193–198.

Lee, D. N. Visual information during locomotion. In R. B. MacLeod & H. Pick (Eds.), *Perception: Essays in honor of James Gibson.* Ithaca, N.Y.: Cornell University Press, 1974.

Longuet-Higgins, H. C., & Prazdny, K. The interpretation of a moving retinal image. *Proceedings of the Royal Society of London,* 1980, *208,* 385–397.

Mackworth, A. K. How to see a simple world: An exegesis of some computer programs for scene analysis. In E. Elcock & D. Michie (Eds.) *Machine Intelligence.* Chichester: Ellis Horwood, 1977.

Marr, D., & Poggio, T. Cooperative computation of stereo disparity. *Science,* 1976, *194,* 283–287.

Marr, D., & Poggio, T. Analysis of a cooperative stereo algorithm. *Biological Cybernetics,* 1978, *28,* 223–239.

Marr, D., & Poggio, T. A computational theory of human stereo vision. *Proceedings of the Royal Society of London,* 1979, *204,* 301–328.

Pentland, A. P. Finding the direction of illumination. *Journal of the Optical Society of America,* 1982, *72,* 448–455.

Phillips, R. J. Stationary visual texture and the estimation of slant angle. *Quarterly Journal of Experimental Psychology,* 1970, *22,* 389–397.

Restle, F. Coding theory and the perception of motion configurations. *Psychological Review,* 1979, *86,* 1–24.

Sedgwick, H. A. *The visible horizon.* Ph. D. Thesis, Cornell University, Ithaca, N. Y., 1973.

Todd, J. T. Visual information about moving objects. *Journal of Experimental Psychology: Human Perception and Performance,* 1981, *7,* 795–810.

Todd, J. T. Visual information about rigid and nonrigid motion: A geometric analysis. *Journal of Experimental Psychology: Human Perception and Performance,* 1982, *8,* 238–252.

Todd, J. T., & Mingolla, E. The perception of surface curvature and direction of illumination from patterns of shading. *Journal of Experimental Psychology: Human Perception and Performance,* 1983, *9,* 583–595.

Todd, J. T., & Warren, W. H. Visual perception of relative mass in dynamic events. *Perception,* 1982, *11,* 325–335.

Torrance, K. E., & Sparrow, E. M. Theory for off-specular reflection from roughened surfaces. *Journal of the Optical Society of American,* 1967, *9,* 1105–1114.

Turvey, M. T. Contrasting orientations to the theory of visual information processing. *Psychological Review,* 1977, *84,* 67–88.

Ullman, S. *The interpretation of visual motion.* Cambridge, Mass.: MIT Press, 1979.

Ullman, S. Against direct perception. *The Behavioral and Brain Sciences,* 1980, *3,* 373–415.

Waltz, D. Generating semantic descriptions from drawings of scenes with shadows. In P. Winston (Ed.), *The psychology of computer vision.* New York: McGraw-Hill, 1975.

Woodham, R. J. *Reflectance map techniques for analyzing surface defects in metal castings.* Technical Report AI–TR–457, Artificial Intelligence Laboratory, Massachusetts Institute of Technology, Cambridge, Mass., 1978.

Woodham, R. J. Analysing images of curved surfaces. *Artificial Intelligence,* 1981, *17,* 117–140.

6 Perceiving Architectural Space: From Optic Arrays to Isovists

Michael Benedikt
Clarke A. Burnham
University of Texas at Austin

ISOVISTS AND OPTIC ARRAYS

In his *The Senses Considered as Perceptual Systems* (1966), J. J. Gibson proposed the idea that the *optic array,* rather than the retinal image, was the proper starting point in the investigation of visual perception. While acknowledging the existence of optic arrays in the physical sense, many psychologists maintain that the optic array is a redundant construct. On the grounds that information in the array necessarily ends up mapped onto a convex two–dimensional surface (e.g., retina or film) anyway, they argue: Why not simply begin with the pattern of light and dark and color on this surface? The reason may be that it is indeed difficult to visualize an optic array for what it is—a three–dimensional physical entity, a converging and passing through of rays of light at a point in space, existing independently, or prior to, the existence of an eye or camera at that point.

In a later formulation Gibson (1979, p. 70) explained the optic array as a set of "nested solid angles" corresponding to surface elements in the environment rather than as a set of infinitesimally thin rays each, potentially, doing its own thing. But this formulation has difficulties too. For one, an "angle," especially a "solid angle," is merely a quantity and has no shape: a solid angle of, say, π steradians can be created by infinitely many configurations of surface element size, shape, and observation position. Second, in specifying solid angle shapes and their interrelations in space and time, one is again reduced to discussing these as projected onto a surface—such as a sphere around the point of observation. Thus, though there is merit in pointing out (1) the "surrounding" quality of the visual world (cf. also Benedikt, 1980); and (2) the fact that optic arrays are "out there waiting" to be perceived by all manner of eyes and minds; it seems to us that a further step needs to be taken to distinguish thinking about optic arrays from thinking about, say, retinas in eyes, or film in cameras, or digitized picture planes.

Imagine a rectangle (representing a room) and the space within it. Draw a straight line between any two points on the rectangle; draw another, and another, until the space of the rectangle is effectively filled with criss-crossing lines between all pairs of points. Now choose any point within the rectangle and you find that a large number of lines pass through that point, one of which is shared with another different set of lines passing through a point nearby. If we consider these lines to represent light rays (i.e., photon streams) of varying wavelength and intensity being scattered and bounced by the edges of the rectangle (i.e., the walls of the room), then you have a picture of an optic array—a set of rays that happens to pass through the point of interest.

But where does a given ray begin and end? Is a ray that happens to pass through our point the same ray that it was before it bounced off the wall? If it is, then almost every ray in the room qualifies as belonging to our optic array, as it would eventually pass through our point. Clearly this isn't going to work. The solution lies in considering a ray only after its "last bounce," that is, in considering only the set of lines—rays—joining our point to the nearest light-scattering surface in every direction. Now, the *isovist* is simply this optic array, with wavelength and intensity information omitted.

Omitted? What remains in this picture? The very distances themselves from the point of interest to the nearest surfaces. That is, to every bearing (θ, ψ) from a point of potential observation, x, in the world there corresponds a distance, l, from the point to the nearest surface such that we have a unique ordered set

$$L_x = \{1 \ \theta_2, \ \psi_2\}_x$$

which is the isovist at that point. Put another way, the isovist is simply the precise "piece of space" visible from a point in the environment.

Note that the isovist cannot properly, or to advantage, be mapped on to a surface. It is best seen as it is: a shaped chunk of space with a special point within. Now add back to this, if you will, radial wavelength and intensity "lines" and you have a complete picture of what three–dimensional optic array is.

In *The Senses Considered as Perceptual Systems*, Gibson went to some lengths to discuss the numerous strategies nature has evolved to pick up information from the optic array—eyes of design different to ours (without retinas, for example). These considerations lent credence to thinking of the optic array as something prior to or more fundamental than retinal images. With our new and more complete description of what an optic array is, the strategy can be taken further. For what do bats "see" if not isovists, "depth arrays," if you will. All creatures and mechanisms relying on sonar or radar see isovists. It does not seem unreasonable to us to suggest that a large part of our visual and, yes, retina-based processing is, in a sense, "directed at" seeing the isovist, since the isovist or depth array is, in and of itself, salient information to most mobile organisms in the terrestrial environment.

This is all very well, but you may ask: how does an observer come to *know* this ordered set of distances which together give him knowledge of the proximity of surrounding surfaces? This, of course, is a central problem for many perception psychologists and researchers in computer vision. *To move forward with isovists, however, we need not solve this problem.* The isovist exists independently, objectively, and can be measured in shape and size anywhere in any normal environment. It is at once primitive and contingent, an entity we can observe and pay attention to as such, and an entity on account of which we are able to see spatially at all. The shaded areas in Fig. 6.1, V_x and $V_{x'}$, are two-dimensional representations of the isovists from two points, x and x' within the semienclosed environments. We have derived the description of an isovist from the description of optic arrays. Alternative formulations of isovists are possible, however, and perhaps even preferable (Benedikt, 1979; Davis & Benedikt, 1979).

ISOVIST MEASURES

We would like to show that isovists (and hence, we venture, optic arrays) exist not only physico-mathematically but psychologically in our experience of the visual world. To do this one needs to develop some quantitative measures of isovist *shape* and *size*. (For a detailed exposition of these, see Benedikt, 1979 and Davis & Benedikt, 1979.)

In any environment the shape and size of isovists are liable to differ from point to point and in accordance with the layout of the environment itself. Here are the measures we have developed to characterize two-dimensional isovists.

A_x : the area of the isovist at a point x.

P_x : the length of the visible boundary

Q_x : the length of the nonvisible radial components of the total isovist boundary. (These are the radial components separating the visible space from the space one cannot see from point x.)

$M_{2,x}$: the second moment (variance) of the isovist's boundary about the mean boundary distance.

$M_{3,x}$: the third moment (skewness) of the isovist boundary about the mean boundary distance.

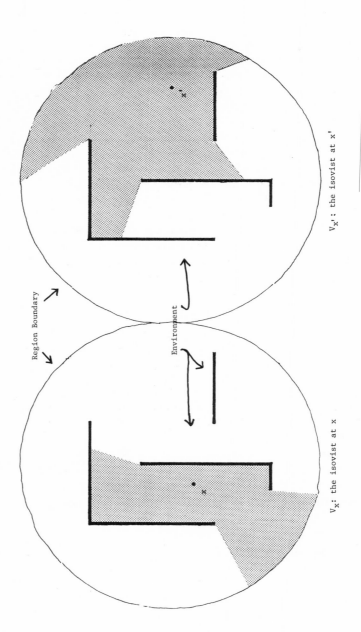

$V_{x'}$: the isovist at x'

Region Boundary

Environment

V_x: the isovist at x

FIG. 6.1.   Isovists from x and x' within the same environment.

Every point in an environment has a particular value for each of these measures and, conversely, each point is to some extent characterized by that set of values. An examination of Fig. 6.1 should clarify these measures. The isovist from x' has a larger area (A) than the isovist from x. More wall length can be seen from x than x'; the perimeter (P) of V_x is greater than the perimeter of $V_{x'}$. Occlusity (Q) is greater from x' than x; the total length of the nonbounded radials to the walls of the environment and the region boundary is greater for $V_{x'}$ than V_x. $V_{x'}$ has more variability (M_2) than V_x; the distribution of the lengths of the radials from x' to the walls of the environment and the region boundary has more variability than the comparable distribution from x. The two isovists differ slightly in skewness (M_3). The distribution of the lengths of the radials from x appears to be positively skewed with most of the lengths being relatively short and a few relatively long whereas the distribution of lengths from x' is more normal.

The next step, then, is to systematically vary the values of such isovist measures (by experimentally manipulating environments and viewpoints) so as to effect corresponding variations in the perception of the environments. This is the basis of our program of research. The dependent variable we chose to study was that of "spaciousness": How large or small an environment seemed on account of its shape and one's position in it. This variable was chosen, in part, because of its relevance to design problems. Can one rearrange objects in space, holding the containing area constant, so that the containing area will appear more or less spacious?

METHOD

The purpose of the experimentation was to determine which, if any, of the isovist measures would contribute to perceived visible space (Experiment I) and estimated total space (Experiment II). Using a paired comparisons design, we ran experiments in which subjects judged which member of a pair of isovists had more visible space (Experiment I) or more total space (Experiment II). The two members of each pair had *different* values on one of the isovist measures and were *similar* on the other isovist measures. Thus, one member of a $P+/P-$ pair had a relatively large perimeter, the other had a relatively small perimeter, and both were equal in visible area (A), occlusivity (Q), and the variance (M_2) and skewness (M_3).

Stimuli

The spaces are best characterized as four-column histograms with unit height, a total floor area of 18 square units, and the presence of at least one unit in each column (see Fig. 6.2). Thus one space could be designated as 3 8 1 6 and another

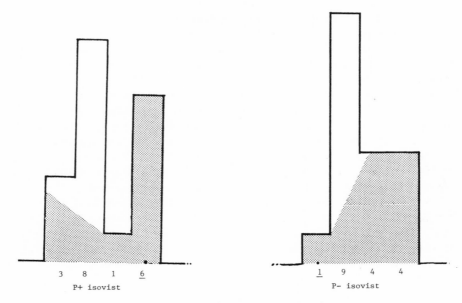

3	8	1	<u>6</u>		<u>1</u>	9	4	4

P+ isovist   P- isovist

FIG. 6.2.   Isovists differing in visible perimeter.

as <u>1</u> 9 4 4. The numbers represent the length of the columns and the underlined column indicates the position from which these spaces were viewed. From the center of the base of the underlined columns, the 180 isovists of these two spaces differ in visible perimeter (3 8 1 <u>6</u> is $P+$ and <u>1</u> 9 4 4 is $P-$). Floor plans of these two isovists are shown in Fig. 6.2. The shaded areas are the isovists when these spaces are viewed from the center of the base of the underlined column.

Several considerations dictated the use of such four-column histograms as our spaces. The spaces are architecturally reasonable—they look like rooms. One can see the entire space by viewing it from the base of each of the columns but any single view is not necessarily sufficient—this will be important in future research. And the entire population of such histograms ($N = 560$, without counting symmetrical spaces) was thought to be large enough to produce pairs of spaces which would satisfy the design of these experiments.

The five isovist measures were computed from the center of the base of each column for each of the 560 histograms. The 4×560 values obtained for each measure were converted to percentiles. We then selected the specific members of each pair to maximize the percentile difference on one isovist measure and to minimize the percentile differences on the other four measures. The selected isovists differed by about 50 percentile points on the measure of interest and by about 5 percentile points on the other measures. Three different pairs were selected for each isovist measure to help ensure the generalizability of the results.

Models of the selected spaces were constructed from white cardboard on wooden bases to the scale of 6 in. (15.24 cm.) per unit. The floor of the model was a rectangular grid pattern (too fine for counting) and the ceiling an "egg carton" light diffuser. The floor and ceiling textures provided perspective and density cues to distance.

The apparatus for displaying the models is shown in Fig. 6.3, with the right wall removed to show the interior of the model. While a subject was making a judgment, the laboratory room lights were extinguished. When the subject placed his/her chin on a small plate located at the base of the columns, a bank of six lights evenly illuminated the space. Thus the subject only saw the interior of the spaces from the position of the chin rest. The chin rests were moved to the appropriate column bases at the beginning of each trial to present the subject with the selected isovists. Subjects in both experiments viewed the stimuli monocularly while wearing an eye patch over one eye. The position of the chin rest was adjusted so that the viewing eye was at the center of the column base, the position from which the isovist measures were computed. While the spaces were being changed between trials a screen prevented the subject from seeing into the laboratory room.

Design and Procedure

Three pairs of stimuli were selected for each of the five isovist measures. Five different orders were used for the presentation of the isovist measures and the

FIG. 6.3. Subject viewing a model.

order of the specific pairs was counterbalanced with the order of the measures. Thus there were 15 different stimulus sequences. In addition, the assignment of a member of a pair of stimuli (e.g., the $P+$ or the $P-$ space) to the left or right viewing position was randomly determined, as was the member the subject viewed first.

There were a total of 20 experimental trials; the stimulus pairs used for the first five trials were repeated during the last five. The responses to first five trials were used to estimate the reliability of the judgments. The subjects were permitted to view each member of a pair as long as they wanted to, and to go back and forth between the left and right spaces as many times as they wanted to until they made their decisions. The instructions for Experiment I told the subjects to judge the stimuli on the basis of visible space: "In which room can you actually see more space from the selected viewing position; take into account all the space you can see from the left to right wall but do not worry about the parts of the room you cannot see." The instructions for Experiment II told the subjects to judge the size of the room as a whole: "You will only see a portion of the room, but we want you to estimate how big the whole room seems to be, taking into account all the space you can see from the left to the right wall and your estimate of the parts of the room you cannot see." In both experiments the subjects responded verbally by stating whether the room on the left or the room on the right was larger.

Subjects

There were 16 different subjects in each study. Half of them were male and half were female. They were university students; some responded to an advertisement and were paid, and the others participated to fulfill an introductory course requirement.

RESULTS

Reliability

Each subject saw one of the stimulus pairs for each isovist measure twice, once during the first five experimental trials and again during trials 15–20. The stability of the subjects' responses may be estimated by computing the percentage of times they gave the same response to these five pairs. For Experiment I the reliability was 79% ($t = 6.89$, $df = 15$, $p < .001$); it was 66% for Experiment II ($t = 2.15$, $df = 15$, $p < .05$). The t-tests indicate that both of these figures differ from a null hypothesis value of chance (50%).

Isovist Measures

During the 15 experimental trials each subject viewed three different pairs of stimuli for each of the five isovist measures and selected a member of the pair as having more visible space (Experiment I) or more total space (Experiment II). For each experiment then, each isovist measure could achieve a score from each subject of 0, 1, 2, or 3. These numbers were transformed to percentages. If the average percentage, computed over the 16 subjects in Experiment I, was less than 50%, the scoring for the isovist measure was reversed. The results for both experiments are shown in Fig. 6.4. The labels for the isovist measures indicate the direction of the effect of the measure on perceived space. Thus high values of A ("$A+$") and M_2 ("M_2+") and low values of P ("$P-$") and Q ("$Q-$") were associated with judgments of greater perceived space.

A statistical analysis (t-tests, $df = 15$) of the responses for Experiment I, comparing the obtained distribution of responses for each measure against the null hypothesis value of 50%, indicated that all the isovist measures except M_3 were statistically significant. For Experiment II, all except Q and M_3 were statistically significant. The relationship between the measures and the dependent variable had the same linear ordering for both experiments but was con-

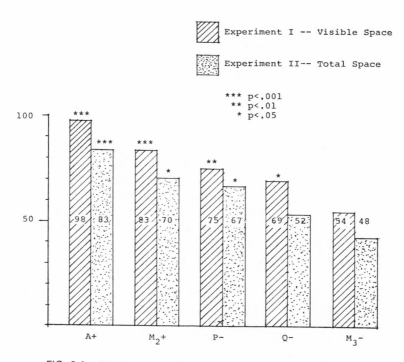

FIG. 6.4. Effectiveness (percentage of choices) for isovist measures.

sistently lower in Experiment II. This decrease was significant only for isovist measure A ($t = 2.57$, $df = 30$ $p < .05$).

Sex and Subject Differences

The only hint of a sex difference occurred for isovist measure Q in Experiment I. The female subjects selected the Q member of the stimulus pair 17% of the time; the males selected it 46% of the time. This difference approaches significance ($t = 1.90$; $df = 14$, $p < .10$). However, this difference was not evident in Experiment II, where the comparable percentages were 46% for females and 50% for males. There was no differences between the responses of the subjects who were paid and those fulfilling the course requirement.

DISCUSSION

In Experiment I, the high score of A was to be expected—the isovists varied on A and subjects were asked to judge A. Hardly less strong, however, was the effect of M_2+ (i.e., high M_2) followed by $P-$ (low P) and $Q-$ (low Q), while M_3 had no significant effect.

Now M_2, all other things being equal, tends to go up in value as one nears the walls and corners of a room. From walls and corners, respectively, more space can be seen in one "eyeful". Because subjects were explicitly asked to inspect the whole space, we might conclude that people are not good at "adding up spaces" that are distributed over a 180° field of view. If this is true, we are anxious to find out in a forthcoming experiment whether people are correspondingly bad at "adding up spaces" over time, i.e., when an overall layout is viewed part by part sequentially.

The positive effect of $P-$ and $Q-$ suggests that we perceive an area of a given size as more spacious when we see less wall surface, rather than more, and when we see less space potentially around corners rather than more.

So it would seem that if you wished to maximize the apparent size of a view from a given position, you should maximize A and M_2, minimize P and Q, and ignore M_3. An isovist that fits this specification is one from the corner of a large square room. We have informally tested this hypothesis (a "4.5, 4.5, 4.5, 4.5" viewed from position 1) and have discovered that this isovist does *not* seem larger than, say, a "3, 4, 5, 6" from position 2. Dare we say there is more to this than meets the eye? We do not have the opportunity here to discuss at sufficient length the reasons for, and consequences of, this observation.

In Experiment II subjects were asked to judge how big the room as a *whole* seemed from the incomplete view they had. They were asked to make an inference about the total space, based on a partial view of the space. Here A "wins" again, this time for no a priori reason, followed by M_2+ and $P-$. Notice that the effectiveness scores (percentage of choice) *maintained the same order as in Experiment I,* but decreased for each measure; Q did not differ from chance and M_3 remained as ineffective as it was before.

Our simplest explanation is this: In judging or sensing the size of a whole, known-to-be-bounded environment from a partial view, we do not give the benefit of the doubt to what we cannot see but know may be there. Thus the more you see $(A+)$, the less you suppose remains to be guessed about. Vacillation about the size of a "remainder" explains statistically the lowered effectiveness of $A+$. M_2+ and $P-$, by this explanation, do not directly affect the overall size judgment but, rather, affect it only indirectly by contributing to the perceived size of the isovist at hand. This enhancement of the size of the isovist then goes on to act as outlined earlier.

The percentage decrement for $Q-$ was larger than that of the other measures. We think it is plausible that, under pressure explicitly to evaluate the unseen, $Q+$ would begin to contribute, and in a sense "fight," with $Q-$'s enhancement of perceived spaciousness.

CONCLUSIONS

We are not yet in a position to generalize our results to all architectural environments with any confidence. We are now investigating the effects of dynamic viewing, that is, of how isovist information is integrated over time. Ultimately we will test for the validity of our results with full size rather than model spaces. Only then will we be prepared to give advice to architects.

In the meantime, however, we think our research indicates that isovists—as captured by our shape and size measures of them—do indeed affect our perception. Insofar as isovists are related to optic arrays, we hope that we have lent further credibility to Gibson's formulation of how to approach the problem of how we see the world.

Isovists "belong" to the physical world. They describe it objectively, if partially. Learning how to usefully describe the physical environment is surely a crucial step in discovering how our perception and actions are circumscribed by it.

ACKNOWLEDGMENT

Research supported by the National Science Foundation, Grant DAR 7817451.

REFERENCES

Benedikt, M. L. "On mapping the world in a mirror" *Environment and Planning B* 1980, 7, 367–378.

Benedikt, M. L. "To take hold of space: isovists and isovist fields" *Environment and Planning B* 1979, *6*, 47–65.

Davis, L. and Benedikt, M. "Computational models of space: isovists and isovist fields" *Computer Graphics and Image Processing* 1979, *11*, 49–72.

Gibson, J. J. *The Senses Considered as Perceptual Systems*. Boston: Houghton Mifflin, 1966.

Gibson, J. J. *The Ecological Approach to Visual Perception*. Boston: Houghton Mifflin, 1979.

7 Acoustic Information for Objects, Places, and Events

James J. Jenkins
University of South Florida

INTRODUCTION

One day last spring when the writing of this chapter was much on my mind, my wife and I were sitting in the garden drinking coffee and enjoying the morning sunlight. I suddenly realized as my wife and I talked that I was at that moment hearing her voice and following her conversation and that at the same time I could be aware that the radio inside was playing music, that two dogs in the next yard (out of sight) were playing together (and that one was a puppy and the other a mature, large dog), that the breeze was rustling the leaves in the tree overhead, that a variety of birds were singing and chirping, that an airplane was approaching overhead from the northwest, that the dog in the yard behind me was complaining about something, that a lawn mower was running somewhere in the neighborhood, and that traffic was cruising past on the main road a half a block away. And, I protest, I was still following the meaning of our conversation! All of this via variations of air pressure sensed at two little holes in my head! I was again reminded of the truly marvelous capacity of the auditory system to pick up acoustic information and identify its coherent aspects.

A very different example but an equally compelling one turned up in my reading. The writer is M. R. Schroeder at the Dahlem Conference on Recognition of Complex Acoustic Signals (1977):

> Zillions have been spent to improve long-range underwater detection, but when some stumbling crew member in a submerged submarine (lying in wait with its engines shut off) drops a wrench, only the human listener can identify the unexpected sound and draw the uncomfortable conclusion. (p. 184)

115

It is customary for reviewers interested in audition to begin by complaining that other scientists devote too much attention to vision and relegate audition to a minor sense. Arnheim (1936/1972), for example, says,

> The sensory preponderance of the visual over the aural in our life is so great that it is very difficult to get used to considering the aural world as more than just a transition to the visual world. (p. 136)

I notice that there is a tendency to think of events as if they were by nature "really" visual, and then to add that, of course, one might have some acoustic information about them. In fact, events are just events. They have a variety of consequences; some optical, some acoustic, some vibratory, some odorous, etc.

In this chapter, however, I want to stress the advantages of being concerned with the auditory system and acoustic information. Some of these advantages have occasionally been overlooked.

USEFUL DIMENSIONS OF ACOUSTIC INFORMATION

First, there are advantages for an organism in the use of acoustic versus, say, optical information. For example, listening is a fine way to obtain information unobtrusively. Thus, animals can listen for a predator without attracting unwelcome attention by exposing themselves to the predator. (Of course, some predators play the same game!) Further, listening does not depend on an external source of energy such as light, although it does, of course, depend on a medium of transmission. Thus, listening works in the dark, through and around many kinds of barriers, and under water. Still further, sounds ordinarily provide information about what produced them and where the source is located; these are critical kinds of information for animate organisms.

Because acoustic alerting does not ordinarily depend on the organism having carefully oriented receptors, the auditory system is a good "interrupt" system for warnings, alerts, appeals, new information and the like. We all know this in some sense and it is even recognized in our laws. Yelling "Fire!" in a crowded theater is widely regarded as a serious offense if there is no fire, but displaying a printed sign that said "FIRE" in the back of a darkened theater would probably be regarded as merely bizarre behavior. Those who have lived in apartments know first hand the effective interrupting properties of loud parties, loud record players, and loud television sets (although we are rarely upset by the garish pictures on our neighbors' living room walls or the brightness of their television set.)

Second, there are advantages for the scientist. One great advantage of working with acoustics is that the signal itself keeps reminding one that the nature of the world is event-like. Sound is action, happening, movement. There is no such thing as a frozen moment in sound. If there is a frozen moment, then there is no sound. So in the auditory domain there is no strict parallel to the tachistoscope and it is, perhaps, a little less likely that researchers will hold a "snapshot theory". Arnheim says, "Activity, then, is the essence of sound and an event will be more easily accepted by the ear than a state of being" (p. 136.). In general, a sound is news that something is happening; a dog is barking, a siren is whirling, a motor is running, the wind is blowing the leaves, the snow is crunching underfoot, an awning is flapping, a nail is being pulled, etc.

Third, there are advantages for the theorist. The domain of acoustics provides good examples of complex notions that are hard to illustrate in other areas, and that are instructive to theorists. Consider the notions of "structural invariant" and "transformational invariant" so often invoked by Shaw and his students. One of the best examples that I know is that of musical theme (as structural invariant) and variation (as a transformational invariant). All of us know that themes have constancy over many different instantiations and that variations can be styles of changes that themselves can be perceived as invariants. Two of our students, Leah Larkey and Greg Wakefield (1981) have shown that even musically naive subjects do recognize identities of both kinds.

Another excellent example of a transformational invariant is the Doppler effect, which gives information for relative motion by modulating an acoustic carrier signal of any sort whatsoever. As an illustration, consider two bells, one on a locomotive and one on a railroad crossing signal. For the pedestrian waiting at the crossroad, the crossing bell is constant in pitch; the bell on the approaching locomotive, however, increases in intensity as it nears him and then drops suddenly in pitch and then in intensity as the train rushes by. For the engineer on the train, exactly the opposite effect obtains. The bell on the locomotive is a constant and the crossing bell shows the appropriate changes in pitch and intensity as the train passes. For a motorist travelling along the railroad track frontage road in the opposite direction to the train, both bells will show the Doppler effect but the bell on the locomotive will undergo a much greater transformation in pitch than the crossing bell. Acoustic information for relative movement is present over time, regardless of the specific nature of the source. Whistles, engine sounds, bells, and rattling of the couplings all undergo transformation. It is the style of change that is the information for relative motion.

Finally, there are advantages for the artist. The acoustic domain is of great interest because it supports one of our most impressive art forms, music. This is sound for sound's sake; acoustic events developed and refined for the sake of their auditory quality. Anthropologists tell me that both music and drumming are cultural universals. For our species at least (and perhaps for others) sounds are of interest in and of themselves without the need for any external reference.

LEGACIES OF PAST RESEARCH

But this is not to argue that all is well in the study of ecological acoustics. In spite of the many reasons for its investigation and reasons for its success, much of the research with acoustics is limited to impoverished signals that carry no intrinsic meaning and little aesthetic quality. And many experiments strive to approximate the frozen moment in time by the use of very brief stimuli delivered through earphones in sound-conditioned chambers. Such experiments are usually motivated by the scientific desire to understand how the auditory system works. To this end, physically simple stimuli are employed in the belief that they will serve as efficient probes of the characteristics of the system.

Two legacies have had a powerful influence on our thinking about the ear and auditory stimulation: our atomistic heritage and our mechanistic heritage. The first leads us to model processes "from the bottom up", so to speak. As Warren and Shaw point out in their chapter in this volume, the choice of the unit of analysis is made on physical grounds in the faith that "simple" physical components must be the appropriate units of perceptual analysis. The second legacy leads us to examine systems part by part to see how each component works. The faith in this case is that the total system will be understood as the sum of these components. While these are both admirable strategies, and strategies that have been remarkably successful in many other pursuits, the researchers at this conference will recognize that the strategies are sharply limited with respect to sensory systems in general and the auditory system in particular. Nevertheless, three of our eminent predecessors have set the stage for the prevailing treatment of the auditory system: Fourier, Ohm and von Helmholtz.

Fourier contributed an idea and a method of startling power. He showed that a periodic waveform of any sort whatsoever could be analyzed into a series of sine waves; that is, it could be represented as a sum of a series of very simple waves of specific amplitude and phase. (Modern computers have now made the mathematics of Fourier's contribution available to every one and the utility of Fourier's analysis has been demonstrated in domains as different as the study of earthquakes and the analysis of birdsong.)

Ohm's contribution to the topic of interest is known as Ohm's acoustic law (somewhat less well known than his law of electrical phenomena.) Ohm's "other" law asserts that the ear is an analyzing instrument that is capable of resolving complex stimulation into its simple components. The usual demonstration of Ohm's law is that a listener can hear a musical chord and "factor out", or detect separately, its individual notes. Indeed this achievement is so well known to us that we scarcely realize its complexity. Reflect for a moment that the ear has a tiny mechanical system (ear drum, ossicles and window) through which all the vibrations must pass serially. There is only one channel of complex shaking movement that is transmitted, no matter how rich or complicated the sound. Yet, the auditory system can redivide this complex shaking into separate components at different frequencies that correspond to their different sources.

Von Helmholtz went the next step and proposed a model of the ear which included resonating parts that responded to particular frequencies of the incoming signal just as a given tuning fork in an array of tuning forks responds when its particular frequency is present. (A more homey demonstration is available at the nearest piano. If one sings a note loudly into the open piano while someone holds the sustaining pedal down, that note in the piano will resonate for an appreciable period after the singer stops.)

Thus a model of the ear as an analytical instrument gradually developed. The ear seemed to be an analog instrument that performed essentially the same task that Fourier analysis performed. That is, it took complex signals and rendered them into simple components which were then sent on to the brain to be reassembled, combined and augmented into meaningful perceptions. The task of understanding audition was then seen to be the task of charting the ear's response to sine waves (pure tones) of various frequencies and different amplitudes and studying its response to time and phase differences. The underlying assumption was that when this task was complete, complex stimuli would be readily accounted for by some form of summation or concatenation of the components.

An enormous amount of research has been devoted to such efforts in the past 100 years and a great deal has been learned about sound transmission, both in the ear and in our electronic communication media (telegraph, telephone, radio, television and recording). The physics of sound transmission has made giant advances as has our understanding of the ear, but the work is by no means completed.

The root of the problem seems to be that a purely mechanistic analysis of the ear does not offer general solutions to explain its functions. As Colin Cherry (1978) points out:

> We may speak of the ears or the eyes as "mechanisms" (using terms taken from mechanics, electrical engineering or physics). Whatever may be the adequacy, or validity of such description, all that I wish to stress here is that if such a description is made, we must not expect the "mechanism" to possess the same structure for different tests. Such a model may be adequate for one series of tests, yet be found to fail as a description with other tests . . . . However, this is not to say that the properties of, for example, the ears cannot be described by sufficient physical measurements, recorded data, graphs, etc. Rather it implies the risk of false conclusions if the results of any one series of tests are generalized and assumed to be relevant to other sets of conditions. (p. 130)

Part of what Cherry is saying is that what the ear appears to us to be is a function of the tasks we set for it. The ear is not a mechanism which can be taken apart, component by component, studied for its properties and then reassembled with the expectation that it will have just those properties when it is engaged in any arbitrary complex activity.

While an overzealous commitment to atomistic and mechanistic analyses may lead one away from realistic psychological problems, and while it is always tempting to wax polemical about other people's shortcomings, we must also recognize that enormous amount of excellent work have been devoted to real problems of practical importance such as noise abatement, the acoustics of orchestral halls, the design of hearing aids, improvements in communications technology and the like. And we must also recognize the careful work that has been done on classical problems such as the localization of sound, problems that are of obvious importance in any discussion of the functional auditory system.

At the same time many problems remind us that an account of auditory perception in terms of simple elements is insufficient:

1. Pure tone audiograms are only partially effective in predicting people's difficulties in understanding speech.

2. Speech signals that are radically different in terms of the usual physical analysis may be heard as "the same thing."

3. Speech signals that are remarkably similar in terms of the usual physical analysis may be heard as "different things."

4. Learning, or "attunement," must play an important role in speech perception (e.g., in identifying phonemes in one language versus another) and there may be critical periods for such attunement.

5. Points of high information in speech as well as other sounds often appear to be those of rapid spectral modulation (where the detailed structure is difficult to extract by physical measuring devices) rather than steady states (where the structure is relatively easy to extract physically). Rapid transients at onsets and offsets seem to be particularly important in both speech and music.

6. While listeners can indeed analyze a signal, they can also hear the unanalyzed complex—the whole orchestra, the chord itself, etc. That is, there is a "reverse Ohm's law" (Helmholtz' "synthetic listening") that must be explained as well as the traditional Ohm's law.

7. Presented with "pure tones", listeners report hearing harmonics; presented with a set of harmonics, listeners report hearing the missing fundamental.

This list could be made indefinitely long.

The reader will note at this point the underlying similarity of my point to the one made so elegantly by Johansson in his paper (this volume). We might call it Johansson's Law of Perceptual Richness (or, more simply, Johansson's Conjecture): While natural information may be enormously complex mathematically, it may be readily and efficiently perceived by the biological organism that has evolved to employ that information. Conversely, mathematically simple stimulation may be too impoverished to yield stable or unambiguous perceptual results. As he put it succinctly in his paper with regard to vision, " . . . what is simple for the visual system is complex for our mathematics and what is mathematically simple is hard to deal with for the visual system." I argue that the same must be said of the auditory system.

What I want to do in this chapter is sketch out a possible taxonomy for considering the study of acoustic information that supports the perception of objects, places and events in the real world. It is a "first try" and, of course, is ragged and incomplete. Other arrangements will surely prove to be more useful as we gain more knowledge but, perhaps, this will serve as a framework for immediate discussions of acoustic information.

A POSSIBLE TAXONOMY OF ACOUSTIC INFORMATION

It seems to me that we can divide the phenomena we want to discuss into the following categories:

1. Information in ambient acoustics. Usually, these are sounds that are generated by sources other than the listener.

2. Information in intraspecies acoustics. Although these are a subset of the first category, they are selected for special attention because they are usually sounds produced for some other member of the species to hear. That is, these are sounds that serve "intentional" communicative functions.

3. Information in echoes. In this case the sound is generated by the listener for the listener's own hearing

4. Acoustic art. In this case sound is produced for its own aesthetic value (as in music) or it is produced to simulate information in one of the first three categories (as in sound effects.)

5. Special topics. This is a residual category for special topics of importance such as the combination of acoustic information with information presented in other modalities and unusual special uses of listening.

I will try to give some examples of the material in each of these categories and then conclude with some very general questions that characterize research opportunities.

Information in Ambient Acoustics

Recall the story with which this chapter began. As my wife said at the time, the auditory world is a "full" world. It is packed with information; it surrounds one; it fills the entire environment. Many people report feeling shut off from the world when their ears are plugged by an experimenter (or when their spring cold does the same thing.) The world of the deaf (we conjecture) must be to some degree vacant or empty. For the active, orienting, enquiring listener the world offers a staggering wealth of acoustic information under all but the most unusual conditions (such as being in an anechoic chamber or a space ship.) The acoustics provided by the world contain at least partial answers to questions such as, Where am I?, What is that?, Where is it?. Is it moving?, How is it moving?, and the like.

Recently, some of my seminar students at the University of Minnesota experimented with blindfolded walking using only a cane for guidance. In a few weeks of practice they discovered that there were many acoustic landmarks in the psychology building: Differences in the sounds of the ventilators in different parts of the building, water fountains purring, people's voices as one passes an open door, the interplay of near and far sounds as one passes an intersecting hallway, the clack of office machines, footfalls of passers-by on different floor coverings, elevator doors clanging, the tattoo of feet on steps, metal as opposed to wooden doors closing, etc. We were impressed with how much information was readily available.

The students discovered further that the noises, resonances and echoes gave them information concerning the size of rooms and the number of people present. They also discovered that some noises are distinctive for the time of day, occurring only on periodic schedules. (The classic example of yesteryear was the milkman clinking his bottles as he delivered the milk at the same time every morning.)

We also observed experienced blind persons at street intersections. We learned that they oriented to the street by listening to the sound of passing cars and determined the rhythm and the state of the traffic signals by listening to the sounds of the cars stopping and starting

All of these phenomena draw our attention to the fact that we can identify a host of environmental sounds and use them for self orientation in time and place, for orientation toward people and things, for information about enclosures and apertures and for ascertaining the state of certain events occurring in the world around us. In one sense these phenomena are so common and obvious that we scarcely find them worth investigating, but an attempt to build a machine to perform the same tasks will convince us that we do not know in any detail what information supports such a variety of perceptions.

VanDerveer's (1979) work is a first step in the direction of cataloging some of the facts that we must account for. She found that listeners could identify with a high degree of accuracy the sources of 30 common natural sounds. In general, listeners responded by naming a mechanical event that produced the sound and reported sensory qualities only when source recognition failed. She also found that similarity in temporal pattern was important in determining errors of classification. Warren and Verbrugge (1981) interpret these data as supporting the claim that the temporal structure of sound is specific to the mechanical activity of the source. They conjecture that the auditory system might best be viewed as being designed for the perception of source events via higher-order acoustic functions, rather than for the detection of quasi-stable sound elements. (See also Schubert, 1974.)

Warren and Verbrugge search for higher-order acoustic properties that support the perception of "breaking" versus "bouncing" in recordings of the acoustic consequences of dropping glass bottles of various sizes to each of these two fates. Their results show that the two events may be distinguished by differences in the temporal patterning of component pulse onsets, together with the initial burst of rupturing; but not by cross-sectional spectral properties. (Particularly interesting to me were the conditions under which neither breaking nor bouncing were perceived; for example, iterating a recording of one "bounce pulse" at equal intervals, rather than at diminishing intervals, destroyed the bouncing effect entirely and replaced this perception with that of a mechanical event, like a jack hammer.)

As noted previously, information for the location of sound sources is one aspect of the world of ambient sound that has been well explored. Many summaries of this literature are available (e.g., Konishi, 1977; Mills, 1972; Neff, 1968) so little mention need be given that literature here. In general, wide-band signals are more accurately located than narrow-band signals; that is, more complex signals are better localized than simple signals. (There may be an important lesson here.) It is also important to notice that there are many sources of acoustic energy that support spatial localization. Intensity, temporal and spectral differences in the signals arriving at the two ears are the most often cited sources of information contributing to accuracy of localization. It is interesting to note further that while any one source of information may be ambiguous under certain conditions, a listener who is free to move and turn can readily distinguish many otherwise uncertain signals.

Ethologists contribute some interesting examples of peripheral auditory apparatus specialized for the detection of biologically significant sounds. A particularly impressive case is the noctuid moth (Roeder, 1966), which is a favorite prey of bats. These moths have special detectors that are sensitive to the frequencies of bat chirps. The detectors are, so to speak, "wired through" to motor structures in such a way that the moth dives when the bat sound is detected at a given amplitude and localized to the rear of the moth. (For a recent summary of moth versus bat, see Fenton & Fullard, 1981).

It is also a frequent report of neurological studies that biologically significant sounds evoke more neural responding than clicks or steady tones. For example, 15% more units in a cat's auditory cortex respond to cat vocalizations and bird calls than to tones. In the squirrel, vocalizations of other squirrels elicit responses from 90% of the units studied, as opposed to 70% of the units for tones and far fewer for clicks. (See Newman, 1977; Scheich, 1977)

Both prey and predators can play the auditory game, of course. It is well known in folklore that owls can find prey by audition. That fact was verified by Payne and Drury (1958; see also Payne 1971) who demonstrated that owls could catch mice in total darkness using only acoustic information. Konishi (1973a, 1973b) showed further that owls could better localize wide-band noises than narrow-band noises. Knudsen (1981) discusses the experiments he and Konishi performed and the kinds of information the owl uses in its nocturnal feats of localization.

We have already mentioned that a transformation in frequency through the Doppler effect provides information as to changes in rate or direction of movement for a source that generates a stable characteristic spectrum of sound. Thus acoustic stimulation may also supply information about relative movement.

It may also be true that changes in the relative amplitude of a source provide information related to time to contact, via, perhaps, the same characteristic equations that describe looming and zooming in the visual world. As yet, however, experimental evidence for this hypothesis is lacking.

In summary, ambient sound may supply answers to such basic questions as: Where am I? What is that? Where is it? Is it moving relative to me? (perhaps, particularly, is it going to come into contact with me?).

Intraspecies Acoustic Communication

Let us now turn to another fascinating and biologically important category, sounds that are produced for other members of the species to hear. Such sounds may be thought of as propositions and questions like the following:

"Here I am! I'm me! Look out for danger! Here's food! I'm lonely and insecure. Keep away! Where is everybody? Anybody want to mate?"

There is no denying that such communications serve vital biological functions. Some commonly cited functions are:

- territoriality
- mate attraction
- mate recognition
- filial communication
- social group maintenance
- identifying one as a member of a category, e.g., a particular sex, age, mood, etc.
- identifying one as a specific individual
- warnings of various sorts
- news of importance to the social group—food, water, etc.

Actions of listeners often depend crucially on such communications. Some communications seem to set off behaviors such as fleeing, fighting, approaching, investigating (getting more information) or remaining "at ease" directly. An interesting example is found in the alarm calls of vervet monkeys (Struhsaker, 1967). These monkeys have a series of alarm calls that elicit differential behavior in the hearers; that is, they are not just general alarm calls. They are in some sense either directions for an action like, "Flee to the trees!" or labels such as

"There's a leopard!" Such calls differentiate between leopards, eagles, pythons, and baboons.

Seyfarth, Cheney, & Marler (1980) are investigating the ontogeny of these calls and find, as is usually the case, both genetic and environmental influences. In the beginning, infant vervets give alarm calls to more different species than do adults. That is, they overgeneralize the calls. They do not give them randomly, however. Leopard alarms are given to a variety of terrestrial creatures. Eagle alarms are given to eagles, hawks, and other birds. Python alarms may be given to any snake. Baboon calls, however, appear to be intrinsically limited and are given only to baboons. After experience with the monkey band and with adult calling behavior, the infants narrow down the variety of animals to which they give warning calls until their behavior becomes similar to that of the adults. In this case one sees the growth of specificity. (It might be noted that this kind of study gives evidence concerning perceptual equivalence and concept attainment in monkeys. Obviously, the classes that are functionally equivalent for the infants can be identified by observing the stimuli that elicit the infants' calls.)

Everything that was said about localization can be seen as being applicable here. For many of the functions listed above it is necessary to determine the location of the communicator (especially for territoriality, mating, and food-finding). Just having the knowledge that there is someone to fight, or to mate, or something to eat is not nearly as efficacious as knowing, in addition, where the fighter, potential mate or potential dinner is located. Yet, as Marler (1977) points out, in the presence of a predator, it might be a grave disadvantage to be localizable. He reports that for many species, warning calls have slow rise times, which make localization more difficult, while other, more sociable, calls have fast rise times which maximize locatability.

A timely reminder to prevent us from concluding that nature has made communication automatic is the observation that even among the lower animal species there are contextual conditions that modulate the response to the communication event. For example, Owings and Leger (1980) have shown that even among the lowly California ground squirrel there are discriminably different vocalizations for terrestrial predators, raptors (birds of prey), and agonistic encounters and even different variations among some of these categories (snake calls are different from calls for carnivores and badger calls are separate from those for bobcats, coyotes and dogs). Responses of other squirrels are not automatic, however (Leger, Owings & Boal, 1979). Responses vary as a function of the number of calls in the series (1, 3, or 5), the intensity of the calls (80 or 90 decibels), and the location of the listening squirrel (near boulder, near burrow or on boulder). These investigators also cite the work of Holmes (personal communication) who reports that hoary marmots monitor the location of refuge sites; they run after an alarm call only if the distance to safety is greater than five meters!

Reynolds (1975) points out that among chimpanzees, behaviors following "communications" are highly modulated in response to many contextual factors. "Some individuals, for example, who are known to be nervous nellies, consistently have their alarm calls ignored." Reynolds goes on to say that the response of a primate to a call is not simply a function of the characteristics of the call but involves a great deal of additional information such as who said it, the hearer's relation to the caller, and the circumstances under which it was uttered and heard. Among other variables concerning caller and hearers, he lists the following status variables as being important in modulating responses to calls: infant–adult, male–female, estrous female–anestrous female, dominant–subordinate, mother–child, consort–nonconsort, and separated infant–nonseparated infant.

Finally, of course, we must mention human speech. Because Studdert-Kennedy treats this topic elsewhere in this volume, I will only point out that the marvel of communication through the speech code is only one aspect of the information that is available in the acoustic stream of speech. There is also information (I believe) for the age, sex and identity of the speaker, the mode of speech (whispered, spoken, growled, shouted, etc.), the language spoken, the dialect of the language, accent, rate of speech, the speaker's emotions, perhaps the speaker's education and class, the location of the speaker, the distance of the speaker and, finally, of course, what it is that the person is saying. All of this is packed in the same signal and all of it is more or less available to us.

Echolocation

Echolocation is the active examination of the environment by acoustic means for information concerning objects, places and events. The most dramatic examples of echolocation are found in bats, porpoises, and whales, all of which produce sounds (in what appears to be a highly purposeful manner), the echoic return of which provides information about many aspects of their environments. Human beings make use of the general echo principle when they shout into a cave to tell how far it goes, or drop a stone into a well to tell how deep it is. More directly parallel, of course, is the case of echolocation by the blind, using their own actions to generate sound (heel clicks, finger snaps, hissing and clicking noises of the mouth, etc.) in order to obtain information about their environment. A special artificial case which has been much studied is the use of sonar to locate objects under water. (The parallels of sonar to biological echolocation systems have been specifically examined, Altes, 1976).

From the usual examples, I was led to the supposition that only mammals (under sufficient selection pressure) could develop sophisticated echolocation. And it is true that all mammals that live in the oceans do employ echolocation to some degree. But the literature discloses that some birds (cave dwellers) and some fish also use echolocation (Griffin, 1958).

While echolocation in humans has been the subject of some study, particularly the thorough work of Dallenbach and his colleagues at Cornell (Supa, Cotzin, & Dallenbach, 1944; Worchel & Dallenbach, 1947; Cotzin & Dallenbach, 1950) which first disclosed the true nature of "facial vision" and studied the nature of the acoustic signals involved, and the more artificial laboratory studies of Rice at Stanford, (Rice & Feinstein, 1965; Rice, 1967), the most detailed information we have concerns the bat. The many different species that live under a variety of conditions, that eat radically different diets, and that thrive in different environments, have shown us a diversity of ways to employ echolocation. The bat has become highly specialized for (1) the production of particular classes of sound, (2) the pick-up of variations of these sounds and, presumably, (3) the sophisticated extraction of information from these sounds. (For general accounts of the studies of bats, see Neuweiller, 1977; Simmons, 1977.)

Consider the most fundamental searching operation: Where is the target and is it moving? Most bats combine two types of sounds in their acoustic productions: a constant frequency section which may be quite lengthy (up to 90 milliseconds (msec)) and a frequency modulated section which is typically quite short (less than 5 msec) although it may be 15–100 kHz wide. The frequency modulated section is always downward in pitch, never upward. Although bats can produce upward modulated signals, they never use these signals for echolocation purposes. (There may be both neurological and acoustic reasons for that.) The constant frequency signal is quite sensitive to the velocity of the target via the well known Doppler effect. The frequency shift tells the bat whether or not the target is moving and also codes the velocity of the target. This is very useful in hunting in a cluttered environment. The frequency modulated signal, on the other hand, is not very velocity sensitive but is excellent for inspecting the shape, texture and size of targets. And regardless of signal type, the time of the return of the echo gives information for distance. The bat appears to be sensitive to time lags of 30 to 60 microseconds.

Detailed study of particular species of bats has revealed finely tuned auditory sensitivities in the frequency regions closely associated with the bat's call. Indeed, some very clever interactions have been discovered. For example, in one species of bat that uses a long constant frequency signal, there is very sharp tuning of the auditory system around the signal frequency. The tuning is so sharp that one would suppose that as the bat's speed increases, the echo would shift in frequency and fall outside the sensitive region. That is not the case, however. As the bat increases its speed, it lowers the frequency of its call with the result that the returning echo is kept in the critical region of its auditory system.

The performance of the bat is quite impressive especially when one considers that the animal operates in a sea of noise created by other bats and environmental events. When one attempts to jam the bat's system with white noise, there is virtually no effect even at very high intensity levels. Even when the noise is concentrated in the frequency range of the bat's own signal, the animal can successfully employ his echo-ranging capabilities when the noise is, say, 10,000 times as intense as the bat's signal. This implies, of course, a highly coordinated and calibrated system developed for just this task. When one recalls further that acoustic signals are altered in quality by changes in temperature, humidity, turbulence, rain and fog, it is easy to regard the bat's performance as miraculous. One conclusion that must be drawn is that bats apparently monitor the quality of their information and the needs of the situation and modulate their behavior accordingly. New information results in modification of subsequent transmission. In his classic book, Griffin (1958) tells us, for example, of changes in the rate of emission of the acoustic signal by the bat during the course of an experimental flight:

> On release (take off) the bat transmits briefly (1/10 sec) at 80/sec, goes into cruising mode, 30/sec; approaches the maze of wires—where his rate goes up to 50–60/sec; then as he goes through the wires, he drops to cruising rate again.

Griffin also gives examples of bats "not paying attention" when flying a familiar path. In a highly familiar surrounding, if an obstacle is placed in a customary flight path, bats are likely to crash into the obstacle even though they are emitting calls at their usual cruising rate. After the crash, they emit calls at a very high rate, as if there is a lot of "investigation" or reexamination of the environment.

Some bats change their type of call depending on their temporary situation. They may cruise with constant-frequency calls (CF) and switch to frequency-modulated calls (FM) as they close in on their prey. Or another species may cruise with a combined FM–CF signal, go to CF to search for prey, and switch to FM to identify and pursue the prey. In addition they may modulate the repetition rate from as few as 10 calls/sec while cruising to as many as 200 calls/sec as they approach the prey. In some sense the investigator can tell what the bat is looking for (listening for) by the kind of call it emits.

The detailed grain of the information that the bat extracts is impressive even to seasoned investigators. Some bats can detect a difference of less than 1 millimeter in the depth of holes that are 8 millimeters in depth and 30 centimeters distant. (Porpoises are found to have comparable accuracy in water when one corrects for the higher speed of sound in water.)

Fig. 7.1 is adapted from Simmons (1977) to summarize much of what is known concerning the acoustic correlates of the bat-environment relationship. The diagram directs our attention to the impressive amount of information that is available to, and apparently used by, the organism.

In reading this literature I have returned again and again to Johansson's conjecture. Complicated, rapidly varying signals containing complex patterns of information are "simple" for the organism that has evolved to make use of them. Signals that are mathematically simple, on the other hand, seem to be less well processed and have more limited utility for the organism.

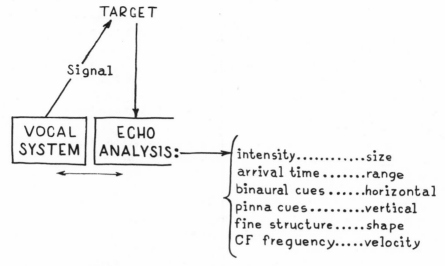

FIG. 7.1   Object perception by acoustic imaging in bat echolocation. The sound is generated by the larynx and vocal tract and emitted through the open mouth or the nose leaf. The sound travels outward, primarily to the front, encounters a target, and is reflected back to be picked up at the two ears. The shape of the external ears augments directional information. Target identity and trajectory are available through higher order processing. Subsequent transmissions are modified on the basis of incoming information. Mechanical and neural mechanisms in the auditory system are activated in synchrony with sound emission to reduce the level of direct self stimulation, and the vocal apparatus receives short latency control information directly from the auditory system. (Adapted from Simmons, 1977)

As an aside, we should note that the study of bats sometimes reveals our persistant anthropomorphism. It is interesting in reading the report of the Dahlem Conference on Recognition of Complex Acoustic Signals to note the discussion of the problem that is posed by considering how the bat converts sound into "an image" so that sound can be turned into useful spatial information. I can imagine a conference of "bat psychologists" asking how it is that human beings transform visual information into sound so they can navigate in the truly auditory world!

Art

Because of limitations in my background I have little to say except to call attention to this area. Conference participants like Balzano and Jones are highly capable and experienced in this area and must carry the responsibility for treating music. Arnheim (1936/1972) reaches back to Goethe for a quotation that suggests the special status that music may have in the realm of acoustic events:

> True music is for the ear alone. I want to see anyone I am talking to. On the other hand, who sings to me must sing unseen; his form must neither attract nor distract me.

Music seems to belong in a space or world of its own. It moves in time, dynamics, and pitch in ways that are difficult to describe and to constrain. I believe that we have much to learn from its study and I am delighted that we have such forward-looking representatives here.

We have done a few experiments with musical material that suggest that some of the cognitive components of music are shared with nonmusical cognitions. For example, the well-known experiments of Bransford and Franks (1971) and Franks and Bransford (1971), that show integration of verbal ideas into one complex idea and the integration of parts of visual patterns into a complex visual pattern, have analogs in the musical realm. A group of my students (Chew, Larkey, Soli, Blount, & Jenkins, 1982) has shown that chorales of four instruments behave in the same way as complex sentences with four ideas or a complex visual design having four components. If the chorales are played with one, two and three instrumental parts present, the listener falsely recognizes the full four-part chorale as one that he has heard. As in the original Bransford–Franks experiments, the listener's confidence in recognition is a function of the number of parts being played in the piece at the recognition test. The more parts present, the higher the confidence that the particular passage was heard earlier, whether it was actually presented or not.

In addition, Larkey and Wakefield (1981), as I mentioned earlier, have shown that subjects can reliably react to themes and variations independently (invariants of structure and transformations) and will predict and falsely recognize combinations of theme and variation that they have not actually heard.

I would like to draw attention here to a domain of sound art that psychologists have largely neglected, namely, sound effects, so ubiquitous in radio, television, stage and cinema. Sound effects were developed to a high level in the "golden age of radio" and most of the books on sound effects that I found in our library date from that period. This is not to be taken as an indication that the art itself has been lost or neglected; perhaps it merely indicates that sound effects have moved into the status of trade secrets. Surely anyone who has seen a science-fiction movie must recognize that art is at work in providing sounds for machines, weapons and creatures that have no existance in this world. What is the appropriate sound for a "light saber", for a gleaming streak from a "ray gun", or for the pounding of the complex foot of a giant "snow walker" tank? What is the appropriate sound (or lack of it) that accompanies the "jump to light speed" of the hero's rocket ship? These are fundamentally artistic questions, and where sound art goes, the psychology of acoustic information should follow.

Some of the manipulations of the radio sound effects experts give us food for thought and materials for experimentation. The following list of just some of the uses of sound effects is impressive.

Sound as Stage Setting.   Here the radio expert found his first challenge, to set the atmosphere or mood of the radio material that was to follow. The expert tried to define the place (by sounds that occur only in limted environments), the historical period, the time of day and the like. An idealized example might be the creaking of a carriage wheel clattering over cobblestones, echoing off buildings close by, muffled by heavy fog, with the faint sound of a fog horn in the distance and a distant voice with an English accent—obviously a setting for a Sherlock Holmes episode.

Sound as Action.   Here the task was to create action for the unseeing audience with sounds of running feet, pouring water, slamming doors, revolver shots, bodies falling, objects breaking, trap doors releasing and so on. These are, perhaps, the best known and most obvious sound effects. Related to these in a negative sense is "sound out of action", that is the announcer's voice with information or commentary; a voice in a sound-treated room that seems to be floating in the void, clearly separated from any of the real action being portrayed.

Sound Symbols.   These are conventionalized sounds that audiences have been trained to understand as having a given meaning: The clock striking midnight, music swelling to indicate a break in the action or a change in scene, the train whistle that signals a trip, the clock ticking for the passage of time, etc.

Proportion.   This term indicates an exaggeration in sound that produces a comic effect. The classic examples in the United States are the landslide effect that accompanied Fibber McGee's closet door opening, and the echoing and clanging sound of Jack Benny's vault doors as he went down to get a few dollars. These sounds are out of proportion to the situation, and rely on exaggeration for their effect.

Sound Dominance.   By this the sound-effects expert meant a change in volume, contrast, repetition or duration that signaled a change in perspective, apparent movement, change of pace, increases or decrease in complexity, or a break in rhythm. Although this notion seems to be relatively complex, a simple example might be the shifting of relative amplitudes between a conversation at one table in a cocktail lounge and the conversation at the next table as if the observer were passing by the first table to a position next to the second. The movement of the observer is carried in the relative change in amplitudes of the sound sources

Spectral Modulation.   From the early days of radio the sound experts understood that filtering sounds to change their spectral composition produced effects akin to changing their distance. Thus, the distant shot was low-pass filtered and diminished in amplitude while the nearby ricochet of the bullet was high-pass filtered and loud. This modulation corresponds with the natural spectral shift that takes place with distance.

Change of Scene.   Change of scene is often accomplished by appropriate changes in resonance, that is, the amount of echo and reverberation that is included in the sound (along with other information, of course.) In a recent radio drama I heard the following changes of scene: The major character, a man, went to his car. The background was city street noises. Amid these noises I heard footsteps, car door slam in close quarters, abrupt disappearance of city noises, sound of engine starting as it might sound inside the car, sound of man talking to himself in a very reverberant enclosure, engine noises at low volume as man talks, then fade out of talk and engine noise (to indicate passage of time), engine noise fades in and then, following braking noises, stops. Man talks to himself in resonant enclosure, car door opens, faint chirping of birds, man's voice with no resonance, footsteps on sidewalk, knocking on door, door opens, woman's voice, man's voice passing from no enclosure to room size enclosure, bird chirps stop, door closes, conversation takes place with the couple at easy speaking distance. Obviously, a great deal of information was transmitted through the nonverbal use of sound.

Rhythm.   This term refers to the tempo or pace of the production and seems to cover everything from the signalling power of background music to the rate at which characters talk and events take place in the drama.

In listening to modern radio drama I have been impressed with the subtlety of the manipulations of sound to achieve effects. Sound-effects technicians have learned to use the resources of modern sound-recording with a light touch to achieve effects without drawing attention to the means by which the effects are achieved. It appears to me that we have much to learn from them about the information that can be carried in the acoustic signal.

Coherence of Multisensory Systems

From our backyard locale, my wife and I heard a remarkable burst of song— some kind of warbler. At length we located a small bird on a high wire at the end of the yard. Could it be that this tiny bird was the source of the song? We thought it unlikely, but we were rapidly convinced by the synchrony of the bursts of song and the movements of the bird. The visual and the auditory reinforced each other. Coherence of acoustic and optical information specified the bird as the source of the song without a doubt.

How closely wed are the various senses? From casual experience we must suppose them to be closely knit, and experimental data confirm the supposition. It is well known (e.g., Muir & Field, 1979) that infants will turn toward and look to the side from which a sound originates. Mendelson and Haith (1976) report further that when an infant is eyposed to a lighted visual field with no figures in it (a Gansfeld), the infant's eyes ''jitter''. However, if a voice speaks to the child, the jitter stops. Spelke (1976, 1979) showed that four-month-old babies, given a choice of two films to watch, would watch the film that matched a sound track that they could hear. There seem to be invariants of tempo or synchrony in the two sensory domains that unite them.

Walker (1980) similarly showed that infants are sensitive to congruity in the optical and acoustic displays of emotion. Films of a happy woman and films of a depressed or angry woman were displayed to infants while one or the other soundtrack was played. Again the infants watched the appropriate film, in this case even when the films were out of synchronization with the acoustics!

Bahrick (1980) showed that four-month-old infants differentiated the collision of rigid, hard objects from the collision of plastic, spongy ones on the basis of acoustic specifications. (See E. J. Gibson, in press, for a complete discussion.)

In a convincing series of studies McGurk and MacDonald (1976, MacDonald & McGurk, 1978) demonstrated that visual information concerning the articulation of speech can cause listeners to hear syllables that are not actually present in the acoustic signal. Thus, if the voice from a television monitor is saying /ba/, but the lip configuration that the listener sees on the screen is appropriate for /da/ or /va/, the listener will report hearing one of the latter sounds. Obviously, in the ordinary, natural situation we have a close and necessary correlation between the visual and the auditory information for speech sounds. But we are usually little aware that we monitor or use the visual. The experiment suggests not only that the visual is important but also that the visual can override the auditory and determine what the subject perceives. In some sense, this experiment says that information is just information and that the perceptual system does not especially note or mark its source. This is a well-known claim, of course, in the writings of James J. Gibson, and it seems to be finding increasing support in the experimental work of many psychologists.

Unusual Applications

By "unusual applications" I mean the application of listening to obtain information that is divorced in space–time from the verification of that information by other sensory modalities. A classic instance is thumping a watermelon to determine whether it is ripe or not. A more elaborate example is auscultation of the heart, or simply listening to heart sounds.

Over 200 years ago Lannec discovered the richness of heart sounds and invented the stethoscope for listening to such sounds. He described the fundamental rhythms of the heart—the first and second heart sounds—and began an inventory of heart murmurs. By the late 1800s heart sounds were recorded by mechanical means, and in the first decade of this century the first phonocardiographic records were obtained and analyzed. This meant, of course, that heart sounds now furnished information for both the eye and the ear. In the 1950s a classic work on heart sounds with detailed spectrographic analyses was published by McKusick (1958) and a decade later Luisada (1965) published an extensive work on phonocardiography.

For the psychologist, auscultation furnishes an interesting and important problem (see also Farber and Mark, this volume). Some issues that might not be readily apparent can be suggested:

1. Physicians differ widely in their skill and confidence in auscultation. Some say that they hear very little at all; others are highly skilled in obtaining and interpreting information. Everyone agrees that expertise requires years of experience. Thus, auscultation offers a valuable opportunity to study perceptual learning.

2. Auscultation is a classic case of the pursuit of information. Action in the service of perceptual ends is obvious in the physical examination. The skilled listener applies his stethoscope with different degrees of pressure and listens at various sites. Variations in the sounds between sites are found to have special meanings. Further, sounds at one site suggest new movements and tracing out of significant sounds as they radiate away from the heart.

3. Auscultation represents an interesting fusion of one's knowledge of anatomy and haemodynamics with acoustic information. For the novice, auscultation is hard work and is essentially problem solving, with extensive errors. To the expert, it is somehow "listening to the heart itself"—not so much reasoning and conscious deliberation, but attunement to the event structure that is available.

We are beginning to study heart sounds in pediatric cardiology. Auscultation of the newborn or young child is much more difficult than one might suppose. Even a stereotyped murmur that would be easily heard at a heart rate of 60 beats per minute, tends to disappear (for the novice) at 120 beats per minute, a common rate for infants' hearts.

Consider another example, the mechanic who listens to a car engine diagnostically. Some mechanics can work from the general characteristics of the sound. Some take a steel rod or long screwdriver and, placing one end of it on various parts of the engine and the other end close to one ear, diagnose the source of the difficulty.

Other examples include such tasks as deciding that a bearing in an electric motor is burned out by its sound, or detecting that the brushes of a motor are worn, or discovering that a wine cask is half full, etc.

CLOSING REMARKS

Finally I wish to conclude these remarks by posing some very general questions that I believe to be important. Do not suppose that I favor working on general questions rather than pursuing particular problems. That is not at all the case. In fact I incline to the belief that we are most likely to advance science by working on real problems in the world, partly so that we can see whether we are making any progress. But these questions are everywhere present and I believe that no matter where one works, it might be wise to look at the general issues from time to time. These global, general questions may be susceptible to solution.

1. Is it possible to focus the ear? All the evidence suggests that the ear is anything but a passive organ. It appears to be capable of special spectral and temporal sensitivity when particular spectral or temporal events are expected. Is it truely an active organ, searching for information?

2. Is it generally true that Johanssons's conjecture holds in audition? That is, is it true that mathematically complex acoustic events have a great advantage over mathematically simple acoustic events in the amount of acoustic information transmitted and the ease with which it is available to us? Are points of rapid change and spectral complexity usually the most informative? (D'Amato & Salmon, 1981, recently reported, to their obvious amazement, that both monkeys and rats learned to respond differentially to auditory stimuli more readily when the stimuli were two complex tunes than when the stimuli were two widely different sine waves [tones]. Here, even when there is no reason to suppose a biological advantage to the particular stimuli used, complexity again turned out to be "easier" than simplicity.)

3. What accounts for the coherence of sources? Why do acoustic events hang together? What accounts for the enormous selectivity of the ear that lets it pick out an important source and trace it through other noise? A well-known variant of this question is, why can the speech of a given person be heard at a cocktail party? (For a somewhat different example, why are bats so resistant to "jamming"? How can they operate in a noise field where their own signal is only one thousandth to one ten thousandth of the ambient noise?) Conversely, under what conditions do acoustic arrays come apart into "separate" signals? (For example, under what circumstances does "streaming" occur?)

4. To what extent do the phenomena in audition parallel those in vision? Will the same equations predict time-to-contact in audition that predict time-to-contact in visual looming and zooming? Is there an auditory texture in parallel to visual texture?

I must conclude with a plea for attending to the auditory world. Even at this conference, I hear the neglect of the auditory world in favor of the visual world. Yet I hope my paper will suggest to the reader that study of the auditory world is both important and fruitful. It has many problems that are begging for research and the research promises to be very exciting.

ACKNOWLEDGMENTS

I write this chapter as a near neophyte in the field of acoustic research. However, I hope that the chapter will convey some of the richness of research possibilities in the field and suggest some directions in which the research might move.

I owe much to the stimulation I have received from others in connection with discussions of ecological acoustics. Eleanor Gibson, Edward Reed, Robert Verbrugge, and William Warren have all given me nudges and suggestions that I have found useful. J. Bruce Overmier and Neal Viemeister have valiently tried to keep me from error although I have not always followed their advice. None of these colleagues is to blame, of course, for the shortcomings of this work.

The writing of this paper has been supported in part by a grant to James Jenkins and Winifred Strange from the National Institute of Mental Health (MH-21153) and by the Center for Research in Human Learning at the University of Minnesota, which is supported by that University and by grants from the National Institutes of Health and the National Science Foundation.

REFERENCES

Altes, R. A. Sonar for generalized target description and its similarity to animal echolocation systems. *Journal of the Acoustic Society of America, 1976, 59,* 97–105.

Arnheim, R. *Radio: An art of sound.* New York: Da Capo Press, 1972. (Originally published London, 1936).

Bahrick, L. E. *Infants' perception of properties of objects as specified by amodal information in auditory-visual events.* Doctoral dissertation, Cornell University, 1980.

Bransford, J. D., & Franks, J. J. The abstraction of linguistic ideas. *Cognitive Psychology, 1971, 2,* 331–350.

Bullock, T. H. (Ed.). *Recognition of complex acoustic signals.* Dahlem Konferenzen, Berlin: Abakon Verlagsgesellschaft 1977.

Cherry, C. *On human communication* (3rd ed.). Cambridge, Mass.: MIT Press, 1978.

Chew, S. L., Larkey, L. S., Soli, S. D., Blount, J., & Jenkins, J. J. The abstraction of musical ideas. *Memory & Cognition, 1982, 10,* 413–423.

Cotzin, M., & Dallenbach, K. M. "Facial vision": The role of pitch and loudness in the perception of obstacles by the blind. *American Journal of Psychology, 1950, 63,* 485–515.

D'Amato, M. R., & Salmon, D. Tune discrimination in monkeys (Cebus apella) and rats. *Bulletin of the Psychonomic Society, 1981, 18,* 51 (A).

Fenton, M. B., & Fullard, J. H. Moth hearing and the feeding strategies of bats. *American Scientist, 1981, 69,* 266–275.

Franks, J. J., & Bransford, J. D. Abstraction of visual patterns. *Journal of Experimental Psychology, 1971, 90,* 65–74.

Gibson, E. J. The concept of affordance in development: The renascence of functionalism. In W. A. Collins (Ed.), *Minnesota Symposium on Child Psychology* (Vol. 15: *The concept of development*). Hillsdale, N.J.: Laurence Erlbaum Associates 1982.

Griffin, D. R. *Listening in the dark: The acoustic orientation of bats and men.* New Haven: Yale University Press, 1958.

Knudsen, E. I. The hearing of the barn owl. *Scientific American, 1981, 245,* (6), 112–125.

Konishi, M. How the owl tracks its prey. *American Scientist, 1973, 61,* 414–424.(a)

Konishi, M. Locatable and nonlocatable acoustic signals for barn owls. *American Naturalist, 1973, 107,* 775–785. (b)

Konishi, M. Spatial localization of sound. In T. H. Bullock (Ed.), *Recognition of complex acoustic signals* (see Bullock, above), 127–143.

Larkey, L. S., & Wakefield, G. H. *Learning musical themes and variations.* Unpublished Manuscript, University of Minnesota, 1981.

Leger, D. W., Owings, D. H., & Boal, L. M. Contextual information and differential responses to alarm whistles in California ground squirrels. *Zeitschrift für Tierpsychologie, 1979, 49,* 142–155.

Luisada, A. A. *From auscultation to phonocardiography.* St. Louis, Mo.: C. V. Mosby Co., 1965.

MacDonald, J., & McGurk, H. Visual influences on speech perception processes. *Perception & Psychophysics,* 1978, *24,* 253–257.

Marler, P. R. The structure of animal communication sounds. In T. H. Bullock (Ed.), *Recognition of complex acoustic signals* (see Bullock, above), 17–35.

McGurk, H., & MacDonald, J. Hearing lips and seeing voices. *Nature,* 1976, *264,* 746–748.

McKusick, V. A. *Cardiovascular sound in health and disease.* Baltimore, Md.: Williams & Wilkins Co., 1958.

Mendelson, M. J., & Haith, M. M. The relation between audition and vision in the human newborn. *Monographs of the Society for Research in Child Development,* 1976, *41,* (167).

Mills, A. W. Auditory localization. In J. V. Tobias (Ed.), *Foundations of modern auditory theory* (Vol. 2). New York: Academic Press, 1972, 303–348.

Muir, D., & Field, J. Newborn infants orient to sound. *Child Development.* 1979, *50,* 431–436.

Neff, W. D. Localization and lateralization of sound in space. In A. V. S. De Renck & J. Knight (Eds.), *Ciba Foundation Symposium on Hearing Mechanisms in Vertebrates.* London: Churchill, 1968, 207–233.

Neuweiller, G. Recognition mechanisms in echolocation of bats. In T. H. Bullock (Ed.), *Recognition of complex acoustic signals* (see Bullock, above). 111–126.

Newman, J. D. Biological filtering and neural mechanisms: Group report. In T. H. Bullock (Ed.), *Recognition of complex acoustic signals* (see Bullock, above), 279–306.

Owings, D. H., & Leger, D. W. Chatter vocalizations of California ground squirrels: Predator and social-role specificity. *Zeitschrift für Tierpsychologie,* 1980, *54,* 163–184.

Payne, R. S. Acoustic location of prey by barn owls (Tyto alba). *Journal of Experimental Biology,* 1971, *56,* 535–573.

Payne, R. S., & Drury, W. J., Jr. Marksman of the darkness. *Natural History,* 1958, *67,* 316–323.

Reynolds, P. C. Comments on Marler's paper. In J. F. Kavanagh & J. E. Cutting (Eds.), *The role of speech in language.* Cambridge, Mass.: MIT Press, 1975, 38–40.

Rice, C. E. Human echo location. *Science,* 1967, *155,* 656–664.

Rice, C. E., & Feinstein, S. H. Sonar system of the blind: Size discrimination. *Science,* 1965, *148,* 1107–1108.

Roeder, K. D. Auditory system of noctuid moths. *Science,* 1966, *154,* 1515–1521.

Scheich, H. Central processing of complex sounds and feature analysis. In T. H. Bullock (Ed.), *Recognition of complex acoustic signals* (see Bullock, above), 161–182.

Schroeder, M. R. Machine processing of acoustic signals: What machines can do better than organisms (and vice versa). In T. H. Bullock (Ed.), *Recognition of complex acoustic signals* (see Bullock, above), 183–207.

Schubert, E. D. The role of auditory perception in language processing. In D. D. Duane & M. B. Rawson (Eds.), *Reading, perception, and language.* Baltimore: York Press, 1974.

Seyfarth, R. M., & Cheney, D. L. The ontogeny of vervet monkey alarm calling behavior: A preliminary report. *Zeitschrift für Tierpsychologie,* 1980, *54,* 37–56.

Seyfarth, R. M., Cheney, D. L., & Marler, P. Monkey responses to three different alarm calls: Evidence of predator classification and semantic communication. *Science,* 1980, *210,* 801–803.

Simmons, J. A. Localization and identification of acoustic signals, with reference to echolocation: Group report. In T. H. Bullock (Ed.), *Recognition of complex acoustic signals* (see Bullock, above), 239–277.

Spelke, E. Infants' intermodal perception of events, *Cognitive Psychology,* 1976, *8,* 553–560.

Spelke, E. Perceiving bimodally specified events in infancy. *Developmental Psychology,* 1979, *15,* 626–636.

Struhsaker, T. T. Auditory communication among vervet monkeys (cercopithecus aethiops). In S. A. Altmann (Ed.), *Social Communication Among Primates.* Chicago: University of Chicago Press, 1967, 281–324.

Supa, M., Cotzin, M., & Dallenbach, K. M. "Facial vision": The perception of obstacles by the blind. *American Journal of Psychology,* 1944, *57,* 133–183.

Van Derveer, N. J. *Acoustic information for event perception.* Paper presented at E. J. Gibson Celebration, Cornell University, June, 1979.

Walker, A. S. *The perception of facial and vocal expressions by human infants.* Doctoral dissertation, Cornell University, 1980.

Warren, W. H. Jr., & Verbrugge, R. R. Auditory information for breaking and bouncing events: A case study in ecological acoustics. *Haskins Laboratories: Status Report on Speech Research,* SR–67/68, 1981, 223–240.

Worchel, P., & Dallenbach, K. M. "Facial vision": Perception of obstacles by the deaf-blind *American Journal of Psychology,* 1947, *60,* 502–553.

8

Perceiving Phonetic Events

Michael Studdert-Kennedy
*Queens College and Graduate Center
City University of New York
and
Haskins Laboratories
New Haven, Connecticut*

In her report on the auditory processing of speech, prepared for the Ninth International Congress of Phonetic Sciences in Copenhagen, Chistovich (1980) wrote of herself and her colleagues at the Pavlov Institute in Leningrad: "We believe that the only way to describe human speech perception is to describe not the perception itself, but the artificial speech understanding system which is most compatible with the experimental data obtained in speech perception research" (p. 71). Chistovich went on to doubt that psychologists would agree with her, but I suspect that many may find her view quite reasonable. However, they would probably not find the view reasonable, if we were to replace the words "speech perception" and "artifical speech understanding system" with the words "speech production" and "speech synthesis system". Perhaps that is because even an articulatory synthesizer does not look like a vocal tract, while our image of what goes on in the head is so vague that we can seriously entertain the notion that a network of inorganic plastic and wire might be made to operate on the same general principles as an organic network of blood and nerves.

Of course, this is impossible, not only because the physics and chemistry of organic and inorganic substances are different, but because machines and animals have different origins. A machine is an artifact. Its maker designs the parts for particular functions and assembles them according to a plan. The machine then operates on principles that its maker knows and has made explicit in the plan. The development of an animal is just the reverse. There is no plan. The animal exists before its parts and the parts emerge by differentiation. In the

139

human fetus, a hand (say) buds from the emerging arm, swells and gradually, by cell death and other processes, differentiates into digits. There is no reason to suppose that the principles of behavioral development are different from those of morphological development. On the contrary, structure and function are deeply intertwined in both evolution and ontogeny. Behavior emerges by differentiation, according to principles implicit in the animal's form and substance.

In short, the appropriate constraints on a model of human speech perception are biological. The model must be compatible with what we know of speech acquisition and of speech perception and production. The first, because the origin of structure in the infant determines its function in the adult. The second, because what the infant hears determines what the infant says; and if perception is to guide production, the two processes must be, in some sense, isomorphic.

An artificial speech understanding system is therefore of limited interest to the student of human speech perception. Such a device necessarily develops in the opposite direction to the human that it is intended to mimic. For while the human infant must discover the segments of its language—words, syllables, phonemes—from their specification in the signal, the machine is granted these segments a priori by its makers. As a model of speech perception, the machine is tautologous and empty of explanatory content, because it necessarily contains only what its makers put in. Unfortunately, all our models of speech perception are essentially machine models.

What theories of event perception have to offer to the study of language, in general, and of speech perception, in particular, is a framework for a biological alternative to such models. Three aspects of the approach seem promising. First is the commitment to discovering the physical invariances that support perception, with an emphasis on the time-varying properties of events. Second is the view of event perception as amodal, independent of the sensory system by which information is gathered. This is important for several reasons, not least for the light it may throw on the bases of imitation and on the underlying capacities common to the perception of signed and spoken language. The third aspect is the general commitment to deriving cognitive process from physical principles and thus, for language, to understanding how its structure emerges from and is constrained by its modes of production and perception.

None of these viewpoints is entirely new to the study of speech perception. What is new is their possible combination in a unified approach. I will briefly discuss each aspect, but before I do, I must lay out certain general properties of language and central problems of speech perception.

LANGUAGE STRUCTURE

As a system of animal communication, language has the distinctive property of being open, that is, fitted to carrying messages on an unlimited range of topics.

Certainly, human cognitive capacity is greater than that of other animals, but this may be a consequence as much as a cause of linguistic range. Other primate communication systems have a limited referential scope—sources of food or danger, personal and group identity, sexual inclination, emotional state, and so on—and a limited set of no more than 10–40 signals (Wilson, 1975, p. 183). In fact, 10–40 holistically distinct signals may be close to the upper range of primate perceptual and motor capacity. The distinctive property of language is that it has finessed that upper limit, by developing a double structure, or dual pattern (Hockett, 1958).

The two levels of patterning are phonology and syntax. The first permits us to develop a large lexicon, the second permits us to deploy the lexicon in predicating relations among objects and events (Liberman & Studdert-Kennedy, 1978; Studdert-Kennedy, 1981). My present concern is entirely with the first level. A six-year-old middle-class American child already recognizes some 13,000 words (Templin, 1957), while an adult's recognition vocabulary may be well over 100,000. Every language, however primitive the culture of its speakers by Western standards, deploys a large lexicon. This is possible because the phonology, or sound pattern, of a language draws on a small set (roughly between 20 and 100 elements) of meaningless units—consonants and vowels—to construct a very large set of meaningful units, words (or morphemes). These meaningless units may themselves be described in terms of a smaller set of recurrent, contrasting phonetic properties or distinctive features. Evidently, there emerged in our hominid ancestors a combinatorial principle (later, perhaps, extended into syntax) by which a finite set of articulatory gestures could be repeatedly permuted to produce a very large number of distinctively different patterns.

Let me note, in passing, that manual sign languages have an analogous dual structure. I do not have the space to discuss this matter in any detail. However, we have learned over the past 10–15 years that American Sign Language (ASL), the first language of over 100,000 deaf persons, and the fourth most common language in the United States (Mayberry, 1978), is a fully independent language with its own characteristic formational (''phonological'') structure and syntax (Klima & Bellugi, 1979). Whether signed language is merely an analog of spoken language (related as the bat's wing to the bird's) or a true homolog, drawing on the same underlying neural structures, we do not know. But there can be no doubt that as we come to understand the structure, function, acquisition and neuropsychological underpinnings of sign language, what we learn will profoundly condition our view of the biological status of language, in general.

Here, returning to my theme, I note simply that each ASL sign is formed by combining four intrinsically meaningless components: a hand configuration, a palm orientation, a place in the body space where it is formed, and a movement. There are some fifty values, or ''primes'', distributed across these four dimensions and their combination in a sign follows ''phonological rules'', analogous to those that constrain the structure of a syllable in spoken languages. In short, both spoken and signed languages exploit combinatorial principles of lexical formation. Their sublexical structures seem to ". . . provide a kind of impedance match between an open-ended set of meaningful symbols and a decidedly limited set of signaling devices" (Studdert-Kennedy & Lane, 1980, p. 35).

THE ANISOMORPHISM PARADOX

If words are indeed formed from strings of consonants and vowels, and signs from simultaneous combinations of primes, we must suppose that the listener, or viewer, somehow finds these elements in the signal. Yet from the first spectrographic descriptions of speech (Joos, 1948), two puzzling facts have been known. First, the signal cannot be divided into a neat sequence of units corresponding to the consonants and vowels of the message: At every instant, the form of the signal is determined by gestures associated with several neighboring elements. Second, as an automatic consequence of this, the acoustic patterns associated with a particular segment vary with their phonetic context. The apparent lack of invariant segments in the signal matching the invariant segments of perception constitutes the anisomorphism paradox.

The recalcitrance of the problem is reflected in the current state of the arts of speech synthesis and automatic speech recognition. Weaving a coherent, continuous pattern from a set of discrete instructions is evidently easier than recovering the discrete instructions from a continuous pattern. Speech synthesis has thus developed to a point where a variety of systems, taking a sequence of discrete phonetic symbols as input and offering a coherent, perceptually tolerable sequence of words as output, is already in use. By contrast, automatic speech recognition is still, after thirty years of research, at its beginning. Current devices recognize limited vocabularies of no more than about a thousand words. Moreover, the words must be spoken carefully, usually by a single speaker, in a small set of syntactic frames, and be confined to a limited topic of discourse. None of these devices approaches within orders of magnitude the performance of a normal human listener.

We may gain insight into why automatic speech recognition has so far failed from the corollary fact that no one has yet succeeded in devising an acceptable acoustic substitute for speech. In the burst of technological enthusiasm that followed World War II, a characteristic endeavor was to construct a sound alphabet that might substitute for spoken sounds in a reading machine for the blind. Of the dozens of codes tested, none was more successful than Morse Code, which a highly skilled operator can follow at a rate of about 35 words a minute, as against the 150–200 words a minute of normal speech. Yet with a visual alphabet reading rates of 300–400 words a minute are commonplace. Why should this be?

Part of the answer perhaps lies in differences between seeing and hearing. Eyes comfortably scan a spatial array of static, discrete objects for information; ears are attuned to dynamic patterns of spectral change over time rather than to the abrupt "dots and dashes" of an arbitrary code. Speech has evidently evolved to distribute the acoustic information that specifies its discrete phonetic segments in patterns of change that match the ear's capacities. Yet, ironically, theories of speech perception, like the models implicit in automatic speech recognition devices, have all assumed that the signal is a collection of more or less discrete cues or properties. Not surprisingly, with this cryptoalphabetic assumption, these theories then have difficulty in recovering an integrated percept.

Resolving The Paradox

There are two possible lines of resolution of the paradox. We may reformulate our definition of the perceptual units or we may recast our description of the acoustic signal. In what follows, I will briefly sketch two current approaches which, extended and combined, may lead toward a resolution along both these lines.

Note, first, that we cannot abandon the concept of the phoneme sized phonetic segment, and the features that describe it, without abandoning the sound structure and dual pattern on which language is premised. Moreover, there is ample evidence from historical patterns of sound change (e.g., Lehmann, 1973), errors in production (Fromkin, 1980), errors in perception (Bond & Garnes, 1980), aphasic deficit (Blumstein, 1978) and, not least, the existence of the alphabet, that the phoneme is a functional element in both speaking and listening (for fuller discussion, see Liberman & Studdert-Kennedy, 1978). What we can abandon, however, is the notion of the phoneme sized phonetic segment as a static, timeless unit. We can attempt to recast it as a synergistic pattern of articulatory gesture, specified in the acoustic signal by spectrally and temporally distributed patterns of change.

Here, it may be useful to distinguish between the information in a spoken utterance and in its written counterpart (a similar distinction is drawn in another context by Carello, Turvey, Kugler, & Shaw, 1983). Both speech and writing may serve to control a speaker's output: We may ask a subject either to repeat the words he hears or to read aloud their alphabetic transcription, and the two spoken outcomes will be essentially identical. But the information that the subject uses to control his output is quite different in the two cases.

The form of the spoken utterance is not arbitrary: Its acoustic structure is a necessary consequence of the articulatory gestures that shaped it. In other words, its acoustic structure *specifies* those gestures, and the human listener has no difficulty in reading out the specifications, and thus organizing his own articulations to accord with those of the utterance. By contrast, the form of the written transcription is an arbitrary convention that specifies nothing. Rather, it is a set of instructions that *indicate* to the reader what he is to do, but do not specify how he is to do it (Carello et al., 1983; Turvey, personal communication). A road sign indicates "Stop," a tennis coach instructs us, "Keep your eye on the ball," but neither tells us how to do it. Their instructions are chosen to symbolize actions presumed to be in the repertoires of motorists and tennis players. If these actions were not in their repertoires, the instructions would be useless. Similarly, the elements of a transcription—whether words, syllables, or phonemes—are chosen to symbolize actions presumed to be in the repertoires of speakers. If they were not in their repertoires the instructions would be useless. Our task is therefore to describe those actions and to understand how they are specified in the flow of speech.

Thirty years of research with synthetic speech have demonstrated that the speech signal is replete with independently manipulable "cues", which, if varied appropriately, change the phonetic percept. Two puzzling facts emerge from this work. (See Repp, 1982, for an extensive review.) First, every phonetic distinction seems to be signaled by many different cues. Therefore, to demonstrate that a particular cue is effective, we must set other cues in the synthesis program at neutral (that is, ambiguous) values. We then discover the second puzzle, namely, that equivalent, indiscriminable percepts may arise from quite different combinations of contexts and cues. Thus, Bailey and Summerfield (1980) showed that perceived place of articulation of an English stop consonant /p, t, k/, induced by a brief silence between /s/ and a following vowel (as in /spu/ or /ski/), depends on the length of the silence, on spectral properties at the offset of /s/, and on the relation between those properties and those of the following vowel. How are we to understand the perceptual equivalence of variations in the spectral structure of a vowel and in the duration of the silence that precedes it? More important, how are we to understand the integration of many spectrally and temporally scattered cues into a unitary percept?

The quandary was recognized and a rationale for its solution proposed some years ago by Lisker and Abramson (1964, 1971). They pointed out that the diverse array of cues that separate so-called voiced and voiceless initial stop consonants in many languages—plosive release energy, aspiration energy, first formant onset frequency—were all consequences of variations in timing of the onset of laryngeal vibration with respect to plosive release, that is, voice onset time (VOT).

> Laryngeal vibration provides the periodic or quasi-periodic carrier that we call voicing. Voicing yields harmonic excitation of a low frequency band during closure, and of full formant pattern after release of the stop. Should the onset of voicing be delayed until some time after the release, however, there will be an interval between release and voicing onset when the relatively unimpeded air rushing through the glottis will provide the turbulent excitation of a voiceless carrier commonly called aspiration. This aspiration is accompanied by considerable attenuation of the first formant, an effect presumably to be ascribed to the presence

of the tracheal tube below the open glottis. Finally, the intensity of the burst, that is, the transient shock excitation of the oral cavity upon release of the stop, may vary depending on the pressures developed behind the stop closure. Thus it seems reasonable to suppose that all these acoustic features, despite their physical dissimilarities, can be ascribed ultimately to actions of the laryngeal mechanism. (Abramson & Lisker, 1965, p. 1)

If, now, we extend this principle of articulatory coherence to other collections of cues for other phonetic features—for which, to be sure, the details have not yet been worked out—we can, at least, see how the cues may originate, and may even cohere perceptually as recurrent acoustic patterns. Moreover, we have a view of the perceptual object—consistent with Gibson's (1966, 1979) principles—as an event that modulates acoustic energy. In other words, the perceptual object is a pattern of gesture perceived directly by means of its radiated sound, or, if we are watching the movements of a signing hand, by means of a pattern of reflected light. This view, developed at Haskins Laboratories over the past 30 years, takes a step toward resolving the anisomorphism paradox by treating the perceptual object as a dynamic event rather than a static unit, but does nothing to address the problems of invariance and segmentation in the acoustic signal. For this we must turn to the work of Stevens (1972, 1975) and of Stevens and Blumstein (1978; Blumstein & Stevens, 1979, 1980).

Stevens' (1972, 1975) approach is entirely consistent with Gibson's view that "Phonemes are in the air" (Gibson, 1966, p. 94), in other words, that the acoustic signal carries invariant segments isomorphic with our phonetic percepts. For Stevens, the perceptual elements are the features of distinctive feature theory (Jakobson, Fant, & Halle, 1963). He has adopted an explicitly evolutionary approach to the link between production and perception by positing that features have come to occupy those acoustic spaces where, by calculations from a vocal tract model, relatively large articulatory variations have little acoustic effect, and to be bounded by regions where small articulatory changes have a large acoustic effect. (As a simple example, the reader might test the acoustic consequences of whispering the word *east,* moving slowly from the high front vowel /i/ through the alveolar fricative /s/ to the alveolar stop /t/.)

Most of Steven's work in recent years has been concerned with acoustic properties that specify place of articulation in stop consonants, for the good reason that the acoustic correlates of this feature have seemed particularly labile and subject to contextual variation (Liberman, Cooper, Shankweiler, & Studdert-Kennedy, 1967). For example, in a well-known series of studies (Stevens & Blumstein, 1978; Blumstein & Stevens, 1979, 1980), Stevens and Blumstein derived by acoustic analysis a set of three "templates", characterizing the gross spectral structure at onset, integrated over the first 26 milliseconds (msec) after stop release, for the three syllable-initial English stop consonants [b,d,g]. They described the templates in the terminology of distinctive feature theory as diffuse-falling for [b], diffuse-rising for [d], compact for [g]. They tested the perceptual effectiveness of these brief, static spectra by synthesis, before or as part of either steady or moving formant transitions in three vowel environments, [i,a,u]. The studies are too complex and subtly devised for summary here, but the general outcome was that most subjects were able to identify the stops with 80%-100% accuracy from the first 20–30 msec after consonant onset. Nonetheless, accuracy did vary with vowel environment and, in some syllables, subjects evidently made use of what Blumstein and Stevens term "secondary" properties, such as formant transitions, to identify the consonants.

Before we examine the implications of this last fact, we should note three important aspects of this approach to the invariance problem. First, in accord with distinctive feature theory and with the acoustic analyses of Fant (1960, 1973), Stevens and Blumstein assume that phonetic information is primarily given in the entire spectral array. "Cues" are not extracted; rather, the phonetic segment is directly specified by the signal. Second, the weight assigned to the spectrum at onset is justified by recent evidence from auditory physiology (e.g., Delgutte, 1982; Kiang, 1980; Chistovich, Lublinskaya, Malinnikova, Ogorodnikova, Stoljarova, & Zhukov, 1982) that the (cat) ear is particularly sensitive to abrupt spectral discontinuities, and that the number of fibers responding to the input is increased immediately following such a discontinuity. Third, Stevens and Blumstein acknowledge the role of "secondary"—and potentially context-dependent—sources of information in patterns of spectral change (i.e., formant transitions), but attempt to exclude them by positing innate property detectors. These detectors filter out the secondary properties, it is said, and enable an infant to extract the "primary" invariances, leaving the secondary properties to be learned from their cooccurrence with the primary (Stevens & Blumstein, 1978, p. 1367).

Here, in this third aspect, we see that Stevens and Blumstein have not, in fact, completely freed their theory of perceptual atomism. By dividing the properties into "primary" and "secondary", they slip back into requiring some process of perceptual integration, accomplished, they propose, by the tautological process of "cooccurrence" or association. Moreover, the detectors themselves are purely ad hoc, tautologous entities (or processes) for which there is no *independent* evidence: Their existence is inferred from the fact that infants and adults respond in a particular way to stimuli that may be described as having certain properties. If we have learned nothing else from behaviorist philosophy, we should at least have learned to eschew the "Conceptual Nervous System."

Yet the detectors are supererogatory to the enterprise that Stevens and Blumstein are launched upon. The importance of their work is that they have taken the first systematic, psycholinguistically motivated, steps toward describing the invariant acoustic properties of a notoriously context-dependent class of phonetic segments. What is missing from their approach is not an imaginary physiological device, but a recognition that the signal is no more a sequence of static spectral sections than it is a collection of isolated cues. Rather the signal reflects a dynamic articulatory event of which the invariances must lie in a pattern of change.

And, indeed, moves toward this recognition have already begun. Kewley-Port (1980, 1983) has shown that an invariant pattern may be found in running spectra at stop consonant onset, and that identification accuracy for synthetic stop sylla- bles improves, if they are synthesized from running spectra, updated at 5 msec intervals, rather than from static spectra sustained over 26 msec (Kewley-Port, Pisoni, & Studdert-Kennedy, 1983). Blumstein, Isaacs, and Mertus (1982) have found that the perceptually effective invariant may lie, not in the gross spectral shape, as originally hypothesized, but in the pattern of formant frequencies at onset. This suggests that characteristic formant shifts of the kind described in the earliest synthetic speech studies (e.g., Liberman, Delattre, Cooper, & Gerstman, 1954) may yet prove to play a role: for example, an upward shift in the low frequencies for labials, a downward shift in the high frequencies for alveolars. In fact, Lahiri and Blumstein (1981) report a cross-language (English, French, Malayalam) acoustic analysis of labial, dental and alveolar stops that seems to be consistent with this hypothesis. The distinctions were carried by maintenance or shift in the relative weights of high and low frequencies from consonant release over the first three glottal pulses at voicing onset. All these studies move toward a dynamic rather than a static description of speech invariants.

We may see then, in (distant) prospect, a fruitful merger, consistent with theories of event perception, by which invariances in the acoustic signal are discovered as coherent patterns of spectral change, specifying a synergism of underlying articulatory gestures. From such a resolution of the invariance para- dox there would follow a resolution of the segmentation paradox. For implicit in a view of the perceptual object as a coherent event is a view of "cues", "fea- tures" and, indeed, "phonemes" as descriptive, rather than substantive, catego- ries of speech. The utility of features and phonemes for describing the structure of spoken languages would remain, as would—in some not yet clearly formu- lated sense—the functional role of the phoneme sized phonetic segment in the organization of an utterance. But phonemes and features in perception would be seen, in origin, not as substantive categories, formed by specialized categorical mechanisms, but as emergent properties of recurrent acoustic pattern. As we will see later, this view of perception is coordinate with current research into the origins of phonological systems.

IMITATION AND THE AMODALITY OF SPEECH PERCEPTION

Let us turn now to another body of research that encourages a view of speech perception as a particular type of event perception: research on lip reading in adults and infants. The importance of this work is that it promises to throw light on imitation, a process fundamental to the acquisition of speech.

The story begins with the discovery by McGurk and MacDonald (1976; MacDonald & McGurk, 1978) that subjects' perceptions of a spoken syllable often change, if they simultaneously watch a video display of a speaker pronouncing a different syllable. For example, if subjects hear the syllable [ba] repeated four times, while watching a synchronized video display of a speaker articulating [ba, va, ða, da], they will typically report the latter sequence. This is not simply a matter of visual dominance in a sensory hierarchy, familiar from many intermodal studies (Marks, 1978). Nor is it a matter of combining phonetic features independently extracted from acoustic and optic displays—for example, voicing from the acoustic, place of articulation from the optic. For, although voicing is indeed specified acoustically, place of articulation may be specified both optically and acoustically, as when subjects report a consonant cluster or some merged element. Thus, presented with acoustic [ba] and optic [ga], subjects often report [b'ga], [g'ba] or a merger, [da]. (See Summerfield, 1979 for fuller discussion).

The latter effect was used in an ingenious experiment by Roberts and Summerfield (1981) to demonstrate that speech adaptation is an auditory not a phonetic process, and, more important for the present discussion, to show that auditory and phonetic processes in perception can be dissociated. The standard adaptation paradigm, devised by Eimas and Corbit (1973), asks listeners to classify syllables drawn from a synthetic acoustic continuum, stretching from, say [ba] to [da], or [ba] to [pa], both before and after repeated exposure to (that is, adaptation with) one or other of the endpoint syllables. The effect of adaptation, reported in several dozen studies (see Eimas & Miller, 1978 for review), is that listeners perceive significantly fewer tokens from the continuum as instances of the syllable with which they have been adapted.

Roberts and Summerfield (1981) followed this paradigm with a synthetic series of syllables ranging from [bɛ] to [dɛ]. Their novel twist was to include a condition in which subjects were adapted audiovisually by an acoustic [bɛ], synchronized with an optic [gɛ], intended to be perceived phonetically as [dɛ]. In the event, six of their 12 subjects reported the adapting syllable as either [dɛ] or [ðɛ], four as [klɛ], one as [flɛ], one as [ma]. Not a single subject reported the phonetic event corresponding to the adapting acoustic syllable actually presented, [bɛ]. Yet, after adaptation, every subject displayed a drop in the number of tokens identified as [bɛ], roughly equal to the drop for the control condition in which acoustic [bɛ] was presented alone. Thus, while subjects' auditory systems were normally adapted by the acoustic input, their conscious phonetic percepts were specified intermodally by a blend of acoustic and optic information.

We might extend the demonstration that phonetic perception is intermodal (or, better, amodal) by citing the Tadoma method in which the deaf-blind learn to perceive speech by touch, with fingers on the lips and neck of the speaker. Tactile information may even help to guide a deaf-blind individual's own articulation (Norton, Schultz, Reed, Braida, Durlach, Rabinowitz, & Chomsky, 1977). But the lip-reading studies alone suffice to raise the question of the dimensions of the phonetic percept. The acoustic information is presumably carried by the familar pattern of formants, friction noise, plosive release, harmonic variation and so on; the optic information is carried by varying configurations of the lips and, perhaps, of the tongue and teeth (Summerfield, 1979). But how are these qualitatively distinct patterns of light and sound combined to yield an integrated percept? What we need is some underlying metric common to both the light reflected and the sound radiated from mouth and lips (Summerfield, 1979). Such a notion will hardly surprise students of action and of event perception (e.g., Fowler, Rubin, Remez, & Turvey, 1980; Runeson & Frykholm, 1981; Summerfield, 1980). But, as I have already suggested, it is worth pursuing a little further for the light that it may throw on the bases of imitation.

Consider, first, that infants are also sensitive to structural correspondences between the acoustic and optic specifications of an event. Spelke (1976) showed that 4-month-old infants preferred to watch the film (of a woman playing "peekaboo," or of a hand rhythmically striking a wood block and a tambourine with a baton) that matched the sound track they were hearing. Dodd (1979) showed that 4-month-old infants watched the face of a woman reading nursery rhymes more attentively, when her voice was synchronized with her facial movements than when it was delayed by 400 msecs. If these preferences were merely for synchrony, we might expect infants to be satisfied with any acoustic-optic pattern in which moments of abrupt change are arbitrarily synchronized. Thus, in speech they might be no less attentive to an articulating face whose closed mouth was synchronized with syllable amplitude peaks and open mouth with amplitude troughs than to the (natural) reverse. However, Kuhl and Meltzoff (1982) showed that 4–5 month old infants looked longer at the face of a woman articulating the vowel they were hearing (either [i] or [a]) than at the same face articulating the other vowel *in synchrony*. Moreover, the preference disappeared when the signals were pure tones, matched in amplitude and duration to the vowels, so that the infant preference was evidently for a match between a mouth shape and a particular spectral structure. Similarly, MacKain, Studdert-Kennedy, Spieker, and Stern (1983) showed that 5–6 month old infants preferred to look at the face of a woman repeating the disyllable they were hearing (e.g., [zuzi]) than at the synchronized face of the same woman repeating another disyllable (e.g., [vava]). In both these studies, the infants' preferences were for natural structural correspondences between acoustic and optic information.

Interestingly, in the study by MacKain et al. (in press), the infants' preferences were only statistically significant when the infants were looking to their right sides. Kinsbourne (1973) has proposed that attention to one side of the body activates the contralateral hemisphere and facilitates processes for which that hemisphere is specialized. Given the well-known specialization of the left hemisphere for motor control of speech, we might suspect that these infants were displaying a left-hemisphere sensitivity to intermodal correspondences that could play a role in learning to speak. This hypothesis would gain support if we could establish that the underlying metric of auditory-visual correspondence was the same as that of the auditory-motor correspondence required for an individual to repeat or ''imitate'' the utterances of another.

To this end we may note, first, the visual-motor link evidenced in the capacity to imitate facial expression and, second, the association across many primate species between facial expression and pattern of vocalization (Marler, 1975; Hooff, 1976; Ohala, in press). Recently, Field, Woodson, Greenberg, and Cohen (1982) reported that 36-hour old infants could imitate the ''happy, sad and surprised'' expressions of a model. However, these are relatively stereotyped emotional responses that might be evoked without recourse to the visual-motor link required for imitation of novel movements. More striking is the work of Meltzoff and Moore (1977) who showed that 12–21 day old infants could imitate both arbitrary mouth movements, such as tongue protrusion and mouth opening, and (of particular interest for the acquisition of ASL) arbitrary hand movements, such as opening and closing the hand by serially moving the fingers. Here mouth opening was elicited without vocalization; but had vocalization occurred, its structure would, of course, have reflected the shape of the mouth. Kuhl and Meltzoff (1982) do, in fact, report as an incidental finding of their study of intermodal preferences, that 10 of their 32 4–5 month old infants ''. . . produced sounds that resembled the adult female's vowels. They seemed to be imitating the female talker, ''taking turns'' by alternating their vocalizations with hers'' (p. 1140). If we accept the evidence that the infants of this study were recognizing acoustic-optic correspondences, and add to it the results of the adult lip-reading studies, calling for a metric in which acoustic and optic information are combined, then we may conclude that the perceptual structure controlling the infants' imitations was specified in this common metric.

Evidently, the desired metric must be ''. . . closely related to that of articulatory dynamics'' (Summerfield, 1979, p. 329). Following Runeson and Frykholm (1981) (see also Summerfield, 1980), we may suppose that in the visual perception of an event we perceive not simply the surface kinematics (displacement, velocity, acceleration), but also the underlying biophysical properties that define the structure being moved and the forces that move it (mass, force, momentum, elasticity, and so on). Similarly, in perceiving speech, we do not simply perceive its ''kinematics'', that is, the changes and rates of change in spectral structure, but the underlying dynamic forces that produce these changes. Some such formulation is demanded by the facts of imitation on which the learning of speech and language rests.

ORIGINS OF THE SOUND PATTERN OF LANGUAGE

We come finally to a third aspect of current phonetic study, compatible with theories of action and event perception. The goal of the work to be discussed may be simply stated: to derive language from nonlanguage. The topic is broad and complex. My comments here are brief, no more than a sketch of the approach.

As we have seen, every language builds its words or signs from a small set of meaningless elements, its phonemes or primes. These elements are themselves constructed from a small set of contrasting properties or distinctive features. For modern phonology, phonemes (or syllables) and their constitutive features are axiomatic primitives that require no explanation (Jakobson, Fant, & Halle, 1963; Chomsky & Halle, 1968). A central goal of linguistic study is to describe a small set of 15–20 "given" or "universal" features that will serve to describe the phonological systems of every known language. The goal has proved difficult to achieve, in large part because the various sets of features that have been proposed as potential systemic components have lacked external constraints—for example, physiological constraints on their combination (Ladefoged, 1971).

If there is indeed a universal set of linguistic features that owes nothing to the nonlinguistic capacities of talkers and listeners, their biological origin must be due to some quantal evolutionary jump, a structure producing mutation. While modern biologists may look more favorably on evolutionary discontinuities than did Darwin (e.g., Gould, 1982), we are not justified in accepting discontinuity until we have ruled continuity out. This has not been done. On the contrary, the primacy of linguistic form has been a cardinal, untested assumption of modern phonology—with the result that phonology is sustained in grand isolation from its surrounding disciplines (Lindblom, 1980).

An alternative approach is to suppose that features and phonemes reflect prior organismic constraints from articulation, perception, memory and learning. Thus, F. S. Cooper proposed that features were shaped by the articulatory machinery. Typical speaking rates of 10 to 15 phonemes per second could ". . . be achieved only if separate parts of the articulatory machinery—muscles of the lips, tongue, velum, etc.—can be separately controlled, and if . . . a change of state for any one of these articulatory entities, taken together with the current state of others, is a change to . . . another phoneme. . . . It is this kind of parallel processing that makes it possible to get high-speed performance with low-speed machinery" (Liberman, Cooper, Shankweiler, & Studdert-Kennedy, 1967, p. 446). A similar view was elaborated by Studdert-Kennedy and Lane (1980) for both signed and spoken language.

The most concerted attack along these lines has been developed over the past decade by Lindblom and his colleagues (e.g., Liljencrants & Lindblom, 1972; Lindblom, 1972, 1980, 1983). Their goal has been not simply to specify the articulatory and acoustic correlates of certain distinctive features (as in the work of Stevens and Blumstein, discussed previously), but to show how a *self-organizing* system of features and phonemes may arise from perceptual and motoric constraints.

The early work (Lindblom, 1972) began by specifying a possible vowel as a point in acoustic space, defined by the set of formant frequencies associated with states of the lips, tongue, jaw and larynx. A computer was programmed to search the space for k maximally distinct vowels according to a least squares criterion. The vowels found were then compared with those observed in languages having k vowels: Despite certain obvious deficiencies, the fit of the predicted to the observed data was remarkably good. Later studies (e.g., Lindblom, 1983) have improved the fit by incorporating the results of work in auditory psychophysics (cf. Bladon & Lindblom, 1981), together with certain articulatory constraints, and by relaxing the search criterion to one of "sufficient" rather than maximum distinctness. The last move permits more than one solution for a k-vowel system, as indeed the observed language data require. For the present discussion, the most interesting outcome is that the derived sets of vowels form systems that invite description in terms of standard features, despite the fact that the notion "feature" was never at any point introduced into the derivation.

Recently, Lindblom has extended the procedure to derive the phoneme from sets of consonant-vowel trajectories through the acoustic space between consonant and vowel loci (Lindblom, MacNeilage, & Studdert-Kennedy, 1983, forthcoming). This work brings to bear both talker constraints (sensory discriminability, preference for less extreme articulation) and listener constraints (perceptual distance, perceptual salience) to select the syllable trajectories. Again, the interesting outcome is that when a set of trajectories is selected from a large number of possible trajectories, the syllables are not, as they might well have been, holistically distinct: Each chosen syllable does not differ from every other chosen syllable in both consonant and vowel. Rather, a few consonants and a slightly larger number of vowels occur repeatedly, while other consonants and vowel combinations do not occur at all. Thus, just as the feature emerges as a byproduct of phoneme selection, so the phoneme emerges as a byproduct of syllable selection.

This work rests on a number of assumptions that might be challenged (for example, the precise nature of talker and listener based constraints) and on a wealth of phonetic detail that might be questioned. Its importance does not rest on the correctness of its assumptions nor on the accuracy of its predictions—both may, and surely will, be improved in the future. Its importance lies in its style of approach: substance-based rather than formal. For if we are to do the biology of language at all, it will have to be done by tracing language to its roots in the anatomy, physiology and social environment of its users. Only in this way can we hope to arrive at an account of language perception and production fitted to animals rather than machines.

ACKNOWLEDGEMENTS

Preparation of this chapter was supported in part by NICHD Grant No. HD–01994 to Haskins Laboratories. I thank my teachers in these matters: Carol Fowler, Scott Kelso, Alvin Liberman, Björn Lindblom, Sverker Runeson, Quentin Summerfield and Michael Turvey. My thanks also to Bruno Repp for much stimulating discussion, and to Nancy Frishberg for providing a simultaneous translation in American Sign Language of the first portion of the paper, as it was read at the conference.

REFERENCES

Abramson, A. S., & Lisker, L. Voice onset time in stop consonants: Acoustic analysis and synthesis. *Proceedings of the 5th International Congress of Acoustics*, Liege: Imp. G. Thone, 1965.

Bailey, P. J., & Summerfield, Q. Information in speech: Observations on the perception of [s]+stop clusters. *Journal of Experimental Psychology: Human Perception and Performance*, 1980, *6*, 536–563.

Bladon, R. A. W., & Lindblom, B. Modeling the judgment of vowel quality differences. *Journal of the Acoustical Society of America*, 1981, *69*, 1414–1422.

Blumstein, S. E. The perception of speech in pathology and ontogeny. In A. Caramazza & E. B. Zurif (Eds.), *Language acquisition and language breakdown*. Baltimore: Johns Hopkins, 1978.

Blumstein, S. E., Isaacs, E., & Mertus, J. The role of the gross spectral shape as a perceptual cue to place of articulation in initial stop consonants. *Journal of the Acoustical Society of America*, 1982, *72*, 43–50.

Blumstein, S. E., & Stevens, K. N. Acoustic invariance in speech production. *Journal of the Acoustical Society of America*, 1979, *66*, 1001–1017.

Blumstein, S. E., & Stevens, K. N. Perceptual invariance and onset spectra for stop consonants in different vowel environments. *Journal of the Acoustical Society of America*, 1980, *67*, 648–662.

Bond, Z. S., & Garnes, S. Misperceptions of fluent speech. In R. A. Cole (Ed.), *Perception and production of fluent speech*. Hillsdale, N.J.: Lawrence Erlbaum Associates, 1980.

Carello, C., Turvey, M. T., Kugler, P. N., & Shaw, R. E. Inadequacies of the computer metaphor. In M. S. Gazzaniga (Ed.), *Handbook of cognitive neuroscience*. New York: Plenum, 1983.

Chistovich, L. A. Auditory processing of speech. *Language and Speech*, 1980, *23*, 67–75.

Chistovich, L. A., Lublinskaya, V. V., Malinnikova, T. G., Ogorodnikova, E. A., Stoljarova, E. I., & Zhukov, S. Ja. Temporal processing of peripheral auditory patterns. In R. Carlson & B. Granstrom (Eds.), *The representation of speech in the peripheral auditory system*. New York: Elsevier Biomedical Press, 1982.

Chomsky, N., & Halle, M. *The sound pattern of English*. New York: Harper & Row, 1968.

Delgutte, B. Some correlates of phonetic distinctions at the level of auditory nerve. In R. Carlson & B. Granstrom (Eds.), *The representation of speech in the peripheral auditory system*. New York: Elsevier Biomedical Press, 1982.

Dodd, B. Lip reading in infants: Attention to speech presented in- and out-of-synchrony. *Cognitive Psychology*, 1979, *11*, 478–484.

Eimas, P. D., & Corbit, J. D. Selective adaptation of linguistic feature detectors. *Cognitive Psychology*, 1973, *4*, 99–109.

Eimas, P. D., & Miller, J. L. Effects of selective adaptation on the perception of speech and visual patterns: Evidence for feature detectors. In R. D. Walk & H. L. Pick, Jr. (Eds.), *Perception and experience*. New York: Olenum, 1978.

Fant, G. *Acoustic theory of speech production.* The Hague: Mouton, 1960.

Fant, G. *Speech sounds and features.* Cambridge, Mass.: M.I.T. Press, 1973.

Field, T. M., Woodson, R., Greenberg, R., & Cohen, D. Discrimination and imitation of facial expressions by neonates. *Science,* 1982, *218,* 179–181.

Fowler, C. A., Rubin, P., Remez, R. E., & Turvey, M. T. Implications for speech production of a general theory of action. In B. Butterworth (Ed.), *Language production.* New York: Academic Press, 1980.

Fromkin, V. (Ed.) *Errors in linguistic performance: Slips of the tongue, ear, pen and hand.* New York: Academic Press, 1980.

Gibson, J. J. *The senses considered as perceptual systems.* Boston, Mass.: Houghton Mifflin, 1966.

Gibson, J. J. *The ecological approach to visual perception.* Boston: Houghton Mifflin, 1979.

Gould, S. J. Darwinism and the expansion of evolutionary theory. *Science,* 1982, *216,* 380–387.

Hockett, C. *A course in modern linguistics.* New York: Macmillan, 1958.

Hooff, J. A. R. A. M. van The comparison of facial expression in man and higher primates. In M. von Cranach (Ed.), *Methods of inference from human to animal behavior.* Chicago: Aldine, 1976.

Jakobson, R., Fant, C. G. M., & Halle, M. *Preliminaries to speech analysis: The distinctive features and their correlates.* Cambridge, Mass.: MIT, 1963.

Joos, M. Acoustic phonetics. *Language Monograph No. 23,* Vol. 24, Suppl., 1948.

Kewley-Port, D. Representations of spectral change as cues to place of articulation in stop consonants. *Research in Speech Perception, Technical Report No. 3.* Bloomington: Indiana University, Department of Psychology, 1980.

Kewley-Port, D. Time-varying features as correlates of place of articulation in stop consonants. *Journal of the Acoustical Society of America,* 1983, *73,* 322–335.

Kewley-Port, D., Pisoni, D. B., & Studdert-Kennedy, M. Perception of static and dynamic cues to place of articulation in initial stop consonants. *Journal of the Acoustical Society of America,* 1983, *73,* 1779–1793.

Kiang, N. Y. S. Processing of speech by the auditory nervous system. *Journal of the Acoustical Society of America,* 1980, *68,* 830–835.

Kinsbourne, M. The control of attention by interaction between the hemispheres. In S. Kornblum (Ed.), *Attention and performance* (IV). New York: Academic Press, 1973.

Klima, E. S., & Bellugi, U. *The signs of language.* Cambridge, Mass.: Harvard University Press, 1979.

Kuhl, P. K., & Meltzoff, A. N. The bimodal perception of speech in infancy. *Science,* 1982, *218,* 1138–1144.

Ladefoged, P. *Preliminaries to linguistic phonetics.* Chicago: University of Chicago Press, 1971.

Lahiri, A., & Blumstein, S. E. *A reconsideration of acoustic invariance for place of articulation in stop consonants: Evidence from cross-language studies.* Paper read at 102nd Meeting of the Acoustical Society of America, Miami Beach, Fla., November 30–December 4, 1981.

Lehmann, W. P. *Historical linguistics.* New York: Holt, Rinehart, & Winston, 1973.

Liberman, A. M., Cooper, F. S., Shankweiler, D. P., & Studdert-Kennedy, M. Perception of the speech code. *Psychological Review,* 1967, *74,* 431–461.

Liberman, A. M., Delattre, P. C., Cooper, F. S., & Gerstman, L. J. The role of consonant-vowel transitions in the perception of the stop and nasal consonants. *Psychological Monographs,* 1954, *68,* 1–13.

Liberman, A. M., & Studdert-Kennedy, M. Phonetic perception. In R. Held, H. W. Leibowitz, & H.-L. Teuber (Eds.), *Handbook of sensory physiology, Vol. VIII: Perception.* New York: Springer-Verlag, 1978, 143–178.

Liljencrants, J., & Lindblom, B. Numerical simulation of vowel quality systems: The role of perceptual contrast. *Language,* 1972, *48,* 839–862.

Lindblom, B. Phonetics and the description of language. In A. Rigault & R. Charbonneau (Eds.), *Proceedings of the 7th International Phonetics Congress*. The Hague: Mouton, 1972.

Lindblom, B. The goal of phonetics, its unification and application. *Phonetica, 1980, 37,* 7–26.

Lindblom, B. Phonetic universals in vowel systems. In J. Ohala (Ed.), *Experimental phonology.* New York: Academic Press, 1983.

Lindblom, B., MacNeilage, P., & Studdert-Kennedy, M. Self-organizing processes and the explanation of phonological universals. In B. Butterworth, B. Comrie, & O. Dahl (Eds.), *Explanations of linguistic universals*. The Hague: Mouton, 1983.

Lindblom, B., MacNeilage, P., & Studdert-Kennedy, M. *The biological bases of spoken language.* San Francisco: Academic Press, forthcoming.

Lisker, L., & Abramson, A. A cross-language study of voicing in initial stops: Acoustical measurements. *Word, 1964, 20,* 384–422.

Lisker, L., & Abramson, A. S. Distinctive features and laryngeal control. *Language, 1971, 47,* 767–785.

MacDonald, J., & McGurk, H. Visual influences on speech perception processes. *Perception & Psychophysics, 1978, 24,* 253–257.

MacKain, K. S., Studdert-Kennedy, M., Spieker, S., & Stern, D. Infant intermodal speech perception is a left hemisphere function. *Science, 219,* 1347–1349.

Marks, L. E. Multimodal perception. In E. C. Carterette & M. P. Friedman (Eds.), *Handbook of perception, Vol. VIII.* New York: Academic Press, 1978.

Marler, P. On the origin of speech from animal sounds. In J. F. Kavanagh & J. E. Cutting (Eds.), *The role of speech in language*. Cambridge, Mass.: MIT Press, 1975.

Mayberry, R. I. Manual communication. In H. Davis & S. R. Silverman (Eds.), *Hearing and deafness* (4th ed.). New York: Holt, Rinehart, & Winston, 1978.

McGurk, H., & MacDonald, J. Hearing lips and seeing voices. *Nature, 1976, 264,* 746–748.

Meltzoff, A. N., & Moore, M. K. Imitation of facial and manual gestures by human neonates. *Science, 1977, 198,* 175–178.

Norton, S. J., Schultz, M. C., Reed, C. M., Braida, L. D., Durlach, N. I., Rabinowitz, W. M., & Chomsky, C. Analytic study of the Tadoma method: Background and preliminary results. *Journal of Speech and Hearing Research, 1977, 20,* 574–595.

Ohala, J. Cross-language uses of pitch. *Phonetica,* in press.

Repp, B. H. Phonetic trading relations and context effects: New evidence for a phonetic mode of perception. *Psychological Bulletin, 1982, 92,* 81–110.

Roberts, M., & Summerfield, Q. Audiovisual presentation demonstrates that selective adaptation in speech perception is purely auditory. *Perception & Psychophysics, 1981, 30,* 309–314.

Runeson, S., & Frykholm, G. Visual perception of lifted weight. *Journal of Experimental Psychology: Human Perception and Performance, 1981, 7,* 733–740.

Spelke, E. Infants' intermodal perception of events. *Cognitive Psychology, 1976, 8,* 553–560.

Stevens, K. N. The quantal nature of speech: Evidence from articulatory-acoustic data. In E. E. David & P. B. Denes (Eds.), *Human communication: A unified view.* New York: McGraw-Hill, 1972.

Stevens, K. N. The potential role of property detectors in the perception of consonants. In G. Fant & M. A. A. Tatham (Eds.), *Auditory analysis and perception of speech.* New York: Academic Press, 1975.

Stevens, K. N., & Blumstein, S. E. Invariant cues for place of articulation in stop consonants. *Journal of the Acoustical Society of America, 1978, 64,* 1358–1368.

Studdert-Kennedy, M. The beginnings of speech. In K. Immelmann, G. B. Barlow, L. Petrinovich, & M. Main, (Eds.), *Behavioral development: The Bielefeld Interdisciplinary Project.* New York: Cambridge University Press, 1981.

Studdert-Kennedy, M., & Lane, H. Clues from the differences between signed and spoken language. In U. Bellugi & M. Studdert-Kennedy (Eds.), *Signed and spoken language: Biological constraints on linguistic form.* Deerfield Park, Fla.: Verlag Chemie, 1980.

Summerfield, Q. Use of visual information for phonetic perception. *Phonetica,* 1979, *36,* 314–331.

Summerfield, Q. The structuring of language by the requirements of motor control and perception. In U. Bellugi & M. Studdert-Kennedy (Eds.), *Signed and spoken language: Biological constraints on linguistic form.* Deerfield Park, Fla.: Verlag Chemie, 1980, 89–114.

Templin, M. *Certain language skills of children.* Minneapolis: University of Minnesota Press, 1957.

Wilson, E. O. *Sociobiology.* Cambridge: The Belknap Press, 1975.

9 Language and Event Perception: Steps Toward a Synthesis

Robert R. Verbrugge
University of Connecticut

If one pieces together the literature on event perception, one catches glimpses of a world in which objects loom, people walk, wheels roll, heads age, and forms collide. One does not, by and large, catch glimpses of a world in which people think, imagine, and communicate with one another. This cannot (one hopes) reflect a lack of interest in these phenomena, or a low evaluation of their importance. Cognitive and communicative actions are integral to a wide range of events that we perceive and participate in, and thus must be an integral part of the subject matter of event perception.[1] Thought and speech also play an important

---

[1]A note on terminology: The terms *action, event,* and *process* will be used somewhat interchangeably in this paper; they have different, but overlapping, meanings. In colloquial terms, *actions* are things we do. *Communicative actions* include speaking, gesturing, signing, writing, and drawing diagrams; they are essentially social actions, because they are usually done in relation to other people. *Cognitive actions* include thinking, day-dreaming, and recollecting; although these are less perceptible by others, they are not necessarily any less systematic or environmentally constrained than "overt" actions. *Events* are things that happen; they are natural occurrences. *Communicative events* include communicative actions of individuals (speaking, gesturing, etc.), interactions among people (conversations, lectures, plays, insults, etc.), and interactions between people and symbols (e.g., our interactions with texts, diagrams, road signs, or musical scores). All cognitive actions are *cognitive events;* they are no less natural happenings than rolling stones or diving gannets. *Processes* are biological events; the term is meant to emphasize the physiological nature of these events. *Communicative processes* include both the more overt actions of the body (speaking, gesturing, etc.) and the more covert actions of the body (listening, comprehending, preparing to speak, etc.). *Cognitive processes* include thinking, imagining, comprehending, etc. In parallel with James' (1890) approach to the "stream of consciousness," I view *processes* as having dual aspects: continuous and partitioned, transitive and substantive, flying and perching. I do not wish to view thinking or comprehending solely as *achievements* ("acts"). Thus, my use of these terms differs somewhat from that of Shaw and Alley (in press), Warren & Shaw (this volume), Johansson (this volume), and other authors in the event perception field.

role in experiments on event perception, where they can have a powerful influence on how participants perceive displays and report on their experiences.

The relative inattention to cognitive and communicative events seems to stem from a strategic choice to focus first on inanimate and animate events that lend themselves more easily to analysis, and then gradually to extend the approach to more difficult cases. This strategy may prove to be not only laudable, but essential. Even so, given the central role of cognition and communication in human action, it is important at every stage in the development of event perception theory to evaluate the prospects for extending it into the areas of thought and language. In this paper I would like to summarize some of the prospects and problems I see in relating event perception to the comprehension and production of language.

It is common in linguistic theory to view natural languages as having a "duality of patterning" (see Studdert-Kennedy, this volume).[2] At some levels of analysis, one finds permutable units (such as consonants and vowels) that are not individually meaningful. At other levels of analysis, one finds units (such as words and phrases) that do seem inherently meaningful. A similar contrast emerges when one considers speech as an event, rather than an object of structural description. From one perspective, speech is an articulatory event, a patterning of change in the respiratory system, the larynx, and the supralaryngeal articulators (jaw, lips, tongue, etc.). A description of speech at this level can be framed independent (to a large degree) of the meaning of what is being said. From the second perspective, speech is a communicative event and thus is a type of social event. From this perspective, speech is not the action of a vocal system, but of a person in a social setting. At this level of description, an analysis of the meaning or significance of what is being said is essential.

Distinguishing the articulatory and communicative aspects of speech is somewhat artificial, but it may help to identify where the greatest problems lie in applying event perception approaches to language. On the face of it, it would seem relatively easy to apply these approaches to the perception of speech as an articulatory event. Articulation can be thought of as a "source event" that structures the media of sound and light in systematic ways; proper analysis of these media might show them to contain sufficient information for perceiving the linguistically significant aspects of articulation (e.g., those that correspond to consonants, vowels, or syllables). Developing this kind of analysis in detail has not proven easy, of course (for a discussion of the problem, see Studdert-Kennedy, this volume; Fowler, Rubin, Remez, & Turvey, 1980; Verbrugge,

---

[2]Throughout this paper, the terms *language* and *linguistic* refer to "natural languages" (such as English or Swahili), both in spoken and written forms. The terms *communication* and *symbolization* refer, more generally, to any communicative action (involving words, gestures, diagrams, signals, or whatever). *Symbols* are objects and events produced or used as part of communicative actions (e.g., when speaking, writing, drawing, signaling, etc.). Peirce's (1931) use of the term *symbol* is more restricted (see discussion later in this paper); my use of the term is closer to his generic term *sign*.

Rakerd, Fitch, Tuller, & Fowler, in press). Even so, framing at least the outlines of an event approach to articulation does not seem to do violence to the general framework developed for perceiving such events as walking and biological growth.

Extending the principles of event perception to speech as a communicative event is more problematic. To understand this, we need to begin by considering the types of experiences we have when listening to someone else speak. We experience linguistic actions (questioning, describing, proposing, etc.). We experience intentions to affect us (to warn us, console us, give us directions, etc.). We experience aspects of the speaker's emotional state, attitudes, physical and emotional well-being, and so on. We experience changes in our own readiness to perceive, do, and say certain things. When people tell stories, describe plans, give directions, etc., we experience "virtual events" (i.e., we can imagine events that are not coincident in time and space with the communication setting itself). In short, when we are immersed in communication, the "object of perception" is a social event (including the speaker, the setting, and our relation to them). What we experience is even more extensive: It includes not only the social event per se, but an array of virtual events as well. By and large, we are not aware (and have no need to be aware) of the articulatory and acoustic bases for these experiences.

Some aspects of these experiences may succumb naturally to a more-or-less conventional event analysis; for example, the detection of anxiety or happiness in a speaker's voice may be based on systematic acoustic consequences of the effects they have on articulation (e.g., Tartter, 1980). Other aspects seem more difficult; in particular, it is difficult to understand how our imaginings arise. The experiences prompted by language seem to have little or nothing in common with the articulatory events that prompt them. In fact, they may not be similar to any events in the communication setting at all. The basis for these experiences is patterning in sound and light, and yet the experiences are not of that which patterns the sound and light (the person talking). In this important respect, our experience of speech as communicative action seems to demand a process different in kind from the perception of speech as articulation. If so, we have encountered an important problem to overcome when applying event perception analyses to language. The problem extends to other forms of communicative action as well. For example, the gestures of American Sign Language can be characterized in kinematic and optical terms that conceivably provide a specific basis for perceiving the sign *as gesture* (Shaw & Cutting, 1980). But an event analysis written in these terms alone does *not* provide a basis for understanding how the gesture can serve to "constrain and direct another person's thinking" (Shaw & Cutting, 1980, p. 59).

It is possible that these problems arise from the strategy of adopting two divergent perspectives on communication: one viewing it as a physical or biological event, the other viewing it as a (meaningful) social action or experience.

This strategy is worrisome, because it suggests that very different kinds of descriptors, causal mechanisms, and qualities of knowledge may apply to these two aspects of a single communication event. It also suggests that current approaches to event perception are inherently too limited in scope to explain how we can apprehend the significance of a communication event. This would be ironic, and difficult to accept, since one of the missions of ecological theory is to find a lawful basis for our perception of the *significance* of events (cf. Gibson, 1979; Shaw & Turvey, 1981). The primary goal of this chapter is to develop the basis for a *unified* approach to our comprehension of communicative events and our perception of events in general, and in the process, to dissolve the category boundaries that now appear to divide comprehension from perception. Finding a common ground requires two general lines of analysis. The first is to evaluate conventional perspectives on language, and to develop a perspective that shows language to be similar to other events in the kinds of interactions it can have with its participants. The second is to evaluate recent approaches to event perception, to determine whether they provide sufficient tools for building a theory of communication events; where they are insufficient in their current form, options for broadening and modifying them need to be considered. These two lines of analysis are pursued in parallel throughout this chapter. If the directions taken here are productive, we may be able to avoid the disjointed approach to communication just described. We may also be able to avoid some undesirable dichotomies in approaches to perceptual knowledge (e.g., the view that people function in qualitatively different modes when engaged by *symbols*, as opposed to perceptual *information*).

THE PROBLEM OF SPECIFICITY

Many event analyses (e.g., Gibson, 1966, 1979; Turvey & Shaw, 1979) argue that information about events is necessarily *specific* to them. Without such information, veridical perception and adaptive action would be impossible in principle. In the case of perceptual experience, this implies a tight, nonarbitrary coupling between the experience of events, the media affected by events, and the events themselves (cf. Shaw & Bransford, 1977; Shaw, Turvey, & Mace, 1982). More precisely, this coupling has at least two distinctive properties. First, specific information is *unique;* this implies that some patterning in light and sound could only have arisen from a source event of a particular type, and is an invariant consequence of that type of event. To a properly attuned organism, the resultant structure in light or sound uniquely identifies the type of source event. Second, specificity implies that the patterning in light and sound is a *physically necessary* (lawful) consequence of the event—that is, it is strictly determined by the objects involved, their transformations, and their interaction with light and sound. These two attributes, uniqueness and physical necessity, imply that information is structure-preserving, though not in the sense of an iconic preservation of form, or "first-order isomorphism" (cf. Turvey, 1977). Rather, it "preserves" structure, because it is uniquely and lawfully related to the event that shaped it and to the animal that detects it.[3]

The notion of specificity allows us to sharpen the problem of applying event analysis to language. As noted previously, it seems comparatively straightforward to conceive of the possibility that articulation has systematic acoustic consequences that are specific to the linguistic units being articulated. If relations of this kind can be identified, models of speech perception could be based on unambiguous information for the separation and identification of phonemes and syllables, and would thus have a very different cast from those that assume that cues are nonspecific. The perception of other aspects of speakers' personalities and actions may be similarly direct, based on optical and acoustic patterning that necessarily reveals its source.

---

[3]This chapter addresses the concept of *lawful specificity* and evaluates its applicability to communication events. This type of specificity was the focus of most of Gibson's work on perception and has also been the central focus of most neo-Gibsonian research and theory. However, it is important to note that:

1. Gibson discussed other types of specification, including *conventional specification,* or specification by *rule* (e.g., Gibson, 1966). In the case of language, the rules include arbitrary associations between words and events; the mapping between words and events is potentially ambiguous and its validity may be localized (e.g., to a particular society). In contrast, specification by *law* is based on the causal effects of events on the media around them; these effects are *invariant* and are governed by physical laws *of universal validity.*

2. The concept of "lawful specification" has been sharpened (and hedged) in more recent writings of some neo-Gibsonian authors (e.g., Shaw et al., 1982). These authors stress the context-dependent nature of information; they would prefer to say that information is *pragmatically* unique, that it is physically necessary *under appropriate boundary conditions,* and that it is *dependent on the current attitude and prior attunement* of an organism. They believe this makes explicit what was implicit in Gibson's efforts to develop an *ecological* physics.

3. Gibson focused largely on *perspective* specification (perception of the immediate environment), but he recognized that the current environment could provide systematic support for other varieties of experience: anticipation of the future course of events (*prospective specification*) and recollection of the past course of events (*retrospective specification*) (cf. Gibson, 1979). In the case of perspective specification, at least, the information was held to be *complete* (i.e., it was logically sufficient to define all aspects of the events experienced); this was true even for the organism whose attention had been *educated* to detect those aspects of events. Although Gibson did relatively little to extend these approaches to expectation, recollection, and learning, some neo-Gibsonian authors have begun to do so (e.g., Shaw et al., 1982; Shaw & Alley, in press). These authors apparently do not accept the view that information must be logically *complete* if it is to support veridical perception or successful action. Rather, information is whatever is *pragmatically sufficient* to support perceiving or acting; it need not be *complete* on this occasion if it has been complete over prior occasions of like kind. This approach is very similar to the one I develop in this paper (based on what I call *indexical specification*). One consequence of this approach, as I view it, is that we cannot align language comprehension strictly with *conventional* or *retrospective* specification, align perception strictly with *lawful* and *perspectively complete* information, or contrast the two on either of these bases.

However, the notion of specificity does not obviously apply to the relation between words and events (objects, actions, layouts, etc.). As a result, there is no apparent basis for a specific effect of words on a listener. In fact, the relation between words and things has seemed to most scholars to be the epitome of a nonspecific relation, exhibiting neither uniqueness nor physical necessity. When words are detached from their natural contexts and considered in isolation, the relation between words and things seems to fail the *uniqueness* test. For example, it is often argued that any one of several words can be used to refer to a single object (as illustrated by the different terms used in different languages) and that a single word can be used to refer to many objects (as illustrated by proper names or polysemy). The nonuniqueness of language also seems to gain support from the observation that words and sentences (isolated from context) can provoke a variety of experiences. For all of these reasons, it has been argued that words are *ambiguous* as specifiers of events in our environment or virtual events in a listener. The test of *physical necessity* also seems to fail, since the shape or sound of a word is not a necessary physical consequence of the event to which it may refer, and thus there is no apparent basis for a necessary relation between the word and the event it leads us to imagine. The relation between words and events therefore seems *arbitrary*. If these arguments hold, the ambiguity and arbitrariness of words would together imply that words are not *structure-preserving* or *specific* to events (in the senses described above). When viewed in isolation, they do not appear to preserve either meaning or structure in any determinate fashion. Thus, according to the traditional analysis of isolated words and things, words must be treated as nonspecific. If they are to serve as a basis for apprehending meaning, they would have to do so by a very different mechanism from that which supports detection of (specific) information.

Depending on one's philosophy of language, the problem of specificity can be posed in a number of contexts: the relation between words and things, words and events, words and ideas, words and intentions, words and behavior, words and experience, and so on. The preceding analysis has adopted the more traditional focus on the *representational relations between words and physical things*, and the consequences of these for the relation between words and *mental things* (such as images or ideas). My own preference is to focus on relations between *words and a listener's experiences and actions;* representational relations would not be the central or only focus of analysis. A listener's experiences include perception of the speaker's cognitive actions and communicative intention, and they include the virtual events and cognitive actions that are regulated in part by what the speaker says. Virtual *objects* are only part of the virtual events the listener experiences, and these experiences are only part of the total regulatory consequences of attending to another person's speech. From this perspective, then, the relation between words and *images,* or words and *things,* is only a limited part of the problem for analysis.

Due to the pervasive "representational" metaphor for language (cf. Verbrugge, in press), there has been a scholarly preoccupation with the denotative and referential properties of language (the relations between words and things). In effect, the relation between wordsounds and referents has been accepted as the most appropriate parallel to the relation between light patterns and objects. Tests for specificity developed for one side of this parallel have often been extended analogically to the other side. Language and perception have been seen as either fundamentally similar or fundamentally dissimilar, depending on how these tests turn out. An alternative starting point for analysis would be to focus on the relation between wordsounds and *communicative actions,* and to compare this with the relation between light patterns and *events.* This immediately reveals greater specificity to language than is apparent from the referential view; as noted previously, the acoustics of speech are specific to many aspects of the speaker and the communicative action. This illustrates how important it is to choose analogical parallels carefully; the choice directly shapes the conclusions we draw about fundamental commonalities or differences between language and perception.

The referential view of language has provided analogical support for many theories of perception in the Western tradition. Many philosophers and psychologists have viewed the proximal stimulation for perception as being language-like: a system of symbols that are both ambiguous and arbitrary with respect to the distal event to be perceived. Perception has been viewed predominantly as a process of symbol interpretation, in which symbols must be disambiguated and supplemented by meaning and structure. The analogy between sensations and words was very explicit in Berkeley's analysis of vision, and it has reappeared in the theories of Helmholtz (e.g., his discussion of "sense-symbols"), information processing (e.g., the notions of "sensory codes" and "decoding"), and many others since. Perception has been viewed as a species of symbol interpretation because the relation between objects and sensations, like that between referents and words, was held to be intractably nonspecific.

Research on perception by Gibson and his followers has sought to take a radically different premise as its departure point: that perceptual experience is based on lawfully specific information, as here defined. With this new assumption about the relation between distal events and proximal stimulation, the old analogy between perception and language comprehension fails. We are left with the prospect that two very different kinds of processes can occur: one permitting direct perception, the other demanding interpretation of symbols.[4] One risk is

---

[4]In Gibson's scattered references to language, it is clear that he accepted an epistemological division of this kind (e.g., 1966, pp. 90–96, 242–246, 280–282; 1979, pp. 260–262, 284–285, 295–297; 1982, pp. 289–293). He distinguished *perceptual cognition* (knowledge of the environment) from *symbolic cognition* (knowledge about the environment). His distinction is similar to Russell's (1948) distinction between *knowledge by acquaintance* and *knowledge by description.* For Gibson, the two processes are radically different in starting point, quality, and mechanism. Perceptual cognition is a direct (one-step) resonance of a perceptual system to information that is a causal product of the event it specifies. Symbolic cognition is a mediated (two-stage) process based on

that this distinction will lead to a disjointed view of people: capable of stable, determinate, veridical knowing as perceivers, but capable only of partial, uncertain knowing as symbol users. As a description of people, this overstates the ease and certainty of perception, understates the potential of symbol use as an avenue of knowing, and fails to acknowledge the tight interaction between the two in most of what we do. As an epistemology, this dual approach seems unacceptably chimerical. It does not seem appropriate to me to set aside cognition and symbol use as processes radically different in kind from perception. Symbol use is as much a natural, biological activity as perceiving; indeed it plays an essential role in many of our achievements in perception and coordinated movement.

There are many ways to consider bridging the gap between event perception and language comprehension that appears to be opened by the Gibsonian approach. The boldest possibility is to reverse the traditional analogy, and view language comprehension as a species of event perception. This would require a dramatic change in our view of language (seeing it somehow as a specific medium) and in our view of language comprehension (seeing it as an activity that is free of interpretive mediation). Such a redefinition is certainly worth trying, and steps in that direction are taken in this paper. However, it is not clear that all aspects of communication events will permit such a redefinition, without serious loss or distortion. The more promising alternative may be to combine a redefinition of language with a broadening of the principles of event perception, making it clear in the process how the two can be viewed as compatible and mutually supportive. In particular, it may be essential to broaden the role of cognitive and symbolic processes in theories of event perception and action, and to understand how perception, recollection, and skilled performance are possible under conditions of "partial information."

These topics are speculative and complex. Rather than attempting a thorough or general treatment of them, I would like to discuss two specific types of

---

learned, arbitrary associations between symbols and the events they specify. Perceptual cognition is based on physical law, it is limitless and comprehensive in its power of specification, and it is *tacit* (i.e., we are not aware of what guides it, and it cannot be exhaustively described in words). In contrast, symbolic cognition is based on social convention, it is limited and partial in its power of specification, and it is *explicit* (i.e., we are aware of what guides it, and its limited meaning is spelled out exhaustively). Gibson's treatment of language is based on the following conceptions, assumptions, and terminology: Language *conveys, contains, embodies,* and *transmits* information (e.g., 1966, p. 281; 1979, p. 260; 1982, p. 291); language is a code in which words *substitute for* things (1966, p. 281); language is fundamentally *descriptive* in function: It *names* things in the environment and *predicates* properties of them (1966, p. 281); language only describes things we are *aware* of (1979, p. 260); descriptions *exhaust* what they specify to a listener (1966, p. 281); the relation between words and things parallels the relation between perceptual stimuli and events (1966, p. 244); words are *arbitrary* conventions based on *social agreement* (1966, p. 91); symbols are cultural products, not part of the natural environment (1982, p. 292); the use of symbols (symbolic cognition) is unique to *humans* (1966, p. 91). I disagree with all of these conceptions of language (for reasons that I detail as this paper proceeds). If we truly "make a fresh start" on language (cf. Gibson, 1982, p. 292), the rationale for a distinction between two modes of cognition may disappear.

linguistic expression and some of the implications these have for relations between language comprehension and event perception. I return toward the end of the paper to the more general problem of viewing symbolization and perception as compatible.

DEICTIC LANGUAGE

A close relationship between language and event perception can be observed in the "deictic expressions" that frequent conversational speech. In general terms, deictic expressions are words or phrases whose meaning is determined by some aspect of the communication setting (cf. Weinreich, 1963; Fillmore, 1971; Lyons, 1977). Space (or place) deixis involves the use of terms that depend on the relative locations of the people and objects in the communication setting; this includes terms like *beyond, here, there,* and *beside.* Time deixis involves terms that "locate" events relative to the time at which the communication event occurs—for example, *now, tomorrow, yesterday,* and *next week.* Person deixis is controlled by the identities of the people talking, the people to whom or about whom they are talking, and their relative social status—for example, *I, they, we,* and *Sir.* In general, the meaning or validity of a sentence containing deictic expressions depends crucially on some aspect of the specific communication event in which the sentence occurs; thus, its meaning or validity cannot be characterized adequately in isolation from that event.

As a simple example, imagine that as you look across an open field you see a bed of tulips close by, then a pond, and in the distance, your old friend Muriel. You could say, "The pond is beyond the tulips." Muriel could say, "The tulips are beyond the pond." Who is correct? Which statement is true with respect to the "state of affairs" being described? Either can be, depending on where the speaker is in relation to the events being described. In isolation, the two statements can appear incompatible; if, in a formal semantic analysis, one treats "beyond" as a nonreflexive relation, then the two statements must be treated as contradictory. Hidden in this analysis, however, is an assumption about the situation of use; it assumes constancy of point of observation. Given that assumption, it is certainly the case that only one of the statements can be true; Muriel can only say one of them without fear of contradiction. But it is equally clear that speakers and observation points vary. As a result, what may seem formally incompatible is ecologically permissible; both sentences can be true if they are interpreted in relation to the people speaking them.

In general terms, this implies that constraints on the "semantic well-formedness" or "truth value" of deictic expressions cannot be defined adequately in isolation from the communication settings in which they are used. Crucial constraints on interpretation can only be defined in that context. Semantic analyses that pretend to be context neutral will always be found to make hidden pragmatic assumptions. It would seem preferable to make these explicit, and to characterize meaning in relation to how people perceive the spatial, temporal, and interpersonal structure of events that include speech. In fact, deictic expressions may not be exceptional in this regard; dependencies of meaning on pragmatic context (real or imagined) may be true of all expressions (e.g., see Bransford & McCarrell, 1974).

Deictic expressions demonstrate that close functional linkages need to be sought between event perception and language use. These linkages need to be identified both for language production (linguistic action) and language comprehension. In the production of deictic language, a speaker's use of certain terms is guided by perception of spatial relations among people and objects, the temporal patterning of events relative to "now," and the identities and actions of people. Proper use of a term is constrained by these environmental patterns, so it is crucial that they be perceived accurately by the speaker. In this sense, event perception may be said to guide linguistic action.

Deictic language also illustrates the power of language in guiding comprehension. Deictic terms can produce an experience of a particular kind of relation between a listener and the environment. If we are sitting on the grass chatting, and I say "There was a squirrel behind you," you will experience a particular kind of "virtual event" that is systematically related (in space) to your position and body orientation and (in time) to the "now" of our talking about it. Thus, deictic expressions can activate an attunement to our environment much like that which occurs during "direct perception."

A sentence studied by Fillmore (1973) provides a further illustration of this point: *May we come in.* When you read this sentence in isolation, its full significance is indeterminate, of course, because you don't know who "we" are, where "we" are, or what's happening. Even so, the sentence definitely constrains the situation in which you might imagine this sentence being uttered. Briefly (and typically), it specifies a situation in which two or more people are outside an enclosure and seek permission to enter from someone who is inside the enclosure and has authority to grant such permission. Within these constraints, any number of specific events can be imagined. What is remarkable is how powerful four words can be in establishing a fairly complex system of constraints at the outset.

The power of words to effect a perceptual attunement is especially clear when a sentence is used inappropriately. For example, imagine that I am inside my home and you are standing outside and ring the bell. If I open the door and say "May we come in?" I throw you into confusion. My words entail a situation incompatible with what you perceive. The situation you experience by direct perception is incompatible with the experience aroused by the words I have spoken (i.e., it is incompatible with the environmental relations that should constrain my utterance of those words). You have a choice of playing (metaphorically) into my constraints, laughing it off as a joke, or concluding I am mad. In any case, the kind of disorientation one experiences in such a circumstance indicates strongly that language can have effects that are qualitatively similar to direct perception. Even though the two processes of ''activation'' may be distinct, we may find important commonalities between perception and language in the ''qualities'' of knowing they permit.

METAPHORIC LANGUAGE

The power of language to facilitate a change in knowledge or skill is especially clear in the case of metaphoric language. In very general terms, metaphoric expressions treat one thing as if it were another. In production, a speaker can use a metaphor to communicate the perception of a familiar structure in an unfamiliar context, and to communicate efficiently some property of a person or event being discussed. When a metaphor is comprehended, it can aid discovery of a similarity between dissimilar events, and permit rapid understanding of some property being described. Two simple examples are these: The sentence *The mountain highway was a snake* might express one's perception that the structures of highway and snake were similarly curvey, or that the event of driving the mountain highway was similar to the motions of a snake. The metaphor *The children galloped into the living room* may lead a listener to imagine the children moving with all the speed, noise, and abandon of a herd of wild horses.

Metaphors are typically characterized in terms of three components, not all of which need to be explicit in the sentence: the *topic* or *tenor* (the focus of attention), the *vehicle* (what the topic is compared to or perceived as), and the *ground* (the commonalities between topic and vehicle). For example, in the metaphor about the mountain highway, the highway is the topic, snakes are the vehicle, and the ground may include curviness and sinuous motion.

The relations between metaphoric language and event perception can be considered in three contexts (which are admittedly only partially separable): the role of metaphor in guiding ''virtual experience,'' its role in preparing a person for direct perception, and its role in preparing a person for coordinated movement (action). By ''virtual experience'' I mean any one of the perception-like or action-like processes that have no complement, or only a minimal complement, in the person's immediate environment—for example, those that occur when we recollect, dream, plan, and imagine. (For want of better terms, I will contrast these ''virtual'' experiences with ''direct'' perception and action. ''Direct'' here implies that one's experience or action complements a source event in the immediate environment. The term ''virtual'' is not meant to imply that imaginal processes are any less real than direct perception or overt action.[5])

---

[5]Throughout this paper, the terms *cognition* and *experience* are *not* intended to imply the existence of a mental or formal structure that is separable in kind from biological events. These terms presuppose a monistic system of natural law, remodeled where necessary to accommodate them, not a dualism or transcendentalism.

The powerful effect of metaphor on imagination is exploited not only by poets, but by everyone who uses metaphor in their writing and conversation. Like deictic language, metaphor can activate imaginal experiences that are constrained by its linguistic forms and that may either fit or conflict with one's conventional ways of attending to events. There is no consensus about the nature of the constraints, however, nor about the kind of cognitive process initiated by metaphor. One facet of the process that I find intuitively compelling (and unduly neglected in the literature) is the fanciful transformation of the topic that very often accompanies comprehension of both similes and metaphors (Verbrugge, 1980). When subjects are presented with a sentence such as *Highways are snakes* and asked to describe what they think of or imagine when reading the sentence, they often report experiences in which the topic has been partially transformed into the vehicle. For example, the highway may become a long snake, with a slippery back with a line running down the middle, winding through the mountains.

Perceiving the topic *as* the vehicle, to whatever degree possible, seems to facilitate apprehension of structure that may previously have been unattended to. In some cases, this novel perception can be sufficient unto itself, drifting by in a story or dream, with no obvious impact on perception or action. In other cases, however, it can alter one's readiness to perceive and act in particular ways, and thus can have the important pragmatic function of facilitating changes in knowledge and skill.

Metaphor can affect direct perception by altering one's attention to structure in events. For example, the sentence *That highway is a real snake* might lead a traveler to anticipate a very twisty or slick stretch of road ahead. The driver is likely to be more attentive to the road, may be more aware of curves than would otherwise have been the case, and will definitely be surprised if the road turns out to be straight and smooth (i.e., if virtual experience conflicts with direct experience).

A nonhypothetical example of the perceptual effects of metaphor is provided by Schön (1979). A group of researchers in the 1950s were working on the development of a synthetic-bristle paintbrush, and had tried a number of ideas without successfully matching the quality of natural-bristle brushes. One fine day, one of the researchers noticed something about brushes he had not attended to before, and commented that "A brush is like a pump." After playing with this observation, the group realized that they had been attending to brushes essentially as surfaces that wipe paint. They found their design work facilitated by attending to brushes as composed of hundreds of hollow spaces that fill with fluid, which in turn can be forced (pumped) out under pressure. Design was now guided by attention to the kinds of hollows in a brush and to fluid forces, rather than to surface properties of bristles or of the brush as a whole. This example demonstrates clearly how a novel perceptual experience can be expressed in metaphoric language (a simile, in this case), and how those words, in turn, can alter the perceptual experiences of other people.

Given the close relationships between perceiving and acting, it would be surprising if metaphor did not also have powerful effects on our actions. Effects of this kind are already evident in the examples provided above. The warning "That highway is a real snake" may lead a traveler to drive more cautiously, to be ready to turn frequently through a winding layout, or to brake gently on a road that may afford little traction. The simile "A brush is like a pump" altered the actions of a group of researchers in complicated ways for many months.

There are many other types of context in which the impact of metaphor on action can be observed. Metaphor (often called "imagery") can play an important role in learning new skilled movements. A tennis coach, teaching a learner to serve, may ask her to imagine she is throwing the racket, not hitting the ball. A dance teacher, describing how to raise an arm, may ask the student to imagine a balloon swelling under the armpit. A piano teacher may ask that arpeggios be played with a "floating" elbow. It is remarkable how powerful "images" of this kind can be in facilitating the right kind of coordinated movement. Comprehension of a metaphor can apparently lead to alterations in the pattern of relations among the limbs and to changes in the body's dynamics. In effect, the student's body is the topic of the metaphor. If the metaphor achieves the desired effect, the body will be transformed by structural and dynamic properties of the vehicle (image) provided by the teacher. Short of success, the metaphor will at least provide an imaginal experience that the learner can try to sustain as a guide during subsequent efforts to achieve the desired action. The practical experience of many teachers and learners suggests that this symbiosis of language, imagination, and action can dramatically speed acquisition of a skill.

It is important to note that this power of metaphor extends well beyond the kinds of skilled actions mentioned here. In particular, the role of metaphor in shaping and altering social actions is of great importance to those who seek to understand or alter personality dynamics, to understand styles of action in professions and cultures, or to promote personal or social change.

LANGUAGE COMPREHENSION

Deictic and metaphoric expressions illustrate some close linkages between language comprehension and event perception, linkages that may be general to all forms of verbal expression. As I have tried to demonstrate in the two preceding sections, these expressions raise important questions about the relationships among communication, imagination, perception, and action. Some of the questions relate principally to the process of language comprehension, others to the control of linguistic action (production). The two processes are closely related and often complementary. The remainder of this paper focuses on the comprehension process, with the related production issues moving in and out of the background as necessary.

The examples of deixis and metaphor point to the following question as central to the problem of comprehension: *How does one person's speech constrain another person's perception, thought, and action?* It is clear from the examples presented above that language can alter a listener's (or reader's) perceptual attunement to structure in events, and can also alter their preparedness for coordinated movement of a particular kind. How are these effects achieved? This is a very difficult question. In the following pages, I hope to suggest some directions we might move in search of an answer, without pretending in any way that these suggestions are definitive.

Language as Catalyst

One useful approach to comprehension is to think of it as a process of *catalysis* (cf. Verbrugge, 1980; Waters, 1981). Language may be said to catalyze thought processes or virtual experiences, an analogy to catalysts in chemical reactions, which promote and constrain a reaction process without themselves being "consumed" in the process. Like chemical catalysts, words are rarely the substance of the process they affect, but they can *trigger* a flow of imagining and *constrain* the flow in very specific ways. Words are also like catalysts in that they constrain a process without in any sense containing a representation of the process or its results. Thus, it is inappropriate to say that words *contain* meaning, or *convey* meaning, or *embody* meaning, or *represent* meaning, contrary to so much of our ordinary language about language (cf. Reddy, 1979; Verbrugge, in press). The catalysis metaphor also suggests that it is inappropriate to view meaning as something assigned to an arbitrary word symbol by a system that autonomously embodies structure (e.g., a mind). The relation between a catalyst and the process catalyzed is not arbitrary. The two are naturally coconstraining; each is structured and each entails something about the other. If we can view words and people in a similar way, as coconstrained constituents of a single process, we will have a means of avoiding the pitfalls of both the "objective" approach to meaning (something contained in structured *words*) and the "subjective" approach to meaning (something supplied by an autonomously structured *mind*). In particular, we need to define language structures in reference to the cognitive processes that they presume, and we need to define cognitive processes in reference to the kinds of linguistic actions that can catalyze them.

An important facet of understanding a communication system, therefore, will be an analysis of the constraining (catalytic) effects of its symbols on virtual experience, preparedness for perception, and preparedness for action. In some systems, the analysis may be comparatively simple. In vervet monkeys, for example, a threat-alarm bark is uttered when a troop member sights a major predator (such as a lion); in other troop members, this signal catalyzes prepared-ness for perceiving a major predator (''attention'') and it catalyzes appropriate evasive action (flight to the nearest cover). The effects of other alarm calls in the vervet monkey repertoire can be characterized in similar terms (cf. Struhsaker, 1967; Marler, 1977; Jenkins, this volume). The general strategy in studies of this kind is to identify the internal and external circumstances of signal production by an animal, and to observe the effects of a signal on attention and action in other animals. This kind of analysis has been applied to communication signals in a wide variety of nonhuman species (cf. Green & Marler, 1979), though it still receives secondary attention relative to structural analyses of signaling systems considered in relative isolation.

Although a functional analysis of the human communication system may be more complex, involving the constraining effects of words, morphemic rela-tionships within words, and syntactic relationships among words, it too can profitably be cast in terms that explicitly make reference to processes in language users. For example, a linguistic analysis of deixis could include a description of the attunements to spatial, temporal, and interpersonal relations that deictic words and phrases selectively activate. An analysis of metaphor could include a description of the transformational style of thought process triggered by meta-phor, as well as the influence of such structural characteristics as word order (e.g., *A is a B* vs. *B is an A*) and sentence form (e.g., simile vs. metaphor), both of which can be shown to affect imagination systematically (cf. Verbrugge, 1980). It is important to note, however, that analyses of this kind only seek to identify the general *constraints* (or boundary conditions) that are common to a community of users; they do not attempt to describe the resulting cognitive processes in full detail. Additional detail experienced by a listener may arise from other sources: direct perception, user-dependent constraints of the words being listened to, or a recollection that is triggered by the words.

An analysis of the regulatory effects of language might be expected to reveal the ''affordance structure'' of communication events for listeners and readers (cf. Shaw et al., 1982). Gibson has argued that we generally perceive objects and events in terms of the actions they *afford*—for example, steps afford climbing, an apple affords grasping and chewing, a bouncing ball affords pursuit and capture, etc. (cf. Gibson, 1979; Michaels & Carello, 1981). The significance of an event for action is seen as integral to our perception of it. In its strong form, this approach argues that perceiving and acting are *pragmatically successful* to the extent that they are mutually compatible at every grain of analysis; more precisely, it treats them as isomorphic ''duals'' of one another (cf. Turvey & Shaw, 1979; Turvey, Shaw, & Mace, 1978; Turvey, Shaw, Reed, & Mace, 1981; Shaw et al., 1982). This implies that the information sufficient for perceiv-ing some event must be complementary to the information sufficient for acting toward that event. It also implies that the *affordance structure* of the environment (i.e., the kinds of actions it affords to some organism) must be complementary to the *effectivity structure* of the organism (i.e., its capabilities for action in the environment). For example, if a person perceives that a flight of stairs affords climbing, then sufficient optical information must be available to specify the coordination and energy expenditure needed to climb them (cf. Warren, 1982). According to the duality postulate, the constraints that define a successful stair-climber's *action system* are symmetric to the information available to the stair-climber as *perceiver*. Thus, a tight symmetry is observed between the coordination and control of climbing, on the one hand, and the information available about the environment, on the other.

When applied to language events, an analysis of affordance structures has some useful carryover. A speaker's verbal actions have many effects on a listener's actions that might be considered part of their affordance structure: The speaker's actions will constrain the listener's verbal actions (e.g., during a conversation), they may activate intentions and guide nonverbal actions of the listener (dodging a ball, coordinating a golf swing, etc.), and they may potentiate the listener for actions at a later time (e.g., in response to a request or a set of directions). While these constraints on overt action seem analogous to the concept of affordance, they already deviate from its "pure" form. The patterning of a listener's actions is only partially symmetric to the structure of the speaker's actions, and thus can only partially be determined or specified by them. In addition, the effects of speech on overt action only begin to describe the effects of speech or writing on a person. The more covert effects on recollection, imagination, attitudes, feelings, expectation, thought, etc., are not easily characterized in terms of actions that are fully constrained by an affordance structure of speech or writing. It seems reasonable to argue that cognitive activities and affective processes are as much actions of a biological system as the overt, skeletomuscular movements that the term "action" usually implies, but it does not seem appropriate to say that these covert processes are constrained entirely by the language events that affect them. In fact, these processes often have no clear "dual" in the person's environment at all. Thus, whatever advantages there may be to treating person and environment as *symmetric* or *dual* to one another, it does not seem possible to treat listeners and talkers in similar fashion. The constraints on the actions of a listener are not exhausted by the perceived constraints from the talker as a social environment. A related problem is the difficulty in defining what constitutes a "useful" or "pragmatically successful" response to a conversation or text. Duality is viewed as logically necessary only in the case of *successful* actions (cf. Shaw & Turvey, 1981), and it may therefore provide little guidance for understanding occasions where the success of communication is partial, undefinable, or irrelevant.

For all of these reasons, zealous application of the duality postulate to cognitive and communicative events may seriously reduce our capacity to understand them. If applied too vigorously, the concept of duality would have the ironic effect of promoting a kind of *representational* view of people, treating them as no more than skilled mirrors of their environments. (Or, to be more precise, it risks treating people as no more than attuned effectivity structures that are dually isomorphic to their affordance structures.)

As noted above, cognitive and affective processes present a problem for a theory of perception and action based on the duality postulate, since only partial symmetries are apt to hold between perceptual antecedents and action consequents in many contexts. One alternative solution is to limit "affordances" to overt actions that are under the immediate regulation of (specific) information about the environment. This risks narrowness of scope, since it may preclude the possibility of explaining many important classes of events and actions, including communication, thought, and the appreciation of art and literature. The second alternative is to broaden the range of events to which the concept of affordance structure applies. The "risk" here is that this will require broadening the principles that relate environments to actions (cf. Shaw & Cutting, 1980; Turvey & Shaw, 1979; Turvey et al., 1978). These principles need to be broadened to include the constraining effects of partially specific events on thought and action, and the effects of imaginal processes on coordination and control. Analyses of the optical control of such overt actions as walking or climbing do not embody all of the principles needed to account for the regulatory effects of events that are only partially symmetric to the actions they catalyze. I believe we will find this to be true not only for symbolic actions and many other social events, but also for many of the "physical" events that influence thought and action. If the partial symmetry observed for communication events is not unique to those events, it cannot be taken to justify a category distinction between "conventional specification" for linguistic events and "lawful specification" for physical events.

A Role for Redintegration

One of the most important problems for this approach to language comprehension is to identify how specific catalytic relationships between words and thought develop. In short, what is the origin of the constraints holding over listener and speech, reader and text? An approach to an answer may be afforded by considering comprehension as an instance of a more general kind of process called "redintegration." Redintegration is a process in which part of an event experienced earlier activates experience of the whole event on some later occasion. For example, encountering a friend may be sufficient to trigger recollection of a series of events from the night before, of which the friend was only a part. In a sense, all experiences of recollection that are initiated by some commonality between present and past events involve redintegration.

The activation of virtual experiences by words may be viewed as a process of recollection, and more specifically, of redintegration, if we consider words and their patterning to be the commonality between present and past events. During development, linguistic actions are integral to the events experienced by a child.

Specific kinds of relations within words and among words are recurrent constituents of physical and social events experienced by the child. These relations come to constrain the child's perceptual experience, as well as the child's own actions (linguistic and otherwise). Redintegration could be said to occur when words alone activate perceptual and actional attunements, even when many aspects of the original social and physical settings are absent. Again, if certain kinds of linguistic actions have been related systematically to specific classes of perceptual invariants, then those actions alone may be sufficient to activate attunement to those invariants on later occasions.

It is difficult to talk about such a process without sounding like a traditional associationist. Redintegrative mechanisms were central to the logic by which associationism sought to explain perception, thought, and learning. Such processes as assimilation, unconscious inference, prompted recall, and transfer of training all occurred when an associated part of some event evoked an experience or action that had earlier been evoked by the whole event. Treatments of redintegrative processes can be found throughout the literature on associationism (e.g., Hamilton, 1859; Russell, 1921; Hollingworth, 1926). For anyone who is convinced that associationist theories are inadequate for characterizing language learning, skill acquisition, the development of perceptual knowledge, and other important psychological processes, it may seem highly undesirable to resurrect the concept of redintegration in the current context. It might seem especially undesirable to a theorist who seeks to account for successful perception and action without incorporating processes that supplement partial information. For example, the central (but not exclusive) focus of Gibsonian theory and research has been on those occasions where environmental constraints on perception and movement are complete and specific, not partial; under these circumstances, it has been argued that no special adumbrative process is necessary to mediate perception (e.g., Turvey, 1977). A major puzzle for neo-Gibsonian theory is to explain how perception can be veridical and unambiguous in circumstances where information is *not* complete (cf. Shaw et al., 1982; Shaw & Wilson, 1976). We may argue that the missing constraints are supplied through *redintegration,* but in doing so we risk returning to concepts of memory and association that have failed in the past to provide credible explanations of redintegrative phenomena.

In the current context, then, words like "redintegrated" and "associated" send warning flags flying. How can we profit from the past, but avoid its pitfalls? Let me suggest a few approaches.

First, there are many occasions of human experience and action that are based on only "partial support" in our immediate environment (i.e., they fail to exhibit the lawful specificity taken as prototypic of natural occasions by neo-Gibsonian theory). We all experience the kinds of recollections that inspired traditional associationism. To a degree, the experiential base for associationism seems undeniable, even if we deny the utility of the theory devised to explain those experiences.

In perception, our experiences may be more specific than is warranted by the available information—as when we navigate through a familiar room at night when the lights are out, or when we perceive the shape of a tuba upon hearing its sound from an adjacent room, or when a doctor perceives an abnormal heart valve based on a whisper in the heartbeat, or when a subject in a perception experiment perceives an outline drawing as a baby's head. In all of these cases, perceptual experiences are triggered by information that (on the current occasion) is incomplete. Information may be specific to part of what we experience, but insufficient to support all of what we experience. It does not seem appropriate to me to attribute the supplementary aspects of these experiences to an act of *judgment* distinct from perception (cf. Shaw et al., 1982); they are integral to the perceptual experience itself and are systematic products of prior occasions (including verbal communications) that have attuned the observer.

Similarly, our *actions* may often be predicated on information that is in some sense "incomplete." This may be especially true of skilled performance in a familiar setting (such as driving down a familiar road), where attention to a few invariant aspects may be sufficient to keep one's actions coordinated with the environment. A similar selectivity is exhibited by an echo-locating bat that has flown repeatedly through a maze. If an obstacle is placed in a familiar path in the maze, the bat may fly right into it (Griffin, 1958). Since the same obstacle in an unfamiliar path would have been skillfully avoided, the problem is not the bat's ability (in principle) to detect the obstacle, nor the availability (in principle) of information about it. Instead the bat's collision seems to demonstrate how skilled actions may be guided by only partial constituents of the setting in which the skill has been learned. There are also occasions when humans or other animals take actions when environmental information to guide them is incomplete in principle. Such actions as hunting for deer or foraging for fruit can be highly systematic, for example, even when information about the spatiotemporal distribution of the food source is inconsistent or incomplete. When a food source is not directly specified, when plucking or devouring is not afforded by the immediate environment, an animal's actions must be regulated more by internal processes, by nonspecific external signs, and by attunements for events that are, as yet, unseen, unheard, and unsmelled. Similarly, the response of an animal to an alarm call can be highly systematic and effective, but it is guided more by attunement to an unseen predator than by the structure of the signal itself.

In general, occasions of "partial support" for recollecting, perceiving, and acting seem to be both important and frequent. Analysis of these occasions will require more care than is suggested by my brief examples, but such an analysis is crucial if we are to understand the broadest range of biological activities, including cognition and communication. It would be a mistake, therefore, to take the canonical examples of event perception as *prototypic* situations—i.e., to assume that situations of lawfully specific information embody all of the principles we need for a general theory of human action. Such occasions may be a necessary basis for certain types of knowledge and adaptation, but it would be as misleading to treat them as prototypic or universal as it was for the associationists to treat nonspecific occasions as prototypic and universal. If the world is replete with situations in which information is incomplete or nonspecific (in any sense we can agree on), then redintegrative processes in people are a necessary biological complement to the environments they face and must be given serious theoretical attention.

A second problem in considering redintegration involves the kind of mechanism presumed to exhibit such a process. Traditional associationism assumed a system that recorded recurrent combinations and successions of elemental sensations; all such relations among elements were assumed to be arbitrary. This kind of system has been criticized for centuries for its inability to characterize nonarbitrary constraints or relations over parts, and for its inability to explain how we learn to use structures that are not reducible, in principle, to associations (e.g., Chomsky, 1957). But if we reject associative devices as our model for biological systems, we need not also reject redintegrative phenomena. I would suggest that, whatever types of systems are proposed, we should ask that they exhibit redintegration under appropriate conditions. Redintegrative processes should be part of our "job description" for modeling such systems. Adequate explanations of recollection, expectation, language, perception, and action may be impossible without them.

A final set of problems concerns arbitrariness and completeness. The kind of redintegration I am discussing here does not presume arbitrary relations among constituents of events, nor does it assume that the support for perception and action is always and intractably nonspecific. Thus it differs from the kind of process envisioned by most associationists. Consider first the problem of arbitrariness. Redintegration is apparently more effective when aspects of an event are "organized" or "constrained" than when they are related arbitrarily; the recent literature on verbal memory, for example, provides numerous demonstrations of this (cf. Bransford, 1979). The conditions that govern redintegration of nonassociative types of organization have not been systematically identified, however. With regard to the problem of completeness, note that a revised redintegration model could require that information has been complete on some earlier occasion, or over a series of earlier occasions. Thus, the occurrence of a redintegrative process may presume a developmental history in which the invariant relations among constituents of an event have been specified fully (cf. Kugler, Kelso, & Turvey, 1980).

In general, then, it may be possible to incorporate "memory" phenomena into an event perception framework without assuming arbitrary relations among animals and events or a lack of specificity during learning. One effort in this direction is a set of proposed postulates for learning, generalization of knowledge, and memory (Shaw & Alley, in press; Turvey & Shaw, 1979, pp. 218–219). While these postulates look superficially like classic laws of associative transfer, they make very different assumptions about the kinds of relations that must hold between organisms and their environments if adaptive forms of recollection and skill are to be possible at all.

Language as Index

The concepts of catalysis and redintegration are clearly only a start toward understanding language comprehension, but they do suggest some deeper similarities between comprehension and event perception. A useful way to approach these similarities is to consider events (including word-events) as *signs*. Peirce's three-way distinction among types of signs is a particularly helpful starting point for such an analysis (cf. Alston, 1964; Peirce, 1931). Unfortunately, Peirce's intent is often inconsistent or obscure (cf. Burks, 1949). The following are simplified definitions that derive from Peirce's: *Icons* are signs that resemble what they signify—such as a blueprint, a caricature, a map, or an onomatopoeic expression; *symbols* are signs that are arbitrarily related to what they signify— some examples are words, stop signs, bar codes, and punctuation marks; finally, *indexes* are signs that are related to what they signify by some natural constraint—such as thunder, a footprint, a bad cough, or a bird's nest. Thus, indexes differ from icons in that they need not resemble what they signify, and they differ from symbols because they are not arbitrarily related to what they signify. It is important to note in all these cases that signification cannot simply be defined over two variables (a sign and a significate), but must be defined over at least three variables (a sign, a significate, and an agent); signification assumes a biological agent or other system for which the sign is significant. It is also important to note that signification is a type of *constraint* on the interactions among these physical and biological variables (i.e., it is a "third" in Peirce's system). Signification does not require a distinctive mental *thing* (a "meaning") to mediate between signs and referents (cf. Dewey & Bentley, 1949; Shaw & Turvey, 1981).

Approaches to event perception can be distinguished, in part, by how proximal stimulation is viewed as a *sign* of events. While some ancient theories were strongly iconic, more contemporary approaches view these relations as non-iconic, view only a limited subset of properties as structure preserving, or view "structure preservation" as being more abstractly a second-order isomorphism (e.g., Shepard, 1975) or a duality (e.g., Shaw & Turvey, 1981). The conventional wisdom in philosophy and psychology for the last few centuries has largely been to view proximal stimulation as so incomplete, distorted, and ambiguous relative to the distal event that it is essentially an arbitrary *symbol* of the event. In contrast to this, the thrust of the Gibsonian approach is to view proximal information as an invariant and physically necessary consequence of the distal event. The significant patterning in an optic array, for example, does not *resemble* the event that structures the light, nor is it *arbitrarily* related to the event; it is naturally constrained by the event. By definition, then, *information is indexical*.

It should be noted, however, that the Gibsonian sense of "information" has often been more restrictive than Peirce's sense of "index." In discussions of lawful specification, "information" has tended to imply both uniqueness and physical necessity (e.g., necessity due to the physics of light reflection), while "index" tends more generally to imply constrained co-occurrence.[6] As noted above, pure cases of specificity, where information is complete and unique as well as physically necessary, may not be prototypic of natural circumstances of observation and action, and thus they may not be prototypic of the kinds of indexes that guide perception and action. Many circumstances seem more contingent—such as the relations between storms and thunder, animals and footprints, food and locales, events and verbal actions. It may be possible in all such cases to view sign and significate as being naturally constrained, without the added requirement that the two-term relation between sign and significate must be unique or physically necessary. A natural linkage between sign and significate is sufficient to give the sign indexical potential for an animal, whether their relation is invariant or simply covariant. If so, then all occasions of perception and recollection can be viewed as indexical—both the "fully supported" ones, and the more "redintegrative" cases where an attuned agent experiences storm on hearing thunder, predator on seeing footprint, or hell on reading Dante.

The status of *language* as a sign system has also aroused considerable disagreement historically. As noted above, discussions of this issue have focused predominantly on the representational relation between nouns and referents. It is generally agreed that nouns do not represent their referents iconically, in any of the nouns' manifestations (articulatory, acoustic, optical, etc.); the only exception to this is onomatopoeic expressions. Nouns are typically viewed as *symbols*, in that their form is arbitrarily related to that of their referents.

It is possible, however, to view nouns (and verbal actions in general) as *indexes*. Linguistic actions are not arbitrarily related to their settings or to other actions of the person who is talking. The relations are systematic and con-

---

[6]According to Shaw and Turvey (1981), this indexical form of specificity is closer to what Gibson intended in his discussions of perceptual information. They view the strong interpretation of lawful specificity (uniqueness and physical necessity) as a strawman that differs markedly from the fullbodied intent of Gibson's writings and of their own earlier writings on the subject. Whether this is wishful revisionism or an accurate picture of original intent, I will leave to others to decide. Gibson's strong distinction between lawful specification (based on invariance) and conventional specification (based on local co-occurrences) should certainly give us pause in this regard. If by "lawful" he really meant something more like "indexical," it would be difficult to understand his vigorously defended distinctions between two modes of cognition, and between writing and pictures (see references cited in footnote 4).

strained; they are properties of social events that are perceptible (indeed, they must be perceptible if language is to be learned or to have reliability as a communicative basis for knowing). Words are not merely indexes to *things*, but indexes of social events and settings. Their occurrence is constrained by the speaker's social action, intention, and cognitive processes, and by the speaker's relation to the other people, objects, and events in the social setting. Given sufficient experience with these constraints, both speakers and listeners come to relate to words in ways that are increasingly autonomous of the social events of which the words are indexes. These indexes can act redintegratively on a listener, producing attunements to the current speaker and setting, or inducing experiences of particular kinds of virtual events.

In Peirce's analysis, only a small subset of words were considered *indexes:* words that are "existentially" related to one's immediate environment (cf. Burks, 1949). For example, if you say "that teddybear over there" (perhaps also pointing at the bear in question), the utterances "that" and "there" are constrained by (and coexist with) certain objects and spatial relations in your environment, and are therefore indexes. For the same reason, your pointing is also an index. For Peirce, indexes were limited to deictic expressions and gestures of this kind, and all other words were treated as *symbols*. My extension of the term *index* to cover all of language is based on what I see as an "existential" relation between *all* words and their natural occasions. Words are existentially related to events in the current social setting (including processes in the speaker and the listener), and they are existentially related to previous social settings by the developmental continuity of the listener. If prior attunement and current redintegration can provide a natural "cooccurrence" of present and past, then all words (indeed, all symbols) are indexical, by extension of Peirce's own definition.[7]

If one speaks of constraints holding between linguistic actions and settings, the situation may not seem strictly analogous to the relations between thunder and storms. One might be tempted to argue, for example, that physical law permits only one index, while a language setting permits any one of several indexes (as is suggested by the variability of word-forms across languages). We need to bear in mind that indexical signification is a constraint over at least three terms, including a perceiver or listener. This has consequences for our analysis of both the nonlinguistic and the linguistic settings. First, we must note that thunder (or any other acoustic or optical information) is not significant except to an animal who has become attuned to the natural relation between sign and

---

[7]This use of the term "index" is also compatible with Peirce's view that the interpretation of signs is an *activity* of a person in a world (a *thought*), not a three-term relation between signs, objects, and *ideas* (cf. Shaw & Turvey, 1981; Dewey & Bentley, 1949). Thinking is a natural *component* of signing events; it is not a special "mental" thing that must be added to make signing actions meaningful.

significate. In this sense, linguistic actions are similar to other events that provide information for perception and action; a listener must become attuned to the natural relations between speech and social settings. In the case of language, the necessary attunements develop over years of talking and listening in a particular social environment, in which the natural relations between speech and setting are highly invariant and slow to change. Second, in both linguistic and nonlinguistic events, the relation between indexes and listeners (or perceivers) is nonarbitrary. Perception, thought, and action are all constrained in highly systematic ways. In this sense, someone who listens to instructions or reads a novel is little different from someone who hears thunder or sees a footprint. Language constrains users in nonarbitrary ways.

A person who has developed in a particular social context is like a chemical mixture in the following sense: The dynamics of the system permit only certain catalysts to guide the system in particular ways. In chemical reactions, catalysts cannot be interchanged without loss of function. It is similarly erroneous to speak of *words* as interchangeable (as is done routinely in discussions of words and things). They *appear* interchangeable only if one systematically shreds the natural communication event: first, by separating words from listeners (whose gradually changing attunements presuppose a *particular* language); second, by separating words from their speakers (whose skills have developed in a particular social environment, making *particular* words integral to their cognitive and social actions); and third, by separating objects ("things") from the remainder of their social setting. Naked from analysis, words and things appear arbitrarily related. Their relation can be seen as naturally constrained if, as a minimum, we view them as embedded in social events of naming (and events that derive from these). Verbal actions in these events are what they are because the natural history of human development (over months and millenia) has led them to be what they are. They are not interchangeable *in principle*.

The individual and cultural development of linguistic actions raises an interesting point of contrast with chemical catalysts: The patterning of linguistic actions and the patterning of cognitive processes both undergo development, and in complementary ways. Unlike the average "test-tube reaction," people and their catalysts *develop* together. A better analogy in the chemical sphere might be the relation between intracellular processes and DNA; these presumably have evolved together and are mutually regulating (cf. Pattee, 1969, 1972, 1980; Weiss, 1969). The plasticity of words and their cognitive effects to *change* does not imply that they are arbitrarily related, any more than the chemical constituents of cells are arbitrarily related.

If language is a system of social actions, which are as much a part of our natural environment as rolling stones and bouncing bottles, then we should be able to explain language comprehension and event perception using common principles of biological organization. The concept of index provides one common ground for developing such principles. As biological processes, comprehension and perception both exhibit indexical relations to the events in which they are immersed. For each type of process, these relations vary in specificity (as a function both of the setting and of the person's attention or training), and thus both may exhibit redintegration or internal regulation to varying degrees. From an indexical perspective, then, it may be possible to view language comprehension as similar in kind to event perception, requiring no special principles for explaining either its development or its matured function. Note, however, that this fundamental commonality can only be discerned if we view language as an event that is integral to our environment (not an arbitrary associate of it), and if we give a broader role in ecological theory to cognitive processes, redintegration, and the regulation of action by nonspecific indexes. Without taking these steps, we risk a theory of perception that is radically incomplete, and a theory of language that is radically incommensurable with it.

LANGUAGE IN AN ENANTIOMORPHIC MIRROR

If the approach I have sketched here proves fruitful, much of our conventional wisdom about language will need to be reconsidered and possibly abandoned. As part of this reanalysis, it is a useful exercise to invert each facet of conventional wisdom and to give its opposite some serious consideration. In this section I offer a series of assertions about what language is not, in each case negating a property that is conventionally attributed to language. My hope is that we can come to see language more clearly by looking at what it is not. Language may be the virtual image in the following enantiomorphic mirror.

Language is Not Fundamentally Ambiguous

Language can evoke a highly determinate experience, perceptual readiness, or style of action. Its power of specification may be fairly abstract, evoking attunement for particular types of relations (e.g., pump-like relationships within a brush, or spatial relations in a communication setting). Fine-grained detail may be supplied by other sources or, if unnecessary, not supplied at all. While linguistic constraints may be abstract, they can nonetheless be *unique*. For the seasoned listener, the catalytic effect of words can be very precise.

Thus, ambiguity may be no more prototypic of communication than illusion is of perception. Indeed, the long-term survival of language and the pervasive role if plays in social action suggest that its reliability as a means of knowing must be very high. If communication failure, like misperception, is taken as prototypical, we create unsolvable problems for explaining adaptation, learning, and coordination of action at the social scale. "Linguistic ambiguity" emerges most commonly when words or sentences are excised from their dynamic contexts, which include the communication setting and the actions and cognitive processes of both the speaker and the listener. Structural analysis of sentences alone is blind to the full array of constraints that can preclude ambiguity under natural conditions.

Language is Not Fundamentally Arbitrary

One might defend this assertion by arguing that linguistic actions are natural events, defined at a social–biological scale, and as such cannot be arbitrary. They are what they are because species evolution and social development have taken them there. They express natural constraints effective now and in the past. To speak of words as being interchangeable is to be purely hypothetical; they are not interchangeable in principle.

The embeddedness of linguistic actions in natural settings has been discussed in earlier sections of this paper. To summarize again: When one considers the constraints that govern the interactions among events, linguistic actions, and skilled listeners, the relation of words to events and listeners is seen to be nonarbitrary. Words are integral to social events (not arbitrary correlates), and words complement processes in listeners in nonarbitrary ways. This renders words more indexical than symbolic.

The conventional view of words as arbitrary seems to arise from three sources. First, it arises from viewing language as a formal system, not a natural, biological process (I return to this point later). Second, it arises from a style of analysis that isolates words from their settings and users, thus cutting across natural lines of constraint and leading erroneously to the conclusion that these elements are arbitrarily related. This style of analysis (common in semiotics, structuralism, formalism, etc.) exhibits what James (1890) called the "psychologist's fallacy"; in this case, what the analyst concludes to be arbitrary is functionally nonarbitrary for the language users themselves. Finally, the apparent arbitrariness of language arises from an overemphasis on language as a representational system (see the next section). For many words, one cannot even identify "referents" with which to compare their form, and few sentences are purely descriptive in function. In spite of this, the representational relation between words and things, sentences and events, has often preoccupied attention. When one realizes how little of the function of language is representational, the problem of whether words embody or derive from the properties of things becomes simply irrelevant. The solution to that problem does little to illuminate the constraining effect of a question, warning, imperative, etc., on a listener.

These first two assertions about language imply that there can be a *specificity* to language comparable to that asserted of perception. If language can be both unique and nonarbitrary as a specification, then it approximates the hallmarks of specificity described earlier in this paper: uniqueness and physical necessity. Although "physical necessity" may be too strong a term to apply to language (and many other environmental indexes as well), it is not too strong to say that language exhibits "natural constraint" or that it provides highly systematic support for social perception and action. In fact, language can be more precise in its power of specification than the surface reflections of events or their vibratory effects on air. The constraints of "May we come in" are activated with great economy, as are the effects of a well-chosen metaphor. Language can have great precision in isolating particular structures for attention, and guiding the style of action in a listener. A word can be worth a thousand pictures.[8]

Language is Not Fundamentally Representational

Implicit in many discussions of language (and other symbol systems) is the view that language "represents" by providing a substitute description of some objects, events, or other states of affairs. As previously noted, however, the uses of language go far beyond its descriptive functions. Representational actions are only a small portion of the social repertoire of language. For this reason, the analysis of linguistic symbols as surrogate descriptors of events has been only partially successful. Efforts to identify meaning in terms of the referential properties of words, phrases, and sentences have encountered numerous problems (e.g., see Alston, 1964; Brown, 1958). No general treatment of language in these terms is apparently possible. The view of language as symbolic redescription is thus, at best, incomplete and cannot provide the basis for a general understanding of language as specification.

The view of language as a descriptive surrogate seems to derive from the more general view that human symbols are estranged from the natural world. Rather than being an integral part of natural events, they merely accompany or parallel these events. Their meaningfulness as "substitutes" for those events is assessed solely in terms of how well they "correspond" to them. An alternative view (developed earlier in this paper) is that symbols emerge as *constituents* of natural events. Verbal, gestural, and written symbols are closely coordinated with other aspects of the events we experience. More strongly, symbols are often essential to these events; an enormous range of social actions cannot be defined without them. As constituents of events, symbols cannot be treated simply as arbitrary accompaniments or "correspondents" to events. They only appear so when they are severed from the actions of symbolization that include them, and from the broader range of terrestrial events with which these actions are closely coordinated.

A particularly treacherous form of the representational view treats symbols as if they embody or contain something (cf. Reddy, 1979; Verbrugge, in press).

---

[8]Note that in Gibson's discussions of language, verbal descriptions are generally treated as far more limited than graphical depictions in their power of specification (e.g., 1979, pp. 260–261, 284–285). This renders us helpless to explain the extraordinary power of a poem or novel. As Gibson himself noted on occasion, description need *not* be inferior to depiction; each may be optimal for different kinds of information (e.g., 1966, pp. 242–243; 1982, p. 292).

This leads to questions like the following: What is in a representation? What meaning is in a sentence, or in a text? How much of a theory is represented in mathematical or logical form (and how much "surplus meaning" is there)? All of these theoretical questions treat symbols as self-contained substitutes for something that is represented, whether the substitute is viewed as iconically related to it or not. If meaning is viewed as a property of interactions among symbols, events, and symbol users, then it never makes sense to speak of what is *in* a symbol itself, nor may it matter whether it "exhausts" that which it "represents." The important question is what catalytic role it plays for some function for a person who has come to use the symbol through participation in a community of users. Natural communities of users range from large societies sharing a common language (such as French) to small elites sharing common notation systems (such as linguists, chemists, or logicians). The functions served by their linguistic actions range far beyond "description." In no case can their symbols be viewed simply as stand-alone stand-ins for something else.

The parallels and contrasts drawn between language and sensory stimulation often focus on a representational issue—the problem of specificity or correspondence to states of affairs. Much of this paper, for purposes of argument, has taken that issue as its central focus. Yet in developing an indexical approach to language, it has seemed too limiting to focus solely on the *descriptive* function of language (i.e., its power to evoke an imaginal experience, or a perception-like attunement to events). The range of influences of language on cognitive (and other) actions is far more extensive. Does language then diverge from event perception by virtue of having a broad range of signification functions, compared to event perception, in which the only kind of signification involves *detecting events* (states of affairs)? This does not seem the appropriate conclusion. Optic arrays do not simply permit the *perception of* objects, events, or affordances. They do not simply support perceptual experiences or actions that are complementary to events. Ambient light, sound, and chemicals all play a wide variety of roles in triggering and guiding internal processes and overt actions. Thinking of proximal stimulation primarily in *representational* terms may be as limited a basis for perceptual theory as the representational view of words has been for language. This suggests, in turn, that *specificity* is not as fundamental an issue as many have perceived it to be.

Language is Not Fundamentally Mediated

The argument has been advanced that, if the information about events and their affordances is definitive, then it becomes unnecessary to postulate certain kinds of mediational processes (such as supplementation from memory) as constituents of perception (e.g., Shaw et al., 1982; Turvey, 1977; Turvey & Shaw, 1979). If linguistic signification can also be definitive, it is worth considering the possibility that language comprehension is similarly unmediated.

Given the prevalence of information-processing approaches to comprehension, it is clearly as radical to argue that language needs no "epistemic mediation" as it has been to argue the same of perception. It is also at least as difficult. In the context of perception, there are numerous uses of such terms as "direct" and "mediated" (cf. Shaw & Bransford, 1977), and there is no consensus regarding the degree to which cognition may "penetrate" perception, or whether it is sensible to treat these as separable processes at all (cf. Fodor & Pylyshyn, 1981; Pylyshyn, 1980; Turvey et al., 1981). These problems are no less severe in the context of language.

Even so, some strong similarities between comprehension and perception suggest that nonmediated approaches to language also deserve serious consideration. Like event perception, symbol-guided virtual experience often has an immediacy, automaticity, and epistemic directness. Both comprehension and event perception require an "education of attention" (Gibson, 1966) to significant indexes. Occasions of communication failure in language may be as unusual or atypical as are occasions of illusion or misperception. For both perception and comprehension, one can argue that cognitive processes are more prominent when specification is incomplete or contradictory (e.g., where a deictic utterance fails to specify a crucial relation or specifies a relation inconsistent with perception).

In some senses, then, it may be useful to think of language processes as unmediated, or at least to see them as no more mediated than perceptual processes. For the moment, then, I will sketch this feature into our enantiomorphic image. I suspect, however, that as we develop an indexical approach to comprehension and perception, the issue of mediation will become secondary or vanish from our mirror altogether. Stating the issue requires two troublesome kinds of analysis: a separation between cognition and perception (to permit consideration of their "interaction"), and parallel consideration of structure in the environment and structure in an animal (to determine whether one is supplementing the other, or is isomorphic to it). If we speak of mediation in the context of *indexical* regulation, it seems unlikely that we will want to assume either of these kinds of analysis. The characteristics that we attribute to cognition and perception are blended inseparably in a *single* biological process, which need not be *isomorphic* to the indexes that regulate it. Our use of the term "mediated" will need to be based on different criteria, and it will probably be no more than a matter of degree. For example, we could think of our interactions with indexes as varying in degree of redintegration, or in the degree to which autonomous processes predominate over external regulation. "Unmediated" would be the (impossible) limiting cases on such continua. We may decide that, if a system exhibits indexical regulation and autonomous changes in goals and actions, it is inherently mediational.

Language is Not Fundamentally Formal

Language is very often identified with the formal notation systems devised for representing some of its regularities. At least metaphorically, it is viewed as a "formal system," a reified object or system of objects that can be characterized independent of the "use" of these objects in natural contexts. Thus, for example, it has been common to distinguish *language*, the formal system of rules, from *speech*, the biological action (e.g., Chomsky, 1957; Saussure, 1966). This effectively detaches language structure from the realm of natural law. Structure in speech as biological action is attributed to an underlying "knowledge of the formal system," rather than arising as an expression of biological law. This is unsatisfying as "explanation" (cf. Kugler, Kelso, & Turvey, 1980). First, rather than explaining regularities in action in terms of more general principles, it simply attributes regularities to a mental agent that controls action. The structure embodied in this mental agency is taken to be self-explanatory and transcendent of natural law. Thus, as a second problem, this style of explanation prematurely limits the development of natural law and the application of its principles and research methods to language phenomena. Third, it does not provide an account of how the necessary cognitive structure could have arisen in the natural world. If regularities in linguistic action are not the long-term expression of natural constraints, then they can only be attributed mysteriously to a mind or spirit of transcendent origin. Finally, as noted previously, a "formal" definition of language encourages the view that symbols are separate from natural events and are arbitrarily related to them.

An alternative is to view language as a type of action, a style of dynamic organization in a biological system (defined at both individual and social grains of analysis). Regularities in speech would be expressions of this organization; they would not be symbolized within the speaker as a set of rules for planning and controlling action. This, in principle, keeps linguistic actions within the realm of natural law, and provides a stimulus for broadening natural law if it cannot now accommodate such actions as part of its expression. This approach suggests, further, that the development of symbol systems is purely a product of natural processes, and not the product of autonomous changes in a formal system. To understand the evolution of symbol systems, we need to understand the *ecology* of symbolization, including the circumstances that warrant individual or social use of symbols. Similarly, to understand the development of symbolic skills in individuals, we need to understand the environments that warrant symbolic action and that provide the information to guide it. If we view language as a perceptible form of human action, then it must be included within the scope of any theory of perception or action that aspires to generality. Any "ecological" analysis that fails to provide a natural home for linguistic processes and actions is radically incomplete.

There is already an extensive literature on language as action, including analyses of nonverbal "body language," the communication of affect and intent by voice quality and style of speech, the patterning of conversations, the effects of social setting on speech, the social effects and functions of speech, speech articulation as a form of coordinated movement, and so on. Often, however, these are viewed as "pragmatic" problems, which are to be divorced from a characterization of the pure "formal" system itself. Some aspects of body language have been called "paralinguistic," for example. If language is viewed as a coherent action, there is no privileged status for the structure of its "verbal" aspect (morphemes, words, phrases, sentences, etc.). One cannot isolate these from the speaker and social setting, and achieve a closed analysis of linguistic constraints. During the last few decades there have been numerous attempts to develop formal models of syntax and semantics in isolation from pragmatic constraints. The lack of convergence and closure in these models can be interpreted as eloquent testimony against the view that language is essentially a formal system. Viewed as a natural event, language may more easily succumb to closed analysis. This would not only be a delight for the theorist, but it would explain how language users are able to communicate without ambiguity using sentences that in formal isolation are ambiguous.

SUMMARY AND CONCLUSIONS

This paper has taken as its challenge an apparent gulf between principles that apply to language comprehension and principles that apply to event perception (in particular, those that derive from the work of J. J. Gibson). It is worrisome that the event perception approach has had so little to say about human communication and cognition, in spite of efforts to ground the approach on epistemological principles of great generality. Perhaps it is not surprising that principles of event perception have had so little application to language; concepts like specificity, affordance, and direct perception are difficult to apply to communication. But what does this difficulty imply? It may imply that seeking a common ground is pointless, that the gulf is real and unbridgeable, and that a distinct epistemology is needed for communication. Alternatively, it may imply that current principles are too limited to cover the necessary territory; with a different or broader set of principles, the gulf might disappear. Unfortunately, both of these alternatives imply a lack of generality of current theory in areas that should be central to human ecological analysis: communication and cognition.

Rather than accepting a fundamental difference between language and perception, we need first to question our assumptions about both of them, with the hope of uncovering some fundamental commonalities between them. The effort is worthwhile, because it lessens the risk of developing a psychology that is disjointed in its view of human action, or that simply ignores the problems of language and cognition, or that makes it more difficult to treat language and cognition as natural processes.

The possibility of finding a common ground for linguistic and nonlinguistic events is supported from several perspectives (which have been explored in some detail throughout this paper). Each type of event can provide types of information that range in quality from physically necessary to naturally constrained, from unique to equivocal, from invariant to somewhat systematic, from complete to partial. Each type of process can be relatively unmediated, or can show varying degrees of influence by directed thought. Each can show varying degrees of redintegration, manifested either in an attunement to the current environment or in virtual experiences (e.g., recollected or imagined events). In short, the natural circumstances for perceiving linguistic events may be no different in kind from the natural circumstances for perceiving any other events.

Our approach to finding commonalities between language and event perception should not be to seek a reduction of one to the other, as they are currently understood (e.g., treating comprehension as a species of direct perception, or treating perception as a species of symbolic communication). The preferable course is to broaden and refashion our conceptions of both of them. On the side of perception, both a broadening of scope (e.g., to include linguistic events) and more moderate claims to generality are desirable. In particular, the scope of the following concepts needs to be considered carefully:

1. The concept of *physical necessity* (as a lawful basis for perceptual information). This concept seems well suited to analysis at the physical scale (e.g., surface reflections of light), but does not apply well to a variety of informative events and natural constraints at the ecological scale (including speech and other indexes). The concept seems well suited to more "molecular" levels of analysis (e.g., the optical control of limb movements), but it does not apply well at more "molar" levels of analysis (e.g., the events that regulate hunting for deer). Although physical necessity may be a fundamental support for regularities in some ecological events or psychological processes, it would be both reductive and incomplete to argue that *all* such events and processes must show that kind of lawful specificity. The concept may help us understand how we can perceive speech, or a familiar voice, or a printed page, as such, but it only begins to explain the informative value of these events; it does little to explain, for example, how we understand spoken directions, or talk by phone about yesterday's lunch, or follow a new twist in a plot. Restricting the term "perception" to those occasions in which information is lawful, complete, and expressed in overt action (cf. Turvey et al., 1981, p. 282 ff) prematurely limits the scope of theory. Principles developed for these occasions do *not* provide a sufficient basis for addressing more implicit forms of (cognitive) action or other "varieties of awareness" (Turvey et al., 1981, p. 244).[9]

---

[9]In a recent paper, Shaw & Turvey (1981) argue that the basis for our perception of an event (or the basis for performing an action with respect to it) need not be a *complete* specification of the event. (For example, a mother who notices a foot protruding from behind a sofa may perceive her *child* hiding behind the sofa and may talk to the child.) They argue further that perception in such circumstances is determined in part by autonomous processes (e.g., "psychological attitudes");

2. The concept of *affordance.* This concept is valuable for understanding perceptual systems in relation to action and adaptation, and for helping to ground meaning in the natural world. However, applying the concept universally, in its current form, does not seem appropriate. It does not help us understand how such social events as speech, writing, or artistic performance can be *significant* without affording social actions that are perfectly complementary in kind. These events often have no obvious ''dual'' in action at all.

3. The concept of *duality.* This concept is useful in guiding attention to the mutual constraints between animals and their environments, and for defining the conditions that are necessary, in principle, for successful perceiving and acting. However, it is difficult to apply this concept, without loss or distortion, to a wide range of cognitive processes and communicative actions. In the case of a conversation, for example, it does not seem possible, at any level of abstract analysis, to show that the information constraining a listener's actions is fully isomorphic (''dual'') to available information about the speaker's actions. Finding dual structure is even more difficult when one tries to define the constraints that yoke a reader to a written text. If a particular action of listening or reading is in some sense ''successful,'' then the postulate of duality argues that an isomorphism *must* hold between the listener (or reader) and their communication setting; to that degree, it would be appropriate to try to describe what is isomorphic. It seems highly unlikely, however, that the isomorphism could be found in available information about the *current* environment (the speaker's actions or the book in hand). The listener's or reader's ''success'' would have to be defined with reference to a long history of relevant *prior* occasions; the information distributed over these earlier occasions would show the isomorphism to actions that we call ''successful'' on the current occasion. But even with this broader span of environmental constraints, we could only partially describe what constrains a listener's or reader's experiences and actions on a particular occasion. For these reasons, it seems likely that the concept of duality will apply too incompletely to communication events to make it of general theoretical value, and it may apply at too abstract a level of description to provide much guidance for fine-grained description, for causal modeling, or for empirical research. Treating the formal structure of dualities as a necessary framework for inquiry in ecological psychology is therefore very risky. Overzealous application of this

---

these affect what parts of an event are sufficient to support action with respect to the whole of an event. Finally, the environmental support for an action is contingent on circumstances; perceptual knowledge is defined by whatever motivates useful action in a particular circumstance. These conditions for perception appear to depart significantly from earlier senses of ''specification'' (where information was held to be complete, structure-preserving, necessary, unique, and complementary to action), and they appear similar to the kinds of circumstances I have focused on in this paper. The authors' approach to situations of ''ostensive specification'' may provide some of the broadened set of principles we need for a perception-based theory of cognitive and communicative actions.

formalism at all grains of analysis could blind us to important texture in the events we wish to understand.[10]

In general, I am concerned that current approaches to event perception, which have focused mainly on the analysis of physical events and overt actions, do not have sufficient scope to accommodate language and cognition. Lawful specificity may be fundamental to many events we participate in, but it only begins to explain the full range of events and processes that constitute the human ecosystem. An analysis of occasions for which information is complete and definitive may help us understand some aspects of the environmental control of action or experience, but it provides little guidance for understanding thought, recollection, imagination, symbolization, comprehension, and many other important processes that function well in the context of "partial" information. We are warned that any deviations from the principles of ecological realism are unacceptable (e.g., Turvey & Carello, 1981), but there is a risk that inflexible adherence to these principles in their current form may preclude an explanation of cognitive and communicative processes, and thus, in turn, may severely limit our ability to explain human perception and action. I am not advocating a return to mentalism or dualism, nor an abandonment of the general goals of an ecological or realist theory. I prefer to view language and cognition as fundamentally *natural* events (to be defined at physiological, biological, and social–biological scales). My concern, again, is that the current canonical examples of event perception and action do not embody all of the principles needed to explain language and cognition as expressions of natural law at the ecological scale. We need to broaden our set of exemplars and readjust the scope of theory to accommodate them.

While we seek to broaden the set of principles that we use to understand perception, we also need to reevaluate our conceptions of language, if a common ground between them is to be found. This requires challenging some deeply rooted conceptions of communication and symbolization—in particular, those that treat symbols as objects or formal systems isolated from human actions, that treat language as a system of arbitrary and ambiguous representations, and that treat meaning as a resident of symbols or minds. This conventional wisdom needs to be challenged at every turn. In the preceding pages, I have sketched some alternative perspectives that may help free us from these conventional attunements and help us to perceive the common grounds we are looking for.

---

[10]One might point here, by way of warning and parallel, to the zealous pursuit of *binary oppositions* in structuralist linguistics. While this formalism has no doubt facilitated structural description at a high level, one can argue that it has provided little guidance for understanding the specific physical and biological texture of phonemes or for understanding the specific contents and subtleties of written texts.

The best observation point seems to be one that permits us to view language as a form of social action. This immediately allows some common ground with perception to be identified, even without the broadening discussed above. For example, we can think of a communicating person as a perceptible event about which there is considerable specific information in light and sound—information about an articulating, gesturing, asserting, feeling, thinking being. If theories of perception and action can be broadened appropriately, they will provide a common ground for understanding many other aspects of communication as well, including the cognitive processes that guide the flow of speech and comprehension, the regulatory effects of symbols on perception, thought, and action, and the comprehension of derivative forms of communication (e.g., written text or other notation systems).

These goals may be aided by viewing words as *indexes* of social actions. Specifically, words can be viewed as *natural signs* of the following: cognitive activities of the speaker, actions directed toward the listener, other aspects of the social setting, and events and relations in the broader environmental setting of which the actions are a part. By redintegration in a trained listener or reader, words alone can evoke attunements to previously experienced kinds of actions, events, and relations, in novel combinations of unimaginable variety.

Understanding how language functions as an index may carry over to many other kinds of natural events that provide a nonarbitrary guide to thought and action. Indexes are systematically related to events of which they are a part. They can serve as catalysts, selectively triggering, facilitating, or regulating the flow of thought and action. They can guide redintegrative processes, and thus permit experiences and attunements that go well beyond what is specifically supported by the ambient environment. Finally, their significance can only be defined in determinate fashion when they are considered in relation to ''internal'' processes that are partially autonomous of them (biological processes such as thought or anger). Their potential to provide information or serve as a catalyst cannot be determined simply by assessing whether they are ''specific'' to other events in the environment. These properties of indexes apply to our perception of any type of event that guides thought and action, not simply to our perception of linguistic events. In all of these ways, then, language comprehension and event perception are fundamentally similar.

The indexical approach developed here has been motivated by the need for a more comprehensive theory of event perception, one that can provide a natural home for language and cognition. The approach certainly needs sharpening in detail, terminology, and argument, and it will no doubt strike many theorists of perception and language as an undesirable direction in which to head at all. Nonetheless, the problems that motivate this approach are important ones, and cannot reasonably be ignored or postponed. They have to be faced early if we are to develop a comprehensive psychology rooted in natural law.

ACKNOWLEDGMENTS

I would like to thank Reuben Baron, Charles Blaich, Steven Braddon, James J. Jenkins, Kathleen McCormick, Richard Schmidt, Robert Shaw, and David Williams, among others, for discussions that have helped me find a path through this maze. I am especially grateful to Charles Blaich, Kathleen McCormick, Richard Schmidt, Robert Shaw, and William Warren for their insightful and very helpful comments on earlier drafts of this chapter. More broadly, I would like to acknowledge the inspiration I have drawn from the work of J. J. Gibson, H. H. Pattee, R. E. Shaw, E. C. Tolman (who has been here before), and M. T. Turvey. While all of these individuals have helped to attune me, I am responsible for the path I have finally chosen.

Correspondence should be addressed to Robert R. Verbrugge, Department of Psychology U-20, University of Connecticut, Storrs, CT 06268.

REFERENCES

Alston, W. P. *Philosophy of language*. Englewood Cliffs, NJ: Prentice-Hall, 1964.

Bransford, J. D. *Human cognition*. Belmont, Calif.: Wadsworth, 1979.

Bransford, J. D., & McCarrell, N. S. A sketch of a cognitive approach to comprehension. In W. Weimer & D. Palermo (Eds.), *Cognition and the symbolic processes*. Hillsdale, N.J.: Lawrence Erlbaum Associates, 1974.

Brown, R. W. *Words and things*. New York: Free Press, 1958.

Burks, A. W. Icon, index, and symbol. *Philosophy and Phenomenological Research*, 1949, *9*, 673–689.

Chomsky, N. *Syntactic structures*. The Hague: Mouton, 1957.

Dewey, J., & Bentley, A. F. *Knowing and the known*. Boston: Beacon, 1949.

Fillmore, C. J. Santa Cruz lectures on deixis. Unpublished manuscript, 1971.

Fillmore, C. J. May we come in? *Semiotica*, 1973, *9*, 97–116.

Fodor, J. A., & Pylyshyn, Z. W. How direct is visual perception?: Some reflections on Gibson's "Ecological Approach." *Cognition*, 1981, *9*, 139–196.

Fowler, C. A., Rubin, P., Remez, R. E., & Turvey, M. T. Implications for speech production of a general theory of action. In B. Butterworth (Ed.), *Language production*. New York: Academic Press, 1980.

Gibson, J. J. *The senses considered as perceptual systems*. Boston: Houghton Mifflin, 1966.

Gibson, J. J. *The ecological approach to visual perception*. Boston: Houghton Mifflin, 1979.

Gibson, J. J. Notes on direct perception and indirect apprehension. In E. Reed & R. Jones (Eds.), *Reasons for realism: Selected essays of James J. Gibson*. Hillsdale, N.J.: Lawrence Erlbaum Associates, 1982.

Green, S., & Marler, P. The analysis of animal communication. In P. Marler & J. G. Vandenbergh (Eds.), *Handbook of behavioral neurobiology* (Vol. 3: *Social behavior and communication*). New York: Plenum, 1979.

Griffin, D. R. *Listening in the dark: The acoustic orientation of bats and men*. New Haven: Yale University Press, 1958.

Hamilton, W. *Lectures on metaphysics and logic* (4 Vols.). Edinburgh: W. Blackwood and Sons, 1859.

Hollingworth, H. L. *The psychology of thought*. New York: Appleton, 1926.

James, W. *The principles of psychology*. New York: Holt, 1890.

Kugler, P. N., Kelso, J. A. S., & Turvey, M. T. On the concept of coordinative structures as dissipative structures. I. Theoretical lines of convergence. In G. E. Stelmach & J. Requin (Eds.), *Tutorials in motor behavior*. Amsterdam: North-Holland, 1980.

Lyons, J. *Semantics* (Vol. 2). Cambridge: Cambridge University Press, 1977.

Marler, P. Primate vocalization: Affective or symbolic? In G. H. Bourne (Ed.), *Progress in ape research*. New York: Academic Press, 1977.

Michaels, C. F., & Carello, C. *Direct perception*. Englewood Cliffs, N.J.: Prentice-Hall, 1981.

Pattee, H. H. How does a molecule become a message? *Developmental Biology Supplement*, 1969, *3*, 1–16.

Pattee, H. H. Laws and constraints, symbols and languages. In C. H. Waddington (Ed.), *Towards a theoretical biology* (Vol. 4). Chicago: Aldine, 1972.

Pattee, H. H. Clues from molecular symbol systems. In U. Bellugi & M. Studdert-Kennedy (Eds.), *Signed and spoken language: Biological constraints on linguistic form*. Weinheim: Verlag Chemie, 1980.

Peirce, C. S. *Collected papers* (Vol. 2). Cambridge, Mass.: Harvard University Press, 1931.

Pylyshyn, Z. W. Computation and cognition: Issues in the foundations of cognitive science. *Behavioral and Brain Sciences*, 1980, *3*, 111–169.

Reddy, M. J. The conduit metaphor—A case of frame conflict in our language about language. In A. Ortony (Ed.), *Metaphor and thought*. Cambridge: Cambridge University Press, 1979.

Russell, B. *The analysis of mind*. London: Allen & Unwin, 1921.

Russell, B. *Human knowledge: Its scope and limits*. New York: Simon and Schuster, 1948.

Saussure, F. de *Course in general linguistics*. New York: McGraw-Hill, 1966.

Schön, D. A. Generative metaphor: A perspective on problem-setting in social policy. In A. Ortony (Ed.), *Metaphor and thought*. Cambridge: Cambridge University Press, 1979.

Shaw, R. E., & Alley, T. R. How to draw learning curves: The view from hereditary mechanics. In T. D. Johnston & A. T. Pietrewicz (Eds.), *Issues in the ecological study of learning*. Hillsdale, N.J.: Lawrence Erlbaum Associates, in press.

Shaw, R. E., & Bransford, J. D. Introduction: Psychological approaches to the problems of knowledge. In R. E. Shaw & J. D. Bransford (Eds.), *Perceiving, acting, and knowing: Toward an ecological psychology*. Hillsdale, N.J.: Lawrence Erlbaum Associates, 1977.

Shaw, R. E., & Cutting, J. Clues from an ecological theory of event perception. In U. Bellugi & M. Studdert-Kennedy (Eds.), *Signed and spoken language: Biological constraints on linguistic form*. Weinheim: Verlag Chemie, 1980.

Shaw, R. E., & Turvey, M. T. Coalitions as models for ecosystems: A realist perspective on perceptual organization. In M. Kubovy & J. Pomerantz (Eds.), *Perceptual organization*. Hillsdale, N.J.: Lawrence Erlbaum Associates, 1981.

Shaw, R. E., Turvey, M. T., & Mace, W. Ecological psychology: The consequence of a commitment to realism. In W. Weimer & D. Palermo (Eds.), *Cognition and the symbolic processes II*. Hillsdale, N.J.: Lawrence Erlbaum Associates, 1982.

Shaw, R. E., & Wilson, B. E. Abstract conceptual knowledge: How we know what we know. In D. Klahr (Ed.), *Cognition and instruction*. Hillsdale, N.J.: Lawrence Erlbaum Associates, 1976.

Shepard, R. N. Form, formation, and transformation of mental representations. In R. Solso (Ed.), *Information processing and cognition*. Hillsdale, N.J.: Lawrence Erlbaum Associates, 1975.

Struhsaker, T. T. Auditory communication among vervet monkeys (*cercopithecus aethiops*). In S. A. Altmann (Ed.), *Social communication among primates*. Chicago: University of Chicago Press, 1967.

Tartter, V. C. Happy talk: Perceptual and acoustic effects of smiling on speech. *Perception & Psychophysics*, 1980, *27*, 24–27.

Turvey, M. T. Contrasting orientations to the theory of visual information processing. *Psychological Review*, 1977, *84*, 67–88.

Turvey, M. T., & Carello, C. Cognition: The view from ecological realism. *Cognition*, 1981, *10*, 313–321.

Turvey, M. T., & Shaw, R. The primacy of perceiving: An ecological formulation of perception for understanding memory. In L.-G. Nilsson (Ed.), *Perspectives on memory research*. Hillsdale, N.J.: Lawrence Erlbaum Associates, 1979.

Turvey, M. T., Shaw, R. E., & Mace, W. Issues in the theory of action: Degrees of freedom, coordinative structures and coalitions. In J. Requin (Ed.), *Attention and performance VII*. Hillsdale, N.J.: Lawrence Erlbaum Associates, 1978.

Turvey, M. T., Shaw, R. E., Reed, E. S., & Mace, W. M. Ecological laws of perceiving and acting: In reply to Fodor and Pylyshyn (1981). *Cognition*, 1981, *9*, 237–304.

Verbrugge, R. R. Transformations in knowing: A realist view of metaphor. In R. P. Honeck & R. R. Hoffman (Eds.), *Cognition and figurative language*. Hillsdale, N.J.: Lawrence Erlbaum Associates, 1980.

Verbrugge, R. R. The role of metaphor in our perception of language. *Annals of the New York Academy of Sciences*, in press.

Verbrugge, R. R., Rakerd, B., Fitch, H., Tuller, B., & Fowler, C. A. The perception of speech events: An ecological approach. In R. E. Shaw & W. Mace (Eds.), *Event perception: An ecological perspective*. Hillsdale, N.J.: Lawrence Erlbaum Associates, in press.

Warren, W. H. *A biodynamic basis for perception and action in climbing*. Unpublished doctoral dissertation, University of Connecticut, 1982. (University Microfilms No. 8309263)

Waters, D. P. *Meaning as behavior: Symbolic control in natural systems*. Unpublished manuscript, Department of Systems Science, State University of New York, Binghamton, N.Y., August 1981.

Weinreich, U. On the semantic structure of language. In J. H. Greenberg (Ed.), *Universals of language*. Cambridge: MIT Press, 1963.

Weiss, P. A. The living system: Determinism stratified. In A. Koestler & J. R. Smythies (Ed.), *Beyond reductionism*. Boston: Beacon Press, 1969.

10 The Physics of Controlled Collisions: A Reverie About Locomotion

Peter N. Kugler
The Crump Institute for Medical Engineering
University of California, Los Angeles

Michael T. Turvey
University of Connecticut
and
Haskins Laboratories

Claudia Carello
State University of New York at Binghamton

Robert E. Shaw
University of Connecticut

> *No fact of behavior, it seems to me, betrays the weakness of the old concept of visual stimuli so much as the achieving of contact without collision—for example, the fact that a bee can land on a flower without blundering into it. The reason can only be that centrifugal flow of the structure of the bee's optic array specifies locomotion and controls the flow of locomotor responses. (p. 14)*
>
> *But to understand, to be able to explain and predict, entails the knowing of laws. It is our own fault if we do not know the laws. (p. 15)*
>
> —J. J. Gibson (in Reed & Jones, 1982)

INTRODUCTION

Imagine the following scenario. It is late in the afternoon and since early morning you have been mulling over a long term concern of Gibson's (1950, 1960, 1961,

195

FIG. 10.1. Observing controlled collisions.

1966, 1979), namely, the optical structure ambient to an animal that is generated by the layout of surfaces and by the animal's movements (both the movements of its limbs relative to its body and the movements of its body, as a unit, relative to the surface layout). You are taken by the subtlety of Gibson's point that this optical structure resembles neither the surface layout nor the movements but it is specific to them because it is nomically (lawfully) dependent on them. And you are impressed by Gibson's insistence that these dependencies between properties of the animal-environment relation and properties of the ambient light are instances of laws, indigenous to the ecological scale (the scale of animals and their environments), that make possible the control of activity.

Your thoughts return repeatedly to locomotion, Gibson's favorite example, and to his characterization of locomotion as a matter of controlled encounters (Gibson, 1979) with the substantial surfaces that comprise the objects and places of the animal's niche. In the course of locomoting, an animal's surfaces may contact surfaces of the environment. These contacts are selective and they vary in intensity. There are hard contacts (as in predatory attacks), medium contacts (as in diving into water), soft contacts (as in alighting on a branch) and noncontacts (as in steering between trees). It seems to you that it might prove helpful to know what happens to bodies, in general, when they collide. And to this purpose, you direct your reading to the physics of collisions (summarized in the Appendix).

Your attention begins to wander. Looking out the window you see a bird in flight (Fig. 1). You admire its ability to adjust its flight to the surroundings. Your thoughts meander—"laws," "controlled collisions," "a physics of the ecological scale." You fall asleep and dream. . .

THE REVERIE

You are a physicist investigating a type of visible particle whose identity is unknown to you. Particles of this type range in mass from .001 kg to 10,000 kg. You watch the trajectory of a token particle through a nonuniform, three–dimensional surround as depicted in Fig. 10.2. In some regions of the surround, matter or energy is more concentrated than in other regions. The particle sometimes moves between the particularly dense regions and sometimes it contacts them. The particle's speed is not uniform. There are obvious decelerations and accelerations prior to contact, but these are not uniform either. Sometimes contact is preceded by a marked deceleration so that the contact is gentle—very little momentum is exchanged. Sometimes the deceleration prior to contact is hardly noticeable or there is an obvious acceleration so that the contact is violent or hard—a great deal of momentum is transferred to the contacted region. And sometimes the deceleration is in an intermediate range, such that the contact is neither gentle nor especially violent.

Not all the particularly dense regions of the surround are stationary. Some regions move just like the particle. Other regions move, but without the variations in accelerations that characterize the particle. Basically, the particle's trajectory with respect to the moving parts of the surround is not different from its trajectory with respect to the stationary parts: There is a steering among moving regions and contact—ranging from soft to hard—with moving regions.

Repeated observation of the particle's behavior with respect to the surround leads you to certain tentative conclusions as to its nature.

Conclusion 1.   In tracking the particle's behavior, you monitor the mechanical quantity of momentum. The rate of change of momentum identifies a force or interaction between particle and surround. Usually momentum and its first derivative prove sufficient for the purpose of describing a given particle's trajectory. For the behavior of this particle, however, it seems that there is another mechanical quantity that is much more relevant: The second derivative of momentum or *the rate of change of force*. Characteristically, as the particle approaches a region of the surround, it exhibits a systematic sequence of acceler-

FIG. 10.2.   As the particle moves through a nonuniform surround, it sometimes steers between dense regions (1 and 4) sometimes contacts them gently (2) or violently (3), and does not maintain a uniform speed.

ative changes. You wish to give this mechanical quantity a name. "Jitter" comes to mind but for obvious reasons you are attracted to "control" and you make note of the control quantity's relation to the more familiar mechanical quantities of momentum, impulse, and force (Table 1).

The *control* of a collision (read in the same sense that one would read "the *momentum* of a collision" or "the *force* of a collision") is, therefore, measurable. It would be given by the integration of C within the spatial and/or temporal limits of the collision, assuming that they can be reasonably approximated. Because of the fact that the mechanical quantity of control is a natural extension of the mechanical quantity of force, you are willing to speculate that there is a (scalar) quantity that relates to control in the manner that potential (a term referring to the concentration or distribution of a conserved quantity such as energy) related to force. Ordinary language usage suggests the term *coordination*

TABLE 10.1

Quantity	Symbol	Composition	Dimensions
MOMENTUM	P	MV	MLT^{-1}
IMPULSE	I	$\Delta\, MV$	MLT^{1}
FORCE	F	$\Delta\, MV/T$	MLT^{2}
CONTROL	C	$\Delta\, MV/T^2$	MLT^{-3}

[Where M = mass, V = velocity, T = time, Δ = change, L = length.]

for this quantity. The suggestion is fortunate: Both ''potential'' and ''coordination'' are configurational notions. You are tantalized by this idea that the conceptions of control and coordination may be interpreted as mechanical quantities that are as principled in their relation to one another as are force and potential.

Conclusion 2.   It is evident that while proximity to things in the surround is a determinant of the forces forming the particle's trajectory, it is neither the sole determinant nor the most significant. Conventional particle trajectories are shaped by interactions with regions—usually other particles—which attract or repel a particle to varying degrees depending on the particle's distance from them. A force that is a function only of distance is termed ''conservative.'' The forces affecting the trajectory of your particle seem to depend on time (the time-to-contact) and, perhaps, velocity (the velocity prior to contact). They are *non*-conservative forces. You guess that these forces—which entail a dissipation rather than a conservation of energy—originate in the particle rather than in the surround. There is something special about this particle; it seems to have (on-board) a replenishable source of potential energy that it can deploy.

Conclusion 3.   The number of soft, medium, and hard collisions; and non-collisions, exhibited by your particle during a period of observation is very large. Given so many interactions, you think it worthwhile to adopt a statistical mechanical orientation toward the particle's behavior. It seems particularly promising to inquire about the distribution function that characterizes the many interactions of the particle and surround. In the tradition of Boltzman, Maxwell, and Zipf you look to the distribution function as a way of appreciating the constraints—the quantities that must be conserved—on the interactions of particle-like entities. Relatedly, you see the usefulness of the distribution function for classifying particles. Types of interactions will be broadly distinguished by the quantities conserved over interactions; these differences in conservations will show up as differences in distribution functions given that a distribution function is *completely* determined by the operative conservations.

In the construction of a distribution function one asks, roughly, how many particles (in any arbitrarily chosen volume) will possess a particular value of a particular quantity. Boltzman and Maxwell focussed on gases and the property of velocity. Over the very many interactions of n particles of a gas, the conservations of total mass (nmv^0), momentum (nmv^1) and vis viva (nmv^2, or twice the kinetic energy) determine that the particles will tend to move at one particular speed, more or less. Collectively, the conservations select ("prefer") a distance between collisions (mean free path) and a time between collisions (mean relaxation time). The mean and variance (the "more or less") of the velocity reflect the concentration of the conserved quantities. The mean and the variance of the velocity prove to be characteristics of a gas, and both are affected by its temperature.

Thinking about your particle in comparison to a gas particle you are of the opinion that the contrast between the two is most sharply drawn with respect to momentum change in relation to velocity. Impulses of gas particles are of maximum frequency when the velocity of the particles is zero, that is, at the moment of impact. At any other moment impulse is nonexistent. Statistically, your particle could be assigned a mean free path and a mean relaxation time but, importantly, across the full range of velocities that it exhibits, impulses can be observed. Unlike the gas particles, there is no velocity at which the frequency of impulses is concentrated.

You imagine a distribution function defined over three coordinates: number of particles, velocity, and number of impulses. For a typical gas and for particles of the type you are studying the distribution functions differ significantly. The peaking of impulse frequency at zero velocity that reflects the conservations governing the gas will not be found in the distribution function of your particle type. What does the absence of a peak (the fact that impulse is uniformly distributed over velocity) mean? The distribution function for your type of particle must be the way it is because of the conservations that are operative. This is true by definition. However, the conservations governing your particle's behavior cannot be the typical velocity-linked conservations of mass, momentum and energy. *The conservations governing your particle's behavior are velocity indifferent.*

Conclusion 4. Although you are unable for the present to say much about the selectivity of the trajectory—the fact that some regions function as attractors and some as repellers—it is clear to you that the particle's trajectory *minimizes the mometum transferred to the particle from the surround.* What sort of principle is the particle subject to that demands no momentum bumps? If the particle's interior was complex and if its persistence depended on maintaining that interior, then keeping the level of momentum absorption below some critical value would clearly be important—large transfers of momentum could fracture the particle (see Appendix). At the level of the particle this principle reads: *move so as to conserve a smooth unitary process* ("smooth" meaning no sudden energy or momentum bumps—excessive energy or momentum exchanges—and "unitary" meaning that the characteristic form and function of the particle is preserved). As a physicist, however, you might be uncomfortable with a conservation that is (1) defined at the level of the individual particle; and (2) not identified with a quantity. The traditional conservations of mass, energy and momentum are in reference to measurable physical quantities exhibited by the particle. Further, the invariant nature of these quantities is not defined at the level of the individual particle but minimally at the level of a pair of interacting particles. For example, with regard to momentum conservation, the momentum of each of two individual particles may change with a collision but the summed momentum of the two particles after collision equals the summed momentum of the two particles before collision.

Your discomfort with the notion of a conservation of a smooth, unitary process might be alleviated (but not eliminated) by the observation that some of the so-called quantum numbers conserved in the collisions of subatomic particles denote a qualitative property—the class of the particle—that is invariant at the level of the individual particle. You note how well leptons (approximately eight particles that do not take part in "strong" interactions) conserve their class membership; accelerating a lepton such as the positron to the point where its mass is equal to that of a proton (a member of the baryon class of particles that *do* take part in "strong" interactions) does not result in a metamorphosis. Nevertheless, you would be happier with a more traditional orientation to conservation, given the size of the particle you are studying. You suppose that your particle might be a member of a class. Is there a conserved quantity defined at the level of the class? For example, over the many trajectories of the many members of this class, perhaps the number of members is conserved.[1] If a quantity such as the latter had to remain constant then the minimization of momentum transfer from surround to particle (and hence the conservation of a smooth, unitary process) would be rationalized.

Conclusion 5.   You recognize that a circumstance, such as the one you are studying, in which forces are shaped to achieve one trajectory and to prevent others, usually defines a machine. Somehow a machine conception must be brought to bear on your understanding of the particle. Because a machine is a way of harnessing mechanical forces to do work in determinate directions, a machine can be properly termed a constraint—a restriction on the laws of motion. Very often a machine is constructed with hard, resistant pieces linked by hard, resistant chains. Is your particle a hard-molded machine like this? What

---

[1]Iberall (1977) has suggested that the number of members of a biological species is approximately conserved and a physics that accommodates biology will require the addition of this conservation to the list of conventional conservations.

makes you dubious is that a hard-molded machine is not very flexible and the particle's trajectory indicates that the shaping of force to achieve gentle, medium and violent collisions, or to avoid collisions, *is* flexible. The rate of change in the rate of change of the particle's momentum (i.e., the control) varies from region to region of the surround. The unavoidable conclusion is that the forces are harnessed by a constraint that cannot be hard-molded. To draw the comparison, you might say that the constraint on the nonconservative forces centered in the particle is "soft" rather than "hard" and that the appropriate machine conception is soft-molded rather than hard-molded.

Conclusion 6.   Because you must avoid postulating action at a distance, you make the assumption that *the soft constraint on the particle-based forces is a field.* This field is ambient to the particle. Is it a field associated with a force, a quantum field? Of the four fundamental forces only the gravitational and electromagnetic forces apply, given the magnitude of the particle. The electromagnetic field would seem to be a better bet than the gravitational, but neither is particularly appealing because you are convinced that *if the soft constraint is a field, it cannot be a field associated with a force.* It may well be caused by electromagnetic phenomena but it is qualitatively different from them.[2] Your conclusion follows in part from certain distinctions drawn by Pattee (1972, 1977). Forces and constraints are not things of the same type, even though constraints—like all other aspects of nature—are built from the four fundamental forces. To begin with, the forces are not embodied in anything particular and they apply to everything within the range to which they apply (gravity, for instance, applies everywhere). A constraint, however, has a particular embodiment and applies to a particular thing. Further, whereas the important feature of a force, its magnitude, is dependent on rate (the derivative of a variable or variables with respect to time) the important feature of a constraint, its selectivity (resulting in one directed motion rather than others), is not dependent on rate.

Conclusion 7.   It is a small step from the preceding conclusion to the conclusion that if the field in question is *not* a force field then the fundamental dimensions from which its relevant variables are constructed cannot include mass (M). That is, the field must be kinematic—of fundamental dimensions length (L) and time (T)—or geometric—of fundamental dimension L, but it cannot be kinetic[3]—of fundamental dimensions, M, L, and T. As you have already noted this field must constrain the dissipative forces focused in the particle so as to keep to a minimum the momentum transferred to the particle from the surround. You puzzle over this requirement. Doesn't it mean that the field in question must

---

[2]Gibson's optic array (1961, 1966, 1979) seems to be a field of this type.

[3]Gibson repeatedly pointed out that optical motion is altogether different from material motion—that optical motion has no inertia (for example, Gibson, 1979).

be structured by the kinetics of the surround and the kinetics of the particle? If the field did not faithfully reflect these two kinetic domains then there would be no lawful basis for relating forces originating in the surround to forces originating in the particle and the exchange of momentum could not then be regulated. You suppose, therefore, that the field in question has this capability and inquire what this tells you about the general properties of the field.

To bring things into focus, you assume (1) the particle to be in motion at a constant velocity in one direction; and (2) an absence of motion in the surround. Normally you would represent this by a velocity vector originating in the particle and pointing in the direction of travel. However you find it convenient to think of the field hydrodynamically—as a fluid flowing relative to the particle. So instead of assigning a velocity vector to the particle (because you regard it as the origin) you assign a velocity vector (the negative of the particle's velocity) to each point in the field, where each field point can be anchored to a surround point.

This vector flow field viewed strictly as a kinematic field is always at equilibrium; there is no tendency *on the part of the field* to restore its structure following a disturbance. Further, from the perspective of the flow field, a disturbance is reversible in that any disturbance and its reverse are energetically equal. This reversible, equilibrium character of the flow field is because the flow field is not paying the energy cost, so to speak, of its changes. That bill is being paid by the *kinetic* field—the particle—to which the flow field is coupled: Only changes in energy flux can give rise to changes in flow, and the changes in energy flux in this case are bound to the particle's on-board energy reservoirs or potentials.

The reversibility of the flow field appears to be of paramount importance. If the flow field were not reversible, if it carried potentials that "wound up" the trajectories, then the flow field would itself determine some of the properties it exhibits. A reversible field on the other hand, meets the criteria of linearity—superposition and proportionality—and can, therefore, faithfully map the kinetics that give rise to it. You feel that there may well be a very general principle here: *The availability of a reversible field is a prerequisite for the kind of controlled collisions that your particle exhibits with respect to its surround.*

What properties arise in the flow field caused by the particle's motion relative to the surround? A coarse analysis reveals the following: kinematic properties, consisting of (1) *transformations defined over the entire flow field*—such as outflow from a point and inflow to a point; and (2) the *inverse of the rate of dilation* of a topologically closed region of the field; and (3) geometric properties viz., *singularities,* such as foci of outflow and inflow.[4] Global transformations (1) are specific to the displacement of the particle as a unit relative to the surroundings (moving forward or backward); the inverse of the rate of dilation

---

[4]Properties of this kind were identified by Gibson (1966, 1979) for the optical flow field resulting from the locomotion of an animal in a cluttered environment.

(2)—a property you recall reading about in the astronomer Hoyle's science-fiction novel *The Black Cloud* (1957)—is specific to the time at which the particle will contact a region on its path while the first derivative of this property, which is seen to be a dimensionless quantity, is specific to the deceleration of the particle with respect to the approach region.[5] The foci of flow (3) will be specific to the regions, or to the gaps between them, toward which the particle is moving; that is, the foci are specific to the direction of the particle's trajectory.

It is obvious to you that under normal circumstances, the style and/or rate of transformation will not be uniform throughout the entire kinematic field; rather, there will be discontinuities caused by region boundaries that will identify more precisely the relationship between the moving particle and a particular layout of dense regions (depots of mass). For example, within the global outflow "local" properties will be revealed, such as: (1) a gain of structure inside a closed contour in the field specifies an opening in a dense region through which the particle could travel; (2) a loss of structure outside a closed contour in the field specifies an obstacle to the particle's current trajectory.[6]

Clearly, motion of the particle gives rise to properties that do *not* exist when the particle is immobile. The properties identified above, both kinematic *and* geometric, are annihilated when the temporal dimension goes to zero and the ambient kinematic field is reduced to an ambient geometric field. For example, "streaming" engendered by the particle's motion condenses out geometric, rate-independent points, the singularities, that are not identified by a geometric field analysis. A geometric field analysis at any instant of time would not contain the singularities.

Conclusion 8.   You are drawn to the fact that your cursory examination of the properties of the kinematic field (caused by the displacement of the particle relative to the surround) revealed a dimensionless number: The first derivative of a kinematic field property specifying time-to-contact. What intrigues you is the possibility of an analogy between the dimensionless quantities of the kinematic field (assuming that there are more to be discovered) and the dimensionless quantities that order a kinetic field, such as a hydrodynamic field.

The transition from one state to a qualitatively distinct state of a physical system usually indexes a critical change in the relation between two competing processes. Your favorite example is the transition from laminar flow to turbulence which occurs when the processes (viscous, dissipative, irreversible) that resist fluid motion cannot, in their current organization, balance the processes (inertial, conservative, reversible) that sustain fluid motion. The dimensionless Reynolds number gives an index of the competition between inertial (etc.) and viscous (etc.) processes. High inertial forces favor turbulence, with the pro-

---

[5]Lee (1976, 1980) identified this property for the condition in which a point of observation approaches, or is approached by, a substantial environmental surface.

[6]See Gibson's (1979) discussion of the optical support for the control of locomotion.

nounced internal shearing that that implies. High viscous forces prohibit sustained turbulence by damping motions that lead to discontinuity (e.g., eddies) and thus ensure laminar flow. The inertial processes are governed by Newton's law of inertia and the viscous processes are governed by the law for shear stress of a Newtonian fluid. The Reynolds number, therefore, might be described as indexing the relation between the two laws. On either side of the critical value of the Reynolds number the two laws are mutually cooperative whereas at a critical value one of the two laws dominates the other (that is, a competition occurs).

You are aware that, as a general rule, any major dimensionless number used in physics can be derived directly from the laws known to apply to the phenomenon to which the number refers (Schuring, 1980). A dimensionless number is often referred to as a Pi number (Buckingham, 1914), and when it is derivable from one or more laws it is termed a *principal* Pi number (Schuring, 1980). The important thing you note here is the linkage between physical states of affairs that principal Pi numbers index and the facts of critical values and behavioral modes (or natural categories). As you see it, the shift in balance between two (or more) laws governing a phenomenon from situations in which they cooperate to situations in which one law alone is responsible can produce categorically distinct states. The transition from cooperation to competition between governing laws is tantamount to a natural boundary making device: Behavioral modes are created, critical values of one or more variables are defined.

In sum, the critical values of dimensionless quantities in the kinetic cases mark off distinct physical states. It does not seem likely to you that dimensionless quantities will play this role in the kinematic field of constraint because of the absence of forces—by definition—in the kinematic field. But you cannot be too sure, one way or the other. For the present, however, it seems prudent to emphasize the specificational rather than the physical nature of the kinematic field. This emphasis raises the question: Do dimensionless quantities in the kinematic field mark off—at critical values—distinct *specificational* states?

A soft collision with no momentum exchange between the particle of interest and a nonmoving, dense region on its path requires that the particle decelerate. A deceleration is adequate if and only if the distance it will take the particle to stop with that deceleration is less than or equal to the particle's current distance from the region of upcoming contact. Your calculations show that for any particle of the type you are studying a deceleration is adequate if and only if:

$$P_i(\text{contact}) = \frac{d\tau(t)}{dt} \geq -0.5$$

where $\tau(t)$ is the time-to-contact variable of the kinematic field.[7] You state this

---

[7]Lee (1976, 1980) performed these calculations and highlighted the significance of the first derivative of the time-to-contact variable. Other optically defined dimensionless quantities that order (at critical values) specificational states have been suggested and experimentally examined by Warren (1982).

result as follows: When less than -0.5, the dimensionless quantity, Pi (contact), specifies that the particle will experience a momentum bump if present conditions persist; when equal to or greater than -0.5, Pi (contact) specifies that the particle's contact with the upcoming region will involve no momentum exchange if present conditions persist.

You are encouraged by the results of your analysis. It does seem that *critical values of dimensionless quantities in the kinematic field distinguish between qualitatively distinct specificational states.* And it seems to you that the analogy should be pursued further. For example, you might ask: What kinds of laws go into the construction of pi numbers applicable to the kinematic field?

Conclusion 9.   Because the kinematic field ambient to the particle constrains its trajectory, you infer that the field and the particle must be coupled. This coupling is obviously "soft" rather than "hard." The question to which you now turn is: What must be required of the particle and of this soft coupling if the particle is to be constrainable in a way that makes its collisions controllable? What must be true of the particle so that it can be reliably constrained by the kinematic field?

It appears to you that there are two important and very general conditions on the coupling. One condition is that the coupling be linear. What would have to be true of the particle's interior in order to guarantee a linear coupling? The interior of the particle could be in either a reversible or irreversible steady state. If it were reversible the distribution of conserved quantities would be (nearly) uniform and the interior would be (approximately) at equilibrium. This means that there would be no problem of "connectivity": A disturbance felt by any region of the interior could be transported to any other region of the interior, however remote. On the other hand, if the interior's steady state were irreversible then there would be marked and persistent source-sink gradients. As a consequence, a disturbance felt in one part of the interior may not be transported to other parts. Conservations are not carried up gradients and, conventionally, it is through the transport of conserved quantities that one part of a physical system "informs" another part about what it is doing. A loss of connectivity among the regions that accompanies irreversible steady states means that the overall effects of the kinematic field on the particle's interior—however those effects are realized—could be discontinuous and equivocal. In short, it seems to you that if the steady state of the interior were irreversible and far from equilibrium then there would not be a constant scale for laws relating properties of the kinematic field to force trajectories of the particle. You are led to assume, therefore, that a linear coupling, which would be both flexible and precise, requires a reversible, close-to-equilibrium steady state. This is tantamount to assuming that the state space of the particle's force trajectories are quasiergodic (that is, no strong preferences or dislikes): The particle should not be biased in a way that undercuts the specifying capability of the kinematic field.

The other condition on the coupling is that the criterial "smooth and unitary process" be upheld. This condition would be met only if the coupling involves very little energy (relative to the energy stored and dissipated by the particle). A coupling achieved at high energy expense might take too long (there would be steep external gradients) or it might involve a large momentum exchange and irreversible processes (marked by stress and shock waves). You conclude that there must be an energetically cheap translational gate effecting the coupling of the particle to the kinematic field.[8] Or, said differently, you conclude that the kinematic field is the spatio–temporal structure of a *low*-energy field. Your best hunch is that this low-energy field is the electromagnetic field modulated by the absorption/emission properties of the surround.

Conclusion 10.   Some of your observations of the particle's trajectories are especially puzzling. Two of them are depicted in Fig. 10.3 and 10.4. In one observation (Fig. 10.3), you noted that your particle mimicked the trajectory of another particle of like kind. The two trajectories were, for a time, coupled. This coupling of trajectories did not depend on the distance between the particles. Sometimes you witnessed the coupling when the particles were very close (Fig. 10.3a). At other times you saw the coupling when the particles were separated by a substantial distance (Fig. 10.3b).

---

[8]For animals, the photoreceptor processes perform the role of a translational gate that involves very little energy relative to the animal's daily energy expenditure.

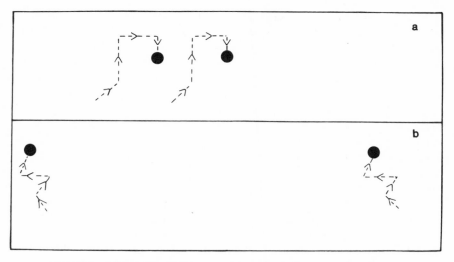

FIG. 10.3.   The particle mimicks the trajectory of another at near (a) and far (b) distances.

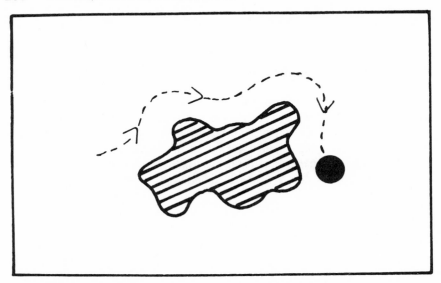

FIG. 10.4. The particle's trajectory follows the border of a dense region of the surround without contacting it.

In the other observation (Fig. 10.4) you noted that your particle's trajectory would follow, without contact, the border of a dense region in the surround. Here it seemed that there was another temporary coupling—between the form of the particle's trajectory and the form of a region.

Why do you find these observations especially puzzling? It is because, as a physicist, you are committed to explaining any coupling (coordination or cooperativity) of one thing with another through conservation principles, and it is not immediately obvious to you what the principles are that apply to the two couplings depicted in Fig. 10.3 and 10.4. If you had observed two, more conventional particles coupled in interaction, then you would have said that (1) some quantity was exchanged between the particles—at the very least momentum and energy; and (2) the coupling was an instance of coordination or cooperativity *because the exchange of quantities between the particles is constrained by the requirement that these quantities be conserved over the pair of particles.* You would explain the loss of degrees of freedom that marks an interaction between particles by an appeal to conservational invariants.

You feel, therefore, that you have no option but to identify the conservations that account for the coupling phenomena depicted in Fig. 10.3 and 10.4. Because the ''mimicking'' phenomenon is indifferent to particle separation, you believe that the conservations in question are unlikely to be energy or momentum related. Conventionally, couplings based on energy exchange depend on the distance between the particles (i.e., the inverse square law).

After a good deal of deliberation and hesitation you suggest the following: One of the conservations accounting for phenomena of the type depicted in Fig. 10.3 and 10.4 must be *conservation of topological form.* (You believe that this conservation is integral to these instances of cooperativity but recognize that this conservation alone cannot account for the loss of degrees of freedom). Your use of topological form is intuitive rather than technical. You mean, most generally, adjacencies and successitivies—that is, neighborhoods in space and time. And you mean, more particularly, properties of the kind captured in contrasts such as inner/outer, sooner/later, lower/higher, closer/further, slower/faster, larger/smaller, and so on. Further, your use of conservation is intended to mean that from one "slice" of the kinematic field that couples the particle to the surround to another, the topological form is constant. This conservation of adjacencies and successivities from a location proximate to the source to a location distal to the source is made possible by the reversible, equilibrium, low-energy nature of the kinematic field. Identifying the two particles in Fig. 10.3 as kinetic fields, it is clear that the adjacencies and successivities arising from one kinetic field are perfectly conserved over the distance that separates the two kinetic fields. The proof is in the adjacencies and successivities arising from the second kinetic field (your particle)—they duplicate those arising from the first.

Conclusion 11. A better stab can now be made at the machine conception befitting the constraining of the forces that determine the particle's trajectory. You have come to the understanding that whatever the machine conception, it cannot apply just to the particle; rather, it must apply minimally to both the particle and to the kinematic field that is lawfully generated by the surround and the particle's displacement relative to it. It is very obviously true that the particle and the kinematic field are distinguishable. They clearly are different materially and, further, the particle, as a source of forces, is a kinetic field. Given that they are so different, you are puzzled by the principle that relates them as a single machine.

Now you are set to thinking: What, after all, is a machine? Turning to examples of hard-molded machines you are struck by the fact that they are always closed kinematic chains, where a chain consists of kinematic pairs of elements, for example, shaft and bearing, bolt and nut, etc. Each element in a pair, because of its resistant material qualities and its form, envelops and constrains the other so that all motions except those desired in the mechanism are prevented. There is kinematic closure. You can appreciate why a thoughtful student[9] of hard-molded machines might say that *a machine consists solely of elements which correspond, pair wise, reciprocally.* Kinematic closure is the central principle governing the construction of hard-molded machines.

---

[9]Such as Reuleaux (1963).

Two other features of hard-molded machines capture your attention. First, in a closed pair of elements the roles of "fixed" and "moveable" can be exchanged (for example, the nut can rotate and translate relative to the fixed bolt or the bolt can rotate and translate relative to the fixed nut). This inversion of roles causes no change in the motion belonging to the pair as you show in a sketch (Fig. 10.5). In both of the situations shown in your sketch the separation between the nut and the head of the bolt is decreasing. Second, although it is common for a pair of elements to be completely closed in terms of bodily envelopment, it is not necessary. The closure that prevents certain motions from occurring can be achieved without material structures; you note, for example, how vertical downward closing forces keep the wheels of a train in contact with the rails.

It occurs to you that this invariant characteristic of hard-molded machines—reciprocally constraining, kinematic pairs—may well be an invariant characteristic of all machines, including the soft-molded machine you are trying to understand. Are the paired elements of this machine, the particle and the field ambient to the particle, kinematically closed? If there is a generalizable principle of kinematic closure, as you suppose, then the particle and the ambient field should pass the inversion test: For example, fixing the entire surround and moving the particle in one direction should have the same consequence as fixing the particle and moving the entire surround in the opposite direction. In the diagram (Fig. 10.6) situation A should be indistinguishable from situation B.

Your empirical validation proceeds as follows: You note a location where the particle frequently comes to rest. (It is natural to assume that this location is a singularity—a stable location of minimal potential energy—in the particle–surround system.) You then arrange matters so that on the next occasion that the particle is immobile at that location the entire surround moves relative to the particle. You observe that the particle displaces in the same direction as the surround.[10] You conclude that the vector flow field lawfully generated by the

---

[10]Lishman and Lee (1973) have shown that in a room where the walls and ceiling can move as a

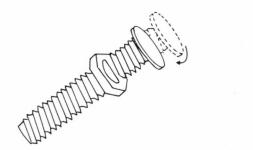
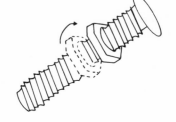

FIG. 10.5.   An example of a hard-molded machine. The distance between the nut and the head of the bolt can be decreased either by turning the bolt relative to the fixed nut as in (a) or turning the nut relative to the fixed bolt as in (b).

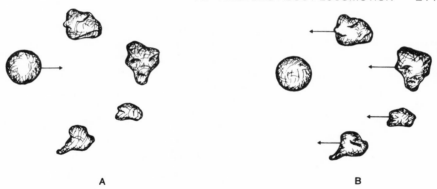

FIG. 10.6.   An example of a kinematically closed soft-molded machine. The distance between the particle and the surround can be decreased either by moving the particle relative to the fixed surround as in A or moving the surround relative to the fixed particle as in B.

displacement of the surround in direction $+X$ specifies a displacement of the particle from the singularity in direction $-X$. Hence, the particle displaces in direction $+X$ toward the singularity.

This kind of kinematic closure differs from the most familiar types. The two familiar type you have already remarked upon might be labeled (1) kinematic closure through resistant bodies; and (2) kinematic closure through forces. The kinematic closure you are now promoting is (3) kinematic closure through specification. The three types are alike in that the realization of any particular motion requires that a special relation hold between the paired elements. You are convinced that if you were observing your particle on a rectilinear trajectory toward a given region of the surround and you intruded on the flow field by some means so as to introduce a prolonged rotational component into the flow field, then the rectilinear trajectory would not be maintained. To realize any given trajectory of the particle, a symmetry must exist between that trajectory and the flow field: For the particle to move clockwise there must be a counterclockwise flow; for the particle to move toward p there must be a flow centered at p, and so on. Although it is very clear to you that for your particle and its ambient field this symmetry always holds, the point that you wish to underline is that *in the absence of this symmetry an "intended" trajectory cannot be satisfied.*

You are absorbed by what the foregoing reasoning implies, namely, that there might well be a similitude for all machines, hard-molded and soft-molded. The invariant feature of machines seems to be kinematic closure achieved by reciprocal contexts of constraint; kinematic closure seems to be founded on a

unit, displacement of the room causes a person standing in the room to topple in the direction of the room's movement.

symmetry between the paired elements. To your journeyman understanding, this symmetry reads: There is a transformation T such that if A and B are the paired elements, then $T(A) \rightarrow B$ and $T(B) \rightarrow A$. You recognize that this transformation T is the mathematical notion of a *duality operation* and that the elements A and B are mathematical *duals*. You pose the question: What is the significance of the duality nature of machines? Tentatively you answer that if the prerequisite for constraining forces to produce selective, determinate motions is a duality structure then *duality must be a symmetry property of the most basic kind.*[11]

Conclusion 12.   In controlled collisions the particle must produce changes in force that are commensurate with changes in the kinematic field. Two examples come to mind: (1) to effect a soft collision any fluctuations in P_i (contact) that carry this quantity below its critical value must be countered by fluctuations in the control quantity, C, that are of commensurate amplitude; (2) if the surround is caused to fluctuate, so as to produce oscillatory global outflow and inflow of the kinematic field, the particle's position will similarly fluctuate, $180°$ out of phase.[12] The particle's commensurate fluctuations are the result of force changes in proportion to flow changes.

Your earlier conclusions about the conditions of the coupling of particle and field are incomplete. They do not identify *a principled physical basis for force differences that are proportional to flow differences.* When considering hydrodynamic flow you normally visualize a process in which an inhomogeneity in potential gives rise to a force that drives a flow. More generally, differences in potential (ΔP) gives rise to difference in force (ΔF) that, in turn, give rise to differences in flow (ΔV): $\Delta P \rightarrow \Delta F \rightarrow \Delta V$. Flows are proportional to forces, and where the Onsager condition holds, sensible deductions can be made in many instances from the macroscopic hyrodynamic flow to the irreversible thermodynamics that is its basis. The problem your particle poses is different from this conventional problem. It reverses the causal path and asks how flows can give rise to proportionate forces. Here, the causal vocabulary looks strained. But you are aware that you have felt this strain throughout your analysis. Thus you have spoken of the kinetic fields (particle and surround) as *causing* the kinematic field and the kinematic field as *specifying* and, cognately, *constraining* the kinetic field.

You remind yourself of some basics: Changes in motion or flow per se cannot cause changes of force; there can be no forces where there are no potential differences; the trajectory of force depends on the form of the potential. You surmise that *if a flow is to affect a force it must do so by modifying the potential from which the force is derived.* Modulating a potential would not necessarily cause a change of force; generally, other conditions must be satisfied. This

---

[11]This point has been argued by Shaw and Turvey (1981).
[12]See Lee (1978).

reservation is consonant with your observation of the influence of the flow field on the particle: only *global* changes in flow lead invariably to changes in force. So, a change in force may or may not occur given a change in flow but what you are after is a lawful basis for these changes whenever they do occur.

The problem has been refocused: *How could a flow affect a potential?* Formally a force F is defined as the negative of the potential inhomogeneity or, more presently, gradient, viz. $F = -\nabla P$, where the gradient symbolized by ∇ is a spatial gradient. If P is identified as the particle's on-board potential which is taken to be nearly homogeneous (given the arguments you made about the reversible, close to equilibrium steady state of the particle—Conclusion 9) then you must look to the kinematic field as the source of the inhomogeneity, that is, as specifying a *spatial operator*, ∇. Now, by taking the first derivative of both sides of the above expression for F you get:

$$dF/dt = -d(\nabla P)/dt;$$

that is, control (see Conclusion 1) is given by the rate of change of the product of the spatial operator and the potential. In the foregoing context the first derivative of $-\nabla P$ defines a temporal gradient. As with the spatial gradient, you take the temporal gradient to be an operator specified by the kinematic field. Assuming commutativity the preceding expression for the control quantity can be written:

$$dF/dt = -\nabla dP/dt = -\partial^2 P/ X_i dt,$$

where ∂X_i is the spatial operator and dt is the temporal operator. In sum, the answer to the question of "how could a flow affect a potential?" seems to require the recognition and understanding of space and time operators on potentials. Given that the units of space and time must be in the scale of the particle—expressed in terms of the mean free path δ and the mean relaxation time τ of the particle's interior—the control quantity ought to be reducible to an expression in P, δ changes and τ changes.

As a further point, the ordering of potential, force and flow that you are suggesting here is different from that which follows from considerations of hydrodynamic flow, namely: $\Delta V \rightarrow \Delta P \rightarrow \Delta F$. It would be prudent, however, to relate the two orderings. You go for the most obvious relation:

$$\begin{matrix} \Delta E & \rightarrow & \Delta V \\ \nwarrow & & \swarrow \\ & \Delta P & \end{matrix}$$

The flow field (ΔV) and energy flux ($\Delta P \rightarrow \Delta F$) are linked in "circular causality." You underscore that these two "paths" of influence are not the same. First, the flux-to-flow path is a change in layout (e.g., a flow is produced when the particle as a unit displaces relative to the layout of the surrounding regions) whereas the flow-to-flux path is through the translational gate you identified in Conclusion 9. Second, comparatively speaking, the flux-to-flow path is energetically expensive whereas the flow to flux path is energetically cheap (see Conclusion 9). (You resist identifying these paths with the cybernetic notions of "forward-fed" causality and "backward-fed" causality. You feel that such a move is regressive given that the notions of feedforward and feedback imply a referent signal, a comparator and, more generally, a separate controller. The origin and functioning of each of these would have to be rationalized by physical principles. [As a physicist you wish to explain the phenomenon of controlled collisions without the introduction of controllers sui generis.] Moreover, you feel that the different labeling of the pathways, as forward and backward, although well motivated in artifactual situations, is arbitrary in natural situations.)

Conclusion 13.   A controlled collision is a physical event in space–time. It is, however, by the conventional theory of physical events, a very odd kind of event. You struggle to formulate its heterodox quality: *A controlled collision is a space–time event in which the final conditions of a particle's motions determine the values that the initial conditions must assume.* (You had observed repeatedly, for example, that when the particle softly collided and when it violently collided with a region of the surround its accelerative change prior to collision was initiated at two different marginal values of the time-to-contact property.) This heterodox quality suggests to you a structure of space–time peculiar to controlled collisions, one that is explicitly shaped by *both* initial and final conditions. As a physicist you are well aware of the need to be clear on the space–time structure of events. Without a prescription for putting space–time boundaries on an event the determination of its causal basis remains very much a guessing game. Within what limits should you try to close the bookkeeping on the relevant summational invariants—the conservations? You turn your attention to conventional physical event theory to see how well it fares in this regard and to see what modifications will be required.

In the conventional theory, "observer" refers to the measurement of the location of an event in space–time. As a local reference system or inertial frame, the observer must be perspective free. Measurements must be made simultaneously and distributively throughout a given region of space–time. The "observer," therefore, must be capable of existing everywhere in a specified region of space–time. Your particle "observes" and "measures" (its surroundings and its relation to them). However, given that it is of finite size (rather than being infinitely small) and can exist in only one place at any one time it cannot be identified with the observer in orthodox physical event theory: *Your particle must have a perspective.* You suspect that this fact will be of importance in the eventual formulation of the laws of controlled collisions.[13]

---

[13]For Gibson (1966, 1979) the structure of an optical flow field is always exterospecific *and* propriospecific—it is always specific to the layout and to the observer.

Corollary to the absence of a real or natural perspective in physical event theory is the absence of an historical perspective. While the present is causally constrained by the immediate past, it is not (to borrow a term from Bertrand Russell) *mnemically* conditioned by the distant past. You sketch for yourself the Minkowskii diagram (Fig. 10.7) that illustrates the causal light cone which is the traditional domain of physical event theory. (Fig. 10.7b is a simplified version of Fig. 10.7a with x, y, z reduced to a single spatial (s) axis.) With the speed of light as the limiting boundary, only those events within the same forward light cone can be causally connected to the present event at the origin, $t = 0$ (because there are no known superluminal signals, events outside the light cone cannot be connected with those inside). The events leading up to the present are nowhere represented. The premise of the orthodox theory is that the past is instantiated in the present and that, together with the laws of motion, is sufficient to predict or explain event outcomes. The particle you have been studying makes you skeptical of this premise. Somehow the final conditions must be brought in—explicitly—to accommodate controlled collisions.

You try to close in on what this would require by producing a series of modifications of the Minkowskii diagram. First, you include a past light cone which converges at $t = 0$—the event from which the forward or future light cone diverges. In your modified sketch (Fig. 10.8) you have rotated the axes so that time flows from left to right. Next, you depict four events in your sketch (Fig. 10.9). The events $E_1, E_2,$ and E_3 are on the same world line where E_3 is causally constrained by E_2 and E_2 is causally constrained by E_1. You take pains to note that the causal constraints are not necessarily transitive for these interactional sequences (that is, E_3 is not necessarily causally constrained by E_1). This is because E_2', which is on a world line with E_3, might cancel (or otherwise alter) the effects of E_1. While E_1 transacts with E_3 in the context of E₃'s historical

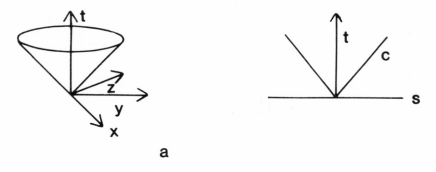

a

b

FIG. 10.7.   (a) The causal light cone determined by time (t) and three spatial dimensions, x, y, and z. (b) The causal light cone where x, y, and z have been reduced to a single spatial axis (s), showing the speed of light, c, as the limiting boundary.

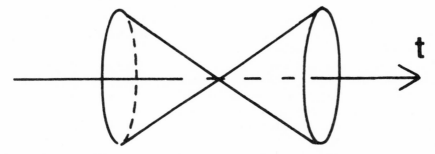

FIG. 10.8.   A modified Minkowskii diagram rotated so that time flows from left to right. It includes a mnemic (past) light cone as well as the standard causal (future) light cone.

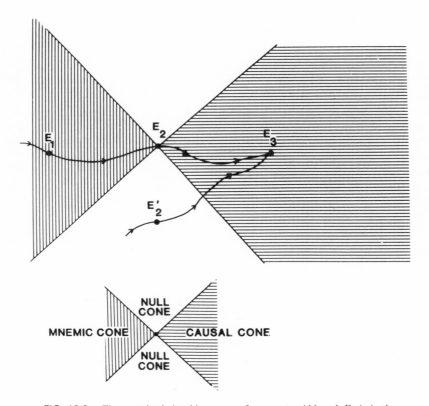

FIG. 10.9.   The causal relationships among four events. Although E_3 is in the causal cone of E_2, it cannot be explained on this basis alone—E_2 exerts an influence on E_3, yet is in the null cone of (and, therefore, unknown at) E_2.

relation to E_2, it does not do so in terms of the historical context of E_2'. The rub, as you see it, is that because E_2' is outside the forward light cone of E_2 (it is effectively simultaneous with E_2), its effects cannot be known at E_2 and, therefore, E_3 cannot be explained on the basis of E_2's causal cone alone.

Because unobservable events may exert an influence on future events, necessary paths of influence cannot be discovered by working forward from initial conditions to final conditions. You recognize, however, that determinant histories may be discovered by working back from the final conditions to the initial conditions. *All* of the influences on E_3 are in its past or mnemic cone. In sum, the causal future of E_2 is only partially accounted for by its forward cone but all of the determiners of E_3 are in its mnemic cone. There is an asymmetry between the information derived from history and the information applicable to the future.

You are inclined to believe that the only appropriate framework for controlled collisions must be composed of the causal and mnemic perspectives together. But is this framework to be one in which these perspectives remain asymmetric? Or, more accurately, is there a different level of analysis that may reveal the symmetry of the event space for controlled collisions? You pose this question because of a major lesson learned from orthodox physical event theory: Putting symmetry at the forefront reveals the structure of space–time and fetters the application of law. Knowing the symmetry that defines a space–time event means that if one element of an event is known, the nature of its symmetric counterpart is also known.

You modify your sketch of the Minkowskii diagram once again, this time creating a bounded region between the causal and mnemic cones of two succeeding events (Fig. 10.10). You are now ready to propose a *symmetry postulate for controlled collisions:* If (1) E_1 (approach to a region) and E_2 (contact) are on the same world line (where E_2 is in the causal cone of E_1 and E_1 is in the mnemic cone of E_2); and (2) there are no events outside the causal cone of E_1 that influence E_2; then E_1 and E_2 together define a new event—call it E_D—for which they are dual perspectives. The past and future cones have been merged into a higher-order event space. Events outside the bounded region have no existence for the particle; they are in neither its history nor its future. Events inside the bounded region have relative existence. The new event E_D is a controlled collision and it will be guaranteed whenever the symmetry conditions (1 and 2) hold.

In a further sketch (Fig. 10.11) you contrast dual events with nondual events. The events E_0 and E_1 are duals, the events E_2 and E_3 are duals, but E_1 and E_2 are not duals because condition (2) is violated (E_2 is influenced by E_1' which is in the null cone of E_1). What you wish to show in this last sketch is that the specification of E_2 will be indeterminate when based on the causal cone perspective of E_1. Moreover, the selection of marginal values at E_1 to determine an outcome at E_2 is not guaranteed to be successful since the basis for controlling the outcome at E_2 is not completely available at E_1. A controlled collision cannot be defined over E_1 and E_2 because they are not duals.

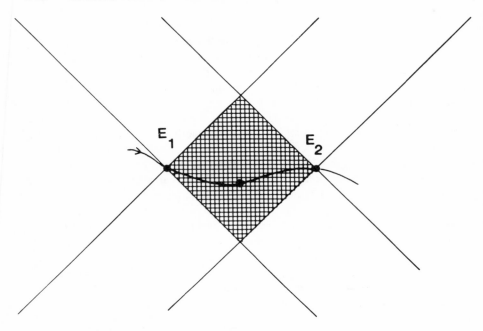

FIG. 10.10.   The bounded region between the causal cone of E_1 and the mnemic cone of E_2 defines a new event, E_D, for which E_1 and E_2 are dual perspectives.

To restore or, more accurately, to reveal a duality you suggest a change in scale (Fig. 10.12). At the grain of a finer space–time mesh there necessarily exists some event E_2, causally proximal and dual to E_1, for which a controlled collision can be minimally defined. This change in scale merely assumes that the particle has limited sensitivity or acuity to distant events on its world line. (In fact, your observations of many particles of varying sizes reveal that there is a strong relationship between acuity and size. The spatial range is a constant proportionality of the vertical magnitude of the particle.[14] Simply put, large particles act with respect to things at a greater absolute distance than do small particles.)

Your point is that, for controlled collisions, any events antecedent to some future event toward which the particle's current behavior is directed (1) must lie within the particle's current causal perspective if they have significant effects on the particle's immediate future; or (2) must be trivial in their effect if they lie undetected in the particle's null cone. Because significant events cannot lie outside the bounded region of a controlled collision, *an appropriate scale of*

---

[14]Kirschfield (1976) reports that for animals there is a simple first-order relation between visual resolution (R) and body-height (H), $R = k/H$, where k is a constant of proportionality.

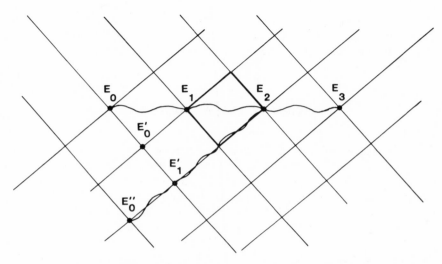

FIG. 10.11. E_0 and E_1 are duals (note that E''_0, though in the null cone of E_0, is *not* on a world line with E_1), as are E_2 and E_3 (note that E''_0 is at the limiting boundary of (and, therefore, is included in) the mnemic tone of E_2). E_1 and E_2 are not duals because E_1 influences E_2 but is in the null cone of E_1.

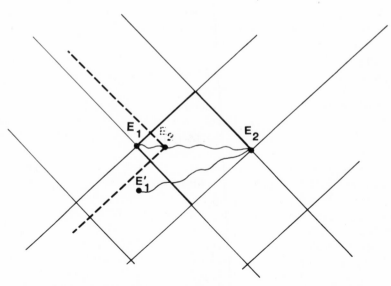

FIG. 10.12. Some E_2 must exist that is causally proximal to E_1. A change in scale reveals the duality over which a controlled collision can be defined.

analysis that satisfies this condition must exist. You insist that symmetry is the guide to finding this scale: Given either the perspective from the initial conditions or the final conditions, the other perspective is specified.

A SUMMARY AND AN AWAKENING

You have discovered quite a lot about your particle but its identity still eludes you. You convince yourself that you have all the information you need to identify this type of particle and it is only some firmly entrenched bias that prevents you from seeing it. You think that you may have given a physical description to the behavior of an entity that is usually considered to be outside the domain of physics. Several of its properties are like those of more standard particles but you have noticed they often include less standard twists. You review the properties you have discovered in the hope that highlighting the "twists" might fuel an insight. (At the very least, it will provide a convenient way to summarize these REM episodes.)

1. The behavior of your particle can be described with a measurable quantity but this quantity is control ($\Delta MV/T^2$) rather than the more standard momentum (MV).

2. Forces determine the trajectory of your particle but they are dissipative rather than conservative forces and they originate not in the surround but in the particle. Moreover, the particle can replenish its energy supply.

3. The distribution function that you constructed as a means of classifying your particle reveals it to be in a class whose behavior is not governed by velocity dependent conservations.

4. Your particle exhibits conservation but it seems to be conservation of population number, rather than the more standard energy or momentum or mass. To accomplish this conservation, it appears to minimize momentum transfers that might fracture the particle.

5. Because your particle harnesses forces to achieve selective trajectories, you consider it to be in the class of machines. But its constraints are soft molded, allowing flexibility in the strength of collisions, rather than hard molded.

6. The soft constraint on the particle-based forces is a field, but it cannot be associated with a force.

7. Because the constraining field is not a force field, it cannot include dimension M and, therefore, is not kinetic; because certain properties that are necessary to the control of collisions are annihilated when t goes to 0, the field must include dimension T and, therefore, is not geometric. The soft constraint must be a kinematic field.

8. Critical values of dimensionless quantities in the kinematic field distinguish between qualitatively distinct states, but these are specificational states rather than physical states as would be the case in a kinetic field.

9. Because the kinematic field constrains the particle's trajectory, it must be coupled somehow to the particle, but the coupling must be linear (so that equivocalities are not introduced) and low energy (so that it does not involve large momentum exchanges and irreversible processes).

10. You explain the coupling through a conservation but it is of topological form (adjacencies and successivities) rather than of energy or momentum.

11. The machine conception (identified in Conclusion 4) must apply minimally to the particle *and* the field as duals, not just the particle. The symmetry is necessary in order to realize and maintain trajectories.

12. The flow field produces proportionate forces in the particle, presumably by modulating a layout of potentials. Whereas the fact that forces produce flows proportionate to the forces is understood, the fact that flows produce forces proportionate to the flows is not.

13. Controlled collisions, which are characteristic of your particle, are physical events but the structure of space–time is shaped by final conditions as well as initial conditions. Where the particle is going colors how it gets there.

What is this soft-coupled duality of particle and surround, wherein collisions are guided by distinct specificational states that bring final conditions to bear on initial conditions, and are controlled by the dissipation of the particle's replenishable energy reserves in such a way as to minimize momentum transfers

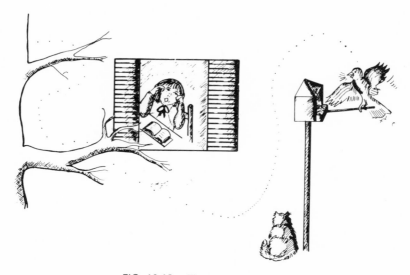

FIG. 10.13. The dreamer awakes.

that could fracture it? You seem to have described a physics of controlled collisions, but for what . . . or whom. . . ?

You are startled awake by the agitated chirping outside your window. The bird is hovering about a feeder in an effort to replenish its fuel supply but a cat has appeared on the scene waiting to replenish itself by effecting a violent, predatory collision on your friend. Fortunately for the bird, you muse theoretically, the imminence of contact with the cat is specified in the optical flow field that links properties of the animal to properties of the environment. You marvel, once again, as it guides its flight to avoid the cat and locate the food, cutting its speed just in time to alight gently on the feeder. Now those are the kinds of controlled encounters that Gibson wanted to understand and that you've been trying to understand. You are suddenly overcome with a sense of déja vu, with a feeling that, at some level, you have understood.

APPENDIX

A. The Theory of Collisions

The concept of collision refers to forces applied to and removed from an object in a very short period of time. The classical theory of collision, based primarily on the impulse-momentum law for rigid bodies, regards the colliding objects as single mass points. All elements of each object are assumed to be rigidly connected and to be subjected instantaneously to one and the same change of motion as the result of the collision. In reality, the forces initiate stress waves which travel at finite velocity away from the region of contact and through the object. These waves reflect from boundaries of the object and interact with stress waves still being generated at the region of contact to create a complex pattern of stresses and strains in the interior. In short, all regions of an object subjected to a collision are *not* exposed simultaneously to the same force conditions (Goldsmith, 1960).

The classical theory is most suited to ideal atomisms whose degrees of freedom are exhausted by the three axes of translation. Atomism is a term suggested by Iberall (1977) for an entity of any magnitude that is atom-like at the scale of the ensemble to which it belongs. It is conventional to say that ideal atomisms have no internal degrees of freedom, where "internal" has the uncommon meaning of "extratranslational." Atomisms of gases such as helium are closest to this ideal. They are single atoms each free to move on the three spatial dimensions. For all intents and purposes, the total energy imparted by collision to a helium atomism may be regarded as going into the translation of the atomism. In terms of the equipartition theorem, the energy received is divided evenly and completely among the atomism's degrees of freedom, which are all translational.

The atomisms of another gas, oxygen, introduce a measure of internal complexity. These atomisms (molecules) consist of two linked atoms. To define the position of each of the atoms of oxygen requires three degrees of freedom for a total of six. However, the linkage between the atoms eliminates a coordinate choice, thereby reducing the degrees of freedom of the oxygen atomism to five. Because translation of the oxygen atomism's center of mass consumes only three of the five degrees of freedom, the two degrees of freedom that remain are "internal." The equipartition theorem would assign three fifths of the energy of collision to the translation of the atomism and two fifths of the energy to the internal bond. Clearly, conservation of energy does not hold if only the energy carried by the translation degrees of freedom is taken into account. It is for this reason that collisions of atomisms with internal degrees of freedom are said to be inelastic and that the conservation of momentum (rather than of energy) is the dominant constraint on their equations of collision.

Consideration of the collisions of diatomic atomisms is a small step toward the collisions of *systems*. In a statistical mechanical sense a system is an ensemble of interacting atomisms with a boundary that prohibits the ensemble from dissolving into the surround. The atomisms of a system may be internally barren (like the helium atomism) or internally complex (of a kind hinted at by the oxygen atomism). As noted, internal complexity is associated with ways of absorbing the energy applied to a unitary thing other than through the translation of its center of mass.

B. The Theory of Fracture

The first major advance beyond the classical theory of collisions (viz., the one–dimensional vibrational treatment of colliding objects) recognized the significant proportion of energy converted into oscillations when the system's natural frequency is long compared to the duration of contact. Subsequent analyses of the multidimensional aspect of wave propagation consequent to collision, and of the stress distribution at the region of contact, were made possible by developments in the theory of elasticity (Timoshenko & Goodier, 1951). It suffices to say, for present purposes, that elasticity refers to the fact that the internally generated forces of restoration are comparable to the externally applied forces of deformation so that there is a return to the status quo ante on removal of the external forces.

In many collisions, however, the conditions of impact are such that the entire cross-section of one or both of the colliding objects will exhibit a final permanent strain of significant magnitude, or one or both of the objects may fracture. Such nonreversible phenomena result from the conversion of kinetic energy into permanent distortion or fracturing of the structure of the object and the eventual dissipation of this energy in the form of heat. The analysis of the irreversible deformations wrought by the propagation of stresses that exceed the elastic limit (so called plastic flows or plastic waves) is a more recent and less developed aspect of collision theory (Goldsmith, 1960).

Evidently, the responses of an internally complex system to collision will be difficult to follow. It is possible, nevertheless, to obtain some useful insights into the collision process by considering (1) the behavior of a system under statically imposed forces; and (2) the relation between impact parameters and system failure, ignoring the internal responses.

The deformation resulting from loading a system statically can be treated as a series of equilibrium states requiring no consideration of acceleration effects or wave propagations. Of major interest is the response to static loading of systems that exhibit a degree of rigidity, that is, systems which preserve their form in the face of perturbations. The requirement, of course, is that the system be elastic through some range of perturbation. Solids have an elastic domain as do multiphase systems that are solid or gel in part, such as living things that are dominated by elastic-plastic-fluid (liquid and gel) processes (Yates, 1982).

The interior of a solid system can respond in one of three ways to an applied force: (1) the linked atomism can be forced further apart or closer together than the equilibrium (minimal potential) distance; (2) atomisms can hop into adjacent vacant lattice sites; and (3) the bonds between the atomisms can be broken (Freudenthal, 1950; Nadai, 1950; Walton, 1976). If response 1 is sufficient to absorb the energy of loading the solid is operating strictly within its elastic domain. Suppose that a static loading is realized as a force applied along an axis (a stress) so as to stretch or compress (more generally, to strain) the system. Then response 1 means that the system as a whole undergoes a coordinate transformation that changes the distances between all the atomisms but not the topology of the system's internal configuration. This response to static loading is reversible. It is, however, a response of finite capacity. At some point the potential energy stored up within the excessively strained bonds reaches a limit (the elastic yield) and new mechanisms for accommodating the applied energy must be found (that is, a new "escapement" arises). One escapement mechanism is the breaking of some bonds between some atomisms (response 3), another escapement is diffusion (response 2) which is enhanced considerably by the structural changes resulting from bond breaking. (In a multiphase system at the elastic limit there is a structural change in at least one phase; for example, in the continuous solid phase of a two phase solid–fluid system such as a gel or in the more rigid phase of a polyphase solid–solid system such as a polycrystalline metal or a polyphase solid–fluid phase system such as a high polymer.)

A brittle system (a physical ideal, an engineering myth) would be infirmed at the elastic limit. There are no plastic deformations (flow processes) in a brittle system and microscopic bond breaking becomes, immediately, macroscopic fracture. For real, ductile systems, however, the yield point only identifies that loading at which fracturing begins on the atomistic level. Once the yield point is reached in a ductile system the mutually reinforcing processes of bond breaking and diffusion can continue to accommodate excessive energy brought in by the static loading. The dissociating of some of the atomisms makes it easier for other bound atomisms to migrate to locations that are more stable than the locations that they currently occupy. This flow process is irreversible: Less energy is required for an atomism to hop from a high to a low potential site than vice versa. However, the consequent relaxing of some bonds brought about by diffusion increases the strain on other, already overstrained, bonds, disposing them to further fracture.

The microfracturing that begins at and proceeds beyond the yield point reduces the long range order or cooperativity of the system (interpreted as bonds that repeat regularly over many thousands of atomic distances). The long range order is replaced by short range order or local cooperatives, not unlike the "flow unit" of a liquid. The diffusion occurs at the surface of these local clusters because the atomisms located there are thermally less stable than their partners in the interior. Clearly, the larger the number of local cooperatives and, therefore, internal surfaces, the greater the diffusion. And the greater the diffusion the more disposed to breaking are the already strained bonds at places in the system where diffusion of atomisms is not possible. In sum, fracturing of the bonds between atomisms is a chain reaction process and eventually a ductile system will fracture at the macroscopic scale.

The emphasis of the foregoing has been the gradual progression of macroscopic fracture, or system failure, as might occur under the repeated or prolonged application of static forces that exceed the system's elastic limit. In the range between the initiation of bond breaking on the microscale and the occurrence of system failure on the macroscale, the system gradually loses its ability to absorb the applied energy. A measure of the energy asorption of a material is given by its stress-strain curve, which relates force per unit area to proportional change in length. The energy per unit volume is approximately equal to the shaded area of Fig. 10.14. Consequently, the strain energy to failure may be approximated as follows: energy/unit volume $= \frac{1}{2} (P_x + \epsilon_x)P_c$. Where P_c is the stress at the yield point and P_x and ϵ_x are the ultimate stress and ultimate strain, respectively, that mark the collapse of the system.

Of course, the loss of ability to absorb energy could be quick, given a collision. The microscopic processes leading to failure from a single brief loading must be a rapid chain reaction of bond breaking associated with elastic and plastic waves propagating from the point of contact and multiply reflecting from the system's boundary. However, as noted, broad conclusions relating failure to the conditions of collision are possible without considering the complex of intermediary processes.

A collision will have an *acceleration* (of the system) $\times$ *time* profile. Three examples of single loadings are given in Fig. 10.15; to achieve a given response amplitude, shorter durations of loading must be compensated by greater accelera-

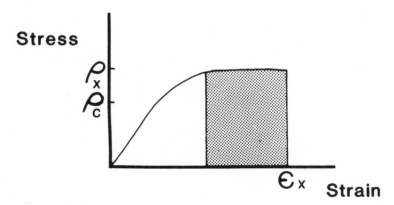

FIG. 10.14.   The energy absorption per unit volume of a material is given by the shaded area of its stress-strain curve.

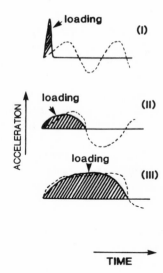

Fig. 10.15. *Acceleration × time* profiles of collisions under three loading durations (after Kornhauser, 1964).

tions. Two parameters are of special significance: the change in velocity and the average acceleration (in units of gravity) that is *just sufficient to produce structural failure*. In Fig. 10.15 the cross-hatched areas express the velocity changes. The average acceleration of any collision is equal to the velocity change divided by duration. A collision sensitivity curve can be generated by plotting criterial velocity change (where fracture occurs) against criterial average acceleration (where fracture occurs) (Kornhauser, 1964). A prototypical collision sensitivity plot is given in Fig. 10.16. The vertical asymptote is related to acceleration pulses that are steady or of long duration. It implies that no failure occurs unless a certain average acceleration is exceeded, regardless of the change in velocity of the system and the duration of the collision. The horizontal asymptote is related to acceleration pulses of short duration. It implies that system failure does not

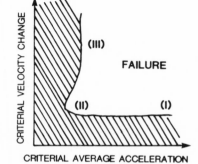

FIG. 10.16. Collision sensitivity plot shows where system failure will occur (after Kornhauser, 1964).

occur unless a certain velocity change is exceeded regardless of the average acceleration value (Kornhauser, 1964).

The location of the vertical asymptote in Fig. 10.16 is a function of the shape of the collision (its *acceleration* × *time* profile). In contrast, the horizontal asymptote is independent of the shape of the loading and is fully characterized by a unique value of velocity change: Collision durations that are short enough to be on the short duration asymptote (marked by (I) and (II) for a given system will result in the structural failure of that system. There is some evidence (Kornhauser, 1964) to suggest that the collision velocity change required for irreversible damage to mammals is relatively indifferent to species and size (25 feet per second is a reasonable approximation). The criterial average acceleration, however, differs markedly with species and size (roughly, 20 g for man and 650 g for mice).

A simple rule of thumb relates the critical velocity change (V_c) and criterial average acceleration (G_c) to the system's natural frequency (ω) (Kornhauser, 1964): $G_c = \omega V_c$. If most collisions between systems and their surrounds are of sufficiently short duration to place the systems on the horizontal asymptote of their collision sensitivity function, then V_c is constant. (For mammals, as noted previously, $V_C = 25 \ f/s$.) In other words, the higher the value of a system's natural frequency, the greater is the system's tolerance to collision (measured in multiples of the gravitational constant).

ACKNOWLEDGMENTS

This work was supported in part by NICHD Grant HD-01994 awarded to Haskins Laboratories. The authors wish to thank A. S. Iberall for his comments on parts of this chapter.

REFERENCES

Buckingham, E. On physically similar systems; illustrations of the use of dimensional equations. *Physical Review,* 1914, *4,* 345–376.

Freudenthal, A. M. *The inelastic behavior of engineering materials and structures.* New York: Wiley, 1950.

Gibson, J. J. *The perception of the visual world.* Boston: Houghton Mifflin, 1950.

Gibson, J. J. The information contained in light. *Acta Psychologia,* 1960, *17,* 23–30.

Gibson, J. J. Ecological optics. *Vision Research,* 1961, *1,* 253–262.

Gibson, J. J. *The senses considered as perceptual systems.* Boston: Houghton Mifflin, 1966.

Gibson, J. J. *The ecological approach to visual perceptions.* Boston: Houghton Mifflin, 1979.

Goldsmith, W. *Impact: The theory and physical behavior of colliding solids.* London: Edward Arnold Ltd., 1960.

Hoyle, F. *The black cloud.* London: Heinemann, 1957.

Iberall, A. S. A field and circuit thermodynamics for integrative physiology: I. Introduction to general notions. *American Journal of Physiology/Regulatory, Integrative, & Comparative Physiology,* 1977, *2,* R171–R180.

Kirschfield, K. The resolution of lens and compound eyes. In F. Zettler & R. Weller (Eds.), *Neural principles in vision.* Berlin: Springer-Verlag, 1976.

Kornhauser, M. *Structural effects of impact.* Baltimore, Md.: Spartan Books Inc., 1964.

Lee, D. N. A theory of visual control of braking based on information about time-to-collision. *Perception,* 1976, *5,* 437–459.

Lee, D. N. The functions of vision. In H. Pick, Jr. & E. Saltzman (Eds.), *Modes of perceiving and processing information.* Hillsdale, N.J.: Lawrence Erlbaum Associates, 1978.

Lee, D. N. Visuo–motor coordination in space–time. In G. E. Stelmach & J. Requin (Eds.), *Tutorials in Motor Behavior.* New York: North-Holland, 1980.

Lishman, J. R., & Lee, D. N. The autonomy of visual kinaesthetics. *Perception,* 1973, *2,* 287–294.

Nadai, A. *Theory of flow and fracture of solids, Vol. II.* New York: McGraw-Hill, 1950.

Pattee, H. H. Laws and constraints, symbols and language. In C. H. Waddington (Ed.), *Towards a Theoretical Biology.* Chicago: Aldine, 1972.

Pattee, H. H. Dynamic and linguistic modes of complex systems. *International Journal of General Systems,* 1977, *3,* 259–266.

Reed, E., & Jones, R. (Eds.). *Reasons for realism: Selected essays of James J. Gibson.* Hillsdale, N.J.: Lawrence Erlbaum Associates, 1982.

Reuleaux, F. *The kinematics of machinery.* New York: Dover, 1963.

Schuring, D. J. *Scale models in engineering.* New York: Pergamon Press, 1980.

Shaw, R., & Turvey, M. T. Coalitions as models for ecosystems: A realists perspective on perceptual organization. In M. Kubovy & J. Pomerantz (Eds.), *Perceptual organization.* Hillsdale, N.J.: Lawrence Erlbaum Associates, 1981.

Timoshenko, S., & Goodier, J. N. *Theory of elasticity.* New York: McGraw-Hill, 1951.

Walton, A. J. *Three phase of matter.* New York: McGraw-Hill, 1976.

Warren, W. H., Jr. *A biodynamic basis for perception and action in bipedal climbing.* Unpublished doctoral dissertation, University of Connecticut, 1982.

Yates, F. E. Outline of a physical theory of physiological systems. *Canadian Journal of Physiology and Pharmacology,* 1982, *60,* 217–248.

11 Dialogue on Perception and Action

Claes von Hofsten
University of Umeå, Sweden

David Lee
University of Edinburgh, UK

C: That was a good walk we had yesterday, wasn't it?

D: Yes there's some lovely countryside around Storrs. Also, in thinking about control of movement I think it helps to be engaged in it. Sitting at the desk and scratching your head doesn't really set the right scene . . . it gets all too . . . well, abstract! You tend to forget what the functions of movements are.

C: That's true . . . the closest you get to the movements themselves is when you model them on a two dimensional sheet of paper. That may also be the

reason why there has been so much interest in the perception of static 2–D displays, geometric illusions and the like. Sort of desk research.

D: Well, that is until Jimmy Gibson (1950) and Gunnar Johansson (1950) came along and injected motion into it all.

C: Yes, the crucial step they took was to bring *time* in as an integral component of perception.

D: It's amazing how people could leave it out isn't it? Perhaps they thought they were simplifying things. It's the age-old fallacy that supposes that if something's simple to describe it's necessarily easy for people to deal with. You know, the sort of thing Runeson (1977) talks about in his paper on smart perceptual mechanisms. Anyway, talking about time, it obviously has to be considered as a basic integral component of action too, not just perception. In fact, of course you can't really separate perception and action.

C: The work of Bernstein and others on coordinative timing of the limbs in walking and running made it quite clear to me how intimately related perception and action are. Ironically, most running and walking studies have involved rather minimal interaction with the environment. The subjects have locomoted in a robot-like way on treadmills. The inter-relation between perception and action really becomes most obvious in everyday situations.

D: Oh yes, when you're running over rough terrain for instance your eyes have to keep going the whole time . . . in timing your actions accurately and so forth. You clearly need to have available very good information about your relationship to the environment. But you know the sort of thing I mean, you've done experiments on it—your reaching experiments, or rather, wobbler-catching experiments (Hofsten, 1980; Hofsten & Lindhagen, 1979). I wanted to ask you something about those experiments, about the timing of the reaches. You found that the infants were rather successful in catching the toy, but have you any idea how accurate the timing was?

C: I am working on that problem now (von Hofsten, 1983) but the analyses of timing are not yet completed. However, it is possible to calculate a 'time window' within which the reach must fit in order to be successful. The youngest infants would typically approach the object with an open hand and only when they had stopped the object would they grasp it. Considering the size of the infant's hand, the 'time window' would be between 100 and 150 ms for a successful catch of a 30 cm per sec object. In a later experiment with eight-month old infants I came across one female subject who repeatedly caught an object moving at 120 cm per sec. In addition, this subject clearly formed her hand in an anticipatory fashion before catching the object, as seen in Fig. 11.1 The 'time window' she had at her disposal must have been less than 50 ms.

D: That reminds me of the experiments of Alderson et al. (1974) on catching tennis balls—adults that is, not babies. Of course, to catch a ball one-handed you not only need to get your hand into the right place but you also have to close your fingers at the right time, otherwise it's going to hit the palm of your hand and

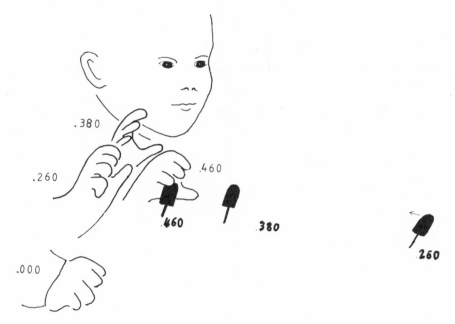

FIG. 11.1.   An infant, eight months old, catching an object moving in front of
her at 120 cm per sec. The duration of the reach was 460 ms. In the picture, the
position of the hand and the object at different time intervals from the start of the
reach are shown. Note that, during the movement, the hand first opens and then
closes around the object.

bounce out or bang you on the knuckles if you close your hand too soon. They
calculated from their films that the timing accuracy of the grasping action had to
be about plus or minus 14 ms. With slip fielders at cricket who have to catch
much faster balls the timing accuracy's obviously going to have to be a lot finer
than that. Remember, also, that work by Tyldesley and Whiting (1975) on table
tennis where he found temporal precision of the order of 4 ms.

C: What about those studies by Sharp and Whiting (1974, 1975)? They had
something interesting to say about timing, didn't they? As I remember it, they
had balls being projected rather like in the Alderson study and the lights being
turned off at particular points in the trajectory of the ball.

D: Yes. What they basically showed was that as long as you could see the ball
for at least 40 ms and at a period in its flight about 300 ms before it reached you,
then performance would be reasonably good. If you could also see the ball for
about 250 ms up to that point that improved your performance because it allowed
time for your eyes to latch on to it. But if the exposure was not long enough for
your eyes to latch on, then performance was no better than with 40 ms exposure.

Also, it added little to be able to see the ball for the last 300 ms, which would indicate that much of the information for controlling the catch was picked up before that time.

C: Sharp's and Whiting's results lend support to the suggestion that human arm movements are regulated by a pulse frequency of about 3 Hz. This frequency also corresponds to the physiological tremor at the elbow of human adults (Fox & Randall, 1970). However, the pulsing seems to be a property of the control structure itself rather than a function of some physical constraints. Trevarthen and his colleagues (1981) as well as I myself have found the same pulsing of arm movements in neonates. There is further evidence showing that eye movements of adults (Yarbus, 1967) are regulated by the same base rhythm.

D: It's perhaps better to talk about regulation *at* rather than *by* the same base rhythm, don't you think? ''By'' implies a central clock controlling it all, whereas it may be, for example, that the observed pulsing is due to lag in the perceptuo-motor cycle or inertial properties of the biological system. Of course, that raises the question why eye and arm movements should show similar pulsing.

C: Eye movements and arm movements seem to have an important property in common. They are both controlled by peripheral vision. When people reach for targets they always fixate the target, never the hand. This is also true for young infants. An experiment reported by Paillard (1980) gives further evidence for this position. Subjects who were only allowed foveal vision did not adapt their pointing behavior to a prismatic displacement. If instead they were allowed only peripheral vision, they did adapt, but only if they could see the continuous movements of their arms. Paillard argued from these and similar results that there are two sensorimotor systems regulating arm movements. The system I already mentioned controls the direction of the trajectory of the moving hand relative to the stabilized orientation of the visual axis and relies essentially on movement information provided by peripheral vision. The other system controls the accurate homing-in of the hand onto the target and relies essentially on positional information provided by foveal vision. Paillard's two systems correspond to an important functional distinction made by Bernstein (1947) between body-related and object-related movements. There are some beautiful experiments by Buyakas et al. (1980) illustrating these points. They placed the subject in a completely dark room and asked him to move his index finger onto a point of light while they monitored his movements. They found that the subject would start out with a rather precise movement which ended, on the average, two degrees of visual angle from the target. However, not being able to see his hand, the subject was lost from there on. Corrective movements were just as often directed away from the target as toward it. The phenomenon has, in fact, been known for some time. As far as I know it was first described by Sandström (1951). He called it ''the eluding light point.''

D: These two control systems you talk about, do you think they function independently of one another?

C: No, even if it is possible to separate them under special conditions it is obvious that they function as an integrated whole in everyday life. The anticipatory adjustments of the hand are delicately timed relative to the movement of the arm. However, it is not only in reaching and batting that timing is an important aspect. Doesn't it seem to enter into most kinds of skilled activities? The timing of a skilled person is delightful to watch. Take for instance downhill skiing.

D: Yes . . . did I tell you we'd recently done a film analysis of ski-jumping (Lee et al., 1982)? The films show the ski jumper right near the lip of the jump. We were interested in the timing of the explosive straightening of the legs just before the lip because, as you know, it's critically important that they get that right. What we found was the standard error of the timing across 14 jumpers was only 10 ms.

C: Do you think the same sort of thing goes on when you're running and jumping—say as in the long jump—that long jump study you did?

D: Yes, I do. As you know we did that study a few years ago and the results clearly showed that the jumpers were visually regulating their gait over about the last four strides in order to hit the take-off board. But it puzzled me for a long time as to how they were doing that, what exactly they were doing and what type of visual information they were using. And it wasn't really until I started to think about the mechanics of running that it dawned on me that perhaps timing was the central essence of it. You see there was something else to explain too and that was the rather consistent stride pattern the athletes achieved during the initial phase of the run-up. If the strides had been a regular length that would have been fairly easy to understand but since they were accelerating their strides were gradually increasing in length. And then there was the smooth transition from this stereotyped phase of the run-up to the visually regulated phase which made me think that perhaps throughout the whole run-up they were regulating just one parameter of their gait. Anyway to cut a long-jump story short, the conclusion that I came to was that the gait parameter they were regulating was the vertical thrust—or more precisely, the vertical impulse that they applied to the ground at each step. During the stereotyped phase of the run they tried to keep the impulse constant, then, as they neared the board, they regulated the impulses and thereby the durations of their strides on the basis of visual information about the time-to-reach the board (Lee et al., 1982).

C: There must also be a lot of fine-grained timing, don't you think so?

D: Certainly. For example, the activities of the leg muscles have to be finely timed relative to the moment of impact of the foot with the ground in order that the leg can act as a shock absorber, as Melvill Jones and Watt (1971) have pointed out. If, for instance, you step off a curb you haven't noticed you can get a very nasty jolt. This type of timing control would certainly seem to be visual.

C: There is no doubt that the information for most timing must be visual. Just imagine blindfolding a downhill skier or a tennis player. . . . A much more tricky question is to define the information used. You have discussed one potentially useful variable in the optical flow for a subject who wants to time his behavior relative to an object he is approaching or that is approaching him.

D: Yes, in these cases time-to-contact is specified in the optic flow field by the inverse of the rate of dilation of the image of the object (Lee, 1976). People— and animals too—seem so good at detecting time-to-contact and do it so rapidly that I think it's very likely that they pick up the information directly from the image dilation.

C: But time-to-contact is also specified indirectly through the distance to the target and the velocity of approach. Do you have any proof that the system does not in fact extract information about distance and velocity and work out time from that?

D: There are several ways to approach that question. First, there's the method Schiff and Detwiler (1979) used, showing people movies of an object approaching. No information about the distance or velocity of the object is displayed, only information about time-to-contact through the rate of dilation of the image on the screen. They found that subjects could detect the time-to-contact quite well, though they tended to underestimate. However, the times used—from 2 to 10 sec—were outside the normal useful range of a second or less required for timing actions like hitting, catching and jumping. Todd (1981) used shorter times-to-contact in his computer displays and found that subjects could discriminate (at the 80% level) times-to-contact differing by 50 ms. The experiment testing subjects' ability to actually detect times-to-contact of less than 1 sec from displays needs to be done. But it certainly looks as though information about distance and velocity is not necessary for the perception of time-to-contact.

Another way to test out the idea, but nobody's done it as far as I know, is to set up a situation where the subject has to judge distance, velocity, and time-to-contact. You could then work out what the error in perceived time-to-contact should be if the perception were based on the ratio of perceived distance to perceived velocity, and compare this with the actual error. I'd predict that the latter will be the smaller. This would support the idea that the perceptions of distance and velocity, even when the information is available, are not entailed in the perception of time-to-contact.

A further approach to the question occurred to me a little while back, walking along the coast near Edinburgh and watching gannets diving into the sea. They dive steeply from up to 100 feet with their wings partly open to steer themselves and just before they reach the water, at up to 50 mph, they streamline their bodies by stretching their wings right back and go in like a spear (Fig. 11.2). They're fantastic! The question which intrigued me was how do they perceive when to streamline themselves for entry. It's an interesting case because they are accelerating under gravity and so the inverse of the rate of dilation of the image of the water—let's call it tau (τ) for short—is not equal to the time-to-contact as it would be if their velocity were constant. For, as you know, tau simply specifies

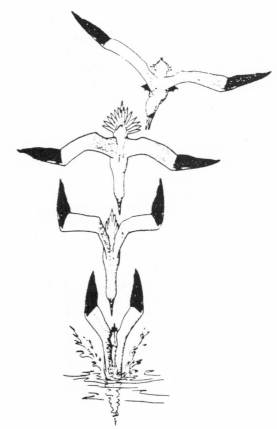

FIG. 11.2.   Wing positions of diving gannet, Sula bassana (length ~0.9 m, wing span 1.7 m). Illustration by John Busby. Reprinted from B. Nelson, The Gannet (Berkhamsted: Poyser, 1978), courtesy of the author and publishers.

the ratio of the current distance away to the current velocity and takes no account of acceleration. This is not to say that time-to-contact under constant acceleration is not optically specified: it is, in fact—by a formula involving tau and its time derivative (Lee et al., 1981). However, the formula is quite complicated and it occurred to me that gannets mightn't have evolved a visual mechanism for effectively computing the formula but instead might have found it adequate to essentially ignore acceleration and visually time their actions as if they were travelling at a constant speed. In short, I thought they might be using a simple "tau strategy," starting to streamline their bodies for entry when tau reached a critical value. This would lead to a particular pattern of behavior quite different from the patterns which would result if they were guiding themselves on the basis of real time-to-contact or height or velocity. The film analysis we did indicated that they were in fact using the tau strategy (Lee & Reddish, 1981).

C: In these examples, information about time-to-contact could very well have been used once and for all—in Schiff and Detwiler's case to decide when to press the button and for the gannets when to streamline themselves. However, if the time-to-contact variable is of such crucial importance as you seem to believe, subjects should be able to use it in their continuous adjustment of preparatory behavior. I remember you carried out some discussions of how the braking of a car could be controlled by the change in time-to-contact (Lee, 1976), but have you got any empirical evidence that subjects make use of this information in their continuous control of behavior?

D: We did, in fact, set up an experiment to investigate this (Lee et al., 1983). It was a sort of upside-down gannet experiment. Instead of dropping people down and seeing when they prepared themselves for landing, we dropped a ball down to them which they had to leap up and punch as it fell. (We did the experiment in the main stairwell in the department, which caused a little consternation!) We chose this task because it requires timing of activity over quite a period—from the start of the crouch-down to the actual punch. We found that basically the subjects behaved like the gannets: The longer the drop time, the sooner before contact did they perform their actions, such as starting the crouch-down, as they would if following the tau strategy (Lee & Reddish, 1981). This is not to say, though, that having started the crouch-down they just let the whole activity rip off in a ballistic fashion, which would have certainly led to error. Our results indicate that they visually controlled the activity right through. The timing of successive phases of the act was less and less influenced by the drop time, as also predicted by the theory, and at the very end the standard deviation of the timing of the punch itself was only about 20 ms.

C: OK . . . time-to-contact does seem to be an important determinant of timing behavior, but it can't be the sole one. After all the subject moving toward an obstacle or an object moving toward the subject as if it were to collide with him is a rather special case. I doubt that time-to-contact is of any use when you try to catch a moving object if the object is not heading directly for your eyes. When the object passes in front of you and you reach out for it, it is your hand that is approaching the object and not your eyes. There will no visual expansion pattern. Yet timing is delightfully exact.

D: That's an important point and I must confess I hadn't given it enough thought. But let's see. I think a spherical model of the optic array is the most appropriate for the general case you want to consider. Suppose there is an object at a point P distance R from the eye O and it is moving at a constant velocity V along a straight path which passes some distance D from the eye (Fig. 11.3). It will have a component of motion towards the eye of $V \cos \theta$, which will cause its image on the spherical projection surface to dilate. Let's consider a small image, which may correspond to a small surface patch of the object. Then the inverse of the rate of dilation of the image perpendicular to its direction of motion, which we can call τ (tau), is equal to $R/(V \cos \theta)$. Dave Young, at Edinburgh, has derived a nice proof of this. Anyway, getting rid of θ and R:

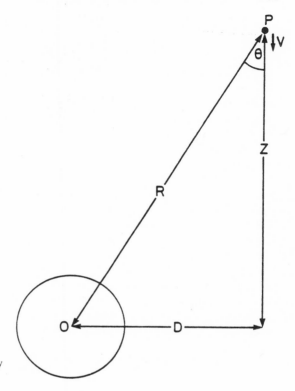

FIG. 11.3 (left).   Optical geometry
of time-to-contact.

$$\tau = (Z/V) \,[(D^2/Z^2) + 1]$$

where Z is the distance remaining before the object will be at the nearest point to
the eye. The time to reach this nearest point may reasonably be thought of as the
time-to-contact, supposing, for instance you are going to hit or catch the object.
The time is given by:

$$T_c = Z/V$$

Now, if we differentiate the above equation for τ with respect to time we get:

$$\dot{\tau} = D^2/Z^2 - 1$$

and if we now substitute for D^2/Z^2 we find that the time-to-contact is optically
specified by

$$T_c = \tau/(\dot{\tau} + 2)$$

We can also see that when Z is large compared with D then $T_c \approx \tau$.

Don't you think that this could account for how your infant subjects timed their catches of the wobbler toy?

C: No . . . I think that you can account for the precise predictive reaching strategy in a much simpler way. If the subject moves her hand with the object at the same time as she moves towards it the resultant movement will be directed at the meeting point with the object, as you can see in Fig. 11.4. In other words, if the reaches are made in reference to a coordinate system fixed to the moving object instead of to the static background they will necessarily be predictive. This strategy seems to be optimal when the object moves perpendicular to the line of sight whereas a time-to-contact strategy would seem optimal when the object moves parallel to the line of sight. Maybe, it is possible to combine these two strategies to account for timing relative to motions in all possible directions. An explanation of predictive reaching as the one I propose is not only simpler than one based on calculation, it also allows for continuous control. I think that is crucial. . . You see, I don't believe in ballistic movements. Movements are always controlled, and what you need is continuous information about the environment to be able to plan your movements and continuous information about your own movements to be able to correct them.

D: In general I agree with you about ballistic movements, though I think it's worth stressing that while people may, for example, continuously *use* visual information about their relationship to the environment to guide their walking,

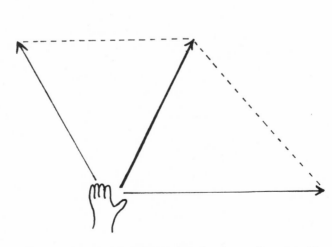

FIG. 11.4 (right).   A movement of the hand directed at the meeting point with the object can also be described as a movement with the object and towards it at the same time.

they don't have to be continuously picking up the information. They can look around as they walk, or even close their eyes for up to 8 sec as Jimmie Thomson (1980) showed, and still steer themselves accurately. What Jimmie's experiments clearly demonstrate I think is that the subjects were continuously guiding their walking or running on the basis of integrated visual and nonvisual information. The visual information was, of course, a little older than the nonvisual, but its richness made up for that.

Also, what you say is related to the ideas of feedback/feedforward and closed-loop/open-loop control which I've always found confusing terms since they imply that actions can be performed either with or without information. Like you I don't think this is the case. Action requires a perceptuo-motor cycle. Furthermore, actions have to be programmed and the program has to be continually regulated to allow for deviations of the activity from its intended course. Therefore a central question is: How is the program regulated? Clearly, it's only the yet-to-run sections that can be adjusted. Therefore, what is required is information that is predictive, in the sense that it can be integrated with the current motor program to yield a prediction of the potential future course of the movement were the program left to run. It's on this sort of basis that upcoming sections of the motor program must be regulated. Stopping a vehicle for an obstacle provides a good example of this. Clearly, in order to stop safely you've got to start braking soon enough. But that in itself is not sufficient. You've also got to brake hard enough earlier on, because if you don't you can reach a situation where you've run out of braking power. You can thus imagine somebody driving along . . . starting to brake . . . braking with a certain force . . . running a certain motor program. What the driver needs is information about whether that program, if carried through, would in fact achieve the goal that it was set to achieve—namely stopping safely. So what the driver needs is information about the inadequacy or adequacy of the program of action that he's currently putting into being. And you'll remember that, interestingly enough, the optical parameter tau (τ) which gives the time-to-contact under constant velocity and is apparently used by gannets and so on pops up again. For it turns out that its time derivative specifies the adequacy or inadequacy of the braking force (Lee, 1976). Thus, braking could be visually guided simply on the basis of τ. In fact, if one calculates what a driver would do if following such a strategy, it matches very nicely some data obtained from test drivers.

C: I think we could both do with another walk now.

D: Or how about a swim?—did I ever tell you about that study. . .

ACKNOWLEDGMENT

Some of the work reported was supported by the Swedish Council for Research in the Humanities and Social Sciences under grants to C.v.H. and by the Medical Research Council (UK) under grants to D.N.L.

REFERENCES

Alderson, G. J. K., Sully, D. J., & Sully, H. G. An operational analysis of a one-handed catching task using high speed photography. *Journal of Motor Behavior,* 1974, *6,* 217–226.

Buyakas, T. M., Vardanyan, G., & Gippenreiter, Yu. B. On the mechanisms of precise hand movements. (In Russian.) *Psichologitsheskij Jornal,* 1980, *1,* 93–103.

Fox, J. R., & Randall, J. E. Relationship between forearm tremor and the biceps electromyogram. *Journal of Applied Physiology,* 1970, *29,* 103–108.

Gibson, J. J. *The perception of the visual world.* Boston: Houghton Mifflin, 1950.

Hofsten, C. von, Predictive reaching for moving objects by human infants. *Journal of Experimental Child Psychology,* 1980, *30,* 369–382.

Hofsten, C. von, Catching skills in infancy. *Journal of Experimental Psychology: Human Perception and Performance,* 1983, *9,* 75–85.

Hofsten, C. von, & Lindhagen, K. Observations on the development of reaching for moving objects. *Journal of Experimental Child Psychology,* 1979, *28,* 158–173.

Johansson, G. *Configurations in event perception.* Uppsala: Almkvist & Wiksell, 1950.

Lee, D. N. A theory of visual control of braking based on information about time-to-collision. *Perception,* 1976, *5,* 437–459.

Lee, D. N. & Reddish, P. E. Plummeting gannets: A paradigm of ecological optics. *Nature,* 1981, *293* (5830), 293–294.

Lee, D. N., Lishman, J. R., & Thomson, J. A. Visual regulation of gait in long jumping. *Journal of Experimental Psychology: Human Perception and Performance,* 1982, *8,* 448–459.

Lee, D. N., Young, D. S., Reddish, P. E., Lough, S., & Clayton, T. M. H. Visual timing in hitting an accelerating ball. *Quarterly Journal of Experimental Psychology,* 1983, *35A,* 333–346.

Melvill Jones, G. & Watt, D. G. D. Observations on the control of stepping and hopping movements in man. *Journal of Physiology,* 1971, *219,* 709–727.

Paillard, J. The multichanneling of visual cues and the organization of a visually guided response. In G. E. Stelmach & J. Requin (Eds.), *Tutorials in motor behavior.* Amsterdam: North-Holland, 1980.

Runeson, S. On the possibility of "smart" perceptual mechanisms. *Scandinavian Journal of Psychology,* 1977, *18,* 172–179.

Sandström, C. J. *Orientation in the present space.* Stockholm: Almqvist & Wiksell, 1951.

Schiff, W. & Detwiler, M. L. Information used in judging impending collision. *Perception,* 1979, *8,* 647–658.

Sharp, R. H. & Whiting, H. T. A. Exposure and occluded duration effects in a ball-catching skill. *Journal of Motor Behavior,* 1974, *6,* 139–147.

Sharp, R. H. & Whiting, H. T. A. Information-processing and eye movement behavior in a ball catching skill. *Journal of Human Movement Studies,* 1975, *1,* 124–131.

Thomson, J. A. How do we use visual information to control locomotion? *Trends in NeuroSciences,* 1980 (Oct.), 247–250.

Todd, J. T. Visual information about moving objects. *Journal of Experimental Psychology: Human Perception and Performance,* 1981, *7,* 795–810.

Trevarthen, C., Murray, L., & Hubley, P. Psychology of infants. In J. Davis and J. Dobbing (Eds.), *Scientific foundations of clinical pediatrics.* London: Heinmans Medical 1981.

Tyldesley, D. A. & Whiting, H. T. A. Operational timing. *Journal of Human Movement Studies,* 1975, *1,* 172–177.

Yarbus, A. L. *Eye movements and vision.* New York: Plenum Press, 1967.

12 Work Group on Visual Perception

Prepared by
Claire Michaels, Lake Forest College
Claudia Carello, State University of New York at Binghamton
Beth Shapiro, University of Denver

Participants
William Mace (Moderator), Trinity College
Michael Benedikt, University of Texas
Alan Gilchrist, State University of New York at Stonybrook
Ron Growney, University of Connecticut
Margaret Hagen, Boston University
Gunnar Johansson, University of Uppsala
Ernest Lumsden, University of North Carolina at Greensboro
Dean Owen, Ohio State University
John Pittenger, University of Arkansas at Little Rock
Sverker Runeson, University of Uppsala
William Schiff, New York University

The issues raised, debated and abandoned, or seemingly resolved by the Perception Work Group can be sorted into four categories: The nature of events, information about events, the methodology of investigating event perception, and practical applications. In what follows, we give an overview of the major issues falling in each of these categories.

THE NATURE OF EVENTS

There seem to be two approaches to the characterization of events. In one, perceptual theory contributes part of the characterization; in the other, events are described in terms that are relatively neutral to theory. Particularly, we discussed

243

at length whether one ought to consider that an event presumed to be known by cognition differs from one known by perception.

This proved to be a difficult problem for several reasons. First, there are those who do not draw a distinction between perception and cognition. Second, those who draw the distinction can do so according to a number of different criteria (e.g., phenomenal experience, type of information, neural mechanisms, time involved, or mental activity). Some felt that a single process makes a good working assumption because it is more likely to coordinate accounts of the phenomena of perceiving, recognizing, remembering and expecting. Others felt that the phenomenological obviousness of the different processes demanded their separation.

Debate on this issue eventually was curtailed by the suggestion that the invariants that specify events may exist at many grains or scales and that a particular perceiving animal selects the appropriate scale by virtue of individual or species properties (e.g., size). The continuity of these scales is evident through such techniques as magnification, stroboscopic illumination, and time-lapse photography, which allow events to be temporally or spatially rescaled (Shaw & Pittenger, 1978; Warren & Shaw, this volume). Within such a formulation, environmental events of importance (e.g., looming) can be considered as a single class of events, though the processes or mechanisms involved in their detection might differ between species. Thus, the description of environmental events themselves can proceed neutrally with respect to processing theories if one allows for scale effects and allows for the possibility that different information may be "picked up" differently (e.g., with or without memory).

A second concern in the characterization of events can be termed their unitization (after Newtson, 1973). This involves the way in which the processes of nature might be organized into nested events. To begin, a useful distinction is provided by the two Swedish words for event. *Händelse* are distinct happenings which, while they can be temporally protracted, are dramatic or have a distinct beginning and end (e.g., a breaking bottle, a concert). *Skeende* are events that have a more continuous, less dramatic flavor (e.g., aging, walking). Inasmuch as we sought to avoid any characterization of events according to processing theory, we avoided the use of perceptual moments and the like to quantize events. Instead, Newtson's (1973) work, wherein perceivers demarcate the beginning and ending of events, seemed more appropriate. As with scale effects, it was expected that the unitization of events will be understood with reference to properties of perceivers, perhaps their actions and intentions.

Closely related to the unitization of events is the role of time itself in event perception theory. While it was argued that time could provide important information (e.g., in visual capture), there was a more pervasive conviction that concentrating on the perception of time itself undermines the event approach. Even though perceivers can accurately judge time given change (e.g., "time-to-contact''), the event should be taken to be the primitive rather than its temporal or spatial descriptions.

INFORMATION ABOUT EVENTS

It was agreed that while persistence and change are intrinsic to events, they can be discussed with regard to three realms: persistence and change in the environment, persistence and change in the proximal stimulus, and the perception of persistence and change. This division serves to illustrate different strategies that have been used by investigators of event perception.

The method of Gunnar Johansson at Uppsala has been to look for lawful relationships between the proximal stimulus and the percept. Although it is the proximal pattern that is described and to which observers must respond, it is also the case that the patterns used by Johansson are based on real physical and biological events (e.g., Johansson, 1973). The grounding in real phenomena is important and suggests two caveats for researchers who work within the proximal approach. First, one should identify what is salient about a natural phenomenon so that subjects are not merely being trained to notice information that normally is not used. This was discussed particularly with reference to the problem of simulation where one's theory is too often the determiner of what variables are studied. Concern was expressed about the generalizability of simulation experiments that necessarily omit information. Statistically significant effects may be found, but the phenomena are often odd or weak. It was suggested, therefore, that we should not rely on statistical significance to discover our phenomena. This points to a slightly different strategy: Investigations should be limited to those phenomena that are important to an organism in its natural environment (Gibson, 1979), and avoid phenomena that are merely suggested by a particular theory or technology (e.g., visual masking). This strategy emphasizes complex, survival-related, generally pragmatic situations or variables. One group member noted, however, that asking for unnatural judgments might lead serendipitously to a useful discovery. As an illustration, it seems that subjects asked to judge the voltage of a shock were so accurate that they were later used as voltmeters.

Second, if one starts with the proximal stimulus without regard to the physical event that might give rise to it, one might be asking for judgments of impossible situations. For example, in his pioneering work on causality, Michotte (1946/1963) had to classify certain observations as anomalous because they seemed contrary to the proximal information. But, in fact, he had ignored the law of conservation of momentum in determining what his displays represented in terms of real collisions. A more careful scrutiny of the relationship between distal events and proximal patterns seems called for, so that the dimensions of constraint on a particular environmental event are reflected in the proximal patterns used in experimental investigations of that event. This concern is made obvious in Runeson's (1977) analysis of collisions which incorporated the dynamics of real mechanical motion, information that Michotte's kinematic analysis had not taken into account. It was suggested that dynamics, not simple motion, are apprehended in event perception.

The three realms of persistence and change came together in our discussion of drawing. A drawing is a record of persistence and change of two kinds: The environmental event that is depicted and the process of the drawing's creation (e.g., Gibson, 1966, 1979). Both levels of information are available to perceivers. There was some debate as to whether the way in which static pictures specify an event is arbitrary or naturally constrained. Clearly, certain methods of depiction have become conventionalized; the question is why those particular conventions originated. Barrand's study on comic book art (Barrand, Roberts, & Tolens, 1972) suggests that only a few techniques seem to be arbitrary conventions; most capture the essential information structured by the event.

The fact that a stationary object such as a picture need not provide only static information reintroduced the discussion of slow events (Shaw & Pittenger, 1978; Warren & Shaw, this volume). It was suggested that the slow events that can be perceived are those that leave traces such as streaming or smears. Importantly, the trace can take the form of the object that is participating in the event. It has already been noted, for example, that a sketch is a trace of the event of drawing. Similarly, a face is a trace of the event of aging. It seems, therefore, that just as change specifies structure, so too can structure specify change.

THE METHODOLOGY OF EVENT PERCEPTION

The methodology most appropriate for an event framework differs from the converging operations (Garner, Hake, & Ericksen, 1956) common in perceptual research today. The assumed confluence of perceiving and acting blurs the traditional distinction of perceptual and response mechanisms. Nevertheless, the continued utility of the distinction was evident in a set of experiments described by Schiff on the conservation of length. Children asked to place pairs of sticks of the same length in a suitably sized box will put both in the same box even though one of the pair might have been judged "longer" in a verbal judgment task.

This prompted a discussion of what kinds of dependent measures are appropriate to event research. Options included not only verbal judgments and overt action, but also variability in each of these as an index of how reliable a phenomenon is. The importance of action can be reflected in verbal judgments if the latter are not restricted to absolute and extrinsic metrics (e.g., meters), but admit body-scaled units as well (e.g., within arm's reach). It was noted that body-scaled information has a nested character such that far things are not perceived in terms of an indefinite iteration of some unit (e.g., 1,000 eye-heights away) but in terms of some larger scale body referent (e.g., if I hike there, I should pack a lunch).

A discussion of illusions as a methodological tool was truncated because of the metatheoretical baggage it carries. Instead, there was strong sentiment that the most appropriate research strategy is to mimic in the laboratory what normally occurs in the environment. An experiment, therefore, can be considered as a test of whether the information presented is sufficient to specify the event. Scoring participants' reports or actions as correct or incorrect, efficient or inefficient, adequate or inadequate, can produce a measure of the sufficiency of the information made available. Although there was not complete agreement, it was argued further that, because an experiment is a test of whether the experimenter isolated the relevant information, judgments of success or failure on the part of the perceiver are inappropriate.   (correctness?)

Research that was described seemed to fall into two general categories. *Demonstration experiments* are attempts to verify that a particular perceptual ability does indeed exist. For example, can perceivers identify human walkers from twelve points of light? Can novices be trained to discriminate wines? Will animals avoid a looming object? In focussing on real phenomena, demonstrations prevent us from trying to explain supposed perceptual abilities that might not naturally exist.

Analytical experiments manipulate available information in order to determine what information is being used and how that information can be isolated (What is the minimal information needed to obtain an effect; what produced the strongest effect?). Similarly, if there are multiple sources of information, they can be made to compete or to be redundant in order to isolate the most important variables. One should be cautious, however, in interpreting experiments that pit normally redundant information sources against each other in an attempt to determine the best or most powerful. Certain combinations so produced are not representative of what occurs naturally (cf. Brunswik, 1956; Mark, Pittenger, Hines, Carello, Shaw, & Todd, 1980) and, therefore, their implications for natural perception are not straightforward.

This issue reintroduced the discussion of statistics, and it was generally agreed that such fine-grained analyses could be useful in isolating information after a phenomenon has been shown to exist, but that the information supporting that phenomenon should already be relevant to some organism (e.g., Schiff & Detwiler, 1979). Thus, statistics seem more appropriate for analytical experiments and investigations of perceptual learning than for demonstrations.

PRACTICAL APPLICATIONS

The work on simulation holds the greatest promise for practical concerns. Displays that enhance salient information can educate attention so that, for example, a pilot might more quickly learn to detect the information relevant to landing an airplane. The artificial "rescaling" of events is also useful in that it can make certain events—those that are too fast (or slow) or too large (or small)—more readily perceptible. For example, stroboscopic illumination of rapid mechanical motion can make certain physical stresses apparent. Other practical applications were discussed, but none were more appreciated than the practical, inexpensive and extremely portable human voltmeter.

SUMMARY

A search for major themes of our week's meetings indicates that an emphasis on the perception of real-world events stands out, both in terms of widespread agreement and the amount of time devoted to it. This concern was reflected in the fact that certain topics were discussed eagerly (e.g., the generalizability of simulation experiments, the appropriateness of statistics, the necessity of paying heed to environmental constraints in constructing experimental displays, the event character of picture perception), but other topics generated little enthusiasm (e.g., illusions). It was generally agreed that there is a shortage of good, manipulable phenomena and that much work should be devoted to generating and pinning down a richer set of examples to which to tie perceptual theory.

It should be noted that the question of whether a useful distinction can be drawn between fast and slow events occupied much time but inspired less unanimity. It seemed to be the case, however, that a common ground for the potential resolution of this problem was established belatedly in the discussion of streaming. It must be left to the next conference to determine whether this was, indeed, the case or whether the well-intentioned reporters have inadvertently tucked group conclusions into a procrustean bed.

REFERENCES

Barrand, A. G., Roberts, J., & Tolens, T. L. *Perceptual aspects of cartooning: The pictorial representation of events*. Paper presented at the 139th Meeting of AAAS, Washington, D. C., 1972.

Brunswik, E. *Perception and the representative design of psychological experiments*. Berkeley: University of California Press, 1956.

Garner, W. R., Hake, H. W., & Ericksen, C. W. Operationism and the concept of perception. *Psychological Review*, 1956, *63*, 317–329.

Gibson, J. J. *The senses considered as perceptual systems*. Boston: Houghton Mifflin, 1966.

Gibson, J. J. *The ecological approach to visual perception*. Boston: Houghton Mifflin, 1979.

Johansson, G. Visual perception of biological motion and a model for its analysis. *Perception and Psychophysics*, 1973, *14*, 201–211.

Mark, L. S., Pittenger, J. B., Hines, M., Carello, C., Shaw, R. E., & Todd, J. T. Wrinkling and head shape as coordinated sources of age-level information. *Perception and Psychophysics*, 1980, *27*, 117–124.

Michotte, A. *The perception of causality*. London: Methuen, 1963. Originally published, 1946.

Newtson, D. Attribution and the unit of perception of ongoing behavior. *Journal of Personality and Social Psychology*, 1973, *28*, 28–38.

Runeson, S. *On visual perception of dynamic events*. Doctoral dissertation, University of Uppsala, 1977.

Schiff, W., & Detwiler, M. L. Information used in judging impending collision. *Perception*, 1979, *8*, 659–664.

Shaw, R. E., & Pittenger, J. B. On perceiving change. In H. Pick & E. Saltzman (Eds.), *Modes of perceiving and processing information*. Hillsdale, NJ: Lawrence Erlbaum Associates, 1978.

13 Work Group on Visual Information

Prepared by   *Ennio Mingolla, Boston University*
Glenn Hamilton, University of Connecticut

Participants   *Joseph Lappin (Moderator), Vanderbilt University*
Myron Braunstein, University of California
James Cutting, Cornell University
Barbara Gillam, State University of New York College of Optometry
Daryl Lawton, University of Massachusetts
Mats Lind, University of Uppsala
Hal Sedgwick, State University of New York College of Optometry
James Todd, Brandeis University

INTRODUCTION

The discussions of this work group were concerned with two related issues: What are the phenomena of perception? What stimulus properties constitute information for perception? These issues were chosen by the group and provided fruitful general questions for discussion. Of course, we did not really answer these broad questions in a direct or comprehensive fashion, for it would not have been feasible to do so in the discussion group format, but the specific problems we discussed were tied to these general issues.

Our discussions were influenced by two significant factors: First, all of the group members have ongoing research interests in the visual perception of moving patterns in general and in the perception of three–dimensional (3–D) structures and events in particular. Thus, the group benefitted from a considerable overlap of experience and interest, though of course theoretical perspectives, investigative strategies, and specific research interests varied among the members. Furthermore, throughout our many discussions it was apparent that group members shared the critical assumption that physical events produce changes in optical stimulation which serve as the principal input for visual perception.

Second, the group decided at an early stage to focus on concrete phenomena rather than on more abstract conceptual or theoretical issues. This strategy turned out to be effective in generating common and fertile grounds for discussion and avoiding some of the friction often associated with more conceptual issues. The following sequence of specific problems was addressed by the group:

1. *Illusions:*What is their status in the characterization and investigation of perception? What do these phenomena tell us about the nature of perceptual information?
2. *Rigidity:* Is the rigidity of 3–D objects a privileged interpretation in the visual system's analysis of changing optical patterns?
3. *Complexity:* What is the proper definition of the complexity of visual stimulation? What evidence justifies Gunnar Johansson's conjecture that rapid and accurate perceptions are associated with stimulus patterns that are mathematically complex?

Embedded in the preceding problems are some general issues about the properties of perceptual information and the characterization of visual perception. As the discussions progressed, several general theoretical conceptions did emerge about the nature of perceptual information, although these convergent conceptions were not anticipated at the outset. Perhaps these emergent concepts are all the more significant for their spontaneity. The following discussions do not resolve these fundamental issues, of course, but perhaps these discussions will stimulate for readers as they did for the discussants some fruitful ideas about information and perception.

ILLUSIONS

Any experiment in visual perception involves the manipulation of information; sometimes that manipulation results in "illusory" judgments by a subject. What makes some visual experiences illusions and not others? Workshop members agreed that an illusion can be characterized as *a perceptual result not accurate in the metric the subject is asked to adopt*. Often the judgment required of the subject is one known to be performed with relative accuracy in conditions different from those present when the illusion occurs.

For example, in the Ponzo illusion the subject is asked to measure length as defined by the metric of physical length of lines on a page. The subject reacts to the entire display as if it were in a three dimensional coordinate system rather than the two dimensional coordinate system of the printed page. While subjects can ordinarily judge relative line length on a page to a certain tolerance, the presence of depth information in converging contours induces a response bias toward identifying the length of a line segment with its length in the metric of the 3–D coordinate system. While a subject is instructed to determine the lengths of lines on the two–dimensional page, the subject's visual system cannot, as it were, stop seeing the visual display in the competing 3–D geometry.

While giving general assent to the preceding characterization, group members recognized that it hardly exhausted all the phenomena of illusions. Motion after-effects and reversible figures, to name only two, may involve more than a juxtaposition of metrics or coordinate systems. The present view of illusions does offer, however, a guiding emphasis on key issues regarding visual information. Illusions remind us that we cannot take the units, metric scales, or coordinate systems used by the perceptual system for granted. As the Ponzo and related illusions demonstrate, whatever the visual system does with a depiction, the metric of physical length of picture contours is either never accessible or rapidly lost.

Group members agreed, then, that the characterization of information for the perceptual system ought not to proceed through a priori imposition of measures which have no intrinsic relation to the perceptual system's function. In particular, such quantities as length and distance need not always be measured in a Euclidean geometry. The units and geometries of perceptual organization must affect the researcher's estimate of the units and geometries appropriate to describing visual displays.

Much research with illusions in recent decades has been performed with an explicit intent to study the role of perceptual mechanisms. It has been felt that by placing perceptual mechanisms in controlled situations requiring competition of functions which are ordinarily collaborative, that the contribution of internal mechanisms can be better appreciated. Thus, when a physical object rotates near us, information from texture, contour gradients, motion parallax, and illumination all redundantly specify the rotary motion. The rotating trapezoid display, however, creates a situation where certain sources of information indicate that the object is oscillating. Manipulations of parameters of the rotating window are designed to determine the relative efficacy of corresponding cues in ordinary situations.

The trapezoidal window example illustrates the second major agreement reached by workshop members concerning illusions. Workshop participants agreed that such illusions may be used profitably for theory testing, but that illusory phenomena make a bad basis for generating theories. A phenomenon known to exist only in certain illusions ought not be the foundation of our understanding of perceptual acts in other contexts. The very name "illusion" connotes a lack of generalizability, suggesting a mismatch of perceptual organization and our initial expectations. If on the other hand one has formulated explicit hypotheses about how certain perceptual mechanisms act, then an illusion may help validate or invalidate the hypotheses. Competing models may equally well explain veridical perception, but the models may predict differing outcomes in the ambiguous or conflicting circumstances of an illusion. Thus while illusions should not be a basis for *generating* theories, they can be instrumental in *testing* competing theories.

THE PERCEPTION OF RIGID MOTION

The perception of rigid motion has long been a favorite research topic for visual psychologists for two main reasons. Motions of rigid bodies in our environment are numerous and often important for us to detect, and rigid motions generally yield much simpler mathematical descriptions and experimental manipulation than nonrigid motions.

Our group began its discussion of rigid motion by considering the work of the Conference's most distinguished scientist Gunnar Johansson. In his classic experiments on the perceptual organization of moving dots, Johansson found that dots tracing elliptical paths on a screen are seen as the end points of an object moving rigidly in depth, provided that their motion is a possible projection of some rigid 3–D motion. In a typical example two dots are seen as endpoints of a rigid rod translating and rotating in depth. In some cases the motions of the connecting rod are rather improbable gyrations violating momentum constraints on real objects, but most subjects still report that the dots move as if they were rigidly connected. The force of such demonstrations led Johansson to speculate that the visual system may somehow preferentially impose the interpretation of rigid motion on such displays. One group member pointed out, however, that the demonstrations typically involve motions of one to four dots on an otherwise empty field. Although Johansson's displays are consonant with his commitment to investigate systematic variations in proximal stimulus patterns, the ability to dynamically transform large numbers of dots through computer graphics makes possible the investigation of more complex conditions. Consequently, greater attention is being paid to rigorous mathematical analyses of how one could in principle distinguish the rigid motion of real objects from nonrigid motion through optical information. Several competing theories exist, and increasingly attention is turning to means of determining which formal models best describe the behavior of the visual system. Two approaches were discussed in detail.

Ullman (1979) has shown that a determination regarding rigidity can be made from only two views of the displacements of five dots under parallel projection, provided corresponding dots can be reliably identified accross the two views. Todd (1982), on the other hand, has described several constraints on the elliptical optical trajectories traced by dots on the surface of a rigidly rotating object. Transforming visual displays whose dot trajectories obey those constraints describe rigid motion and are reliably seen as such by subjects, while displays violating those constraints are reported as nonrigid motions. The key contribution of these and related analyses is the commitment to study the relationship of proximal optical patterns to environmental events. Some group members suggested that the visual system's treatment of optical information can thus better be understood in terms of constraints on optical structure imposed by environmental conditions than through rules of operation on proximal optical patterns per se. Such formal analyses of the optical specification of rigidity show that for many displays an informational basis exists for distinguishing rigid from nonrigid objects, and, therefore, no preference for rigid motion interpretation by the perceiver need be assumed.

The trapezoidal window illusion also came up in the discussion of rigid motion. When the rotary motion of the trapezoidal window is experienced as oscillation, the window often also seems to deform nonrigidly while it oscillates. This latter effect is vexing for theories such as Ullman's and Todd's, because the optical information for rigid motion as described by their theories is present, yet nonrigid motion is reported. However, the oscillation and deformation effects are best obtained in relatively impoverished conditions where textural information on the window's surface is minimized and where the observer is relatively distant from the window (Mingolla & Todd, 1981). Perhaps additional constraints regarding the optics of rigid motion might yield a theory consistent with actual performance of human observers in the Ames illusion and in the detection of rigid motion in other settings. For the present, however, it is clear that whatever the visual system is doing, it does not prefer the interpretation of rigidity in all cases.

Evidence from Johansson's displays, from mathematical analysis of the optics of rigid motion, and from the Ames window is not entirely reconciled at present, but the trend of the group's thinking was that rigid motion is not a privileged perceptual outcome, but one among many possible physical motions and hence one among many possible interpretations of optical information. The visual system seems explicitly designed to register complicated events in a 3–D world. While some psychologists argue that the visual system greatly supplements available optical information or has prejudices regarding its interpretation, it may be that such behavior is not at all characteristic of normal functioning, where the richness of optical information generally compels accurate perception. The characterization of rich optical information is, however, little understood at present, and more work is needed which describes the units and geometry of the optics of complex motions, nonrigid as well as rigid, in terms applicable to the function of the visual system.

COMPLEXITY OF VISUAL INFORMATION

As stated previously, Johansson has observed that certain proximal displays of events that are mathematically complex are quickly and easily perceived. [See

Johansson, this volume]. His displays of point-light walkers aptly illustrate this observation: When the various spatio–temporal paths of the twelve major joints are displayed simultaneously over a brief trajectory, one achieves the perception of a person walking. However, one does not see the spatio–temporal path of a single joint (e.g., the knee) as part of that locomoting person when it is viewed in isolation. Group members noted that the addition of information from several joints seems to facilitate rather than impair the success of perceptual processing.

Most group members did not see this as a recalcitrant paradox because the notions of ''complex'' and ''simple'' are not yet well understood in terms of how a visual system processes input. A display which is simple to the visual system may have a description which is complex in terms of the components described by a psychologist's theory. Presently, formal complexity theory characterizes the complexity of algorithms by plotting increases in processing time as a function of increases in the number of elements to be processed. The application of formal complexity theory to a problem requires a proper and explicit definition of the elements to be processed, but one of the perceptual psychologists' major problems remains the identification of perceptual units. During the discussion, some group members argued, in the case of the point-light walkers, that the trajectory of each joint is not independent of those of the other joints and so each joint might not constitute a distinct unit. These individuals argued that the proper effective unit for this task was *relational* information over the trajectories of several joints. (for describing human gait percep.)

All group members agreed, in any case, that the fundamental units of visual processing have long eluded perceptual psychologists. In the past, units have often been taken to be rather low-level sensory elements from which a perceiver constructs a rich perceptual experience: The point sensations of classical structuralist theories are such elements; the features of current information processing models are slightly more complex units. Group members discussed some experimentation in the last few decades which suggests that proper geometrical analyses can reveal perceptual units whose descriptions are more complex than that of the classical units. Higher order invariants were offered as examples of such units. Some group members noted that if such invariants in optical stimulation indeed constitute the fundamental units for perception, then a resolution of Johansson's paradoxical observation may be at hand. One member suggested that if relations over several human joint trajectories are the minimal proper units for describing human gait perception, then the presentation of a single joint trajectory is better called insufficient than simple, and the invariant relations over trajectories better characterized as adequate than as complex.

Hence, the additional joints depicted do not trace out truly new motions but help to specify the structure and transformation of every joint. The degrees of freedom in this display are less than the number of joints and their possible motions because the underlying anatomical constraints determine the motions of joints and their depicted trajectories. These combined trajectories, then, seem to have an underlying geometric characterization which is far simpler than a function describing any single trajectory in Euclidean coordinates. Point lights attached to a rolling wheel rim are a simple illustration of this point. The rolling of the wheel itself constrains the motion of each individual wheel rim point whose trajectory is that of a mathematically complex trochoid. In this example the translatory and rotary motion of the wheel is perceptually salient, and the trochoidal trajectory of any individual point light is not. The underlying motion of the wheel here is revealed across the motion of all points and one perceives the unitary rolling motion of the wheel which is geometrically simpler than the independent trochoid motions. Conversely, truly complex displays in the perceptual sense may be those which defy a unitary description through such a geometry of constraints.

Several group members noted that progress has been made recently in statistical characterizations of the complexity of visual patterns. Theoretical research by Julesz and his colleagues (e.g., Caelli & Julesz, 1978; Caelli, Julesz & Gilbert, 1978; Julesz, 1981), by Restle (1979), and by Doner (in preparation) are examples of such work. All present agreed that this problem remains an important theoretical and experimental problem for research. The group concluded that much remains to be learned about the role of statistical complexity and the geometric structure of visual events.

CONCLUSION

The description of optical information continues to prove a fundamental task for researchers in visual perception. Dialogue among work group members revealed a shared interest in appropriately characterizing information for the visual system, and many points of consensus regarding how that might be done. Issues concerning units and geometries involved in perception extend beyond traditional psychological areas and into practical issues of representation for computer controlled processes. Dialogues like the one reported here are helping to unify our knowledge of perceptual mechanisms with a broad understanding of visual information for the perception of events.

REFERENCES

Caelli, T. M., & Julesz, B. On perceptual analyzers underlying visual texture discrimination: Part I. *Biological Cybernetics,* 1978, *28,* 167–175.

Caelli, T. M., Julesz, B., & Gilbert, E. N. On perceptual analyzers underlying visual texture discrimination: Part II. *Biological Cybernetics,* 1978, *29,* 201–214.

Doner, J. F. Toward a theory of processing: I. Quantification of stimulus organization. In preparation.

Julesz, B. Textons, the elements of texture perception, and their interactions. *Nature*, 1981, *290*, 91–97.

Mingolla, E., & Todd, J. The rotating square illusion. *Perception and Psychophysics*, 1981, *29*, (5), 487–492.

Restle, F. Coding theory of the perception of motion configurations. *Pychological Review*, 1979, *86*, 1–24.

Todd, J. Visual information about rigid and nonrigid motion: A geometric analysis. *Journal of Experimental Psychology: Human Perception and Performance*, 1982, *8*, 238–252.

Ullman, S. *The Interpretation of Visual Motion*. Cambridge, Mass., MIT Press, 1979.

14 Work Group on Perceptual Development

Prepared by   *Rebecca Jones, University of Minnesota*
Elizabeth Spelke, University of Pennsylvania
Thomas Alley, University of Connecticut

Participants   *Eleanor Gibson (Moderator), Cornell University*
Reuben Baron, University of Connecticut
Catherine Best, Columbia Teachers College
Claes von Hofsten, University of Uppsala
Leslie McArthur, Brandeis University
Peter Pufall, Smith College

INTRODUCTION

The study of perceptual development focuses on the foundations of perception and traces the changes that perception undergoes with growth and learning. Thus from a developmental perspective on event perception, one seeks to discover the origins in infancy of the ability to perceive events, ways in which this ability changes during childhood, and the aspects of this ability that persist throughout development. Although the study of event perception is a relatively new field, a significant amount of developmental research has already been undertaken. In our discussion, we considered some of this research, in order to find out what has been learned and to identify directions for further investigation (see Gibson & Spelke, 1983, for further discussion).

Events are changes in the layout of the substantial surfaces of the environment, such as displacements and deformations. They have a beginning and an end, and are nested within other events (however, see Mace, this volume). Events are specified by information in ambient arrays, and usually this information is available to more than one perceptual system. Some events have consequences for an organism and provide certain possibilities for its action. In J. J.

Gibson's (1979, Ch. 8) terminology, they have *affordances* for behavior. For example, some musical events afford the possibility of synchronous rhythmic movement for humans. In addition, events can reveal the affordances of objects and places; the affordances of some objects may remain ambiguous until an observer encounters those objects within an event.

The above characterization of events leads to several questions concerning the development of event perception. When does the perception of events and their affordances begin, and how does it develop? Specifically, is the perception of events primary in development, or is it achieved on the basis of ontogenetically prior perceptions of static surface layouts? Is multimodal perception of events an early achievement or is it dependent on extensive learning of correlations between modality-specific sensations? Are some of the affordances of events and of objects immediately perceived and acted upon by infants, or are meanings attached to events over the course of development through an associative or constructive process? The expanding literature on event perception suggests that infants begin life with the ability to perceive events multimodally and to act on some of their affordances. Studies of event perception in childhood suggest that these abilities are refined and that perception becomes differentiated as the child actively explores the environment.

EVENT PERCEPTION IN INFANCY

Despite the emphasis on infants' perception of unchanging two–dimensional patterns that has characterized most work on perception in infancy, it has long been evident that infants are attentive to events. For example, Wertheimer's (1961) early observation that his newborn daughter turned her eyes to look in the direction of an event that produced a sound suggested that exploration of events by the auditory and visual perceptual systems is coordinated at the beginning of life. Recent studies support this suggestion (e.g., Muir & Field, 1979) and indicate that coordinated visual and haptic exploration occur as well (e.g., von Hofsten, 1982).

Given that many events are specified by information available to more than one perceptual system, and that infants explore events with different perceptual systems in a coordinated fashion, the question arises as to whether infants perceive unitary events when there is information available multimodally. In a series of studies, Spelke (1976, 1979) has investigated 4-month-old infants' detection of optical and acoustical information specifying the temporal structure of events. The method developed by Spelke is to present infants with two movies side by side with the sound track corresponding to one of the movies centered between the two screens. A concealed observer records the direction of the infant's gaze, and preferential looking to the sound-specified movie is taken as evidence for bimodal perception of the unity of the event. Using this method, Spelke has found that infants perceive an audible and visible event as unitary based on certain characteristics of the event's tempo. For example, she found that infants who saw movies of two unfamiliar toy stuffed animals moving up and down, each arbitrarily paired with different percussive sounds, looked for the sound-synchronized object, even when the sound was not simultaneous with the object's impact on the ground. Thus fairly abstract properties of events, such as their tempo, can be perceived bimodally in infancy.

In further studies using this method, Bahrick (1980) investigated infants' intermodal perception of the substance of objects. She hypothesized that infants would perceive a single meaningful event (i.e., show preferential looking to the sound-specified event) only if both the acoustical and optical information specified an object of the same substance. She showed 4-month-old infants two films, one of two wooden blocks hitting each other and one of two wet sponges hitting each other. The blocks had a sound track of "clacking" noises and the sponges had a sound track of "squishes." She found preferential looking for the sound-synchronized film only when the optical and acoustical information for the object's substance specified the same kind of thing. Apparently the infants could perceive the substance of the objects both through the motions and the sounds, and they perceived a unified event only when the two sources of information were consistent.

Walker (1982) has shown that 5- and 7-month-old infants can perceive the unity of a movie of a person speaking expressively (happy or sad) and its appropriate sound track, also by using the preferential looking paradigm (see also Dodd, 1979; Spelke & Cortelyou, 1981). In investigating the information used in perceiving this event, Walker found that it was not merely a simple timing relation, because the appropriate preferential looking occurred when the movie and its sound track were out of synchrony; nor was it simply the level of activity because the preferential looking was not found when the movies were presented upside down. Walker suggests that it is the mutual affordance that links the two presentations as one event. Finally, Born, Spelke, and Prather (1982) have found that newborn infants, as well as 4-month-olds, detect the intermodal relation when they view a person speaking and a musical performance, and hear a sound that is specific to one of them. Although further work needs to be done to discover what information is being used by the infants, all of these studies, and many others, demonstrate intermodal perception of events by very young infants. Intermodal perception of events is not dependent on extensive learning about the correspondences between modalities; rather, it appears to be a fundamental perceptual ability by which infants explore and obtain knowledge about the world.

Studies of the perception of the affordances of events have revealed that quite young infants perceive some of their affordances and act upon them appropriately. In studies of visually guided reaching, von Hofsten (von Hofsten, 1979,

1980; von Hofsten & Lindhagen, 1979) has shown that infants will reach for moving objects with considerable accuracy, and begin to do so at least as early as they reach for stationary objects. Infants adapt their reaching to the object's motion, reaching toward the position that the object will occupy when their arm is fully extended. Moreover, they adapt their reaching to the speed of the object, even the first time that they see an object moving at a given speed, limiting their reaching attempts to objects that they can, in fact, catch (von Hofsten, 1979, 1980). These findings indicate that infants accurately perceive when a moving object affords catching and manipulating and that they coordinate their actions to realize those affordances.

Objects moving in particular ways afford catching, but objects moving in other ways are obstacles that afford collision. Investigations of reactions to approaching ("looming") surfaces have revealed that infants as young as two weeks will blink when they perceive an approaching obstacle. Later on, infants also withdraw their heads from the object (Yonas & Granrud, 1981; cf. Ball & Tronick, 1971; Bower, Broughton, & Moore, 1971). However, when 3-month-old infants perceive a looming aperture, a surface that approaches an observer rapidly but affords moving through safely, they show no defensive reactions (Carroll & Gibson, 1981). Thus events involving the approach of objects that afford either dangerous collision or safe passage are discriminated and acted upon appropriately early in development, within the limits of the available action systems.

Another important event that can be seen is that of oneself moving through the environment. When an animal locomotes, information for its own path of movement is given in the changing pattern of optical flow (Lee, 1980). Studies by Lee and Aronson (1974) and by Butterworth (1981) indicate that infants and toddlers use optical information to adjust their postures and control their movements; that is, they both perceive and control the event of their own swaying. In these studies, children were presented with optical information specifying their own forward or backward movement (global optical flow with foci of expansion and contraction at eye height) by means of a "swinging room," whose walls and ceiling moved linearly backward and forward. The children compensated for their apparent body sway by moving in the opposite direction, or at least by attempting to so move. For unsteady toddlers this often meant a complete loss of balance, indicating their reliance on optical information in responding to this event, even when other kinesthetic and proprioceptive sources of information specified stability.

Events also reveal the properties of objects and this is a topic that holds great promise for research. In contrast to static displays, events can reveal the boundaries of an object and some of its important properties such as its elasticity, mass, and animacy or inanimacy (see Johansson, von Hofsten, & Jansson, 1980). Research by Kellman & Spelke (1979, 1981) has shown that 4-month-old infants perceive the unity of an object whose center is occluded when the object undergoes a translatory motion but not when it is stationary. Using an habituation-dishabituation paradigm, they found that infants habituated to a stationary rod, when the center of the rod was occluded from their view, showed moderate and equal dishabituation to both an unoccluded broken rod and an unoccluded complete rod. However, those infants to whom the rod was presented translating behind the occluder during the habituation phase behaved like a control group who saw an unoccluded complete rod during habituation, showing dishabituation to an unoccluded broken rod and showing little interest in an unoccluded complete rod. Thus the motion of an object provided information about the boundaries of an object in the region where it was hidden.

Studies by Gibson and her students (Gibson, Owsley, & Johnston, 1978; Gibson, Owsley, Walker, & Megaw-Nyce, 1979; Walker, Owsley, Megaw-Nyce, Gibson, & Bahrick, 1980) indicate that infants can perceive the rigidity or elasticity of an object through deformation events. In one study, they habituated 3½-month-old infants to a foam rubber object undergoing three rigid transformations and then compared looking times to a novel rigid transformation with looking times to a novel nonrigid transformation. They found that infants viewing the former transformation continued to demonstrate signs of habituation, but infants who saw the nonrigid transformation became dishabituated. Parallel experiments with deforming, elastic transformations yielded similar results. These findings indicate that infants can detect several different types of optical transformations that specify the substance of an object. Combinations of properties such as elasticity constitute the affordances of objects, and recent evidence indicates that these may be perceived and acted upon by young infants (Gibson & Walker, 1982).

In sum, the evidence from many different studies leads us to conclude that infants perceive events from the beginning of life and that these events inform them about possibilities for action, aspects of their own movement, and the properties of objects. Further research is needed to specify the information infants use in perceiving events, especially in intermodal perception, and research is also needed to investigate perception of the various properties of events through all of the perceptual systems.

TRENDS IN THE DEVELOPMENT OF EVENT PERCEPTION

Event perception undergoes clear and striking changes with learning and development. Some of these changes are revealed through observations of the child's changing patterns of exploration of events. Others are revealed through investigations of the child's changing ability to detect the information for events. In the course of development, exploration becomes more systematic, and perception becomes more differentiated and economical. Most important, the child comes to discover progressively higher order structure and meaning in events.

From the beginning of life infants have a small but effective repertoire of investigatory activities such as moving their eyes and heads, listening, and mouthing; and they can use these activities to discover properties of the environment. The development of infants' visual exploration skills recently has been a subject of much study. It has been found that when a display suddenly appears as far as 30° in the periphery, even one-month-old infants will localize it accurately (Aslin & Salapatek, 1975). It has also been shown that infants are especially apt to look at a target in their peripheral field of view if it moves (Tronick, 1972), but they do so by making a series of inefficient saccadic movements. With age, both the accuracy of the localization and the efficiency of the scanning improves. The improvement is gradual; children continue to localize and to track targets less efficiently than adults throughout the preschool years (Kowler & Martins, 1982).

The increase in the efficiency of eye movements is paralleled by the increase in the efficiency of reaches to moving objects found by von Hofsten (1979). Younger infants (18 wks.) make a series of jerky movements to reach a target while older infants (36 wks.) make a fairly smooth reach. Reaching continues to undergo developmental change throughout the first year (see, for example, Piaget, 1952; Bresson, Maury, Pieraut le Bonniec, & de Schonen, 1977), and the perceptual guidance of manual skill continues to develop through childhood.

All of the experiments mentioned indicate that infants explore events from the beginning of life in systematic, though limited ways. The infant's capacity for exploring events is especially clear in experimental studies in which actions in the infant's repertoire control the presentation of environmental events. One of the earliest developing exploratory actions is mouthing. Infants explore by mouthing nearly from birth (see Piaget, 1952), and it is likely that they can detect object properties such as texture and substance by mouthing long before they detect them by manipulation. For example, infants detect correspondences between the sight and touch of a rigid or flexible object by one month of age, provided that the object is placed in the mouth (Gibson & Walker, 1982). This is the case even when the optical information for the object's substance is available solely through motion. Because manual exploration does not become skillful before 10 or 12 months, infants do not detect the same intermodal relation when they hold an object in the hand until many months later (Gibson & Walker, 1982).

A large number of experiments indicate that infants as young as one month will engage in active sucking when that sucking provides information about events. For example, infants will suck to bring a motion picture film (a representation of an event) into focus (Kalnins & Bruner, 1973). Similar results have been found with speech or articulatory events (e.g., Eimas, Siqueland, Jusczyk, & Vigorito, 1971). Thus active sucking appears to be an early developing activity by which infants can explore events. Older infants are less apt to suck to produce visible or audible events, presumably because other exploratory systems become available that are more effective.

These studies all indicate that exploratory activities change and develop, as do other patterns of activity. As children come to explore with increasing accuracy and efficiency, they will be able to detect more and more of the relevant properties and affordances of events. We consider a few examples.

In the course of development, children appear to distinguish ever more finely among events. A good, but little studied, example concerns the perception of moving objects. In baseball, skilled batters differentiate with awesome precision among pitches thrown at different speeds, with differing paths and amounts of spin, and skilled fielders are similarly adept at perceiving the trajectories of balls hit into the air. All of us come to achieve some skill in detecting differences in the patterns of motion of a ball. The development of such abilities should prove a fascinating area of study. Ball playing skill is just one illustration of the pervasive tendency of perceptual development toward greater differentiation: an increase in the specificity of discrimination of information (Gibson, 1969, Chs. 6, 20). Furthermore, since events typically are embedded in other events in superordinate and subordinate relations, there are many levels for potential differentiation.

Children also come to perceive events more efficiently. The perception of speech provides an example. Recent evidence seems to indicate that infants discriminate more potential phonemic differences than they will as adults. Experience with a language eventually leads to discrimination of only those sounds that create meaning differences in the language; differentiation within the total potential set improves resultant efficiency (see Jusczyk, 1981, for a review).

Another trend in perceptual development is for children to become increasingly able to detect the higher-order structure in events. An example of perceiving the higher-order structure of an event is perceiving a theme and variations in a musical piece. This is an ability that develops across the life span and is just beginning to be studied from the viewpoint of a developmental perspective on event perception (Pick, 1979). In perceiving music, as in perceiving speech and other events, children become progressively more sensitive to higher-order relationships that unify a complex sequence of changes over time (Gibson & Spelke, 1983).

Finally, children learn more about the affordances of events and they become increasingly able to produce events that reveal the affordances of objects (Gibson, 1982). For example, toddlers and older preschool children are especially apt to play with objects in ways that reveal their affordances. They bang blocks on tables, squeeze clay into multiple shapes, tear and crumble paper, and so forth (Piaget, 1952, 1954, provides many revealing examples). They also discover the special functions of more complex, jointed objects, such as levers, through active exploration and manipulation (e.g., Koslowski & Bruner, 1972). These activities hold special promise for studying how affordances come to be perceived.

CONCLUSIONS

Research on event perception in infancy has established that humans begin to explore and perceive events at the beginning of life, and that this capacity provides a foundation for many other aspects of perceptual development. This research indicates, moreover, that event perception becomes increasingly differentiated and efficient with development, and that children become increasingly sensitive to the higher-order structure and the affordances of events. As perception develops, it continues to be tied to the child's actions.

We have pointed to areas where more developmental research is needed. In closing, we wish to give one of these areas special emphasis. During infancy and childhood, humans discover more and more of the affordances of the world. Affordances appear to be discovered primarily through events, as children act on objects to transform them and detect the information provided by these transformations. Perception is directed to the affordances of events, objects, and places throughout life, and is adaptive only in so far as the perceiver comes to have useful knowledge of these affordances. Studies of the growth of knowledge about affordances in infancy and childhood should shed light on this central aspect of perception. To date, few studies of the development of the perception of affordances have been conducted. Nevertheless, they provide one illustration of the special contribution to the understanding of event perception that a developmental perspective can give. Specifically, a developmental perspective provides a clearer view of skill acquisition and perceptual learning than do experiments with adults, precisely because it focuses on the young organism as a simpler, less skilled actor-perceiver. Thus developmental findings can offer rich insights into the acquisition of various types of special expertise by children and adults, and can help to resolve major theoretical controversies about the foundations of perceiving, acting, and knowing.

REFERENCES

Aslin, R. M., & Salapatek, P. Saccadic localization of visual targets by the very young human infant. *Perception & Psychophysics*, 1975, *17*, 293–302.

Bahrick, L. E. *Infants' perception of objects as specified by amodal information in auditory–visual events*. Unpublished doctoral dissertation, Cornell University, 1980.

Ball, W. A., & Tronick, E. Infant responses to impending collision: Optical and real. *Science*, 1971, *171*, 818–820.

Born, W. S., Spelke, E. S., & Prather, P. *Detection of auditory-visual relationships by newborn infants*. Paper presented at the International Conference on Infant Studies, Austin, Texas, March, 1982.

Bower, T. G. R., Broughton, J. M., & Moore, M. K. Infant responses to approaching objects: An indication of response to distal variables. *Perception & Psychophysics*, 1971, *9*, 193–196.

Bresson, F., Maury, L., Pieraut le Bonniec, G., & de Schonen, S. Organization and lateralization of reaching in infants: An instance of asymmetric function in hand collaboration. *Neuropsychologia*, 1977, *15*, 311–320.

Butterworth, G. The origins of auditory-visual perception and visual proprioception in human development. In R. D. Walk & H. L. Pick (Eds.), *Intersensory perception and sensory integration*. New York: Plenum, 1981.

Carroll, J. J., & Gibson, E. J. *Differentiation of an aperture from an obstacle under conditions of motion by 3-month-old infants*. Paper presented at the meeting of the Society for Research in Child Development, Boston, April, 1981.

Dodd, B. Lip reading in infants: Attention to speech presented in- and out-of-synchrony. *Cognitive Psychology*, 1979, *11*, 478–484.

Eimas, P., Siqueland, E., Jusczyk, P., & Vigorito, J. Speech perception in infants. *Science*, 1971, *171*, 303–306.

Gibson, E. J. *Principles of perceptual learning and development*. New York: Appleton-Century-Crofts, 1969.

Gibson, E. J. The concept of affordances in development: The renascence of functionalism. In W. A. Collins (Ed.), *Minnesota Symposia on Child Psychology*, Vol. 15: *The concept of development*. Hillsdale, N.J.: Lawrence Erlbaum Associates, 1982.

Gibson, E. J., Owsley, C. J., & Johnston, J. Perception of invariants by 5-month-old infants: Differentiation of two types of motion. *Developmental Psychology*, 1978, *14*, 407–415.

Gibson, E. J., Owsley, C. J., Walker, A., & Megaw-Nyce, J. Development of the perception of invariants: Substance and shape. *Perception*, 1979, *8*, 609–619.

Gibson, E. J., & Spelke, E. The development of perception. In J. H. Flavell & E. MArkman (Eds.), *Cognitive development*. Volume 3 of P. Mussen (Ed.), *Handbook of Child Psychology*. New York: Wiley, 1983.

Gibson, E. J., & Walker, A. *Intermodal perception of substance*. Paper presented at the International Conference on Infant Studies, Austin, Texas, March, 1982.

Gibson, J. J. *The ecological approach to visual perception*. Boston: Houghton Mifflin, 1979.

Hofsten, C. von Development of visually directed reaching: The approach phase. *Journal of Human Movement Studies*, 1979, *5*, 160–178.

Hofsten, C. von Predictive reaching for moving objects by human infants. *Journal of Experimental Child Psychology*, 1980, *30*, 369–382.

Hofsten, C. von Eye-hand coordination in the newborn. *Developmental Psychology*, 1982, *18*, 450–461.

Hofsten, C. von, & Lindhagen, K. Observations on the development of reaching for moving objects. *Journal of Experimental Child Psychology*, 1979, *28*, 158–173.

Johansson, G., Hofsten, C. von, & Jansson, G. Event perception. *Annual Review of Psychology*, 1980, *31*, 27–63.

Jusczyk, P. *The development of speech perception*. Paper presented at the Guggenheim Conference on Neonate and Infant Cognition, New York, 1981.

Kalnins, I. V., & Bruner, J. S. The coordination of visual observation and instrumental behavior in early infancy. *Perception*, 1973, *2*, 307–314.

Kellman, P. J., & Spelke, E. S. *Perceiving partly occluded objects in infancy*. Paper presented at the meeting of the Society for Research in Child Development, San Francisco, March, 1979.

Kellman, P. J., & Spelke, E. S. *Infant perception of partly occluded objects: Sensitivity to movement and configuration*. Paper presented at the meeting of the Society for Research in Child Development, Boston, April, 1981.

Koslowski, B., & Bruner, J. S. Learning to use a lever. *Child Development*, 1972, *43*, 790–799.

Kowler, E., & Martins, A. Eye movements of preschool children. *Science*, 1982, *215*, 997–999.

Lee, D. N. The optic flow field: The foundation of vision. *Philosophical Transactions of the Royal Society, London, B*, 1980, *290*, 169–179.

Lee, D. N., & Aronson, E. Visual proprioceptive control of standing in human infants. *Perception & Psychophysics*, 1974, *15*, 529–532.

Muir, D., & Field, J. Newborn infants orient to sounds. *Child Development*, 1979, *50*, 431–436.

Piaget, J. *The origins of intelligence in children.* New York: International Universities Press, 1952.

Piaget, J. *The construction of reality in the child.* New York: Basic Books, 1954.

Pick, A. D. Listening to melodies: Perceiving events. In A. D. Pick (Ed.), *Perception and its development: A tribute to Eleanor J. Gibson.* Hillsdale, N.J.: Lawrence Erlbaum Associates, 1979.

Spelke, E. S. Infants' intermodal perception of events. *Cognitive Psychology*, 1976, *8*, 553–560.

Spelke, E. S. Perceiving bimodally specified events in infancy. *Developmental Psychology*, 1979, *15*, 626–636.

Spelke, E. S., & Cortelyou, A. Perceptual aspects of social knowing: Looking and listening in infancy. In M. E. Lamb & L. R. Sherrod (Eds.), *Infant social cognition.* Hillsdale, N. J.: Lawrence Erlbaum Associates, 1981.

Tronick, E. Stimulus control and the growth of the infant's effective visual field. *Perception & Psychophysics*, 1972, *11*, 373–376.

Walker, A. Intermodal perception of expressive behavior by human infants. *Journal of Experimental Child Psychology*, 1982, *33*, 514–535.

Walker, A., Owsley, C. J., Megaw-Nyce, J., Gibson, E. J., & Bahrick, L. E. Detection of elasticity as an invariant property of objects by young infants. *Perception*, 1980, *9*, 713–718.

Wertheimer, M. Psychomotor coordination of auditory and visual space at birth. *Science*, 1961, *134*, 1692.

Yonas, A., & Granrud, C. *The development of depth perception in infants.* Paper presented at the Guggenheim Conference on Neonate and Infant Cognition, New York, 1981.

15 Work Group on Perception and Action

Prepared by   *William H. Warren, Jr., Brown University*
J. A. Scott Kelso (Moderator), Haskins Laboratories

Participants   *Edward L. Cochran, Adelphi University*
Gunnar Jansson, University of Uppsala
David Lee, University of Edinburgh
Rik Warren, Wright-Patterson Air Force Base

The work group on perception and action was concerned with those events that Gibson called "encounters," that is, events that involve an organism's perceptual-motor activity. Like inanimate events such as rotation or breaking, encounters may be described in terms of structural and transformational invariants and a temporal period over which the event transpires (see Warren & Shaw, this volume). However, the work group was concerned less with how actions are specified to an onlooker than with how actions are appropriately selected (the detection of affordances) and tailored to local conditions (the perceptual control of activity) by the participant. As Lee put it, the problem is one of discovering perceptual information *about* and *for* the act.

The group focussed on the problem of how an action system might be regulated by perceptual information specific to the dynamic requirements of an act. We found ourselves returning again and again in this discussion to three central questions. First, what perceptual information is necessary to guide an action? Second, what in the basic design of the motor system allows perceptual information to guide it? And third, how does the action system adapt to changed conditions, and what is the role of perception in guiding adaptation? Here we briefly discuss each of these issues.

NECESSARY CHARACTERISTICS OF INFORMATION
RELEVANT TO ACTIVITY

For any action—jumping a stream, catching a ball, or landing an airplane—an actor must perform an amount of work in moving against gravity, accelerating or deccelerating limb, body, or object mass, or overcoming friction. To do work requires the dissipation of a certain quantity of energy over the appropriate body segments in a manner coordinated with the local environment. The group described three characteristics of perceptual, and in particular visual, information that appear necessary to explain this coordination.

Information Must be Specific to the Spatial, Temporal, and Energy Requirements of the Act.   While classical perceptual theory has emphasized the perception of static space and luminance (geometric properties), and this conference has emphasized the perception of spatio–temporal variables (kinematic properties), considering the functions of perception for action implicates *dynamic* properties of energy transfer as well (see Runeson, 1977; Warren & Shaw, this volume). To catch a fly ball, one must not only detect information about *where* it will land, and *when* it will arrive there, but also *at what rate* energy must be dissipated over the musculature (i.e., how much power must be applied) to propel one's body mass to that space–time locale (see Kugler & Turvey, this volume; Kugler, Kelso, & Turvey, 1980). A ball is "out of reach" if the fielder cannot dissipate energy fast enough to get to it, and such fly balls are generally perceived as uncatchable. Variables previously considered to be "kinematic," such as Lee's (1976) time-to-collision invariant, might be reconstrued in dynamic terms if referred to energetic constraints (Warren & Shaw, 1981). For example, an organism with a greater ratio of available power to body mass can respond to avoid an oncoming object at a smaller value of time-to-collision. What remains to be explained, however, is how the space–time–energy values appropriate for an action might be visually specified to an actor with particular dynamic constraints.

Minimally, an abstract "information space" must have dimensions of space, time, and energy defined over the system encompassing the actor and its environment. The configuration of a manifold (or surface) within that space is a consequence of the dynamics of the animal-environment system, and its stabilities correspond to regions of economical activity (see Kugler, Kelso, & Turvey, 1982). Perceptual-motor learning may involve isolating such regions through exploratory manipulation of the variables of the manifold. Similar considerations may apply if one is supplying force to a joystick in an airplane or a steering wheel in a car, except that the space–time–energy relations must be rescaled for the actor–vehicle–environment system; and allowance must be made for non-linearities in such systems, as when increasing pressure on the brake pedal beyond some limit does not further deccelerate a car. Again, such properties can be discovered through active exploration.

The Relevant Information, and the Period Over Which Energy is to be Dissipated, are Determined by the Goal of the Action.   The goal or "intentionality" of a particular act determines, out of the plethora of information that is available, precisely the information that is relevant to guide the action. The determination of this information may be the essence of what is meant by goal-directed behavior. In Lee's films of female long jumpers it is the impending contact with the take-off board, not with the edge of the jumping pit, that modulates the step cycle in the last few strides of the jumper's approach (Lee, Lishman, & Thomson, 1981). When the runner hits the board, maximum thrust is applied to launch her into the jump. Here the goal of the action is a jump of maximum distance from the board, and it determines the information that specifies the period over which energy (in this case, maximum power) is to be dissipated.

If, however, the goal is to warm up by "running through" the board, the step cycle is first adjusted to hit the board with less than maximum thrust, and is subsequently adjusted with respect to the edge of the sand pit, where there is a sudden change in the running surface. In this case, reaching the board does not bound the action, and the level of power applied in the thrust phase is held roughly constant. When the pit is reached, however, visual information about changes in the elasticity of the terrain modulates the power in the thrust phase to maintain stepping without breaking stride. In sum, the intentionality of the act has consequences for the pickup of information and for the regulation of energy dissipation.

Information Must be Intrinsically Defined, That Is, Scaled in the Metric of the Action System.   The units in which space, time, and energy are visually specified to an actor are clearly not meters, seconds, and joules. Perceptual information must be scaled with respect to the actor in order to govern the action system directly (Lee, 1980; Shaw & Cutting, 1980; Warren & Shaw, 1981). Although such units have been spoken of as "body-scaled," they may be functionally defined relative to the animal's current activity as well as to its anatomy. Thus, space might be specified in units of eye-height (Lee, 1974; Sedgwick, 1980) or current stride length; time-to-collision in terms of the organism's rate of action (e.g., the time necessary to overcome inertia of the body mass, given the organism's maximal power-to-mass ratio); and energy in terms of the maximal or current rate of dissipation. If information can be described as commensurate with the actor, it becomes unnecessary to compute action values from primitives or convert them from arbitrary units.

The following in-principle example may help to clarify these three points, as it did for the group as we worked with it. Consider a runner who must jump over a stream that lies in her path. First, it is clear that she will need visual information about *where* to jump from and land, *when* to thrust, and *how much* power to apply. Second, the goal of clearing the stream bounds the period of the action, establishing a space–time interval over which energy must be quantized to carry our runner's particular mass over a particular distance. It also determines that information about the near bank will modulate the step cycle, and information about the far bank will modulate energy dissipation.

Third, the space–time–energy values can be expressed intrinsically in the following way. Consider the runner in flight and just about to strike the ground. Let TC_{near} represent the time to contact the near bank at her current speed. The time is specified in the optic flow field at the runner's eye (see Lee, 1976). Further, let T_{flight} and $T_{support}$ represent the flight and support times of her current strides; these times are also optically specified, by the changes in time-to-contact with the bank which occur during the stride. Then the number of strides she is away from the near bank is specified by $TC_{near}/(T_{flight} + T_{support})$. In general, she will have to adjust this ratio to be a whole number so that her foot will land right on the brink of the stream. This she can do while maintaining speed, by regulating the vertical impulse power, or "lift," of her strides, because flight time is directly proportional to the impulse. Thus, if I_{stride} represents the regular impulse she is applying (yielding a flight time, T_{flight}) and T^*_{flight} represents the required average flight time of the remaining strides, then the required average impulse I^*_{stride} is specified as a proportion of the regular impulse by $I^*_{stride}/I_{stride} = T^*_{flight}/T_{flight}$.

Up to this point our runner's problem has been the same as that of a long jumper trying to hit the take-off board. But now, instead of launching off as hard as she can, she ideally needs to apply just the *minimum* vertical impulse, I_{leap}, required to leap the stream. This is also specified as a proportion of the regular stride impulse, I_{stride}. If TC_{far} represents the time to contact the far bank (which, of course, is also optically specified), then the minimum required flight time of the leap is $TC_{far} - TC_{near}$. Therefore, I_{leap} is specified by a ratio of flight times: $I_{leap}/I_{stride} = (TC_{far} - TC_{near})/T_{flight}$. Hence, the dynamic requirements of the action are specified in units intrinsic to the ongoing activity of the action system. An experiment to determine whether such information is actually used by stream jumpers is called for!

Scope of Application of the Analysis.   Some cautions were raised by Rik Warren about the range of applicability of such a dynamic analysis of perception and action. The analysis seems most relevant when applied to problems like catching a fly ball, jumping a stream, or perceiving that something is out of reach. Its relevance is not so obvious for activities not immediately controlled by the muscles, as when a pilot engages in terrain-following flight or a sea captain brings a ship into harbor. In such situations involving mechanical control systems, the problem of the guidance of action (to land the plane or dock the boat) is not strictly identifiable with the problem of motor control (to move the joystick or the tiller). The perceptual information guiding the global action is not easily expressible in terms intrinsic to the dynamic requirements of the local motor act, because their relationship is contingent upon the intervening control system.

The activity of flying a plane requires control adjustments that have physically powerful effects, but are achieved by a minor exercise of the pilot's muscles. The previous discussion treated the problem as requiring nothing more than a mere scaling adjustment in the motor system. But a pilot has many control options and the energy requirements for both the plane and the pilot can vary widely for each option. The requirements for the actor may be so low as to render energy cost considerations irrelevant. The dynamic analysis will have to demonstrate the viability of a motor rescaling mechanism if it is to contend with this problem. Flying an airplane does have some characteristics in common with catching a ball, namely, that the physical and perceptual effects of control adjustments are virtually instantaneous.

A new hurdle for the approach is presented by the activity of steering a ship in a harbor. Ships are not agile. They require huge turning radii and long turning times. The space–time realities of steering ships mean that the physical and perceptual effects of such control adjustments are of such long latencies and slow rates that a dynamic analysis hardly seems applicable in this case. Yet, steering a ship safely is a perceptually controlled activity, and presumably some account of this is possible. In both examples, a dynamic account could involve the recalibration of the action system by perceptual information, so that the actor learns to dissipate a particular amount of energy over a certain limb structure to achieve a particular spatio–temporal change in the optic array. Such a recalibration could be adapted to either fast or slow events. Perhaps a dynamic approach can be extended in this way to address human skill with mechanical control systems, but as far as some group members were concerned this stands as an open challenge.

 The Mobility Problems of the Blind. The discussions of the work group centered upon locomotion and other activities that typically are visually guided with respect to a specified goal. As Gunnar Jansson pointed out, however, a major mobility problem for the blind is the maintenance of direction in the absence of visual information. While it is true that the risks of stumbling on uneven ground or of colliding with obstacles are greater for the blind than for the sighted, problems of this kind are to a considerable degree taken care of by the use of mobility aids such as a long cane or a guide dog. Information about the direction of walking with respect to a goal, however, must be obtained from some other source. Study has shown that while performance with artificially generated auditory or tactual flow fields is impressive, they cannot be expected to be adequate substitutes for visual flow (e.g., Jansson, 1981).

In Jansson's analysis, the problem of maintaining direction for the blind can be described as that of steering along a route toward a goal. A route can usually be analyzed as a sequence of stages, each described in terms of the perceptual information available to guide walking. At the start of each stage, a new direction must be chosen, often on the basis of memory of the area. Direction is then maintained within that stage by perceptual information about: (1) *walking towards* a perceptible goal; and/or (2) *walking along* a perceptible guideline.

The information needed for *walking towards* a perceptible goal, be it an object or an opening, must pertain both to the direction of the goal and to the current direction of walking. Although the direction with respect to a sound source may be indicated by binaural differences in intensity changes during the approach, in general, information about the direction of a distant goal is missing for the blind. An attempt to walk in a straight path without being guided by a perceptible goal often results in "veering" from the path. Available mobility aids are not sensitive beyond a distance of a few meters, and thus they are not useful in guiding walking to a distant goal.

To guide walking over longer distances, the blind commonly *walk along* a guideline such as a curb or wall, a strategy often called "shorelining." In this case, the information needed to maintain orientation to the guide must either relate the direction of current walking to the direction of the guideline, *or* pertain to the current distance between the walker and the guideline and changes in that distance over time. The blind person can often obtain the latter information by unaided touch or hearing, or with the help of an aid such as a cane. The task of *walking around* an obstacle may be considered a combination of walking towards a goal and walking along a guideline: During the maintenance of the general direction of walking towards the goal, the pedestrian merely detours along the boundary of the obstacle.

Jansson's outline of the navigational problems faced by the blind is preliminary to further analysis of the information that must be provided to a blind pedestrian to guide locomotion over long distances.

DESIGN CHARACTERISTICS OF THE MOTOR SYSTEM THAT CONSTRAIN USABLE INFORMATION

In the first section of this report we dealt with how perceptual information might be conceived as *unique* and *specific* to a given activity. Here we ask how certain design constraints on activity tailor the way that information is used. This question should not be interpreted as any attempt on our part to promote a conceptual separation between the informational, 'signalling' aspects of a system and the high powered energy converting machinery (dynamics). Perceiving and acting are assumed to be natural events both defined over large numbers of degrees of freedom; how perception guides activity and how activity constrains perception rest on an understanding of how power and information are mutually linked. What this amounts to, minimally, is coming to grips with the form that constraints on many degrees of freedom take.

Hermann Weyl's book on *Symmetry* (Weyl, 1952) offers a general approach to the problem of degrees of freedom that is not only intuitively appealing, but is also similar to the strategies adopted by Gibson for perception and the Soviet physiologist, Bernstein, for action. Gibson's ecological optics characterized coherence over change in the visual world in terms of invariants under transformation (see also Johansson, 1980; Mark, Todd, & Shaw, 1981; Shaw, McIntyre, & Mace, 1974). Bernstein (or more precisely his followers, Gelfand & Tsetlin—see Bernstein, 1967, Chapter 6) characterized actions as "well-organized" (coherent) when they could be described by two classes of variables: Those that preserve the topological properties of an act such as walking (*essential variables,* parallel to Gibsonian invariants), and those capable of producing scalar changes in individual components of an act without annihilating its structure, such as rate of walking (*nonessential variables,* corresponding to Gibsonian variants). Gibson's and Bernstein's approaches conform with Weyl's guiding design principle: Discover the group of transformations that leave crucial structural relations undisturbed (Weyl, 1952, p. 144).

This proves to be a significant strategy in identifying the *functional units* that emerge from the cooperative behavior of large numbers of muscles (cf. Boylls, 1975; Greene, 1972; Turvey, 1977). Altering the metric values of any given activity (e.g., by increasing rate or muscular effort) offers an opportunity to observe which variables are modulable, and which variables, or relations among variables, remain unchanged. It is worth noting that changing the metrical properties of an act could easily obscure its basic form by altering properties of individual components that might otherwise remain stable. On the other hand, these changes may index the major ways that invariance can be observed: Some variables must change but others must remain the same if the structure of the act is to be preserved, and if a given pattern is to be perceived as an instance of the same act (cf. Kelso, Tuller, & Harris, 1983).

Examination of a number of activities ranging from so-called 'stereotypic' activities like locomotion and mastication ('stereotypic' is a clear misnomer in light of environmental modifiability by bumps in terrain or changes in food consistency), to typewriting, speech, and piano playing (see Kelso, 1981, for a review) reveals a ubiquitous feature of muscle collectives. This feature is the independence of the *relative timing* of activities within a muscle collective (both electromyographic and kinematic) from the force or power exerted by that collective. In short, as one examines actions with many different time scales and involving many different anatomical structures one observes the same preferred mode of operation: Where possible, scale up on power but keep timing constant. This invariance in timing relations (characteristic of essential variables) combined with the flexibility attained by varying control parameters (nonessential variables) may be the hallmark of a functional unit of action (cf. Kugler, Kelso, & Turvey, 1980, 1982).

It should be stressed that these properties of a muscle collective are by no means exotic or arbitrary. Consider the case of an ordinary grandfather clock as a case in point. The mechanism of a clock includes: (1) an oscillatory component such as a pendulum with small damping; (2) a source of energy such as a weight or spring; and (3) a control mechanism, called an escapement, which connects the pendulum to the energy source. Now, in general, temporal stability in a system can only be established and maintained if work is performed. Work is accomplished by a flow of energy from a high potential energy source to a lower potential energy sink, as when energy is transferred from the clock spring to the escapement, replenishing the energy lost in the previous swing of the dampened pendulum via friction and heat. Hence, such systems are *open* in the sense that they exchange energy and matter with their surroundings, as occurs when the clock spring is wound or heat lost. This situation establishes the work *cycle* as a fundamental feature of natural systems; they absorb energy and "turn over" through a cycle of work, as in the release of energy from the spring and the subsequent transit of the pendulum (cf. Iberall, 1975). Systems exhibiting such persistent, self-sustaining cycles are, by definition, nonlinear in nature. Nonlinear oscillatory systems, like clocks, constantly supplied with a source of energy can operate autonomously, independent of initial conditions and despite perturbations and energy losses. These oscillatory systems are called limit cycles, and one of their properties that appeals to the theorist of action is that of mutual entrainment: Linked limit cycle oscillators can each affect the other's behavior. It is in this property that solutions to the degrees of freedom problem in action systems may lie, and much may be gained by identifying muscle linkages as functionally equivalent to limit cycle oscillatory processes (see Holt, Kugler, & Turvey, 1980; Kugler, Kelso, & Turvey, 1980, 1982; Turvey, 1980).

Of special interest to the work group was the question of how a study of this type of organization might allow one to intuit how perceptual information is used to guide movement. Returning to our clock, energy is passed from the spring to the pendulum in the form of an impulse, whose release is triggered by the escapement precisely when the pendulum is in an extreme position. Hence, the moment when the escapement operates depends solely on the position of the pendulum—a point in the work cycle—and not on time. Indeed, the whole operation of the system depends only on internal parameters; the design of the clock dictates that the energy source will be tapped at that point where it is most advantageous to do so (cf. Andranow & Chaikin, 1949; Minorsky, 1962). Thus, no "extrinsic" timing mechanism is required because time is not represented (see Fowler, 1980, for a comparison of "extrinsic" and "intrinsic" models of timing).

This analogy allows us to see that organization of the action system may constrain its own regulation. It suggests that the dynamics of the system place restrictions on where and when information can be most effectively picked up and energy released. In Shik and Orlovskii's (1976) work on cat locomotion, for example, continuous neural stimulation of the region in the mesencephalic nucleus associated with extension of the leg muscles has an effect *only* during the extensor phase of induced locomotion. Energy (information?) is tapped at just that phase of the cycle where it can have an effect. This is the general case as well, in that it is the extensor, force-applying phase that is primarily modulated in the act of locomotion (see Grillner, 1975; Shapiro, Zernicke, Gregor, & Diestel, 1981; Shik & Orlovskii, 1976). Similarly, the elegant work on so-called "reflex reversal" (Forssberg, Rossignol, & Grillner, 1977) indicates that the same information (a tap to the paw) can have behaviorally different effects depending upon *where* the tap is applied in the step cycle. The behavior exhibited is significant in that it is functionally adaptive for the animal. Apply a tactile stimulus during the extension phase and increased activity in extensor muscles occurs; apply the same stimulus during the flexion phase and the hip is flexed further, as if the limb were avoiding an obstacle in its path.

The idea that the design constraints on the motor system dictate when and where information pick-up occurs was discussed by the group in reference to Gunnar Jansson's work on the locomotor activity of blind people. A frequent observation of such individuals is that they employ the long cane to scan the environment on each step. One could imagine an alternative strategy based on some other, more arbitrary, criterion such as optimal sampling rate and/or central processing limitations (e.g., Kahneman, 1973). The latter would not likely be influenced by the biomechanical dimensions of the walker. In contrast, Jansson's blind walkers can be thought of as using the periodicity of walking to *regularize* the pick-up of information. The biodynamics of the walker in this case, along with, one supposes, the walker's familiarity with the terrain, provide strictures on the sampling of information necessary for locomotor guidance. As mentioned earlier, such information appears to be specified—in this case haptically—in units intrinsic to the dimensions of the walker and the dynamics of the walking activity itself. Devising substitution devices for handicapped individuals is a difficult problem, but it would be interesting to see, in reference to the hypothesis above, if varying the dynamics by having the blind person carry a load or increase walking speed would modulate the time and place in the walking cycle at which information pick-up occurred. Most of the work up to now has been largely descriptive.

THE GENERATIVITY AND ADAPTABILITY OF ACTION

The group also addressed the problem of how the action system adapts to changed conditions, particularly the role of perception in guiding that adaptation. Although we were not quite sure of the best terminology in which to couch the conjoint problems of adaptability and generativity in action systems, we did discuss these issues in some detail. The question boils down to this: How are we to understand the ability, common to humans and animals, to achieve the same goal through a variety of kinematic trajectories, with different muscle groups, and in the face of ever changing postural and biomechanical constraints? This phenomenon, sometimes referred to as motor equivalence (Hebb, 1949) or equi-finality (von Bertalanffy, 1953), is known to all of us and is exemplified nicely in recent handwriting demonstrations (Raibert, 1977), in which writing patterns are shown to be characteristic of the same individual even when produced by ana-tomical structures such as the foot or mouth that have never previously been used for writing.

Another example that the group focussed on was speech production, which appears to be a creative or generative activity event when stripped of its symbolic component. For example, it is well known that articulatory maneuvers for pro-ducing speech sounds can be effected in spite of varying initial conditions. An oft-used paradigm for studying this process is to insert a bite-block between the upper and lower teeth of a subject, thereby 'fixing' the mandible. The production of a vowel now requires that the individual adjust to the changed geometrical relationships between the jaw, tongue, and lips. The adjustment under such conditions appears to occur spontaneously. Normal range formant patterns are obtained at the first glottal pitch pulse (around 8 msec), a time too short for acoustic information to play a significant role (see Pick, Siegal, & Garber, 1982).

There is some reason to believe that the preferred account of this phenomenon may lie in the parallel between muscle collectives and nonlinear oscillatory systems referred to earlier. In contrast to other models of the generativity of speech that rely on closed-loop mechanisms, in which a referent value (the 'target' shape of the vocal tract) is selected and compared to initial conditions (the sensed state of the vocal tract) prior to the generation of commands (see Fowler & Turvey, 1980, for a review), a nonlinear vibratory system such as a mass-spring has the equifinality property as an integral part of its dynamics (Asatryan & Fel'dman, 1965). The tendency to approach the same endpoint in the face of changes in initial conditions, and when confronted with on-line perturbations, is a common feature of both speech and limb movement (see Kelso, 1977; Kelso, Holt, Kugler, & Turvey, 1980, for details). This fact sug-gests that although there are many *material* distinctions between the two sys-tems, they are alike in sharing behaviors qualitatively like a nonlinear mass spring. In short, the generativity observed in acts involving speech and limbs may be ascribed to the organization of the musculature underlying the activity rather than, as in conventional models, to a set of instructions sent to the muscles.

The speech production example underscores once again a kernel theme of our discussion, namely that action systems are first and foremost sensitive to their own dynamics. This view may force an account of information in dynamic systems as principally determined by the geometry of the system, after the work of Rene Thom (1970). Just as a physical system, such as a mass-spring, changes its geometry with a change in mass or stiffness, so muscles change their geometry when loaded or when excited or inhibited. Systems that grow (living things) undergo continuous and sometimes (like growth spurts in adolescents and the praying mantis) discontinuous changes in their geometry. The group was left with the exciting, if radical, possibility recently articulated (Kugler, Kelso, & Turvey, 1982), that information for action systems is specific to the geometry of the system's dynamics. As a postscript it is worth noting that we were able to demonstrate to the whole meeting that when the geometry of one of us (Kelso, normal nonconference weight 150 lbs.) was drastically altered by having another member climb on his back (Lee, 170 lbs.), the system (Kelso's) was able to adjust immediately—as was evident in his accuracy in performing a standing broad jump to a chalkmark target on the floor.

REFERENCES

Andronow, A., & Chaikin, C. E. *Theory of Oscillations*, Princeton, N.J.: Princeton University Press, 1949.

Asatryan, D., & Fel'dman, A. Functional tuning of the nervous system with control of movement or maintenance of a steady posture—1. Mechanographic analysis of the work of the joint on execution of a postural task. *Biophysics*, 1965, *10*, 925–935.

Bernstein, N. *The coordination and regulation of movements.* London: Pergamon Press, 1967.

Bertalanffy, L. *General systems theory.* Middlesex, England: Penguin Books, 1968.

Boylls, C. C. A theory of cerebellar function with applications to locomotion, II: The relation of anterior-lobe climbing fiber function to locomotor behavior in the cat. *COINS Technical Report* 76–1: Department of Computer and Information Science, University of Massachusetts, 1975.

Forssberg, H., Rossignol, S., & Grillner, S. Phase dependent reflex reversal during walking in chronic spinal cats. *Brain Research*, 1977, *85*, 121–139.

Fowler, C. Coarticulation and theories of extrinsic timing. *Journal of Phonetics*, 1980, *8*, 113–133.

Fowler, C., & Turvey, M. T. Skill acquisition: An event approach with special reference to searching for the optimum of a function of several variables. In G. E. Stelmach (Ed.), *Information processing in motor control and learning.* New York: Academic Press, 1978.

Greene, P. H. Problems of organization of motor systems. In R. Rosen & F. Snell (Eds.): *Progress in Theoretical Biology,* New York: Academic Press, 1972.

Grillner, S. Locomotion in vertebrates. *Physiological Reviews*, 1975, *55*, 247–304.

Hebb, D. O. *The organization of behavior.* New York: Wiley, 1949.

Iberall, A. S. On nature, man and society: A basis for scientific modelling. *Annals of Biomedical Engineering*, 1975, *3*, 344–385.

Johansson, G., von Hofsten, C., & Jansson, G. Event perception. *Annual Review of Psychology,* 1980, *31*, 27–63.

Kahneman, D. *Attention and Effort.* Englewood Cliffs, N.J.: Prentice-Hall, 1973.

Kelso, J. A. S. Motor control mechanisms underlying human movement reproduction. *Journal of Experimental Psychology,* 1977, *3*, 529–543.

Kelso, J. A. S. Contrasting perspectives on order and regulation in movement. In J. Long & A. Baddely (Eds.), *Attention and performance (IX).* Hillsdale, NJ: Lawrence Erlbaum Associates, 1981.

Kelso, J. A. S., Holt, K. G., Kugler, P. N., & Turvey, M. T. On the concept of coordinative structures as dissipative structures: II. Empirical lines of convergence. In G. E. Stelmach (Ed.) *Tutorials in Motor Behavior.* Amsterdam: Elsevier-North-Holland, 1980, 3–47.

Kelso, J. A. S., Tuller, B., & Harris, K. S. A "dynamic" pattern perspective on the control and coordination of movement. In P. F. MacNeilage (Ed.), *The Production of Speech.* New York: Springer-Verlag, 1983, 137–173.

Kugler, P. N., Kelso, J. A. S., & Turvey, M. T. The concept of coordinative structures as dissipative structures: I: Theoretical lines of convergence. In G. E. Stelmach (Ed.) *Tutorials in Motor Behavior.* Amsterdam: Elsevier-North-Holland, 1980, 3–47.

Kugler, P. N., Kelso, J. A. S., & Turvey, M. T. On coordination and control in naturally developing systems. In J. A. S. Kelso & J. E. Clark (Eds.), *The development of movement coordination and control.* New York/London: Wiley, 1982.

Lee, D. N. A theory of visual control of braking based on information about time to collision. *Perception,* 1976, *5,* 437–459.

Lee, D. N. Visual information during locomotion. In R. B. MacLeod & H. L. Pick (Eds.), *Perception: Essays in honor of J. J. Gibson.* Ithaca: Cornell University Press, 1974.

Lee, D. N. Visuomotor coordination in space–time. In G. E. Stelmach & J. Requin (Eds.), *Tutorials in motor behavior.* Amsterdam: North-Holland, 1980.

Lee, D. N., Lishman, J. R., & Thomson, J. A. Visual regulation of gait in long jumping. *Journal of Experimental Psychology: Human Perception and Performance,* 1982, *8,* 448–459.

Mark, L. S., Todd, J. T., & Shaw, R. E. The perception of growth: How different styles of change are distinguished. *Journal of Experimental Psychology: Human Perception and Performance,* 1981, *7,* 355–368.

Minorsky, N. *Nonlinear Oscillations.* Princeton, N.J.: Van Nostrand, 1962.

Pick, H. L., Jr., Siegal, G. M., & Garber, S. R. Development of speech production as a perceptual-motor task. In J. A. S. Kelso & J. E. Clark (Eds.), *The Development of Movement, Control and Coordination.* New York: Wiley and Sons, 1982.

Raibert, M. *Motor Control and Learning by the State Space Model.* M. I. T.: Artificial Intelligence Laboratory, 1977.

Runeson, S. *On visual perception of dynamic events.* Doctoral dissertation, University of Uppsala, Sweden, 1977.

Sedgwick, H. The geometry of spatial layout in pictorial representation. In M. A. Hagen (Ed.), *The perception of pictures* (Vol. 1). New York: Academic Press, 1980.

Shapiro, D. C., Zernicke, R. F., Gregor, R. J., & Diestel, J. D. Evidence for generalized motor programs using gait pattern analysis. *Journal of Motor Behavior,* 1981, *13,* 33–47.

Shaw, R. E., McIntyre, M., & Mace, W. M. The role of symmetry in event perception. In R. B. MacLeod & H. L. Pick (Eds.), *Perception: Essays in honor of James J. Gibson.* Ithaca: Cornell University Press, 1974.

Shaw, R. E., & Cutting, J. E. Constraints on language events: Clues from an ecological theory of event perception. In U. Bellugi & M. Studdert-Kennedy (Eds.), *Signed language and spoken language: Biological constraints on linguistic form.* Dahlem Konferenzen, Weinheim/Deerfield Beach, Fla./Basel: Verlag Chemie, 1980, 57–87.

Shik, M. L., & Orlovskii, G. N. Neurophysiology of locomotor automatism. *Physiological Reviews,* 1976, *56,* 465–501.

Thom, R. T. Topological models in biology. In C. H. Waddington (Ed.), *Towards a theoretical biology,* Vol. 3. Chicago: Aldine, 1970.

Turvey, M. T. Preliminaries to a theory of action with reference to vision. In R. E. Shaw & J. Bransford (Eds.), *Perceiving, Acting and Knowing.* Hillsdale, NJ: Lawrence Erlbaum Associates, 1977, 211–266.

Turvey, M. T. Constraints on language events: Clues from the organization of the motor system. In U. Bellugi & M. Studdert-Kennedy (Eds.), *Signed language and spoken language: Biological constraints on linguistic form.* Dahlem Konferenzen, Weinheim/Deerfield Beach, Fla./Basal: Verlag Chemie, 1980, 41–56.

Warren, W. H., & Shaw, R. E. Psychophysics and ecometrics. *Behavioral and Brain Science,* 1981, *4,* 209–210.

Weyl, H. *Symmetry.* Princeton, NJ: Princeton University Press, 1952.

16 Work Group on Speech and Sign Language

Prepared by   *Carol Fowler, Dartmouth College*
Brad Rakerd, Michigan State University

Participants   *Harlan Lane (Moderator), Northeastern University*
Hollis Fitch, Institute for Defense Analysis
Nancy Frishberg, New York University
Kerry Green, Northeastern University
Mark Mandall, Northeastern University
Robert Remez, Barnard College
Philip Rubin, Haskins Laboratories
Judy Shepard-Kegl, Northeastern University
Winifred Strange, University of South Florida
Michael Studdert-Kennedy, Queens College
Betty Tuller, Haskins Laboratories
Jerry Zimmerman, University of Iowa

Signed and spoken utterances have at least two aspects that are of interest to a perceiver. First of all, they have a physical aspect, the significance of which is given in the *lawful* relations among utterances, the information-bearing media structured by them, and the perceptual systems of observers and listeners. Second, they have a linguistic aspect, the significance of which is given in the *conventional* or *ruleful* relations between forms and meaning.[1] In part because

---

[1]We do not intend to suggest by the word *conventional* that the linguistic aspects of utterances have been established by popular acclaim. We intend only to distinguish the linguistic aspects from the physical aspects in terms of their "relative arbitrariness." Let's consider a physical example first: The articulatory and acoustic differences between the versions of /d/ in /di/ and /du/ are necessary and lawful, given the nature of vocal tracts. This contrasts with the aspiration difference between the versions of /p/ in "pie" and "spy", the production of which is required of English speakers mainly by convention or rule. We know this to be the case since speakers of other languages (e.g., French) make no such distinction.

our time was limited, and in part because so little work has been done on the conventional significance of events, as opposed to the *intrinsic* significance cf. Gibson, 1966[2] our work group chose to focus on the physical aspect. Nevertheless, we did have a speculative word or two to say about the origins of some linguistic conventions, and we would draw attention to the report of the Event/Cognition group, as well as to Verbrugge's remarks (discussant for the address by Studdert-Kennedy), for more elaborate treatments of this important topic.

Our discussions centered around five topic areas: (1) useful descriptions of signed and spoken events; (2) natural constraints on linguistic form; (3) the origins of some linguistic conventions; (4) the ecology of conversation; and (5) conducting language research from an event perspective. Our review of these topics will highlight what seemed to us to be the obvious applications of the event approach and also its apparent limitations.

USEFUL DESCRIPTIONS OF SIGNED AND SPOKEN EVENTS

We considered the minimal linguistic event to be an *utterance,* and identified as such anything that a talker (signer) might choose to say (sign). Obviously, this definition is unsatisfactory on a number of grounds; however, it does identify the minimal event of interest as being articulatory (gestural) in origin, and rejects as irrelevant those properties of articulation (gesture) that are not intended to have linguistic significance. We first attempted to verify that utterances have the "nested" character of other ecological events and that the nestings are perceived; next we considered how to discover the most useful characterization of utterances for the investigators' purposes of studying them as perceived events.

Signing and Speaking as Nested Events

Natural events are nested in the sense that relatively slower, longer-term or more global events are composed of relatively faster, shorter-term or more local ones.

---

[2]In Gibson's view:

> The relation of a perceptual stimulus to its causal source in the environment is of one sort; the relation of a symbol to its referent is of another sort. The former depends on the laws of physics and biology. The latter depends on a *linguistic community,* which is a unique invention of the human species. The relation of perceptual stimuli to their sources is an intrinsic relation such as one of projection, but the relation of symbols to their referents is an extrinsic one of social agreement. The conventions of symbolic speech must be learned, but the child can just about as easily learn one language as another. The connections between stimuli and their sources may well be learned in part, but they make only one language, or better, they do not make a language at all. The language code is cultural, traditional and arbitrary; the connection between stimuli and sources is not. (p. 91)

For example, a football game is a longer-term event composed of shorter-term plays. It is clear from research—particularly Johansson's (e.g., 1973, 1975) on the perception of form and motion in point-light displays—that viewers are sensitive to the nested structure of events. In his address to this conference, Johansson described an example of light points placed on a rolling wheel. When a single point is affixed to the rim, a viewer who sees only that point gets no sense of the wheel's motion; instead, the percept is of a light moving in a cycloid pattern. However, when a second light is attached, now to the hub of the wheel, the viewer perceives rolling instead of the cycloid motion. Thus, two appropriately placed lights provide sufficient optical information to specify the distal event of rolling.

In geometric terms, rolling involves two kinds of motion: *translatory* and *rotary*. These are temporally nested; a series of rotations occurs as the wheel translates over the ground plane. The translatory component affects the behavior of both light points (since both are attached to the translating wheel), but only the point on the rim is affected by the rotary component as well (since it rotates about the point on the hub). Apparently, perceptual sensitivity to the translation (as specified by the correlated activity of the two lights) forms a sort of "backdrop" for detection of the rotation; in essence, the translational component is "factored out" of the cycloid movement of the rim light, thereby revealing its rotational component.

Now let us consider whether these observations apply to signing and its perception (for additional discussion, see Shaw & Cutting, 1980). In American Sign Language (ASL), signs are generally specified by three properties: the shape of the hand or hands, the place of articulation of the sign within a signing space, and the movement of the hand or hands. Signs can be *inflected* by modulating the movement. For example, a "distributional" inflection indicating that all of the individuals under discussion are affected by some act is produced by sweeping the arm through the central body plane. By signing, say, GIVE, while making such an arm sweep the signer communicates GIVE TO ALL OF THEM. Likewise, a "temporal" inflection, one indicating the repeated occurrence of an act, is produced by rotating the wrist about a body-centralized point; with this gesture, GIVE is modified to mean GIVE AGAIN AND AGAIN.

Finally, and most important for the current discussion, several inflections can be superimposed. Carrying our previous example a step further, it proves possible to sign the complexly inflected verb GIVE TO ALL OF THEM AGAIN AND AGAIN. This is accomplished by rotating the wrist while the arm sweeps through its arc. Notice that when this is done the optical information for the "temporal" inflection undergoes a radical transformation; the wrist no longer rotates about a single point fixed at the center of the body, but rather about a point moving with the sweeping arm. It appears that observers treat the sweeping motion (common to all points of the hand, wrist, and arm) as both specifying one signed event (the "distributional" inflection), and as providing a moving frame of reference for the interpretation of the nested "temporal" inflection.

Spoken language, with its syntactic units—phonological segments, morphemes, words, and syntactic phrases, and its metrical units—syllables, feet,
phonological phrases (see Selkirk, 1980) lends itself readily to the characterization "nested." We will take an example of nested articulatory and perceived
events from a relatively low-level phenomenon, coarticulation. In fluent speech,
the productions of successive phonetic segments overlap such that the articulatory gestures often satisfy requirements for two or more segments at the same time.
Typically, for example, unstressed vowels coarticulate with the stressed vowels
of adjacent syllables. It is therefore tempting to think of the production of the
unstressed vowels as being nested within that of their stressed counterparts, and
to think of unstressed vowels as being perceived relative to their stressed-vowel
context. This way of thinking is promoted by findings (Fowler, 1981) that under
some conditions listeners behave as if they have "factored out" the articulato-
ry/acoustic contributions of the context when judging the quality of unstressed
vowels—more or less as Johansson's subjects seem to have factored out common and relative motions in an optical display.

In trisyllabic nonsense words with medial /ə/, the medial vowel coarticulates
with both of its flanking stressed vowels such that the F2 of /ə/ in, for instance,
/ibəbi/ is higher than it is in /ubəbu/. (Compatibly, F2 is high for /i/ and low for
/u/.) When extracted from their contexts, the medial /bə/ syllables do sound
quite different, but when presented in context they sound alike—more alike, in
fact, than do two acoustically *identical* /bə/ syllables presented in different
contexts.

A nested events account of these data would hold that when the /bə/ syllables
are extracted from the context in which they had been produced, the perceiver
has no way to detect (factor out) the contribution that the stressed vowels have
made to that portion of the acoustic signal in which /ə/ correlates predominate
over the correlates of other segments—no more than Johansson's subjects can
separate the rotary from the translatory components of movements when they see
just the one light on the rim of a wheel. Presentation in the context of flanking
vowels, on the other hand, allows the perceiver to factor out components in
common with those vowels, and to recognize the quality of what is left. This
leads to the perceived identity of the acoustically "different" /bə/ syllables (in
the /ibəbi/ and /ubəbu/ contexts), and to the perceived difference of the acoustically "identical" syllables in the different trisyllable contexts.

Identifying Speech Events: The Problem of Description

Several theories of speech perception—including Gibson's (1966) and one more
familiar to speech investigators, the motor theory (e.g., Liberman, Cooper,
Shankweiler, & Studdert-Kennedy, 1967)—adopt a view consistent with an
event perspective: The perceived categories of speech are articulatory in origin.
Gibson's view is distinguished from the other by its working assumption that the

perceived articulatory categories are fully reflected (however complexly) in the acoustic signal and hence need not be reconstructed by articulatory simulations. What are the reasons for this major disagreement among theorists who agree on the question of what is perceived? One difference is in their description of the acoustic signal, or even the articulatory event.

In speech, articulatory activities and their acoustic correlates are both richly structured, and consequently can be described in a great many different ways. Each of the various descriptions may be most appropriate for *certain* purposes, but none is privileged for *all* purposes, and just one or a few are privileged for the purposes of understanding what a talker is doing and why a listener perceives what he or she perceives. A theorist who is convinced that the acoustic support for perceptual categories is inadequate may be correct; but, alternatively, she or he *may have selected a description of articulatory events and their acoustic correlates that fails to reveal the support.*

There are many reasons why a particular description might be inappropriate for aiding our understanding of speech perception and production. It could specify excessive detail (as when, in Putnam's [1973] example, information about the positions and velocities of the elementary particles of a peg and pegboard are invoked to explain why a square peg won't fit in a round hole). Or, for any level of detail, it could be inappropriate because it classifies components in ways that fail to capture the talker's produced, or the listener's perceived, organization. Appropriate descriptions of vocal activity during speech, then, must capture the organization imposed by the talker; those of the acoustic signal must capture those acoustic reflections of the articulatory organization that are responsible for the listener's perception of it.

Appropriate Descriptions of Perceived Articulatory Categories.   In some time frame, a talker might be said to have raised his larynx (thereby decreasing the volume of the oral cavity), abducted the vocal folds, increased their stiffness, closed the lips, and raised the body of the tongue toward the palate. This description lists a set of apparently separate articulatory acts. In fact, however, the first three of them have the joint effect of achieving voicelessness; these and the next, lip closure, are the principal components of /p/ articulation; and all five acts together are essential to the production of the syllable /pi/. Thus, the aggregate of occurrences in this time frame have a coordinated structure of relations something like the following: ([larynx raising, vocal cord abduction, vocal cord stiffening][lip closure])(tongue-body gesture)].

If an investigator settles for the first description—a list of the activities of individual articulators—then, from his perspective information about the phonetic segments of an utterance is already absent and he cannot expect to find any evidence of it in the acoustic signal. Consequently when a perceiver recovers segments in speech, the recovery must be considered reconstructive. Before settling for this conclusion, however, the investigator can try standing back a little from his first perspective on the vocal tract activity and looking for organizations among gestures that were not initially apparent. These organizations will only be revealed from a temporal perspective broad enough that coupled changes among the coordinated structures can be observed. Certainly if there are coordinative articulatory relations among gestures and if the relations have acoustic reflections, then the listener is likely to be sensitive to the coordinated structure, rather than to the unstructured list of gestures from which it is built. By detecting the structure of the relations among these gestures, the listener detects the talker's structure—here the featural and phonetic segmental structure of the utterance—which is what she or he must do if the utterance is to be understood.

In support of this general approach to phonetic perception, there is some evidence that listeners do perceive aggregates of articulatory acts as if those acts were coordinated segmental structures. One example of this involves the perception of voicing. Following the release of a voiceless stop consonant, the fundamental frequency (f_o) of the voice is relatively high and falls (Halle & Stevens, 1971; Hombert, 1978; Ohala, 1979). Following a voiced stop, f_o is low and rises. Although the reasons for this differential patterning of f_o are not fully understood (Hombert, 1978; Hombert, Ohala, & Ewan, 1979), it is generally agreed that it results from the timing of certain laryngeal adjustments and from certain aerodynamic conditions that the talker establishes in maintaining voicelessness or voicing during the production of the consonant (cf. Abramson & Lisker, 1965). That is, the talker does not plan to produce a high falling f_o contour following release of a /p/. Instead, he plans to maintain voicelessness of the consonant and an unintended consequence of that effort is a pitch perturbation following release. Compatibly, listeners do not normally hear this pitch difference as such (that is, they do not notice a higher pitched vowel following /p/ than /b/). Instead, in the context of a preceding stop, a high falling f_o contour in a vowel serves as information for voicelessness of a preceding consonant (Fujimura, 1971; Haggard, Ambler, & Callow, 1970), even though, when removed from the consonantal context, the f_o contours are perceived as pitch changes (Hombert, 1978; Hombert et al., 1979).

Also suggestive of the perceptual extraction of coordinated articulatory structures are occasions when the perceiver seems to be misled. Ohala (1974, 1981) believes that certain historical sound changes can be explained as results of listeners' having failed to recognize some unplanned articulatory consequence as unplanned. An example related to the first one is the development of distinctive tones in certain languages. These languages evolved from others with distinctions in voicing between pairs of consonants. Over time, the f_o difference described between syllables differing in initial stop voicing became exaggerated and the voicing distinction was lost. Ohala's interpretation of the source of the change is that in these languages listeners tended to hear the f_o differences on the postconsonantal vowels as if pitch had been a controlled articulatory variable, rather than an uncontrolled consequence of adjustments related to voicing.

Therefore, when these individuals produced the vowels, they generated controlled (and larger) differences in f_o of voiced and voiceless stop-initial syllables. Eventually, because the f_o differences had become highly distinctive, the now redundant voicing distinction was lost and the words which formerly had differed in voicing of the initial consonant now differed in tone. According to Ohala, this process occurred during the separation of Punjabi from Hindi.

Appropriate Descriptions of the Acoustic Signal. Because very little is known about how a talker organizes articulation, descriptions of the acoustic signal useful for purposes of understanding perception cannot be guided strongly by information about articulatory categories. However, we do know enough to recognize that the usual method of partitioning the acoustic signal into segments, or into "cues," can be improved on. Such partitioning often obscures the existence of information for the phonetic segmental structure of speech because the structure of measured acoustic segments is not coextensive with the phonetic structure of the utterance. For one thing, phonetic segments as produced have a time course that measured acoustic segments do not reflect. The component articulatory gestures of a phonetic segment gradually increase in relative prominence over the residual gestures for a preceding segment and consequently the acoustic signal gradually comes to reflect the articulatory character of the new segment more strongly than that of the old one. Thus, phonetic segments are not discrete on the time axis, although they can be identified as mutually separate and serially ordered by tracking the waxing and waning of their predominance in the acoustic signal (cf. Fant, 1960).

Acoustic segments, on the other hand, are discrete. (Such segments are stretches of the acoustic signal bounded by abrupt changes in spectral composition.) An individual acoustic segment spans far less than all of the acoustic correlates of a phonetic segment and, in general, it reflects the overlapping production of several phonetic segments (cf. Fant, 1960). Looking at the signal as a series of discrete acoustic segments, then, obscures another way of looking at it: as a reflection of a series of overlapping phonetic segments successively increasing and declining in prominence.

Partitioning acoustic signals into acoustic segments also promotes assigning separate status to different acoustic "cues" for a phonetic feature, even though such an assignment tends to violate the articulatory fact that many of these cues, no matter how distinct their acoustic properties may be, are inseparable acoustic products of the gestures for a single phonetic segment (Lisker & Abramson, 1964; Abramson & Lisker, 1965). The findings of "trading relations" among acoustically distinctive parts of the speech signal indicate that these cues are not separable for perceivers any more than they can be for talkers. For example, certain pairs of syllables differing on two distinct acoustic dimensions—the duration of a silent interval following frication noise and the presence or absence of formant transitions into the following vocalic segment—are indistinguishable by listeners (Fitch, Halwes, Erickson, & Liberman, 1980). Within limits, a syllable with a long silent interval and no transitions sounds the same as one with a short silent interval and transitions. It is as if the transitions in the second syllable are indistinguishable from the extra silence in the first. A perceptual theory in which this observation is natural and expected is difficult to imagine, unless the theory recognizes that detecting acoustic segments per se is not all there is to perceiving speech. We would argue that the cues in these stimuli are indistinguishable to the degree that they provide information about the same articulatory event. Thus, 24 msec of silence "trades" with the formant transitions because both cues specify production of /p/. It is our view that source free descriptions of acoustics will not succeed in capturing what a speech event sounds like to a perceiver, because it is *information* carried in the signal, not the signal itself, that sounds like something.

NATURAL CONSTRAINTS ON LANGUAGE FORM

Shifting perspectives from ongoing articulation and its reflections in proximal stimulation, we considered how, over the long term, properties of the articulators in speech or of the limbs in sign may have shaped linguistic forms. Similarly, we considered how perceptual systems and acoustic or optical media, with their differential tendencies to be structured by various properties of distal events, may have shaped the forms of sign and speech.

Sign has several regular properties suggestive of natural constraints on manual language forms. One (Battison, 1974; cited in Siple, 1978, and Klima & Bellugi, 1979) takes the form of a symmetry constraint on two-handed signs: If both hands move in the production of a sign, the shapes and movements of the two hands must be the same and symmetrical. This constraint is compatible with ancedotal evidence (from novice piano players, for example), and more recently with experimental evidence (Kelso, Southard, & Goodman, 1979; Kelso, Holt, Rubin, & Kugler, in press) that it is difficult to engage in different activities with the two hands. One reason for this may be a tendency for actors to reduce the number of independently controlled degrees of freedom in complex tasks by organizing structures coordinatively (e.g., Turvey, 1977). Kelso's experiments suggest that the two arms and hands tend to be organized coordinatively even when such an organization would seem unnecessary or even undesirable (Kelso et al., 1979; Kelso et al., 1981); when subjects were required to engage in different activities with the two hands or arms, the "different" movements tended to retain similar properties.

A second constraint, called the "Dominance" constraint by Battison, may have a similar origin in general constraints on movement organization. For signs in which just one hand moves and the other hand serves as a base for the movements (a place of articulation), the base hand must either have the same configuration as the moving hand or one of a very limited set of other configurations.

An example of a constraint in spoken languages may be the tendency for syllable structures to respect a "sonority hierarchy" (e.g., Kiparsky, 1979) whereby sonority (roughly, vowel-likeness) increases inward toward the vowel from both syllable edges. Hence, for example, /tr/, a sequence in which sonority increases from left to right, is an acceptable prevocalic sequence, but postvocalically the order must be /rt/.

As for language features owing to properties of perceptual systems and stimulating media, Lindblom's (1980) proposed constraints on the evolution of vowel systems provide an example in spoken languages (see also Bladon & Lindblom, 1981). Lindblom has proposed that vowel systems maximize the perceptual distances among member vowels. Based on estimates of distances among vowels in perceptual space, he succeeds in predicting which vowels will tend to occur across languages in vowel systems of various sizes. This implies a constraint on phonological inventories that perceivers be able to recover distinct phonetic segments when distinct ones are intended. Talkers cannot elect to realize distinct phonetic segments by using articulatory gestures (however distinct they may be themselves) that fail to leave distinguishing traces in the acoustic medium or in the neural medium of perceptual systems. (Analogous articulatory constraints also operate to shape vowel systems. Thus, the relatively densely populated front vowel space and the sparsely populated back vowel space possibly reflect the relatively greater agility and precision of movement of the tongue tip and blade compared with the tongue body.)

Lane proposed that similar perceptual and articulatory constraints may shape the evolution of sign inventories. Facial expressions provide information in ASL and perceivers tend to focus on a signer's face. This creates a gradient of acuity peaking at the face. According to Siple (1978), signs made well away from the face tend to be less similar one to the other than signs made in its vicinity; in addition, two handed signs made in the periphery are subject to the Symmetry and Dominance constraints previously described, which provide redundancy for the viewer who may not see them as clearly as signs produced near the face. Lane suggested that the relative frequency of signs in various locations in signing space might be predicted jointly by the acuity gradient favoring signs located near the face and a work-minimizing constraint favoring signs closer to waist level.

THE ORIGINS OF SOME LINGUISTIC CONVENTIONS

As we noted earlier, the conventional rather than necessary relationship between linguistic forms and their message function is central to the nature of language, freeing linguistic messages from having to refer to the here and now, and thereby allowing past, future, fictional and hypothetical events all to be discussed. For Gibson (1966), this property of language removes it from the class of things that can be directly perceived:[3]

> [Perceptual cognition] is a direct response to things based on stimulus information; [symbolic cognition] is an indirect response to things based on stimulus sources produced by another human individual. The information in the latter is *coded;* in the former case it cannot properly be called that. (p. 91)

The study group did not discuss language comprehension in relation to event theory, perhaps because event theory currently offers little guidance on that subject. However, there was discussion of the origins of some linguistic conventions. Several examples suggest an origin of certain conventional relations as elaborations of intrinsic ones. The example of tonogenesis given earlier illustrates this idea. Ohala proposes that in some languages distinctive tones originated as controlled exaggerations of the pitch perturbations on vowels caused by the voicing or voicelessness of a preceding consonant.

A second example is so-called "compensatory lengthening" (e.g., Grundt, 1976; Ingria, 1979)—a historical change whereby languages concurrently lost a final consonant in some words and gained a phonological distinction of vowel length, with the words that formerly had ended in a consonant now ending in a phonologically long vowel. In spoken languages, the measured length of vowels shortens when they are spoken before consonants (e.g., Lindblom, Lyberg, & Holmgren, 1981). Of course, since vowels coarticulate with final consonants, this measured shortening may not reflect "true" shortening; presumably, acoustic evidence of their coarticulating edges is obscured by acoustic correlates of the overlaid consonant. In any case, the loss of a final consonant leads to measured lengthening of the vowel. If that unintended lengthening was perceived as controlled lengthening (just as, hypothetically, uncontrolled pitch perturbations were perceived as controlled pitch contours), and was subsequently produced as a controlled lengthening, it could serve as the basis for a phonological distinction in vowel length.

A final example in speech apparently has an analogue in sign. Some speech production investigators have proposed that vowels and consonants are produced by relatively separate articulatory organizations in the vocal tract, and that vowel production may go on essentially continuously during speech production, uninterrupted by concurrently produced consonants (e.g., Fowler, 1980; Ohman, 1966; Perkell, 1969). The basis for these proposals is observations that vowel-to-

---

[3]It is interesting in this regard that theories of perception developed within the information-processing framework have relied almost exclusively on verbal materials as stimuli, and are theories that perception is indirect.

vowel gestures that occur during consonant production (Ohman, 1966; Perkell, 1969) sometimes look very similar to vowel-to-vowel gestures in VV sequences (Kent & Moll, 1972). Also, a relatively separate organization of vowel and consonant production with continuous production of vowels may promote such linguistic conventions as vowel infixing in consonantal roots in Arabic languages (McCarthy, 1981) and vowel harmony in languages including Turkish (and in infant babbling [e.g., Menn, 1980]).

Vowel infixing will provide an illustration. In Arabic languages, verb roots are triconsonantal. For example, the root –"ktb" means "write". Verb voice and aspect (e.g., active/passive, perfective/imperfective) is indicated by morphemes consisting entirely of vowels. In McCarthy's recent analysis (1981), the consonantal roots and vowel morphemes are found to be interleaved according to specifications of a limited number of word templates and a small number of principles for assigning the component segments to the templates. Some derivationally related words in Arabic are: *katab, ktabab, kutib,* and *kuutib.* The consonantal root in each case is 'ktb'; the vowel morphemes are /a/ (perfective, active) and /ui/ (perfective, passive); and the relevant word templates are CVCVC, CCVCVC, CVVCVC (where C is a consonant and V is a vowel). The general rules for assigning roots and morphemes to templates are (1) to assign the component segments left to right in the template; and (2) if there are more C slots than consonants or more V slots than vowels, to *spread* the last consonant or last vowel over the remaining C or V slots. The only exception to this generalization is /i/ in /ui/, which is always assigned to the right-most V in the template. Below are two illustrations of verb formation according to this analysis:

Kegl discussed an analogous system in ASL. A particular root morpheme can be associated with different sign templates to express derivationally or inflectionally related versions of the morpheme. The templates have slots for locations (L) and movements (M), where the former specify person and number and the latter specify aspect. To take an example, the template that underlies I GIVE TO HIM is (LM + ML). Movements and locations are assigned to it as in McCarthy's analysis:

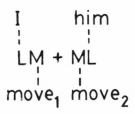

A template can include several L's and M's—more, in fact, than there are distinct movements in a root morpheme. In this case, the movements of the root morpheme are assigned left to right in the template until they are exhausted, and then the right-most movement spreads to fill the empty M slots. In I GIVE TO X, Y, AND Z the template and assignments of root morpheme movements are as follows:

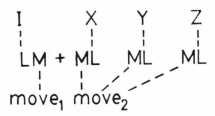

Analyzed this way, the meshing of movements and locations is similar to the meshing of vowels and consonants in languages with infixing and vowel harmony systems. This leads to the question of whether the system is favored as a linguistic device, and, if so, whether it is favored by virtue of the signer's motor organization for producing it. It might be favored, for example, if the motor organization underlying sign production readily produced cyclic repetitions of a movement (as those underlying stepping, breathing, chewing and perhaps vowel production do), and if minimal adjustments to the organization would enable shifts in location without changing the form of the movement.

THE ECOLOGY OF CONVERSATION

A scan of the various conference addresses shows the close ties between the event approach and Gibson's ecological theory of perception. Indeed, Gibson's radical rethinking of classic perceptual problems includes the notion that a perceiver does not operate in a series of "frozen moments," but rather in an ongoing stream of events. We therefore thought it useful to examine the ecology of the speech event, and in doing so we were reminded that both the speaker and the listener (the signer and the observer) have a stake in the success of a communicative episode. This is a rather unique circumstance; it invites both a familiar analysis of the perceiver as an active seeker of information (cf. Gibson, 1966), and a less familiar analysis of the producer as an active provider of informational support.

As to the perceiver's active role, we first of all see behavior intended to enhance signal detection: The head can be rotated to an optimal orientation, the source can be approached, and so on. Beyond this there can be direct communicative intervention; that is, the perceiver can make requests for repetition or clarification. On the producer's part, there are the well known redundancies of language; in essence, more than enough information is provided to ensure the accuracy of communication. Also, perhaps to avoid syntactic ambiguities, the talker may provide careful prosodic marking for clause boundaries and the like (e.g., Cooper & Paccia-Cooper, 1980). And finally, a talker will enunciate more clearly (and a signer gesture more distinctly) when there is a great distance to the perceiver or when the message context makes a particular word unpredictable.

CONDUCTING LANGUAGE RESEARCH FROM AN EVENT PERSPECTIVE

If there is a theme to the event conference, it is surely that psychologists have paid too little attention to the systematic (and potentially informative) nature of change. With respect to speech, this can be seen in the common practice of decomposing the speech stream into a succession of discrete acoustic segments (e.g., release bursts, aspiration, formant transitions, and the like). A whole literature speaks, in turn, of the difficulty in bringing these acoustic segments into some correspondence with linguistic segments. In the case of sign, the perceptual significance of change was overlooked in early attempts to devise sign glossaries: Investigators were preoccupied with cataloguing the featural properties of hand shapes and failed at first to recognize the importance of the gestures being made with the hands (Bellugi & Studdert-Kennedy, 1980; Klima & Bellugi, 1979).

The members of our group agreed that a shift of emphasis is needed: Investigators of both speech and sign should give greater consideration to the time-varying properties of those events. To begin with, this will involve focusing on the dynamics of the source events themselves. These investigations of the source can suggest compatible and appropriate perceptual analyses. Some recent work using Johansson's point-light techniques to study the coordinated activities of the signer, and the perception of lexical movements and inflections (e.g., Poizner,

Bellugi, & Lutes-Driscoll, 1981), seems to offer promising beginnings for such an approach.

Alternatively, analyses of time-varying properties of the signal may provide guidance in understanding the ways in which talkers and signers structure articulatory activity (cf. Fowler, 1979; Tuller & Fowler, 1980). On this issue, our group spent a good deal of time considering the recent work of Remez, Rubin, Pisoni, and Carrell (1981; Remez, Rubin, & Carrell, 1981). They have shown that the phonetic message of an utterance can be preserved in sinewave approximations that reproduce only the center frequencies of its first three formants. These stimuli have no short-time acoustic constituents that vocal tracts can produce and consequently lack acoustic elements heretofore identified by investigators as speech cues. Presumably the stimuli are intelligible because information is provided by relations among the three sinusoids, information that the sinusoidal variations are compatible with a vocal origin.

The importance of these findings is not that they show short-time acoustic cues to be unimportant to speech perception. After all, naive listeners did not spontaneously hear the sinewaves as phonetic events. Instead, the findings are important in showing that time-varying properties of the signal can provide sufficient information for word and segment identification in speech. In this respect, as Remez and Rubin point out (1981), their demonstration is closely analogous to Johansson's demonstrations with point-light displays of moving figures. In both demonstrations, change provides essential information for form.

The conclusion we draw from all of the examples considered here is that students of language should not be misled by the timeless quality of linguistic forms. Signing and speaking are coherent activities and natural classes of events. It is only reasonable to expect that the signatures of these events will be written in time as well as space.

REFERENCES

Abramson, A. S., & Lisker, L. Voice onset time in stop consonants: Acoustic analysis and synthesis. In D. E. Commins (Ed.), *Proceedings of the 5th International Congress of Acoustics.* Liege: Imp. G. Thone, A–51, 1965.

Battison, R. Phonological deletion in American Sign Language. *Sign Language Studies,* 1974, *5,* 1–19.

Bellugi, U., & Studdert-Kennedy, M. *Signed and spoken language: Biological constraints on linguistic form.* Berlin: Dahlem-Konferenzen, 1980.

Bladon, R., & Lindblom, B. Modeling the judgment of vowel quality differences. *Journal of the Acoustical Society of America,* 1981, 1414–1422.

Cooper, W. E., & Paccia-Cooper, J. *Syntax and speech.* Cambridge, Mass.: Harvard University Press, 1980.

Fant, G. *Acoustic theory of speech production.* Netherlands: Mouton, 1960.

Fitch, H. L., Halwes, T., Erickson, D. M., & Liberman, A. M. Perceptual equivalence of two acoustic cues for stop consonant manner. *Perception and Psychophysics,* 1980, *27,* 343–350.

Fowler, C. "Perceptual centers" in speech production and perception. *Perception and Psychophysics,* 1979, *25,* 375–388.

Fowler, C. Coarticulation and theories of extrinsic timing control. *Journal of Phonetics*, 1980, *8*, 113–133.

Fowler, C. Production and perception of coarticulation among stressed and unstressed vowels. *Journal of Speech and Hearing Research*, 1981, *46*, 127–139.

Fujimura, O. Remarks on stop consonants: Synthesis experiments and acoustic cues. In L. L. Hammerich, R. Jakobson, & E. Zwirner (Eds.), *Form and substance: Phonetic and linguistic papers presented to Eli Fischer-Jørgensen*. Copenhagen: Akademisk Forlag, 1971.

Gibson, J. J. *The senses considered as perceptual systems*. Boston, Mass.: Houghton Mifflin, 1966.

Grundt, A. *Compensation in phonology: Open syllable lengthening*. Bloomington, Ind.: IULC, 1976.

Haggard, M. P., Ambler, S., & Callow, M. Pitch as a voicing cue. *Journal of the Acoustical Society of America*, 1970, *47*, 613–617.

Halle, M., & Stevens, K. A note on laryngeal features. *Quarterly Progress Report, Research Laboratory of Electronics* (Massachusetts Institute of Technology), 1971, *101*, 198–213.

Hombert, J.-M. Consonant types, vowel quality and tone. In V. Fromkin (Ed.), *Tone: A linguistic survey*. New York: Academic Press, 1978.

Hombert, J.-M., Ohala, J., & Ewan, W. Phonetic explanation for the development of tones. *Language*, 1979, *55*, 37–58.

Ingria, R. Compensatory lengthening as a metrical phenomenon. *Linguistic Inquiry*, 1979, *11*, 465–495.

Johansson, G. Visual perception of biological motion and a model for its analysis. *Perception and Psychophysics*, 1973, *14*, 201–211.

Johansson, G. Visual motion perception. *Scientific American*, 1975, *232*(6), 76–89.

Kelso, J. A. S., Holt, K., Rubin, P., & Kugler, P. Patterns of human interlimb coordination emerge from the properties of nonlinear oscillators: Theory and data. *Journal of Motor Behavior*, 1981, *13*, 226–261.

Kelso, J. A. S., Southard, D., & Goodman, D. On the coordination of two-handed movements. *Journal of Experimental Psychology: Human Perception and Performance*, 1979, *5*, 229–238.

Kent, R., & Moll, K. Tongue body articulation during vowel and diphthongal gestures. *Folia Phoniatrica*, 1972, *24*, 278–300.

Kiparsky, P. Metrical structure assignment is cyclic. *Linguistic Inquiry*, 1979, *10*, 421–441.

Klima, E. S., & Bellugi, U. *The signs of language*. Cambridge, Mass.: Harvard University Press, 1979.

Liberman, A. M., Cooper, F. S., Shankweiler, D. P., & Studdert-Kennedy, M. Perception of the speech code. *Psychological Review*, 1967, *74*, 431–461.

Lindblom, B. The goal of phonetics and its unification and application. *Phonetica*, 1980, *37*, 7–26.

Lindblom, B., Lyberg, B., & Holmgren, K. *Durational patterns of Swedish phonology: Do they reflect short-term memory processes?* Bloomington, Indiana: Indiana University Linguistics Club, 1981.

Lisker, L., & Abramson, A. S. A cross-language study of voicing in initial stops: Acoustical measurements. *Word*, 1964, *20*, 384–422.

McCarthy, J. J. A prosodic theory of nonconcatenative morphology. *Linguistic Inquiry*, 1981, *12*, 373–418.

Menn, L. Phonological theory and child phonology. In G. Yeni-Komshian, J. F. Kavanaugh, & C. A. Ferguson (Eds.), *Child Phonology* (Vol. 1). New York: Academic Press, 1980.

Ohala, J. Experimental historical phonology. In J. M. Anderson & C. Jones (Eds.), *Historical linguistics II: Theory and description in phonology*. Amsterdam: North-Holland Publishing Co., 1974.

Ohala, J. The production of tone. In V. Fromkin (Ed.), *Tone: A linguistic survey*. New York: Academic Press, 1979.

Ohala, J. The listener as a source of sound change. In M. F. Miller (Ed.), *Papers from the parasession on language and behavior*. Chicago: Chicago Linguistic Society, 1981.

Ohman, S. E. G. Coarticulation in VCV utterances: Spectrographic measurements. *Journal of the Acoustical Society of America*, 1966, *39*, 151–168.

Perkell, J. S. *Physiology of speech production: Results and implications of a quantitative cineradiographic study*. Cambridge, Mass.: M.I.T. Press, 1969.

Poizner, H., Bellugi, U., & Lutes-Driscoll, V. Perception of American Sign Language in dynamic point-light displays. *Journal of Experimental Psychology: Human Perception and Performance*, 1981, *7*, 430–440.

Putnam, H. Reductionism and the nature of psychology. *Cognition*, 1973, *2*, 131–146.

Remez, R. E., & Rubin, P. E. *The stream of speech*. Paper distributed at the First International Conference on Event Perception. Storrs, Ct., June, 1981.

Remez, R., Rubin, P., & Carrell, T. Phonetic perception of sinusoidal signals: Effects of amplitude variation. *Journal of the Acoustical Society of America*, 1981, *69*, S114 (A).

Remez, R., Rubin, P., Pisoni, D., & Carrell, T. Speech perception without traditional speech cues. *Science*, 1981, *212*, 947–950.

Selkirk, E. O. The role of prosodic categories in English word stress. *Linguistic Inquiry*, 1980, *11*, 563–605.

Siple, P. Linguistic and psychological properties of American Sign Language: An overview. In P. Siple (Ed.), *Understand sign language through sign language research*. New York: Academic Press, 1978.

Shaw, R. E., & Cutting, J. E. Constraints on language events: Cues from an ecological theory of event perception. In U. Bellugi & M. Studdert-Kennedy (Eds.), *Signed language and spoken language: Biological constraints on linguistic form*. Dahlem Conferenzen, Weinheim/Deerfield Beach FL/Basel: Chemie Verlag, 1980.

Tuller, B., & Fowler, C. A. Some articulatory correlates of perceptual isochrony. *Perception and Psychophysics*, 1980, *27*, 277–283.

Turvey, M. T. Preliminaries to a theory of action with reference to vision. In R. Shaw & J. Bransford (Eds.), *Perceiving, acting and knowing: Toward an ecological psychology*. Hillsdale, N.J.: Lawrence Erlbaum Associates, 1977.

17

Work Group on Event Cognition

Prepared by   *Claudia G. Farber, New York University*
Leonard S. Mark, Miami University at Ohio

Participants   *Vicki McCabe (Moderator), University of California at Los Angeles*
Gerald Balzano, University of California at San Diego
Steven Braddon, Sacred Heart University
John Doner, Massachusetts Institute of Technology
William Hazlett, Amherst College
Robert Hoffman, Adelphi University
James Jenkins, University of South Florida
Darren Newtson, University of Virginia
Mari Riess Jones, Ohio State University
Robert Verbrugge, University of Connecticut

The central concerns of the event cognition group involved the theoretical and methodological consequences of taking "events" as the primitive units of analysis for a science of knowing. As an event approach may necessitate a reformulation of the role and definition of cognition, as well as the empirical methods used in its investigation, the group elected to survey several areas that must be addressed by any comprehensive theory. Our discussions were at best preliminary because it seemed that our time would be spent most wisely reviewing a number of the participants' interests, rather than focusing on only one or two topics.

DISTINGUISHING PERCEPTION AND COGNITION

Information processing theories have traditionally analyzed discrete snapshots of the world, rather than ongoing events; upon inspection, these are found to be

299

equivocal with respect to the world. This indeterminacy between proximal and distal stimuli has led psychologists to postulate epistemic mediators, such as inference, learning, and memory, to account for the tight correspondence between the world and our knowledge of it. From this perspective, information is regarded as a set of cues about the world that require cognitive elaboration.

Various problems associated with traditional cognitive theories of perception (see Warren & Shaw, this volume) have led a number of us to look toward ''events'' as more appropriate units of analysis for perceptual theory. This endeavor, however, must be accompanied by a consideration of the *natural constraints* on the epistemic relation between a person and his or her environment— i.e., the structure of the information for guiding a person's actions in realizing a goal (see Gibson, 1966, 1979; Warren and Shaw, this volume; Turvey and Shaw, 1978). When these constraints are incorporated into an event analysis, perceptual information need not be ambiguous nor indeterminate and cognitive (epistemic) mediators are no longer required for perception. From this perspective, information is the consequence of a relationship between the perceiver and his or her environment—that is, it specifies actions by the observer that can be supported by the environment.

The perceptual research that has been conducted from the ecological perspective typically involves events in which the information necessary to guide action is specified in the light to the eye. Yet the status of ''mental activity'' must still be evaluated, since phenomenal experience suggests that we infer, remember, imagine, etc. in the absence of apparent physical (e.g., optical) support. If an event approach to perception posits different units of analysis than traditional theories, then the implications for mental processes should be carefully examined. The possibility must be entertained that what is traditionally meant by cognitive processes will change in significant ways.

Just as event perception from the ecological perspective is grounded in constraints on the relationship between the perceiver and its environment, so it may be that cognitive processes operate under similar constraints—including the needs and actions of the observer (see Verbrugge, this volume). Mental activity does not occur in a vacuum, but as part of an adaptive relationship between animal and environment. Thus, there may be constraints on the scope of inferring, remembering, and imagining, as there are on perceiving. This is not to suggest that constraints on cognition are necessarily identical to those governing perception; rather, constraints on perception and cognition are best both motivated from biology (evolution).

The event perspective, therefore, may entail a reformulation of the dichotomy between perception and cognition. It may be the case that the differences between them lie both in the nature of the information used and in the consequent processing demands entailed in different tasks. Cognitive activities may accompany occasions when events are not completely specified or when the available information is symbolic. Thus, cognition may serve to supplement rather than mediate perception and to orient the animal toward other information and possible actions. The identification of those occasions when it is advantageous to employ cognitive processes may serve as a foundation for the study of event cognition.

As it was unrealistic to attempt to develop a comprehensive theory of cognition, the group decided to inventory some of the implications of adopting an event perspective for particular areas of interest: Inference, perceptual learning, metaphor comprehension, memory, concept acquisition, and experimental methodology. These discussions are summarized here.

Inference

We considered the case of inference by examining the conditions under which inference is most likely to occur. Inferential processes may well be necessary on those occasions when events are not completely specified, when the information about an event has been degraded, or when an animal fails to attend to the available information. On the other hand, inference would be maladaptive if, for example, it delayed the start of evasive action in life-threatening situations, such as when a hard object is looming toward a person's head. We agreed with Braddon's suggestion that before inference as a form of propositional reasoning is invoked, certain conditions have to be elaborated. These include: (1) a description of the occasion on which an inference is needed; (2) a means for the organism to recognize the need to draw an inference; (3) a source of perceptual information from which inferences are made (inference does not proceed in isolation from the world); (4) an auxiliary source of information to be drawn on (traditionally this has been long-term memory); (5) a means of selecting information from the auxiliary source that is appropriate to the perceptual information; (6) a means of integrating the two sources of information (3 & 4) (i.e., making an inference); (7) a description of the resultant inference; and, (8) a means for evaluating the adequacy of the inference. Although these problems must be addressed by a theory of inference, they do not themselves constitute such a theory or even decide whether the process of inference from an event perspective will be instantiated differently than in traditional cognitive theories.

Perceptual Learning

The discussion of the implications of the event perspective continued with reference to a problem that must be addressed by any theory of knowing, namely, the acquisition of a skilled perceptual ability. We discussed the growing body of research on skill acquisition, including the diagnostic abilities of pediatric cardiologists, the skills involved in judging fencing matches, the identification of tumors from chest x-rays, and the evaluation of facial disfigurements. Most of the conversation focused on a problem that is currently being studied by Jenkins—how pediatric cardiologists learn to examine children in order to diagnose congenital cardiac problems such as patent ductus atreriosus or atrial septal defect (see Jenkins, this volume).

The cardiologist first needs to determine whether a problem exists and, if so, its nature (diagnosis), and then to prescribe a course of action (treatment). The basic stages in Jenkins' research are as follows: (1) to determine what experts do when they examine patients, for example, where and how they place the stethoscope, what sounds they listen for; (2) to distinguish the sounds that are important in reaching a diagnosis from those that are irrelevant (the sounds of interest are not necessarily the most salient); (3) to characterize the information in the acoustic signal that allows an expert to make a diagnosis; and, (4) once the actions of the experts are understood, to compare them to the actions of novices (medical students) and intermediates (residents) in order to determine the course of skill acquisition.

Although expert cardiologists can listen to a patient's heart or look at an x-ray and know what is wrong, they may be unable to verbalize how the diagnosis was arrived at. It has been found that experts can detect sounds that novices are unable to discriminate. They do not seem to apprehend the acoustic or optic primitives upon which the novices focus, but, rather, the functioning of the anatomic parts that are specified by the available information. The experts search actively for the acoustic signals necessary for establishing a diagnosis and constantly modulate this search based on the information they receive. The problem for psychologists is first to describe the tacit knowledge posessed by experts that allows them to recognize both abnormalities and the range of conditions that qualify as "normal" (i.e., not requiring treatment) and then to describe the process through which this expert knowledge is acquired.

Although an important factor in a cardiologist's training involves the sheer number of cases that have been encountered over the years, it is still necessary to determine what this experience provides. Since experts are able to recognize rare abnormalities that they may have seen but once in 20 years of practice, perceptual learning appears to involve more than encounters with a large number of examples. The "history" of the expert cardiologist also comprises knowledge acquired from articles, courses, and discussions with colleagues. We need to understand how these experiences direct the expert's attention to those parts of the acoustic and optic arrays that specify the condition of the heart.

Event theory may provide an important approach to describing the information used by individuals at all levels of expertise. The group discussed the hypothesis that novices hear the sound of a heart beat as a whole, while experts discriminate numerous sounds within a beat. The difference in sensitivity might be described as attention to a single coarse-grained event (e.g., the contraction of the heart) vs. attention to various fine-grained events nested therein (e.g., contraction of each ventricle, opening and closing of individual valves, etc.). But how might the process of learning to attend be studied?

Metaphor

Metaphor was considered as a tool for understanding how perceivers learn to attend to different aspects of an event. Metaphors can redirect attention to aspects of a situation that may not have been noticed before the metaphor was generated. Consider, for example the metaphor offered by Verbrugge (this volume): A paint brush is a pump. Perceptual information about the pumping action of a brush is available to a person wielding one, but it may not be attended to. A metaphor can facilitate the process of "coming to know" not because it becomes part of a store of knowledge, but because it directs an observer to notice an event in one domain (that of the pump) that can also be perceived anew in another domain (that of the brush)—namely, the event of forcing liquid through a hollow channel. This common event is the *ground* of the metaphor by which the learner's attention is directed to a new aspect of a familiar (or novel) domain. Studies of metaphoric comprehension may allow us to examine the process of how one learns to attend to different aspects of a visual or acoustic display. Understanding how people abstract novel grounds may well assist medical educators in teaching cardiologists to attend to particular acoustic or optic relations that have important diagnostic value.

Memory

In the acquisition of a complex skill the path from novice to expert may extend over a period of many years. This raises the question of the time span of an event (fast vs. slow) and whether recourse to memory is necessary for the apprehension of slow events. A particular instance of a cardiologist listening to a child's heart would generally be regarded as involving perception. But how are we to characterize the totality of the cardiologist's encounters with his or her patients? Does the expert cardiologist "remember" the occasions on which he or she heard a particular sound (or read about a particular problem) and the implications of that sound for a diagnosis? Or, alternatively, is there a way to describe skill acquisition as an extended perceptual event, for example, that the cardiologist is "detecting" or "abstracting over" the invariants common to each of the situations (see Shaw & Pittenger, 1977)? Whether it would be desirable to formulate memory as "perception of a slow event" depends upon whether any of the problematic aspects of theories of memory (the Höffding step, the inadequacies of the storage metaphor, etc) could be avoided. The group recognized this as a central issue for further research and discussion (cf. Jenkins, 1974).

Concept Acquisition

There is also the problem of how an expert diagnostician can recognize novel instances of a known class of events. While some researchers have attempted to examine the perception of novel instances in relation to a cognitive prototype, several members of the group expressed reservations concerning the clarity with which this notion has been defined. A potentially promising approach offered by Shaw & Wilson (1976) uses symmetry group theory as a tool for characterizing the "group generator" of a class, i.e., a subgroup capable of generating all the members (and only the members) of a given class. Yet the discussion led us to realize that, to date, group theory has received limited application to specific events; indeed, only two examples, Shaw & Wilson's orbiting group and Jones' sequencing group have been fully worked out. What emerged from our efforts to consider the application of group theory to concept acquisition was an appreciation of the difficulty of characterizing appropriate symmetry groups for natural events. Application of symmetry group theory demands that the dimensions for describing an event be identified at the outset—a task whose difficulty and importance should not be underestimated.

Research on Event Cognition

An important means for assessing the utility of any proposed reformulation of cognitive theory from an event perspective is to determine its ability to generate research on meaningful problems. During our meetings, group members observed that an event approach has already led several participants to examine significant problems of practical concern: Jenkins' work on training pediatric cardiologists, Newtson's analysis of the information used by fencing judges at various levels of expertise, and Mark, Shaw, Pittenger, and Todd's work on the diagnosis and treatment of craniofacial disorders. Other members of the group have also made substantial empirical contributions to the study of problems in event cognition, including, metaphoric comprehension (Hoffman, 1980; Verbrugge, 1977), music and rhythmic analysis (Balzano, 1982; Jones, 1976, 1981), mental imagery and imagination (Hoffman, 1980), event comprehension (Braddon, 1980; Jenkins, Wald, & Pittenger, 1978), and, delineation of event boundaries (Newtson & Enquist, 1976).

A fundamental question, posed on several occasions, was whether researchers in event cognition should attempt to explain data collected under traditional cognitive and information-processing paradigms. That is, can experimental techniques and phenomena such as reaction time, error frequency, illusions, masking, proactive inhibition, serial position, etc. be reinterpreted in the context of an event approach, or should the data be ignored in favor of developing new methodologies more appropriate to the study of events?

This was generally regarded not as an exclusive choice but as a question of research priorities. Given the apparent distance between work on event perception and the far less developed framework for event cognition, group members approached the problem of explaining extant cognitive data with considerable trepidation. It was recognized that although it may be premature to attempt such explanations, critics are likely to evaluate the efficacy of an event approach by its success with known, rather than new, paradigms.

The key to this dilemma may lie in appreciating that many of the laboratory tasks employed in cognitive psychology study what people are capable of doing under unusual circumstances while an event approach, employing ecologically valid tasks, is directed toward understanding what people usually do. Thus, prior to asking if it is desirable to preserve the information-processing methods of cognitive psychology, it is necessary to consider whether one is interested in human *capabilities* under specially controlled conditions or human *performance* in natural settings.

We did agree, however, that there are problems inherent in some of the experimental work in cognitive psychology, for example, the design of stimuli without concern for environmental constraints. In event research, the experimenter must consider whether the displays presented to subjects are representative of those encountered in real life situations, in terms of both the covariance of important dimensions of information and the significance of the events chosen. Since the acquisition of knowledge involves the intentions of the participant, the significance of both the displays and the task needs to be carefully considered when designing experiments.

CONCLUDING REMARKS

Dissatisfaction with traditional information-processing theories of cognition has led members of the work group to pursue alternative theoretical approaches to phenomena that do not immediately appear to be strictly perceptual. A common thread binding each of our efforts has been the adoption of "events" as the primitive unit of analysis. Our discussion did not produce a reformulation of the role of cognition in a theory of knowing nor did we arrive at a statement of empirical methods to be used in the investigation. What emerged might best be described as a direction for future discussion. The impetus for such discussion is likely to come from several sources: The outcome of theoretical efforts to define the nature of events, the development of a method for their measurement—ecometrics (cf. Shaw & Cutting, 1980; Warren & Shaw, 1981, this volume), continued efforts to demonstrate the richness of perceptual information, and a clearer understanding of the constraints on the relationship between animal and environment and how these constraints arise. The development of a theory of event cognition must be accompanied by experimental work involving natural situations in which cognitive activities play a role. We are encouraged toward this goal by the fact that event analysis has already led many of us to study meaningful, though difficult, problems of this kind.

REFERENCES

Balzano, G. Musical vs. psychoacoustical variables and their influence on the perception of musical intervals. *Bulletin of the Council for Research in Music Education,* 1982, Spring, (70), 1–11.

Braddon, S. *The roles of participation and observation in the perceiving and remembering of figural-symbolic events.* Doctoral Dissertation, University of Connecticut, 1980.

Gibson, J. J. *The senses considered as perceptual systems.* Boston: Houghton Mifflin, 1966.

Gibson, J. J. *The ecological approach to visual perception.* Boston: Houghton Mifflin, 1979.

Hoffman, R. R. Metaphor in science. In R. Honeck & R. Hoffman (Eds.), *Cognitive psychology and figurative language.* Hillsdale, N.J.: Lawrence Erlbaum Associates, 1980.

Jenkins, J. J. Remember that old theory of memory? Well, forget it! *American psychologist,* November, 1974, 785–795.

Jenkins, J. J., Wald, J., & Pittenger, J. B. Apprehending pictorial events: An instance of psychological cohesion. In C. W. Savage (Ed.), *Minnesota studies in the philosophy of science, Volume 9.* Minneapolis, Minn.: University of Minnesota Press, 1978.

Jones, M. R. Music as a stimulus for psychological motion. *Psychomusicology,* 1981, *1*, 34–51.

Jones, M. R. Levels of structure in the reconstruction of temporal and spatial patterns. *Journal of Experimental Psychology: Human Learning and Memory,* 1976, *2*, 475–488.

Newtson, D., & Enquist, G. The perceptual organization of ongoing behavior. *Journal of Experimental Social Psychology,* 1976, *12*, 847–862.

Shaw, R. E., & Cutting, J. E. Constraints on language events: Cues from an ecological theory. In U. Bellugi & M. Studdert-Kennedy (Eds.), *Signed language and spoken language: Biological constraints on linguistic form.* Dahlem Conferenzen, Weinheim/Deerfield Beach FL/Basel: Chemie Verlag, 1980.

Shaw, R. E., & Pittenger, J. B. Perceiving the face of change in changing faces: Implications for a theory of object perception. In R. Shaw & J. Bransford (Eds.), *Perceiving, acting, and knowing: Toward an ecological psychology.* Hillsdale, N.J.: Lawrence Erlbaum Associates, 1977.

Shaw, R. E., & Wilson, B. E. Generative conceptual knowledge: How we know what we know. In D. Klahr (Ed.), *Cognition and instruction.* Hillsdale, N.J.: Lawrence Erlbaum Associates, 1976.

Turvey, M. T., & Shaw, R. E. The primacy of perceiving: An ecological reformulation of perception for understanding memory. In L. G. Nilsson (Ed.), *Perspectives on memory research: Essays in honor of Uppsala University's 500th anniversary.* Hillsdale, N.J.: Lawrence Erlbaum Associates, 1979.

Verbrugge, R. R. Resemblances in language and perception. In R. E. Shaw & J. Bransford (Eds.), *Perceiving, acting and knowing.* Hillsdale, N.J.: Lawrence Erlbaum Associates, 1977.

Warren Jr., W. H. Psychophysics and ecometrics. *Behavioral and Brain Sciences,* 1981, *4*, 209–210.

18 Work Group on Biology and Physics

Prepared by   *Edward Reed, Drexel University*
Peter N. Kugler, University of California at Los Angeles
Robert E. Shaw, University of Connecticut

Participants   *Howard Pattee (moderator), State University of New York,*
Binghamton
Alan Brush, University of Connecticut
Michael Dempster, Oxford University
Arthur Iberall, University of California at Los Angeles
Thomas Terry, University of Connecticut
Geoffrey Bingham, University of Connecticut

INTRODUCTION

The question which motivated the bulk of the group's discussion was "How is physics relevant to the study of events and their perception?" Two extreme positions emerged from our conversations, although perhaps most members of the group would place themselves somewhere between these two views. *Extreme position one:* Properly developed and appropriately scaled physics can explain *everything,* including perception. *Extreme position two:* Physics *cannot* even explain physics (without additional explanatory principles from psychology concerning observation, language, etc.). Perhaps, the key issue dividing these two positions is the problem of *measurement.* Depending on how one defines physics, (and how one understands the operation of measurement), *both* of these positions are *tenable.*

This report will try to rationalize these two alternatives by first presenting an overview of the two positions, and then by presenting three perspectives on measurement theory: The first perspective (offered by Reed) presents a defense of Gibson's view that perceptual information is a qualitative resource (like affordances) and, therefore, can be neither measured nor conserved as energy can. If

307

so, then the founding of psychology, biology and physics jointly on the same conservation laws would be impossible, and a rescaling of dynamic (physical) laws for application at a terrestrial scale in order to provide the nomic (law) context for biology and eventually psychology would not help.

The second perspective on the measurement problem (offered by Kugler) might be said to express a more reductionist neo-Gibsonian view which seeks to extend Gibson's major thesis that traditional physics, as it stands, is not adequate to the task of providing psychological laws at an ecological scale (what Gibson, 1966, 1979, implies in his call for the founding of an ecological physics). This perspective is more optimistic than the first, observing that current developments in physics have now opened up the possibility that physical principles (e.g., conservations and symmetries) may be usefully (ecologically) rescaled to establish the nomic context in which both biological and psychological phenomena can be lawfully explained.

Finally, a third perspective (offered by Shaw) attempts to reconcile the first two perspectives by showing that there is reason to believe that the nature of information parameters supporting perception may in fact take a *dual* form—the form of a *resource* as called for in perspective one and of a measurable quantity as required under perspective two. In addition, he exlores some of the reasons for believing information might be conserved.

As of the writing of the report, however, no consensus had been reached regarding the acceptability of any of the three perspectives. Hence they are presented candidly to you, the reader, unadorned, warts and all, for your consideration.

INTRODUCTION: MEASURING INFORMATION

Hertzian Theory of Explanation

In his *Mechanics* (1896/1956), Henrich Hertz provided a clear expression of the classical view of explanation in physics. On this view, a true physical theory provides a structuring of the physicist's thought processes, such that the necessary consequences of the physicist's thoughts turn out to be the necessary consequents of the things (and processes) about which the physicist is thinking. We will illustrate this both with a figure (Fig. 18.1) and an example. The testing of physical theories occurs as in the figure: Universal patterns (laws) of nature are described by a knower, who *measures* certain physical states and uses the description to predict the latter consequents of those states. To test a prediction requires measuring the relevant parameters of the later physical state and comparing that measurement with the prediction.

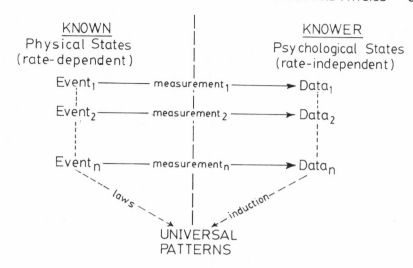

FIG. 18.1.   The Hertzian Theory of Scientific Explanation.

However, this sequence of measurements performed by an observer or scientist is very difficult to incorporate into the physicists' framework because, to be used, measurements must be *coded* into symbol strings. These strings are relatively rate-independent; that is, manipulation of symbol strings may occur at a rate which is noncommensurate with the dynamics of either the manipulator or the referent of the symbols (Pattee, 1979). It is one thing to assert that these measurements can all be described as physical processes—and everyone in the group agreed with this—but is quite another to show how physical laws alone could explain the evolution of the relatively rate-independent symbolic processes involved in measurements.

For example, human beings are quite capable of "predicting" where a moving target will be in order to grab it; in fact, infants as young as 18 weeks do this with considerable accuracy (von Hofsten & Lindhagen, 1979). A Hertzian explanation of this skill would assert that some measurements are taken by the visual system, a prediction generated, a movement then made in accordance with the prediction, and subsequent constraints on the behavior. This is the "information-processing" approach in psychology, a classic example of which (Miller, Galanter, & Pribram, 1960) employs a modified Hertzian model of explanation, as illustrated in Fig. 18.2.

The information processing theorists' modification of the Hertzian model of explanation is significant because, within this Hertzian framework, psychologists can only provide *simulations* of mental processes, not *explanations*. The

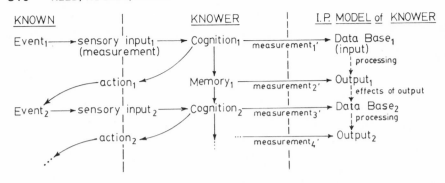

FIG. 18.2.   Psychological Explanation from an Informational Processing Point (I.P.) of View.

reason for this is that no laws of nature are being studied or modelled; the physical and biological evolution of the measurements and their symbol systems are assumed, not explained. Sense inputs are treated as measurements made by an observer—and, simultaneously, the psychologist in his own way attempts to measure these as well—but cognition is considered to be an activity of processing the measured (sensory) inputs according to certain rules in order to create memory representations, in the form of symbol strings or, perhaps, images. The physical laws involved in the processing are not studied by information-processing (I.P.) psychologists, only the logical structure of the rule-based processes. Their basic assumption is that the particular physical embodiment or hardware is not relevant (Simon, 1980). Thus, the I.P. psychologist's explanatory goal is to devise algorithms which simulate the input–output patterns of the observer, ignoring how laws of nature could explain why just such biological processes evolved.

Most physicists do not accept mere simulation as an explanation: The question would immediately arise as to the physical laws underlying the hypothesized algorithms for processing information, as depicted in Fig. 18.3. This approach was exemplified in our group by Iberall, who also suggested that a distinction be made between control and regulation. A *control* system is energetically inefficient because it employs symbol strings to organize its activities, and these rate-independent entities and their storage require vast amounts of energy compared to the behavior controlled. A *regulating* system employs few or no symbol strings, producing its behavior instead on the basis of built-in physical constraints. Again, the problem of how these constraints have evolved loomed as a central issue. Although we discussed in detail two examples of biological growth, the morphogenesis of feathers (by Brush) and of vertebrate crania (by Shaw), it remained unclear how to bring physical theory to the test against examples of regulation and/or control in biological systems.

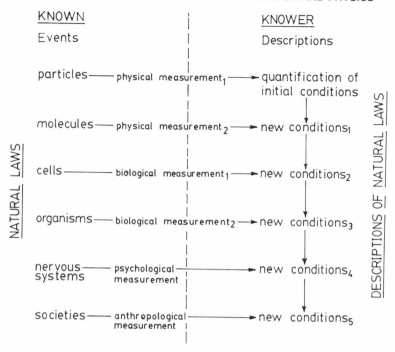

FIG. 18.3.   Physical Explanation in Terms of Natural Laws.

Information, Control and Measurement

The conflict between Pattee's and Iberall's views was unresolved, but some clarification of the contrast was obtained, perhaps paving the way for more concrete tests.

Pattee suggested that information results from measurement, and that a useful criterion for something being information is if it is relatively rate-independent with respect to what is being measured. For example, the organization of nucleic acid into a replicating lineage of chromosomes in an organism persists somewhat independently of the various metabolic cycles of the creature, and this rate-independence of the chromosomal organization is what makes it genetic "information" and allows it to "control" some aspects of those metabolic cycles. Note that it is the genetic *organization* which persists and counts as information, not the chromosome as a material body, which decays with each cell cycle.

According to Iberall, this sort of rate independence is more a function of the measurement units chosen than of the objects under study. The persistence of chromosomal organization, Iberall would argue, should not be analyzed in terms of milliseconds, but in terms of the intrinsic temporal scale of the dynamic processes in which the chromosomes take part. For example, each chromosome pair lasts through a single cell cycle, but the lineage of chromosomes descended from any pair lasts through an entire (diploid) life cycle. Iberall sees such persistences as the segregation of a dynamic field into persistent and changing components which interact, and not as a separation between "controlling" information and "controlled" events. Thus, Iberall claimed that physical laws will be discovered that explain the evolution of rate-independent systems if we use the appropriate measurement units.

Pattee and Iberall agreed that human perception is a type of measurement; but having differing accounts of measurement, they disagreed over the implications of this claim. Whereas Pattee raised doubts that physical laws alone would suffice to explain perception (considered as a form of measurement). Iberall countered by claiming that physical laws for perception would be discovered if and when the appropriate units of measurement are applied to perceiving. Kugler, Shaw and Dempster agreed with Iberall that such laws should be sought. Reed agreed that laws of perceiving probably could be found, but he argued that they would not be simply rescaled physical laws, agreeing with Pattee that the life sciences will have to formulate the bases of their own laws. Reed also disagreed with the rest of the group over considering perception as a form of measurement. Consequently, his perspective on this problem is presented next.

PERSPECTIVE I: WHY INFORMATION CANNOT
BE MEASURED
BY EDWARD REED

Direct perception is not a kind of measurement, but is based on the pickup of nonquantifiable information. The pickup of information underlies the adjustment of all organisms to the affordances of their environment. As Gibson (1977, 1979) pointed out, information is not a function of physical form (as Kugler, Kelso, & Turvey, 1980, argue), nor is it a function of rate independence or symbol strings, as Pattee holds. Rather, information exists when and only when a lawful *specificity* relation holds (Turvey, Shaw, Reed, & Mace, 1981). For example, the densely nested grouping of solid visual angles at any loci for observation—the "optic array"—contains information because it is specific to the habitat in which it is formed. The optic array is, of course, a physical entity, embodying within it a densely nested limitless series of overlappings, adjacencies, and inclusions of visual angles, each of which has a certain persistence despite change. Yet the array is information by virtue of its specificity to its sources, not by virtue of its forms of persistences. To the extent that nested forms or persistences *specify* they provide information, but it is the ecological fact of specificity, and not the physical facts of persisting form which provides the nomic basis for vision. Note that, because the number of nested angles in an array and their possible permutations is nondenumerable, specificity creating optical structure *cannot* be measured. Thus, for Gibson, information pickup cannot be a kind of measurement; instead, it is a detection of an indefinitely rich covariation of persistences and changes, perhaps by a process of differentiating among specificity relations.

Gibson's Approach to Psychology

Whereas Pattee, Iberall, and others took the problem of perception to be that of providing a physical explanation of the measurement processes engaged in by a living observer, Reed dissented. Following Gibson (1979, pp. 8–9), Reed suggested that the theory of perception begins with the distinction between the physical world and the animate environment. The physical world encompasses both the micro- and macroscopic: Even galaxies are made up of fundamental particles and forces. However, to reiterate, the environment has no ultimate constituents, being so densely nested that its constituent levels and units intertwine and overlap indefinitely. Environments have evolved out of the physical world; what demarcates an environment from the physical world is the distinction between animate and inanimate. In an environment the animate is surrounded by the inanimate, and a new kind of entity evolves, the *resource.*

Unlike physical entities, resources are not conserved (although the ultimate physical constituents of resources obey all the conservation principles). Because animate beings are surrounded by nonconserved resources, and because animate creatures reproduce with variations, a new law of nature, natural selection, evolves at the ecological level of reality (Bonner, 1974; Reed, 1981). *Until physics can explain the nonconservation of resources, natural selection and the ecological level of reality will have to be considered as distinct from physics.*

In Gibson's account of perception (Fig. 18.4) resources replace the physicists' "initial conditions." It is not that resources do not *have* initial conditions, nor that they cannot be measured; rather what is important for living and behaving are not the physical states of the environment, but the resources of the environment.

Gibson calls those resources of the environment which potentially support behavior the *affordances* of the environment, and he offers the hypothesis that affordances are what animals perceive. However, to perceive an affordance requires more than the mere existence of the affordance: the environment must also contain a second kind of resource, *information*, which specifies the affordance. Gibson explains that information is contained in patterns of energy distribution in the media of the environment. Again, the physical fact of energy is *not* information, is not a resource for an animal; only specific patterns of energy which emerge in an ecosystem count as information (Gibson, 1961; Hutchinson, 1965). A ray of light specifies not an affordance for behavior but only a radiant

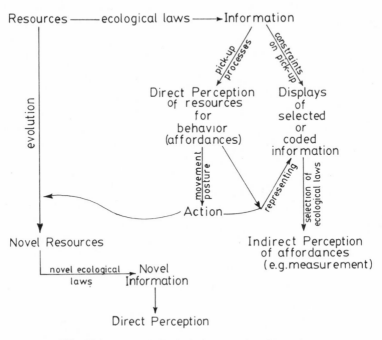

FIG. 18.4.   Gibson's Ecological Approach to Perception.

source. A homogeneous array of light energy specifies nothing, as the Ganzfeld experiments prove (Gibson, 1982). Gibson's theory of perception is based on discovering laws of the environment, demonstrating what information specifies what affordances (Turvey, Shaw, Reed, & Mace, 1981).

If ecological information really specifies environmental affordances, and if animals have evolved both perceptual systems capable of picking up information and action systems capable of being regulated by this information, then neither the physics of measurement nor the processing of symbol strings can explain perceiving. Perception as based on information is neither a physical-causal process nor a symbol-manipulating process; it is a result of and prerequisite for resource use, and a biological analysis is far more appropriate for it than either a physical or a computational analysis.

According to Gibson (1979, pp. 258ff), measurement is a biological capacity involving tools, depictions, and descriptions. A person using a measurement device or strategy (whether as simple as the thumb used to measure distance, or as complex as an X-ray) can *select* out of the indefinite amount of information available a single unit, feature, or dimension. By using pictures, words, indicators, and so on, people can create rate-independent devices (such as clocks and yardsticks) to communicate, abstract, and record properties of the environment. This complex process, called by Gibson "indirect perception of the environment" (indirect because constrained and mediated by tools and/or a selected display) is the basis of all scientific and technological measurement. Gibson (1966) argued that previous perceptionists had modelled their theories of how observers see the environment on this process of indirect perception—hence the common notions of retinal pictures or "coded sensory inputs." Gibson argued that this was the reverse of what actually happens: Direct perception of the environment, based on ecological information, is basic, and indirect perception (including measurement) of the environment based on pictures, displays, and tools is derivative.

PERSPECTIVE II: INFORMATION AS DYNAMIC FORM BY PETER KUGLER

Introduction

The notion that information is the means by which perceptual systems detect properties of the environment is true for all organsims—scientists not excluded. The view that information is a form of specification rather than representation is fundamental to the Gibsonian tradition in psychology. On this I am in perfect agreement with Reed, as was the whole group. Dissension arises, however, regarding the form that specification might take. Reed suggests that it is not merely the physical aspects of persisting forms that account for their capacity to specify but their *ecological* aspects, that is, those aspects of persisting forms in nature that assist an organism in the fulfillment of an intention (construed in the broadest possible way). He attributes the counterview to me that "physical" persistence of form is *all* that information is. This is not quite true. Rather my view is that information is at least instantiated by persisting forms of energy distributions—what Gibson called their invariant properties; but this is not to say that this is *all* information is, if what one means by "physical" is restricted to the kinetic interpretation. For me this is an unwarranted and narrow interpretation.

On the other hand, if we broaden the interpretation to include the kinematic and geometric aspects as well, then we obtain a more adequate and relevant interpretation for the purposes of perceptual theory, but still not a totally adequate one. It is relevant because now the physical concept of information includes a level of abstraction that is sufficiently general to permit the optical structures that are lawfully specific to the environmental properties to play a determinate role in the fashioning and execution of the perceiver's actions. It is this role that physical form plays in serving the action intentions of an organism that qualifies it as "specification," rather than merely as "physical," in the traditionally narrow connotation of the term. Indeed, it is in this sense that we are willing to say that the physical form of information may be "ecological," and to which Gibson himself ascribed the term "ecological physics." On this I do not doubt that Reed and I are also in close agreement. Then where does the dissension begin?

It begins with the claim that ecologically-scaled, physically-based form may be *intrinsically* defined as the form that lawful specification, as such, takes; in other words, I claim that information serves a lawful specification function in perceiving precisely because the physical forms that instantiate it assume a certain dynamic topological form, namely, a form that is intrinsic to, and reciprocally determined by, the organism's properties as a perceiver/actor and the environment's properties that support perceiving and acting.

Thus, the dissension devolves upon whether or not the abstract language of dynamic (physical) topology, being developed for contemporary physics, might prove both adequate and fruitful as a means for couching our psychological theories of information. Iberall, Shaw and I are optimistic on this point; Pattee and Reed are pessimistic. In the following discussion I try to give our reasons for optimism. Prefatory to this discussion, however, is an agreement as to what the theorist's task requires by way of an abstract language in which to state the problems and their solutions.

Defining the Problem: The First Step Towards a Solution

Science, at any phase of maturity, is confronted with a tension between that portion of inquiry that constitutes a description of a problem and that portion of inquiry which constitutes a description of the solution. Problem and solution are intimately connected, and any failure to recognize this close relationship can lead the scientist into dogma. A problem is merely the abstract form of a concrete solution, and a solution is merely the concrete form of the abstract problem: Problem and solution are fundamentally *duals* (in the mathematical sense of duality as opposed to the philosophical sense of dualism).

A common error can occur in the equating of abstraction with the discipline of philosophy. The typical equation is the assertion that when a scientist addresses a problem abstractly that he or she is utilizing the philosophical mode of inquiry. This conclusion is valid only when the test field of interest is philosophy. Abstraction is not an enterprise exclusive to the domain of philosophy, it permeates all domains. When a scientist talks abstractly about an engineering problem, the scientist is not doing philosophy, the scientist is doing engineering. When the scientist talks abstractly about a physics problem, the scientist is not doing philosophy, the scientist is doing physics, and so forth. Abstraction, as a relevant form of scientific inquiry, is dramatically absent from most scientific endeavors of the twentieth century. It is with respect to this issue of abstraction that Gibson offers some of his most valuable insights. Gibson questioned the traditional statement of the problem, arguing that if the problem was wrongly stated then the solution was irrelevant at worst and inappropriate at best. Gibson (1966, 1979) began to question the fundamental assumptions underlying perceptual theories. For, as Gibson points out, most perceptual theories, on extension, lead to the conclusion that animals cannot be said to perceive their environments. For Gibson, perception, as the detection of information about layouts of environments or their change (events), is a *fact* and not a conclusion to be deduced from the premises of a theory. As such, perception of properties relating an animal to its environment is a fact and, therefore, must be accepted as a theoretical postulate.

Starting with the premise that animals can perceive their encounters with their environments, Gibson proceeded to question the correctness of the abstractions assumed by traditional perceptual theories; for these placed in jeopardy any hope of explaining how actors might be in perceptual contact with those environmental facts required to control behaviors. A primary target for criticism centered on representational constructs (in whatever form they might assume: schema, rule, program, frame, set-point, etc.) as being essentially inadequate for accounting for perceptual knowledge (Shaw & Turvey, 1981; Shaw, Turvey, & Mace, 1982; Turvey & Shaw, 1979; Turvey et al., 1981).

Perceptual Realism Versus Scientific Realism

A few words of caution should be added about the scholarship needed to understand the issues surrounding "perceptual realism." "Scientific realism" is often confused with "perceptual realism." This is a serious mistake, a categorical error, and one to be carefully avoided. *Scientific realism* is a philosophical disposition with regard to the method by which scientists carry out the acts of science.

By contrast, *perceptual realism* is a philosophical disposition with regard to the method by which animals perform the act of perceiving. Philosophers of science typically lead us to believe that our philosophy of science is primary and that our methods of science must be parasitic on the philosophy. But this is to place the cart before the horse. Philosophical premises are more apt to fall out of a scientists choice of methods for constructing abstractions (e.g., models).

One of the philosophical premises that may be educed from traditional perceptual theories is that perceiving the facts of the environment necessarily follows a *correspondence theory of truth*. This view of perception is not to be confused with "perceptual realism," but should be viewed as its opposite. For in contrast to the primacy of a philosophy of science, the ecological approach (as advocated by Gibson, Shaw, Turvey and others) argues for the *primacy of perception* (see Turvey & Shaw, 1979).

Premise. It is a fact that animals, as epistemic agents, are in contact with activity-relevant properties. How might this be so? This premise serves as the "boot-strapping" operation for fashioning not only a theory of perception but also for deducing a philosophy of science. This argument is not physically motivated but rather is epistemically motivated. It is a statement about the state of affairs of knowing systems. From this starting point we can begin deducing the necessary physics that would support the argument of perceptual realism: What are the physical requirements of a universe that permit "knowing agents" to evolve? The type of answers this question encourages are more akin to a "coherence" theory than to a correspondence theory.

Attempts to answer this question have led to our interest in a physics based on the concepts of nonlinear mechanics, nonequilibrium thermodynamics, statistical mechanics and qualitative dynamics. Our selection has not been motivated by the current popularity of this brand of physics but rather because it appears to be the only currently available physics that makes room for a psychological theory of knowing agents. The strength of this approach lies in the fact that it makes an epistemological issue the guiding constraint on ontology; the existence of laws is predicated on their making possible explanations of how biological systems can know how to act adaptively. Of course, as psychologists, we are in general not trained in mathematics, physics or biology; yet the breadth of the problem is such that it requires a general understanding of the major issues in the above domains. Therefore, we invite the biologists, physiologists and mathematicians, who share a common interest in the problem of control and coordination of information and dynamics in biological systems, to help us find solutions.

Intrinsic versus Extrinsic Perspectives on Analysis

Too often in science it is the "tools" (e.g. strategies) of the trade that serve to motivate not only the solutions to the problems but also the very nature of the problem. The "tools" define boundary conditions. For a scientist the tools constitute the methods or means by which to measure (or model) a system. These methods of analysis can be classified into two general categories: extrinsic (measurement or modelling) structures and intrinsic (measurement or modelling) structures. The scientist elects one of these strategies before analyzing (measuring or modelling) the system of interest. Importantly, the scientist must have some a priori commitment toward the fundamental design of the system before any analysis (measurement or modelling) of the system is possible.

An extrinsic analysis is based on the assumption that the tools used to measure or model a system are "formally" independent of the system being modelled. Concerning the issue of modelling, Fodor (1980) has identified this requirement as the "formality condition". This requirement is characteristic of Turing-type machines. Symbols and syntax (rules or programs) constitute a basic set of primitives that can be used to model the behavior of any system. Furthermore, the formality condition is valid if and only if it can be assumed that there is only one means of analysis (modelling or measurement) that is universally valid for all systems and for all interactions. Thus this analysis uses a single set of analytic "building blocks" for constructing measures or models for all systems.

Because the units of analysis are arbitrary, formally defined, and extrinsically derived, this is a classical example of a reductionistic program. Such programs rest on the unfounded belief that a single measurement structure applies equally well to all systems regardless of their semantic distinctions. Fodor's formality condition is equally unfounded, implying that the functions over which general purpose computers are defined are sufficient to simulate all the significant properties of living systems. This assumption is analogous to the 19th century belief that classical mechanics provided a formalism (e.g., analytic functions) suitable for modelling all dynamic systems. This proved to be shortsighted, for many dynamic systems turn out to be nonlinear, involving processes not integrable under the laws of classical mechanics. Consequently, there seems little reason to believe that the real-time, parallel functions of *living* dynamic systems can be adequately explained by formal concepts expressible solely as sequentially structured functions of a Turing machine. Perhaps, it is time for psychology to move beyond extrinsically imposed analyses, with their dependency on arbitrarily selected formal constructs, to seek more natural bases for modeling and measurement.

An *intrinsic* method of analysis begins with the assumption that there are no universal units of analysis that apply equally for all systems. Instead, each system uniquely defines its own set of "natural" units and interactions (see Rosen, 1978, for an informed discussion of this issue). The natural units and interaction are defined by properties endemic to the system of interest. There are no a priori assumptions about the geometry of the space in which the system functions, or about what constitutes the system's fundamental predicates (i.e., symbols, syntax, metrics, laws, etc.). From the perspective of an intrinsic analysis nothing is more fundamental than anything else. Rather everything is fundamental, differing only in its relative degree of symmetry, or fit to the patterns of states required for the system to produce a given behavior or exhibit a particular property.

In this analysis, there are only higher or lower orders of symmetries and asymmetries, greater or lesser degrees of fit to the process being analyzed. Patterns are not built up from simple predicates by concatenation rules, rather they are built out of intrinsically defined field symmetries. Pattern recognition is replaced by the notion of pattern differentiation, where one pattern is distinguished from another by their degree of asymmetry and categorized by number of shared symmetries. By using this intrinsic method of analysis Einstein proposed a solution to the problem of how different types of dynamic systems operating in diverse ways in remote regions of space-time might, nevertheless, be compared under a unified theory. In a similar vein, the ecological program seeks an intrinsic analysis of how organisms perceiving and acting differently in diverse regions of the ecological field (econiches) might also be modelled and measured by shared symmetries (laws). In this way, the ecological approach provides the "meta-tools" for developing a unified theory of psychological processes.

In artifactual systems scales and dimensions are fundamental, whereas in natural systems scales and dimensions are variables (that is, new scales and dimensions can be introduced into the system when critical ratios of existing properties of the system are realized). The system precipitates new variables carrying their own intrinsic scales ("order parameters," in Haken's [1977] vocabulary; "new linkages," in Rosen's [1978] terminology; "affordances," in Gibson's language).

Gibson's attack on perceptual theories started with physiological optics, as proposed by Helmholtz and extended by most physiological scientists who address visual perception. A typical approach to physiological optics is to start by identifying the "primitive predicates" from which "more abstract predicates" can be formed. Wavelength and intensity are the regular candidates. Physiological optics then proceeds to demonstrate that organisms perceive more complex properties than wavelength and intensity, such as categories of substances, objects, and events. The noncompatibility of such predicate types is rectified by introducing a set of internal operations which serve to transform simple wavelength and intensity into the complex predicates associated with the perception phenomenon. Feature detectors have been introduced as a means of increasing the vocabulary of simple predicates, allowing some theorists to insert the world, in miniature, into cortical projection areas 16 or 17—a less than helpful move because it postulates a phenomenal world that is just as complex as the one to be explained.

To avoid this problem Gibson began questioning the assumption of the fixed set of the properties which capture the events associated with perception. Addressing the problem of locomotion, Gibson (1958) introduced the concept of an optical flow-field as a dynamic energy distribution that exhibits "higher-order invariant" properties of relevance to the perceptual guidance of locomotion. Optical flow-fields carry information intrinsically scaled both to the animal and the environment. For instance, the perceived rate of flow specifies both the eye-height of the actor and the relative heights and distances of objects with respect to the actor. Furthermore, the point of optical expansion is a special invariant property of a flow field called a "fixed-point property." It can simultaneously specify both the direction toward (or away from) which the perceiver moves, as well the target object that defines the heading. These singular properties, however, are mathematically peculiar in that they must be omitted from the calculus description of the flow field, although they are revealed by dynamic topological analysis of flow. For this reason these and other singular properties defied expression under the laws of classical physics. Although they are produced by flow vectors, they are nevertheless independent of rate of flow; and it is rate of flow that the calculus expresses. To solve the differential equations that express the laws of flow fields requires that these equations be integrated (Indeed, this is what it means to have a solution!).

Unfortunately, integration is not defined over point singularities in a field. Thus some of the most important invariant properties of optic flow-fields that play a role in the perceptual guidance of actions do not fall under the purview of classical physical-law description; about this point there is no disagreement. But rather than abandoning the quest for physical foundations for ecological "physics," and, thereby, creating a misnomer, we might instead continue the search for more adequate foundations to all physics, and, thereby, prevent psychologically significant phenomena from falling through the cracks of science in general.

Are Symbols Independent of Dynamic Laws?

There is, however, another strategy for handling the existence of singular properties that have informational value but do not yield to ordinary physical analysis, and that is to rename the properties so that, presumably, they now fall outside of physics, and can be treated by other methods. One such redefinitional strategy is to treat informative singular properties as nonholonomic constraints. A *holonomic* constraint is simply a property that can be integrated over, and hence comes under the purview of physical laws (since such laws have typically been given a differential form). By contrast, a *nonholonomic* constraint is one that is nonintegrable, and, therefore, must be considered to be independent of physical law, so long as it is narrowly construed in terms of differential forms. Nonholonomic properties that are also informative have been renamed "symbols," and assumed to fall under the aegis of the principle of complementarity in physics.

This principle postulates the existence of a symbol–matter relationship necessary to explain observation and measurement—and, in this sense, is a constraint on physical theory—but at the same time denies that such constraints can be explained by the dynamic laws of physics (Pattee, 1971; 1973; 1982). Consequently, in this view, properties of optical flow-fields that are both singular and have a "symbol" function require linguistic rather than physical description. Those of us who wish to hold out for a reinterpretation of physical law, so that it might ultimately be shown to reassert itself as psychological law under eclogical rescaling, take exception to the "renaming" strategy. Some of the reasons that make this linguistic reformulation problematic are the following:

The term "symbol" carries many qualities that are assumed to be totally and absolutely independent of dynamics. However, this view of information raises more questions than it answers, for it leaves untouched the issue of how symbols arise in nature in the first place. The conventional answer that they are learned as "conventions" is not only circular (because learning requires the existence of information to be learned), but it is irrelevant as an explanation of how prebiotic material, which must originally have been governed only by dynamic law somehow became responsible for the symbol function (information) that arose in biotic material (DNA). This has been Pattee's problem for more than a decade; without resolution and with an abiding air of paradox.

We are bound to ask how symbols arise if not through dynamic processes, and, equally puzzling, how they might be sustained as entities (objects? processes??). In order for symbols to be independent of decay in function, to be stable and reproducible phenomena, and, therefore available for use, some kind of supporting dynamic process seems mandated by definition.

A more parsimonious approach would be to argue (following Iberall) that what we take as the symbol function of a persisting singular property is but a critical scale change in the field dynamics. At a critical scale change, a new macro-scale parameter is precipitated that serves to "organize" the atomisms on the micro-scale.

With regard to perception, Gibson would argue that the new parameter is fundamental to the perceptual system. Traditionally, the new parameter would be considered a "complex" predicate constructed (by mental operations) out of simpler more fundamental predicates (i.e., a symbol). Gibson, however, would argue that there are no complex predicates and no simple predicates, there are only *properties,* all of which when detected are fundamental in their specification. We would argue similarly with reference to actions: There are no simple actions from which complex actions are forged. Complex actions carry their specifications (with regard to their stability and reproducibility) in terms of the precipitation of new order-parameters (new linkages, etc.), not in the concatenation of simple predicates by simple rules.

The link between perception and action lies in understanding two things: coordination of those parameters precipitated by critical scale changes, and the system's "sensitivity" to the new as well as the old parameters. Gibson termed this process "perceptual differentiation"—the ability of the system to take advantage of its emergent properties. The philosophical disposition of this view advocates "property realism," or as Gibson called it, "ecological realism."

With reference to physics, Gibson argued in favor of the "ecologizing" of physics: A search for a physics of properties relevant to the terrestrial scale of animal activity. The beginnings of such a physics is found in Gibson's paper "Ecological Optics" (1961). Rosen (1978) raises this challenge for the physically minded scientist in his questioning of the appropriateness of fundamental units in physics. He argues that we do not need fundamental units that are sacrosanct; rather we need units that are natural. It is this call for natural units, and a commitment to the sensitivity of animals to these units, that is the hallmark of the ecological approach to perception and action.

Next, let us consider how (perceptual) sensitivity to information of a specific type might, in principle, arise in a system as an intrinsic product of its self-organizing processes.

The Dynamic Basis of Perceptual Attunement to Information

Over recent years, it has proven useful in action theory to work from the hypothesis that the complex neuromuscular subsystems of organisms are quite capable of mimicking the behavior of various abstract dynamic systems, such as pendula, springs and other oscillators. For instance, when a particular neuromuscular subsystem exhibits sufficiently stable behavior over a broad class of task conditions that is isomorphic to the topological properties of some model system, we say that its functional organization has "self-assembled" into the mode of operation of the designated system (e.g., a dampened oscillatory mode, in the case of a mass-spring system; or a limit-cycle oscillatory mode, in the case of a self-sustained oscillator). It should be strongly emphasized, however, that the natural system does not embody the physical system it models, rather it simulates the mode of behavior of that system, (say by means of soft tissues, such as elastic muscles and tendons, rather than by surrogate springs or coils). In this sense, the equivalence is abstract and functional rather than concrete and structural.

This analysis begs the question of how a complex (neuromuscular) system, composed of many degrees of freedom, self-assembles into a simple mode of organization consisting of only a few degrees of freedom. The answer to this question must include an account of how the system becomes sensitive to relevant dimensions of information that somehow bring new constraints to bear on the system and, thereby, reduce its excess degrees of freedom. Our growing suspicion is that, in general, the nature of such informational constraints on action systems must be quite abstract. For such constraints (in the case of vision) must map kinetic properties of environmental events (say the momentum of an incoming tackler) across the light supporting media (air, the eye, and nervous system). Such media are capable of sustaining only geometric and kinematic forms of structure, yet the perceiving system (say, a football player) must make the appropriate neuromuscular adjustments that take it into the proper functional mode for remaining stable (say, by warding off the impact of a tackler). As I see it, the basis for lawfully mapping kinetic variables (of the environment), over intervening geometric and kinematic variables, into kinetic variables (of the animal) is *form*—the only thing common to geometry, kinematics, and kinetics.

Furthermore, the very same dynamic processes that are responsible for an emerging mode of organization, through the interplay of the action and perception subsystems, impose a selective attunement on the perceptual subsystem. This attunement increases the system's sensitivity to those dimensions of information required to refine and sustain its mode of functioning until the given task is accomplished and the current intent satisfied. This is the essence of perceptual learning and the education of attention, namely that the system, as an actor, be "self-serving." To do so, however, it must be self-organizing such that the action subsystem is served by the perceptual subsystem which, in turn, is tuned by the action subsystem in accordance with its current mode of organization. One might speculate, then, that Gibson's theory of "resonance" has a natural home in such a view, where the action and perceptual subsystems operate under mutual constraints as if they were "dual," in the sense used by Shaw (Perspective III, this chapter), and "soft-tracked," in the sense of Iberall's (1974) coupled oscillators.

Is Perceptual Measurement of Information Possible?

The problem of measurement (as discussed in the group) centered on two primary issues: (1) measurement as a necessary act by scientists in performing a methodology relative to data collection, (a necessary act if our science is to be tied to observables, as opposed to theory in isolation), and (2) measurement as a necessary component of the epistemic act of perceiving.

As psychologists we have chosen our test field with reference to the problem of the act of perception and its associated measurement problems, but as scientists confronting this phenomena we must also understand the nature of measurement as an act of scientific inquiry. Thus, the problem of measurement must be confronted from both perspectives and, preferably, (as advocated by Shaw, Iberall and myself), the metric chosen will be intrinsic to the system of interest and common to both the scientific measurement process and the perceptual measurement process. If this commonality is not sought, there is a danger that the system will appear more "information-rich" than it actually is.

This error generally leads to the introduction of some form of instantiation of knowledge into the system in forms which were anathema to Gibson, such as schemas, memories, programs, or rate-independent rules. Typical of this problem is the concept of timing in oscillatory systems and the tying of the timing pulses to some internal (rationalism) or external (behaviorism) timer. This problem is resolved if the timing is tied to some intrinsic parameter (other than time) that serves as the metric source. In this manner, time takes on a coherent metric that is unique and specific to the intrinsic parameter, and is continually tailored to changes in the parameter, (such as those incurred by growth or artificially). Iberall (1972, 1978), Yates, (Yates, Marsh, & Iberall, 1973; Yates, 1980) state this issue most articulately; Kugler, Kelso, and Turvey (1980) have applied these concepts to timing in motor systems; Shaw (Shaw & Cutting, 1980; Warren & Shaw, 1981) has applied these concepts generally to show that the tractability of perceptual models depends upon the type of metric chosen.

The conclusion reached by these researchers is that if the wrong metric is chosen by the scientist relative to the system of interest, then the system will appear to require more "information" relative to the task at hand, whereas, under analysis using the appropriate metric, then the phenomena of interest will appear more "lawful" rather than "information-rich." Thus, the concept of measurement is a necessary act in both science, which entails a methodology of measurement, and perception, which is itself a method of measurement, in the sense of being an act for discovering the appropriate transformations over units and dimensions that leave certain properties invariant.

Moreover, when scientific measurement is performed using "natural units" (cf. Rosen, 1978), as is perception, then the two acts of measurement become remarkably similar. It is at the level of a methodology of scientific measurement and a methodology of perceptual measurement that the analogy holds.

Where Do Natural Symbols Come From?

Over the years Pattee's conception of organizational constraints has served as a continuous source for further articulation of the degrees of freedom problem. Unfortunately, Pattee has provided more of an elucidation of the problem than a solution. Nonetheless, this is an important contribution. Pattee seeks a solution to the degrees of freedom problem for complex systems, such as biological or psychological systems, that assumes many rate-independent constraints, or symbols (Pattee, 1972, 1973, 1977). Like Iberall, I believe it a mistake to introduce rate-independent symbols into the solution of the degrees of freedom problem.

Iberall argues that when the symbol is properly analyzed (in terms of "relaxation time" and "mean free path"; or, more simply, the proper units of time and space), then it becomes apparent that the symbol is actually a steady-state variable carried in a dynamic field process. Here the field's relaxation time and mean free path are much slower (in time) and larger (in space) than assumed by the local perspective that views the steady state as a rate-independent symbol. This broadening of perspective of the problem opens up new avenues of explanation.

Fundamentally, all processes are viewed as dynamic in origin; this allows for the possibility of a theory of evolution based on "dynamics," rather than on randomly occurring combinations of highly improbable symbols whose tailoring is provided for by the principles of natural and sexual selection. We believe that any viable theory of organization must be compatible with a theory of evolution of inhomogeneities. Consequently, dynamics as the source for steady states seems a better starting place than symbols.

A second major issue discussed in our group concerned the nature of the mechanism that supports steady-state phenomena. The following general strategy was agreed upon by a majority of the participants: When observing a steady-state situation, (or for that matter, any inhomogeneity in a homogeneous field), start by doing a physical analysis of the system such that the important conservations are identified. Systems dynamically organize relative to these conservations, under appropriate ''open'' conditions, because it is relatively ''cheap'' for an evolving system to ''take advantage'' of a dynamic inhomogeneity. On the other hand, it is very ''expensive'' to create an inhomogeneity, such as a symbol, that is in opposition to the system's dynamics.

If a symbol, by definition, is indifferent to dynamics, then one of two conclusions can be drawn: (1) the symbol is imbedded in a dynamic environment that is totally homogeneous (i.e., no order whatsoever), which rules out the possibility of inhomogeneities in matter, energy, etc.; or (2) that a complementary relationship exists (that is, the symbol and its surrounding dynamics do not relate causally but rather in a complementary, or dual fashion).

Because the universe has pockets of noticeable inhomogeneities (i.e., planets, particles, spiraling motions, etc), it is reasonable to rule out the possibility that symbols are imbedded in totally homogeneous environments (''coarse-graining'' or ''smearing'' do not seem to be reasonable ways of obtaining a homogeneous environment). If alternative (2) is a reasonable conclusion (and assuming that the symbol is not synonymous with a dynamic inhomogeneity, in which case the symbol is not indifferent to dynamics), then we can further conclude that the symbol is setting up some form of competition with the dynamics and, thus is incurring less than optimal dynamic expenditures. In fact such a symbol system, driving a dynamic system (in the form of set-points, rate-independent rules, etc.), would require continuous high energy conversions by the system. Generally, such conditions can persist for only short periods of time. Under this view, then, symbols (or better ''symbol functions'') are *scale-dependent* phenomena, dissolving into dynamic processes at extended scales of analyses.

In contrast, Pattee argues that rate-independent symbols are a viable method for introducing steady-state situations for biological and psychological systems but recognizes that dynamics should be tracked as far as possible. Iberall argues that dynamics is the only means for guaranteeing stability in a system.

Temporary departures may occur from the dynamics, but there is no guarantee that the departure will be stable. It should also be emphasized that a symbol system is absolutely neutral with respect to stability since stability is a rate-dependent phenomenon. This means that symbol functions may not control the rates of dynamic processes but at most may direct or select them by contributing to their initial conditions. But in doing so, symbol initiated or symbol-directed processes must be sustained and stabilized by some appropriate dynamics. Hence, symbols at best function at the behest of dynamics and possess no true autonomy.

Need There Be a Pluralism of Laws?

A note on the issue of physical laws versus psychological laws: From Reed's comments on natural law it would seem that physical law cannot be logically continuous with psychological law. Some of us, however, are fundamentally committed to the position that physical laws are basic to understanding at all levels and scales. When the appropriate levels and scales are selected the consequences of these laws may be dramatically distinct. In particular, when physical laws are viewed at certain scales, such as those found terrestrially, then the observed relations start looking remarkably similar to biological and psychological laws: Put simply, when physics is done at the appropriate scales one derives psychological and biological laws "free." There is nothing discontinuous or incompatable about physical, biological and psychological laws; they merely differ in local boundary conditions and scales.

The physical systems of interest to psychology and biology are persistent, stable, autonomous systems, or (to use Iberall's term), "self-serving systems." There is currently emerging a physics for these systems. This physics is being promoted most notably by Iberall's "homeokinetics," Prigogine's "dissipative structure theory," Haken's "synergetics," and Morowitz's "bioenergetics." Apparently, Iberall's is the most comprehensive in addressing questions of interest to living systems at the scale of ecosystems. In addition, Iberall's methodology of biospectroscopy allows for an analysis of the bookkeeping activities in systems that are generally too ill defined to be approached by other conventional methods. Until these innovative views of natural law are thoroughly mastered, it seems imprudent to conclude prematurely that biological and psychological laws might not come to rest easily alongside physical law under the rubric of natural law.

PERSPECTIVE III: MEASURING INFORMATION
BY ROBERT SHAW

Two Parameters For Information

Reed suggests that information is an immeasurable or qualitative dimension of energy distributions which he terms a "resource." Examples of other types of resources are affordances and living systems. He justifies the claim that information is not a measurable aspect of ambient light by observing that because the optic array consists of a potentially inexhaustible supply of nested solid angles of light contrasts, then it must be a nondenumerable set. There seems to me little doubt that Gibson agreed with this assessment of the status of information as an immeasurable dimension of ambient energy distributions. Gibson (1979) asserts in his last book:

> The information for perception, unhappily, cannot be defined and measured as Claude Shannon's information can be . . . The information in ambient light, along with sound, odor, touches, and natural chemicals, is inexhaustible. A perceiver can

keep on noticing facts about the world she lives in to the end of her life without ever reaching a limit. Information is not lost to the environment when gained by the individual; it is not conserved like energy. (p. 243)

A second reason Reed gives for information, being immeasurable is, presumably, because it functions as a *resource*. Resources have measurable dimensions associated with their physical aspects, for these are *extensive* in character; however, their "use-value," or utility, is qualitative and unextended in character. Elsewhere I have referred to such complementary aspects as being "intensive" in character (Shaw & Cutting, 1981). We return to these aspects of information after consideration of the issue of what kind of resource information might be.

Is Information an Inexhaustible Resource? Is It Conserved?

The title of this subsection raises two distinct but related questions. For example, heat is an important form of an energy resource and, given the sun and other stars, it does seem to be nearly inexhaustible. Early attempts, however, to prove heat was conserved failed, even though when gained by one body, it is indeed lost to the environment. We now know why heat is not itself a conserved quantity: Like all other forms of energy, it can be converted to other forms. Thus, it was soon understood that energy is conserved across all grades but that no grade of energy as such (e.g., electrical, thermal, mechanical) is conserved. Hence, it is quite possible for something to be lost to the environment when gained by one object without that something necessarily being conserved. The condition stated by Gibson is a necessary condition for conservation but is by no means a sufficient one. Indeed, there is a sense in which information *is* lost to the environment of other perceivers when gained by an individual.

At the level of relativity physics each particle, object, or perceiver is characterized by a distinct "world-line," which winds its way through space–time (see Kugler, Turvey, Carello, & Shaw, this volume). A given perspective held by an individual perceiving a particular object or event will be represented uniquely by a "fat" world-line segment. Since all world-line segments are necessarily distinct, no two can occupy exactly the same interval of space–time; therefore, it follows that one perceiver's perspective on a given object will displace all others in the sense that no two perspectives can have identical spatial or historical coordinates, any more than two objects can occupy the same space.

Information is detected over perspectives. Because individual perceivers can never have *identical* perspectival histories, only partially equivalent ones as permitted by socially overlapping situations, then the opportunities for information detection granted one perceiver can never be perfectly shared by another, but rather displace one another. An image that may help convey the sense of this rather abstract argument is that of a crowd of individuals each taking turns watching a baseball game through a knothole in the fence surrounding the playing field. No matter how they try, no two people are really able to see exactly the same game; some will see plays missed by others. Perceiving the environmental "game" of events as it historically unfolds in space–time is similar: No two perceivers have the same opportunity to see exactly the same "plays." It is in this sense that information *is* lost to the (social) environment when gained by the individual–in contradistinction to Gibson's claim. This argument does not prove that information *is* necessarily conserved, but only that it *may* be. Again it is important to note that Kugler has given strong arguments in favor of information as "topological form" being conserved (Kugler et al., 1980; Kugler et al., 1982).

In order to prove that information, like energy, is conserved, one must show that the ratio of the *total set of world-line segments (perspectives) over which information detection events are possible* to the *set of world-line segments over which detection actually takes place* yields a well-defined number; and, furthermore, that this number remains invariant over all required renormalizations due to change in the size of the population of perceivers or of points of observation that they might occupy, within each and every space–time interval one might choose to sample. What this requirement amounts to can be illustrated in the case of the knothole veiwing of the baseball game: Information about the game can be said to be conserved if its *content* (number of players, plays, balls used, innings, fouls, etc.) and the *structure* (batting order, order of substitutions, duration of each inning, and etc.) does not change as a function of the number of people sharing a given knothole or with the number of knotholes. Because a change in these sampling conditions alters neither the content nor the structure of the game event, its world-line, as an information source, remains invariant over any changes in the world-line intervals corresponding to the associated information sampling events. Using Gibson's terminology, we offer the general proposition that *information about an event is conserved under renormalization whenever the same "invariant structure" (transformational and structural invariants defining the event) is preserved under different "perspective invariants" (transformational and structural invariants defining the sampling conditions).*

For those of us who accept the tenets of ecological realism, it is incumbent on us to puzzle over how conservations of different kinds relate to one another. Conservations are in a sense the most real quantities that exist because they do so under the most varied circumstances. Consequently, we must ask how conservation of information relates to other types of conservations, such as conservation of energy, mass, momentum, and angular momentum. If information is truly a conserved quantity, then like the others it must exhibit the same kind of behavior they do, namely, invariance under some (symmetry) group operation. Traditionally, theoretical physics has placed great faith in symmetry group theory as a guide in such matters because each conservation was shown to correspond to a quantity that remains invariant under a distinct operation in a certain symmetry group. For instance, with respect to the so-called "Lorentz" group of transformations, energy is invariant under temporal changes, mass under spatial changes, momentum under translations, and angular momentum under rotations. A reasonable requirement for information to be similar is to show that it, too, is conserved under some symmetry operation. Intuitively, this seems to be so, as the following argument attempts to show.

The conservation laws imply that the amount of the conserved quantity (like energy or momentum) measured at the beginning of an event will be the same as that measured at the end of the event, for a suitably chosen sampling interval. This will not necessarily be the case for a nonconserved quantity (like heat or force). More generally, such quantities are conserved over the transformation from initial to final conditions; that is, in the temporal direction expected of cause and effect. A most interesting feature of the Lorentz group, however, is the fact that it also allows for the inverse temporal transformation from final conditions back to initial conditions. Because this must be considered an acausal direction so far as physics is concerned, (it places the effect before the cause), no physical conservation has been or is likely to be identified with an invariant over the inverse temporal transformation. However, this does not preclude the existence of another kind of conservation.

Could there be a nonphysical quantity which remains invariant over this dimension of space–time—information? Because detailed arguments have been offered in favor of this proposition elsewhere (Shaw & Alley, in press), let me try to make it plausible here only be illustration: When the swimmers or runners explode into action from the starting gun, we do not say that the sound of the official's gun "caused" the competitors to initiate the race but that, precisely speaking, it only "occasioned" their willingness to respond. This is much more than a mere philosophical quibble, for the logical difference between "caused" and "occasioned" is exactly the difference between a physical explanation and a psychological one, between causal and acausal ones, or between those honoring physical conservations and those honoring information conservation.

Racing, like any other action, is intentional, or goal directed. Goals or intents act as inverse temporal operators that allow current physical states of a system to be tuned to future contingencies; in this sense, where causes are part-pending operations on the current states of a system, goals are future-tending. Causes make the system dependent on its determinate past, goals on its nondeterminate future. Another important difference is that the historical chain of causes is opaque to distally past causes, so that the system requires record keeping to see beyond the present, but the anticipatory effects of goal attainment are transparent to the system so long as its current state can, in principle, be constantly updated, or reinitialized, to remain on a felicitous world-line route to the future goal.

The crucial question is, how could the system constantly reinitialize its current state relative to the future goal, and thereby select felicitous or even optimal routes, unless there were information constantly available to specify such choices? To be constantly available the information must be conserved over those future occasions that *will* ultimately link the future goal conditions with the present causal conditions of the system. This is to say, the information that ultimately originates in the final conditions of a felicitous action must be conserved through anticipatory acts, so that it might be used to specify new initial conditions of the system whenever thwarts to the goal-tending aspects of the system may arise. In most cases, perception alone will be sufficient to provide the requisite information for specifying the appropriate choices to be made; however, when adequate information is not available through perceptual means, then rational judgement, correct inference, right opinion, habitual choice, creative intuition, or guesswork may suffice. For it does not matter what vehicle is used to convey information from final to initial conditions, so long as it conserves the information in the process.

Two questions remain to be resolved: If, for the sake of argument, we assume that information is conserved in the manner stipulated, how might it be measured? And what forms might it assume? As we shall see, these are by no means unrelated questions.

Extensive and Intensive Forms of Information

Perhaps, the best way to appreciate the difference between extensive and intensive forms of information is by analogy to what physicists call a Reynolds number.

Generally, such numbers can be thought of as consisting of two coparameters associated with a single dimension—one parameter, the *extensive* one, varies continuously as a function of a ratio of physical variables describing the phenomenon in question, and the other parameter, the *intensive* one, varies discontinuously as a function of how the phenomenon is to be categorized. Hence the extensive parameter permits measurements along a ratio or interval scale while the intensive parameter permits measurement only by a nominal scale or an ordinal scale (depending on whether the categories are being indexed or graded). Consider the role these coparameters play in the case of a Reynolds number for the flow behavior of liquids.

A minimal value for a Reynolds number corresponds to a smooth laminar flow, and increasing values of the number specify distinct categories of turbulence, ranging from simple vortices to complex vortex configurations known as vortex "streets." The analogy to be drawn is that coparameters of information, as with Reynolds numbers, similarly serve two different functions: The extensive one serves to measure how far apart the categories of interest are, and the intensive one serves to index exactly where on the continuum of extensive values the different categories are to be found. Here we see how a single measure, the scale of Reynolds numbers, can have two complementary "use-values'': It can be used *quantitatively,* in the sense of ratio or interval measures, or *qualitatively,* in the sense of ordinal or nominal measures.

Gibson and Reed wish to restrict the measurement of information to nominal scales alone; Kugler and I wish to entertain at least the ordinal scaling of information. In addition, I wish to propose that we also press into service the extensive coparameter of information. Let's consider how this might be done.

An Example

Assume you are ascending in an elevator which stops perfectly level at the second floor but comes to rest just past the third floor, forcing you to step down an inch or so. Now assume that the elevator continues to make this sort of alignment error at the fourth floor, the fifth, the sixth, and so on, except that the error gets larger each time. At first the exiting passengers can step off without noticing the slight misalignment of floors; later, they must watch their step in order to step down safely. Still later, they are forced to jump off the ledge created between the floor of the elevator and the floor of the building. And even later, only the foolhardy hazard to jump for fear of breaking bones. At the final stop, deboarding is best left to the suicidal.

An analysis of this example reveals a strong analogy between the Reynolds number measure for turbulence information and the affordance information specified by sharply elevated surfaces. In both cases the continuous variation of an extensive parameter gives rise to an ordered distribution of intensive categories: Distinct but increasing varieties of turbulence as compared to distinct but increasingly dangerous varieties of disembarcation. And in both cases a linear-extensive parameter relates to its intensive coparameter by a nonlinear function. (See Kugler et al., this volume, Appendix for a discussion of why collisions of increasing impact yield nonlinear traumatic effects on the human body).

There is a subtlety in this analogy, however, that must not be overlooked, or else a serious misunderstanding about the role extensive parameters play may arise: Although intensive parameters, in general, have intrinsic meaning, that is, they may be noticed by the agent involved in the task, the extensive parameter has only an extrinsic interpretation with respect to the agent's detection and use of the information parameters. In other words, the agent can not use them in their raw form; rather they are known solely by the nonlinear effects they impose on their intrinsically specified, intensive coparameter. Another example helps to illustrate the relationship between the coparameters of information.

Warren (1982) has shown that people of various heights prefer stair designs that conform to their body proportions, with taller persons preferring a steeper stair than shorter ones. This preference is reflected by the fact that each person was able to select perceptually from a series of photographs the stair design that, from metabolical measures taken in a later experiment, they were shown to climb most efficiently (See Warren & Shaw, this volume). The validity of their perceptual judgements was tested by having each person climb a series of moving, escalator-like stairmills whose *tread-to-riser ratio* was varied so as to conform to *leg length* by different degrees. The efficiency of the particular stair design for persons of a given leg length was then measured by means of the proportion of carbon dioxide expired per volumetric unit of air breathed.

The important result of the above set of studies is that the space of extensive parameter measures, as mapped by relative leg length and stair design, used in the perceptual task to index categories of stair preferences, also served to index the maxima and minima of the curves determined by another pair of extensive parameters, the metabolic-efficiency and stair-design variables, as used in the actual stair climbing task. Thus the perceptual information, or intensive parameter values, (as indexed by the extensive parameters of the first task), coimplicates the action information—another set of intensive parameter values (as indexed by the different pair of extensive parameters used in the second task). This is both a subtle and complicated point but deserves careful consideration since it has important implications for a theory of measurement.

Information as Higher and Lower Order Specification

We have now encountered two types of information functions, one of which specifies the way in which an extensive parameter, even though it varies continuously, can be used to index the values, or categories, arising nonlinearly along an intensive parameter—as in the case of an ordered series of categories of turbulence, stepping-down places, or stair designs. Let us call this use of the information function "specification by coparameter," or "coparametric specification." In addition, we have also encountered the more abstract, or *higher-order* (to use Gibson's expression), information function that defines an invariance mapping between two sets of coparametric information—one determined by the perceptual system and the other by the action system. Mathematically speaking, a pair of coparameters determined by different systems but related by an invariance mapping comprise a *dual* pair of coparameters. Consequently in other contexts, I have called this a *duality* specification between the action and perception subsystems (Shaw & Turvey, 1981).

The concepts of "coparametric specification" and "duality specification" comprises lower order and higher order forms of information, respectively; the *lower order* form specifies the lower order invarients that Gibson speaks of as "facts of environmental layout" (or change in layout—events); the *higher order* form specifies the higher order invariants of the environment, as compounded from its lower order invariants. He calls these "the affordance properties of the environment." Or correspondingly, the higher-order form of information also specifies to the actor the appropriate "effectivities" by which its action system might realize an affordance made possible by environmental properties. For instance, the covariation of properties of the human hand with those of an apple, such as size, shape, and rigidity, codetermines *both* the graspability of the apple (an affordance property) and tool function of the hand as a grasper (an effectivity property).

Gibson was well aware of the immense difficulties to be overcome by those of us who would be left behind to wrestle with such involved abstractions; but he also recognized the immense contribution to psychological theory these ideas might make if they were but tamed. He believed that even the most severe sceptic could be made to accept the notion of lower order invariants of information that specify facts of surface layout and substances, but that even the most sympathetic critic ". . . may boggle at the invariant combinations of invariants that specify the affordances of the environment for an observer" (Gibson, 1979, p. 140). As if to entice us, however, he goes on to point out that a unique combination of invariants, a compound invariant, is *just another invariant*.

Gibson admonishes us to struggle with the notion of higher forms of information because he wisely concluded that nothing less would do as a basis for a realistic theory of perception. Kugler's notion of information as an invariant aspect of topological forms shared by both the environmental "field" and the organismic "field" seems to capture the appropriate level of abstraction Gibson sought—the level of "formless" invariants (Gibson, 1979; Kugler et al, 1980; 1982).

Information Diagrams

Recently, I have experimented with ways to capture the appropriate levels of abstract mathematical description for affordances and effectivities. The approach I took has roots in the field of descriptive mathematics known as "meta-category" theory (MacLane, 1971); its utility potentially lies in its techniques for formulating abstract, higher order relations by use of simple diagrams. A second advantage over other abstract modelling approaches, such as ordinary category theory, is that one need not commit oneself prematurely to an interpretation of the nature of the underlying sets over which the abstract relations are defined. This means we need not know ahead of time exactly what information *is* before diagramming the relationships among the variables believed to be involved in its use. In this way we can test the consistency of our thinking about information before being required to decide on the best way to measure it. Finally, the resulting diagram may or may not exhibit the group structure required of a conserved quantity. If it should, then a hunting license is granted for conducting the empirical search for the proper measures.

Furthermore, in attempts to diagram affordances as higher order invariants of information, it proved necessary also to incorporate into the diagram more precise interpretations of the relationships among other fundamental concepts, such as perceiving and acting, intensive and extensive, parameter and coparameter, organism and environment, higher order and lower order, facts and information, and, of course, affordance and effectivity. For forcing one to formulate clear commitments to the use of these abstract concepts, no approach seems more promising.

A caveat should be mentioned; the diagrams that result do not represent models of the involved processes, perceiving and acting. They do not tell us *how* the system works but only *what* general constraints the system must satisfy to work in the manner it does. Therefore, this is meta-theory (talk about theories and models), rather than theory (talk about phenomena and laws).

To avoid unnecessary technicalities, the best way to proceed is by example. Therefore, let us return to the case of the errant elevator: Recall that its range of alignment error, as measured extensively, increased over floors from a few fractions of an inch to many feet; however, when referenced against the body proportions of its occupants, a range of categories of potentially dangerous egress situations was intensively specified. The intensive mapping of nominal and ordinal structure onto an extensive scale of continuous variation was compared to the Reynolds number scaling of flow phenomena whereby it is possible to pick out ordered categories of differential turbulence. Both of these examples involve a comparison of three types of scales: An interval scale of extensive variation, a nominal scale of critical values (cv) indexing the boundaries between categories, and an ordinal scale showing how such categories relate to one another. Venn (class) diagrams can be used to depict the fundamental ways in which the three scales differ.

Recall the basic set theoretic relations of *union,* '$\cup$', *intersection,* '$\cap$', and *disjoint union,* '$\uplus$' (as in Fig. 18.5). These relate to the scales as follows:

```
------------------------------------------------------------------
                        EXTENSIVE SCALE
---cv------------------------cv ------------------------ cv---
          NOMINAL SCALE OF CRITICAL VALUES
----|----------CAT1 --------|---------CAT2---------|----
          ORDINAL SCALE OF CATEGORIES
```

The fundamental measurement problem of perceptual theory is to understand precisely how the perceptual system achieves the mapping of extensive parameters of stimulation *into* the intensive categories of information (Shaw & Cutting, 1980), such as, the mapping that takes the continuous scale of Reynolds numbers into the categories of turbulence, or the mapping that takes the scale of alignment error (of the elevator) into the affordance categories of potentially dangerous egress situations (for the passengers). But imagine now that the elevator has an operator who, being of a capricious and sometimes malevolent nature, can turn a control knob the exact angular distance required to select whatever affordance category his mood dictates—ranging from safe to potentially dangerous forms of egress. Here we see that the mapping achieved by the action system is the *inverse* of that achieved by the perceptual system, namely, from the "intent" to select a

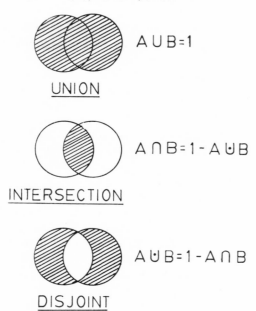

$$A \cup B = 1$$

UNION

$$A \cap B = 1 - A \cup B$$

INTERSECTION

$$A \cup B = 1 - A \cap B$$

DISJOINT
UNION

FIG. 18.5.   Basic   Set   Theoretic
Relations.

particular affordance category *onto* the continuous control parameter of the arm-wrist-hand-knob-elevator system.

Thus, the fundametal measurement problem for action theory is the exact opposite of that indicated for perceptual theory: Where the specification achieved by perception requires mapping the values of an extensive parameter *into* those of an intensive parameter, the specification achieved by action, conversely, requires mapping the values of an intensive parameter *onto* those of an extensive parameter. As a first pass at formally representing the information scales and the mapping between them achieved by perception and action, Venn class diagrams and simple set theoretic notation provide fundamental ingredients out of which to build diagrams.

And, finally, action and perception must involve mutually constraining forms of information, in the sense that the elevator operator must be able to see when the turn of the control knob has achieved the intended mischief. This "handshake" between the perception and action system can be formally modelled by determining the higher order mapping between affordances and effectivities. In the example under consideration, this would be a mapping between the two forms of information mentioned: The information specifying the relative layout of the two surfaces—the floor of the elevator and the floor of the building; and the information specifying the adjustments to the action system required to achieve the desired intent—some particular affordance outcome, such as step-

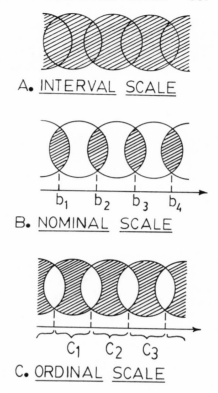

A. INTERVAL SCALE

B. NOMINAL SCALE

C. ORDINAL SCALE

FIG. 18.6. Venn Diagram Representations of Scales.

ping down versus jumping down. These "mappings" can be modelled as follows:

The mapping achieved by the perceptual system alone can be diagrammed as in Fig. 18.7.

And the mapping achieved by the action system alone is similar but has arrows with a different sense as in Fig. 18.8.

In the case that the objects occupying the nodes are sets, then the arrows represent functions; when they are themselves functions, (as in the case at hand), then the arrows represent "functions of functions," or *functors*. Clearly, the arrows in the two diagrams under consideration are functors since the nodes represent scaling functions. The "solid" arrows from node P in Fig. 18.7 captures the fact that perceiving is, at least, a functor consisting of a pair of "projections" *cv* and *cat*, which acts upon the extensive parameter of stimulation X, by means of an "injection" *spec;* this injection function "mixes" organism-dependent (propriospecific) information (e.g., body-scaled information) with environment-dependent information; and from this "mixing" emerges two classes of lower order perceptual invariants: The critical values of the nominal scale of informa-

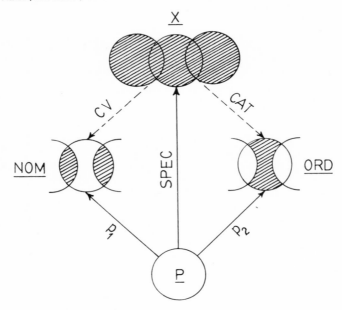

FIG. 18.7   The Mapping Achieved by the Perceptual System Alone.

tion and the category structure as specified on the ordinal scale. These lower order invariants capture, in part, the meaning of Gibson's notion of "formless" invariants that specify properties of substances, their layout, and their change, as well as what Kugler intends by his notion of form as "dynamic topological" invariants of the organism–environment manifold.

The story to be told about Fig. 18.8 is similar but opposite, for here the "solid" arrows represent the action functor which maps the extensive variables of stimulation into the intensive parameters of control, thereby "telling" the actor "how much is enough"—a nominal scaling, or "how much more is needed"—an ordinal scaling—to accomplish a given "intent" to realize some affordance category, (such as making the passengers jump down instead of merely stepping down, or selecting the optimal stair to climb).

Please note carefully the 'dotted' arrows; they represent the important fact that these diagrams "commute." A diagram is said to *commute* whenever there is more than one way to get from one node to another. Assume that you have a diagram with the three nodes a, b, c, and arrows (functions) that take you from a → b, b → c, then by composition (transitivity) the arrow a → c is said to be *naturally* defined. The "dotted' arrows by which the diagrams for action information or perception commute, mark the place of entry into our theories of the notion of "direct" specification; these, then, are the functions that carry the

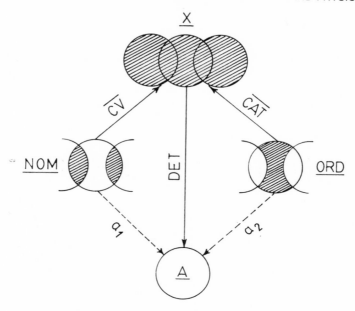

FIG. 18.8   The Mapping Achieved by the Action System Alone.

weight of the claim that perceiving and acting are both epistemic acts that penetrate, through stimulation that is informationally transparent, to the relevant properties of the world.

Note also that the two diagrams for perception and action information involve identical variables but are related by arrows (functions) reversed in direction. This means that the two diagrams are themselves related by a still higher order mapping relationship—on antisymmetric relationship termed a "duality" mapping. A duality mapping is a special case of an isomorphism, just the thing out of which to build higher order invariants, such as affordances and effectivities. The composite diagram expressing the invariance (duality) mapping required to guarantee the mutuality of the complementary pair of diagrams takes the following form:

This composite diagram, when viewed from the perspective of the relation of P to all other nodes, represents information for an affordance specification, and when viewed from the perspective of all the arrows connecting A to the other nodes, represents information for determining an effectivity, (that is, the means by which an action achieves felicity). Taken together, as a composite of dual diagrams, we have the higher order specification of an *ecosystem*. Consequently, the composite diagram with its dual components now satisfies the fundamental

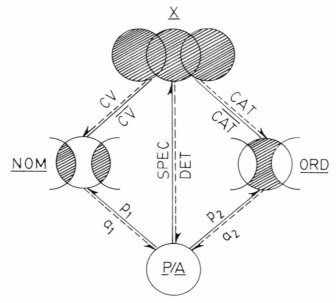

FIG. 18.9   The Duality Mapping Achieved by the Perception and Action Systems Together.

postulate of Gibson's program—the postulate of organism-environment mutuality.[1]

We shall take note of only two of the most significant features of the resulting composite diagram (Fig. 18.9). First, the dotted arrows indicate as before that this diagram, like the others, still "commutes" in just those ways required to make perceiving and acting direct rather than mediated activities. Second, the diagram now has the inverse mapping operations it needed to qualify as a group, and hence as a diagram of those conditions under which information might be conserved.

---

[1]Formally, a diagram of a category represents a monoid with identity, or a semi-group, and, therefore, by definition is not a group because it lacks an inverse operation. A duality mapping, however, is symmetric, such that for any operation in one diagram, then there necessarily exists another diagram with an operation that is the inverse of the first operation. Although neither diagram alone is a group, taken together as a composite diagram, each supplies the other with the missing inverse, and, therefore, qualifies as such. It is this duality, or invariance, mapping between complementary category diagrams that provides the formal interpretation of Gibson's postulate of organism - environment mutuality upon which we have tried to erect our theory of ecological psychology. Indeed, whatever is right or wrong with this approach must, ultimately, be traced to this source. Consequently, no critic who ignores this fundamental postulate deserves, in my opinion, to be taken seriously, for this is the very heart of Gibson's functionalism, as I see it. Unfortunately, to my knowledge, none of the critics of the ecological approach (and there have been many) has yet even addressed this issue.

In category theory, the mapping between two functors is called a "natural transformation." Just as a functor might be thought of as a function taking functions into functions, so a natural transformation can be thought of as a function taking functions of functions into functions of functions. The concept of a natural transformation provides us with the very high level of abstraction required to adequately represent Gibson's view of the information for affordances, or of its corollary concept, effectivities. Little wonder, then, that the field, lacking such necessary tools for the appropriate level of abstraction, has found it so far impossible to assimilate these concepts. This in itself should be motivation enough for us to overcome any reticence we might feel about the use of mathematical description to supplement our use of informal discourse for theory construction.

The meta-theoretical requirements for adequately expressing even familiar ideas (e.g., information and affordances) obviously outstrip the expressive power of the informal theoretical language now currently in vogue. By taking these meta-theoretical requirements for abstraction more seriously, we could, no doubt, resolve many of the inconsistencies in usage of theretical concepts that cause pseudo-controversies (e.g., Cutting, 1983).

Couching our thinking about psychology in terms of abstract information diagrams has the virtue of constantly reminding us that information is not a "thing" but a complex function—a functor; it is not a "node," nor even a relationship between a pair of nodes, rather it is the whole "diagram" of nodes and relations. An affordance, or an effectivity, specified by the information expressed in a single diagram is not, however, defined by the information diagram but by the "natural transformation"—the duality, or invariance, mapping—which coordinates these lower order abstractions under a still more abstract, ecosystem diagram, the composite of the two dual diagrams. An affordance is functionally determined by reading the arrows of the information diagrams in reversed order from that of an effectivity, that is, by reading from Fig. 18.7 to Fig. 18.8, rather than from Fig. 18.8 to Fig. 18.7. Thus we are reminded that an affordance property of the environment is specified by information *for* a properly tuned organism, that is, for one with the appropriate (dual) effectivity; and that the information for the control or regulation of an action must originate *from* an affordance property of the actor's econiche, not simply from the arbitrarily scaled world of physical stimulation.

In short, the abiding theme of the ecological approach to psychology is that information-driven acts—perceiving, acting, remembering, or judging—when properly construed, must be considered to be functionally determined only at the level of abstraction of an ecosystem (Fig. 18.9), and not merely at the level of an organism, as traditional theory would have it. This point has been argued by us numerous times over the years, but, perhaps, not so formally (Shaw & McIntyre, 1974; Turvey, Shaw, & Mace, 1978; Turvey & Shaw, 1979; Shaw, Turvey, & Mace, 1981; Shaw & Turvey, 1981; Shaw & Todd, 1979; Shaw & Cutting,

1980; Turvey, Shaw, Reed, & Mace, 1981; Alley & Shaw, 1981; Warren & Shaw, 1981; Shaw & Mingolla, 1982; Carello, Turvey, Kugler, & Shaw, 1983; Shaw & Alley, in press). The level of abstraction invoked to diagram these higher order functions shows exactly why this must be so. There can be no retreat from this level of theorizing without collapsing the important distinctions for which Gibson fought so hard.

Logon versus Metron Content: Complementary Information Measures

We must also give credit where credit is due, and some credit must surely go to others, like Gabor (1961), who also fought for ways of getting around the seminal but unnecessarily narrow conception of information provided us by Shannon, Weiner, and others.

Perhaps we sell the concept of information short by choosing to reject the possibility of there being a measure that is appropriate to both the nominal sense of specification that Gibson and Reed champion, and the ordinal sense that Kugler and I prefer. For we have seen that the two together implicate an extensive coparameter, and therefore, provide a more powerful measure than either separately. But we have not yet indicated what the nature of this extensive measure might be. Our candidate for this measure is the so-called "logon content" measure suggested by Gabor (1961) as an alternative to Shannon's "metron content" measure of information. Both of these measures give numerical values for the amount of information available, but they do not measure the same thing.

The measure of *metron* content refers to the amount of information, as measured along a single extensive dimension; the measure of *logon* content refers to the number of variables, or parameters, required to "fix" the thing being measured in a coordinate space. For this reason, the measure of metron content is sometimes called a "measure of coordinality." It is, therefore, synonymous with number of degrees of freedom which must be constrained if the thing measured is to be functionally determined, in the mathematical sense, (say, as expressed by functional diagrams that commute). Such a measure has an intimate connection with the notion of information as topological form, for the concepts of "coordinality" and "manifold" are essentially mathematically equivalent to the concept of being functionally determined (e.g., by abstract diagrams). A *manifold* is by definition the topological structure that carries form as the interplay of nominal singularities and ordinal relationships; it is a category of mathematical structures which, like diagrams, can be used to model any system that is completely determined by a set of (functional) parameters.

Conclusion

Fortunately, it seems to me that no cogent reasons have been given to disallow the more liberal definition of information measures discussed. Furthermore, to be fair, it also seems clear that Gibson's intent, expressed in the quote (given in the opening section), was to dissent from Shannon's so-called "metron" content measure, but no mention is made of the less well-known measure of information's "logon" content. Information as nominal specification does not really do justice to Gibson's intent, but should be broadened to include the ordinal aspect as well. When it is, we find that it not only allows intensive scales of information measurement to be defined, but coimplicates an extensive parameter of information measurement as well. For the meaning of the term "to specify," when mathematically interpreted, is exactly that of being functionally determined— whether by topological manifold or category diagram. Simple categorization procedures (unordered set theory) have proven inadequate, in principle, for determining all but the simplest phenomena in science; procedures at least as complicated as ordinal scaling (ordered set theory) are generally required; thus it would seem unwise for psychologists to continue to try to talk about information without benefit of the abstract tools suitable to the task.

Hence, in accepting Gibson's valid rejection of Shannon's metron measure of information, we should not over generalize the complaint to include the logon content as well, or we will be guilty of throwing the baby out with the bath water.

REFERENCES

Alley, T. R., & Shaw, R. E. Principles of learning and the ecological style of inquiry. *Behavioral and Brain Science,* 1981, *4*(1), 139–141.

Bonner, J. T. *On development.* Boston: Belknap, 1974.

Carello, C. Turvey. M. T., Kugler, P. N., & Shaw, R. E. Inadequacies of the computer metaphor. In M. S. Gazzaniga (Ed.), *Handbook of cognitive neuroscience.* New York: Plenum, 1982.

Cutting, J. E. Two ecological perspectives: Gibson vs. Shaw and Turvey. *American Journal of Psychology,* 1982, *95,* 199–222.

Gabor, D. Light and information. In E. Wolf (Ed.), *Progress in optics, 1.* North-Holland, Amsterdam, 1961.

Gibson, J. J. Visually controlled locomotion and visual orientation in animals. *British Journal of Psychology,* 1958, *49,* 182–194.

Gibson, J. J. Ecological optics. *Vision Research,* 1961, *1,* 253–262.

Gibson, J. J. *The senses considered as perceptual systems.* Boston: Houghton-Mifflin, 1966.

Gibson, J. J. On the analysis of change in the optic array. *Scandinavian Journal of Psychology,* 1977, *18,* 161–163.

Gibson, J. J. A history of ecological optics: Introductory remarks at the workshop on ecological optics. In E. Reed & R. Jones (Eds.), *Reasons for realism: Selected essays of James J. Gibson.* Hillsdale, NJ: Lawrence Erlbaum Associates, 1982.

Haken, H. *Synergetics.* Heidelberg: Springer-Verlag, 1977.

Hertz, H. *Principles of mechanics,* Leipzig: 1894.

Hofsten, C. von, & Lindhagen, K. Observations on the development of reaching for moving objects. *Journal of Experimental Child Psychology,* 1979, *28,* 158–173.

Hutchinson, G. E. *The Ecological theater and the evolutionary play.* New Haven, CT: Yale University Press, 1965.

Iberall, A. S. *Toward a general science of viable systems.* New York: McGraw-Hill, 1972.

Iberall, A. S. Discussion paper: Growth, form, and function in mammals. New York Academy of Science, 231:71, 1974.

Iberall, A. S. A field circuit thermodynamic for integrative physiology, III—keeping the books—a general experimental method. *American Journal of Physiology*, 1978, *3*, R85–R97.

Kugler, P. N., Kelso, J. A. S., & Turvey, M. T. On the concept of coordinative structures as dissipative structures: I. Theoretical lines of convergence. In G. E. Stelmach & J. Requin (Eds.), *Tutorials in motor behavior*. New York: North-Holland, 1980.

Kugler, P. N., Kelso, J. A. S., & Turvey, M. T. On coordination and control in naturally developing systems. In J. A. S. Kelso & J. E. Clark (Eds.), *The development of movement coordination and control*. New York, London: Wiley, 1982.

Kugler, P. N., & Turvey, M. T. *Information, natural law, and the self-assembly of rhythmic movement*. Hillsdale, NJ: Lawrence Erlbaum Associates, in preparation.

MacLane, S. *Categories for the working mathematician*. New York, Heidelberg, Berlin: Springer-Verlag, 1971.

Miller, G. A., Galanter, E. H., & Pribram, K. H. *Plans and the structure of behavior*. New York: Holt, 1960.

Pattee, H. H. Can life explain quantum mechanics? In T. Bastin (Ed.), *Quantum theory and beyond*. Cambridge: Cambridge University Press, 1971.

Pattee, H. H. Laws and constraints, symbols and language. In C. W. Waddington (Ed.), *Towards a theoretical biology*. Chicago: Aldine, 1972.

Pattee, H. H. The physical basis and origin of hierarchical control. In H. H. Pattee (Ed.), *Hierarchy theory: the challenge of complex systems*. New York: Braziller, 1973.

Pattee, H. H. Dynamic and linguistic modes of complex systems. *International Journal of General Systems*, 1977, *3*, 259–266.

Pattee, H. H. Complementarity versus reduction as explanation of biological complexity. *American Journal of Physiology*, 1979, *5*(3), R241–R246.

Pattee, H. H. Cell psychology: an evolutionary approach to the symbol-matter problem. *Cognition and Brain Research*, 1982,

Reed, E. Lawfulness of natural selection. *The American Naturalist*, 1981, *118*, 61–71.

Rosen, R. *Fundamentals of measurement and representation of natural systems*. Elsevier North-Holland: New York, 1978.

Simon, H. A. *The architecture of complexity*. Cambridge, MA: M. I. T. Press, 1964.

Shaw, R. E., & McIntyre, M. Algoristic foundations to cognitive psychology. In W. Weimer & D. Palermo (Eds.), *Cognition and the symbolic processes*. Hillsdale, NJ: Lawrence Erlbaum Associates, 1974.

Shaw, R. E., & Todd, J. Abstract machine theory and direct perception. *Behavioral and Brain Sciences*, 1980, *3*, 400–401.

Shaw, R. E., & Cutting, J. E. Constraints on language events: Cues from an ecological theory of event perception. In U. Bellugi & M. Studdert-Kennedy (Eds.), *Signed language and spoken language: Biological constraints on linguistic form*. Dahlem Conferenzen, Weinheim/Deerfield Beach FL/Basel: Chemie Verlag, 1980.

Shaw, R. E., & Turvey, M. T. Coalitions as models for ecosystems: A realist perspective on perceptual organization. In M. Kibovy & J. Pomerantz (Eds.), *Perceptual organization*, Hillsdale, NJ: Lawrence Erlbaum Associates, 1981.

Shaw, R. E., Turvey, M. T., & Mace, W. M. Ecological psychology: The consequence of a commitment to realism. In W. Weimer & D. Palermo (Eds.), *Cognition and the symbolic processes II*. Hillsdale, NJ: Lawrence Erlbaum Associates, 1982.

Shaw, R. E., & Mingolla, E. Ecologizing world graphs. *Behavioral and Brain Sciences*, 1982, *5*, 648–650.

Shaw, R. E., & Alley, T. R. How to draw learning curves: Their use and justification. In T. D.

Johnston & A. T. Pietrewicz (Eds.), *Issues in the ecological study of learning*. Hillsdale, NJ: Lawrence Erlbaum Associates, in press.

Turvey, M. T., & Shaw, R. E. The primacy of perceiving: An ecological reformulation of perception for understanding memory. In L-G. Nilsson (Ed.), *Perspectives on memory research*. Hillsdale, NJ: Lawrence Erlbaum Associates, 1979.

Turvey, M. T., Shaw, R. E., Reed, E., & Mace, W. M. Ecological laws of perceiving and acting: In reply to Fodor & Pylyshyn (1981). *Cognition, 9*, 237–304.

Warren, W. H. A biodynamic basis for perception and action in bipedal climbing. Unpublished doctoral dissertation. University of Connecticut, 1982.

Warren, W. H., Jr., & Shaw, R. E. Psychophysics and ecometrics. *Behavioral and Brain Sciences, 1981, 4,* 209–210.

Yates, F. E., Marsh, D. J., & Iberall, A. S. Integration of the whole organism: A foundation for a theoretical biology. In J. A. Behnke (Ed.), *Challenging biological problems: Directions toward their solution*. New York: Oxford University Press, 1972.

Yates, F. E. Spectroscopy of metabolic systems. *Proceedings of the Society for General Systems Research*, San Francisco, 1980, 65–74.

Author Index

Italics denote pages with bibliographic information.

Subject Index

D,E